A DOCUMENTARY HISTORY OF

The Negro People in the United States

MA

A DOCUMENTARY HISTORY

OF

The Negro People in the United States

Edited by
HERBERT APTHEKER

II

FROM THE RECONSTRUCTION ERA TO 1910

A Citadel Press Book
PUBLISHED BY CAROL PUBLISHING GROUP

Contents

VIII. THE TWENTIETH CENTURY

Index covers Volume I (FROM COLONIAL TIMES THROUGH THE CIVIL WAR) *and Volume II.*

V

The Reconstruction Years

180

STRUGGLES OF THE SOUTHERN NEGRO, 1865

Through the year 1865 economic and political power in the South still remained in the hands of the shaken, but far from crushed, former slaveholding class. Under the Johnsonian Reconstruction governments an attempt was made by this class to firmly establish the subjugation of the Negro people and to make this approximate as closely as possible the situation during chattel slavery.

Faced by this threat, the Negro people—often in unity with the poorer whites—acted vigorously and collectively in an effort to secure and make real their liberation. In 1865 the Southern Negro people set the pattern of struggle that was to guide so much of their subsequent history. They rejected ideas of colonization or flight, welcomed the support of white allies, and protested vehemently against unfair labor practices, violence, peonage and restrictions upon land ownership. They battled to gain possession of the land their toil had made sweet, they sought the right to vote, to testify in courts, to serve on juries, to obtain an education, to bear arms, to increase wages and to eliminate all invidious distinctions based upon color.

To illustrate this, there follow nine documents. The first [a] is a petition, dated Newbern, North Carolina, May 10, which was widely circulated through the State, numerously signed, and presented to President Johnson, and thereafter extensively reprinted in the nation's press.

The second document [b] consists of resolutions adopted May 11 at a mass meeting of Norfolk Negroes, chaired by a dentist, Dr. Thomas Bayne, who had been a fugitive slave. The third document [c] likewise consists of resolutions; these come from a mass meeting of Petersburg, Virginia, Negroes, held June 6, under the leadership of the Rev. William E. Walker, Peter K. Jones, Thomas Scott and others.

The fourth document [d] contains resolutions adopted by Vicksburg, Mississippi, Negroes assembled in mass meeting on June 19. This gathering was chaired by Jacob Richardson of the 49th U.S. Colored Infantry Regiment. The fifth document [e] is representative of the many petitions presented to Congress in 1865 by Southern Negroes. This one contains the opinions of the one hundred and sixty-five delegates to the Tennessee State Convention of Negroes held in Nashville from August 7 through August 11, and was submitted to the U.S. Senate on December 21, by Charles Sumner.

The sixth document [f] is dated Richmond, September 18, and comes from the Negro tobacco workers of that city and its suburb, Manchester. It complains of the conditions they face and urges improvements. The seventh document [g] consists of the address to the North Carolina Constitutional Convention by the State Convention of North Carolina Negroes whose one hundred and fifty delegates met in Raleigh from September 29 through October 3. Prominent in this state convention were James H. Harris, A. H. Galloway, John Randolph, Jr. and the Rev. George A. Rue.

The eighth document [h] shows clearly the keen desire of the Negroes for land. It was evoked by a visit to Edisto Island, South Carolina, by Major-General Oliver O. Howard, as the President's personal representative. The General informed the Negroes that the former rebel landowners had been pardoned and were claiming their property. A committee of three Negroes then prepared a petition to the President, dated October 25, and this is reprinted below.

The ninth document [i] represents one of several public papers issuing from the Colored People's Convention of the State of South Carolina which met in Charleston, November 20–25. The presiding officer of this convention was Thomas M. Holmes; others prominent in the proceedings were Robert C. De Large (later a Congressman), Martin Delany, Jonathan C. Gibbs (later Superintendent of Schools in Florida), Francis L. Cardozo (later Secretary of State and then Treasurer of South Carolina), Alonzo J. Ransier (later Lieutenant-Governor of South Carolina), and the Rev. Richard H. Cain (later a member of the South Carolina legislature and of Congress). The paper printed below was written by R. H. Cain and was entitled, "Address of the State Convention to the White Inhabitants of South Carolina."

[a]

The North Carolina Petition

To his Excellency, Andrew Johnson, President of the United States:

We, the undersigned, your Petitioners, are colored men of the State of North Carolina, of the age of twenty-one years and upward,—and we humbly come to you with our request, and yet in great confidence, because you are occupying a place so recently filled by a man who had proved himself indeed our friend—and it must be that some of his great and good spirit lingers to bless his successor; and then we are assured that you are a man who gives kind attention to all Petitioners, and never turns a deaf ear to any one because he may be in poor or humble circumstances.

In many respects we are poor, and greatly despised by our fellowmen; but we are rich in the possession of the liberty brought us, and our wives and our little ones, by your noble predecessor; secured to us by the armies of the United States, and promised to be permanent by that victorious flag which now flies in triumph in every State of the Union.

We accept this great boon of Freedom with truly thankful hearts, and shall try by our lives to prove our worthiness.

We always loved the old flag, and we have stood by it, and tried to help those who upheld it through all this Rebellion, and now that it has brought us liberty, we love it more than ever; and in all future time we and our sons will be ready to defend it by our blood, and we may be permitted to say that such blood as that shed at Fort Wagner and Port Hudson is not altogether unworthy of such service.

Some of us are soldiers and have had the privilege of fighting for our country in this war. Since we have become Freemen, and been permitted the honor of being soldiers, we begin to feel that we are men, and are anxious to show our countrymen that we can and will fit ourselves for the creditable discharge of the duties of citizenship. We want the privilege of voting. It seems to us that men who are willing on the field of danger to carry the muskets of Republics in the days of Peace ought to be permitted to carry its ballots; and certainly we cannot understand the justice of denying the elective franchise to men who have been fighting for the country, while it is freely given to men who have just returned from four years fighting against it.

As you were once a citizen of North Carolina, we need not remind you that up to the year 1835 free colored men voted in this State, and never as we have heard, with any detriment to its interests. What we desire is, that preliminary to elections in the returning States, you would order the enrollment of all loyal men, without regard to color. But the whole subject we humbly submit to your better judgment, and we submit it with full belief in your impartial integrity, and in the fond hope that the mantle of our murdered friend and father may have fallen upon your shoulders.

May God bless and ever protect you and our beloved country from all assassins, shall be the constant prayer of your faithful friend and humble petitioners.

N.Y. *Daily Tribune*, May 19, 1865.

[b]

Resolutions of Norfolk Negroes

1st. *Resolved,* That the rights and interests of the colored citizens of Virginia are more directly, immediately and deeply affected in the restoration of the State to the Federal Union than any other class of citizens; and hence, that we have peculiar claims to be heard in regard to the question of its reconstruction, and that we cannot keep silence without dereliction of duty to ourselves, to our country, and to our God.

2d. *Resolved,* That personal servitude having been abolished in Virginia, it behooves us, and is demanded of us, by every consideration of right and duty, to speak and act as freemen, and as such to claim and insist upon equality before the law, and equal rights of suffrage at the "ballot box."

3d. *Resolved,* That it is a wretched policy and most unwise statesmanship that would withhold from the laboring population of the country any of the rights of citizenship essential to their well-being and to their advancement and improvement as citizens.

4th. *Resolved,* That invidious political or legal distinctions, on account of color merely, if acquiesced in, or voluntarily submitted to, is inconsistent with our own self-respect, or to the respect of others, placing us at great disadvantages, and seriously retards our advancement or progress in improvement, and that the removal of such disabilities and distinctions are alike demanded by sound political economy, by patriotism, humanity and religion.

5th. *Resolved,* That we will prove ourselves worthy of the elective franchise, by insisting upon it as a right, by not tamely submitting to its deprivation, by never abusing it by voting the State out of the Union, and never using it for purposes of rebellion, treason or oppression.

6th. *Resolved,* That the safety of all loyal men, black or white, in the midst of the recently slaveholding States, requires that all loyal men, black or white, should have equal political and civil rights, and that this is a necessity as a protection against the votes of secessionists and disloyal men.

7th. *Resolved,* That traitors shall not dictate or prescribe to us the terms or conditions of our citizenship, so help us God.

8th. *Resolved,* That as far as in us lies, we will not patronize or hold business relations with those who deny to us our equal rights.

Equal Suffrage. Address from the Colored Citizens of Norfolk, Va., to the People of the United States. Also an Account of the Agitation among the Colored People of Virginia for Equal Rights. With an appendix concerning the rights of colored witnesses before the state courts (New Bedford, Mass., 1865).

[c]

Resolutions of Petersburg Negroes

Whereas, This Rebellion against the constitutional authority of the United States Government has been waged for the purpose of extending and perpetuating the system of American Slavery, and to establish a Southern

Confederacy on its basis; and *Whereas,* God has, in his all-wise Providence, overthrown their Power, and the leaders of this gigantic Rebellion have been taken as prisoners, and some of them have been indicted for treason against the Government of the United States; and *Whereas,* the supremacy of the United States Government has been maintained by the combined forces of the black and white soldiers on many bloody battle-fields; therefore

1. *Resolved,* That we, the colored citizens of Petersburg, Va., and true and loyal citizens of the United States of America, claim, as an unqualified right, the privilege of setting forth respectfully our grievances and demanding an equality of rights under the law.

2. *Resolved,* That we have vindicated our rights to the full exercise and enjoyment of these rights, at Milliken's Bend, Port Hudson, Fort Wagner, Olustee, Petersburg, and last, but not least, had the distinguished honor of being the first regiment to march into that stronghold of rebellion, the city of Richmond.

3. *Resolved,* That New Orleans in 1812, and Red Bank, Valley Forge, and other battles, fought both by land and sea in the Revolution, by the colored man, presents still stronger claims to our right to the ballot box.

4. *Resolved,* That representation and taxation go hand in hand, and it is diametrically opposed to Republican institutions, to tax us for the support and expense of the Government, and deny us at the same time, the right of representation.

5. *Resolved,* That the fundamental basis upon which this, our Republican form of government is established, is, that all such governments derive their just power from the consent of the governed.

6. *Resolved,* That our color or former enslavement is no just cause for our proscription nor disfranchisement, as the word white, nor slave, is not found in the Constitution of the United States.

7. *Resolved,* That our comparative ignorance is not just reason for our disfranchisement, as we can compare favorably with a large number of our white fellow-citizens, both natives and foreigners, in point of intelligence—many of whom can neither read or write, and know nothing of the institutions of the country. We, therefore, hold that any discrimination made against us as a class that does not apply to them, is both unjust and wicked.

8. *Resolved,* That we cheerfully submit to any provision, however rigid, that will apply with equal force to our white fellow-citizen, notwithstanding the fact they have had all the facilities and opportunities for moral and intellectual development.

9. *Resolved,* That we have an abiding confidence in our present Chief Magistrate, Andrew Johnson, but fear much the influence of so-called Unionists, who have hitherto entertained the most inveterate feelings of

hatred against the Government of the United States, but now have taken the oath of allegiance to support the Government, with all their vindictive feelings of hatred against the colored man, as such cannot expect justice at their hands, let reconstruction take place when it may.

10. *Resolved,* That our prayers shall be offered to Almighty God, in behalf of the President and his Cabinet, that their influence and efforts may be used in the future for our political enfranchisement, as they have in the past in securing to us our physical rights.

11. *Resolved,* That in the death of our beloved President, Abraham Lincoln, we have lost a Patriot, a Statesman, and Philanthropist, whose loss we sincerely deplore and that he, in the natural goodness of his heart, proclaimed freedom to the slave, we trust in God, that his successor, President Andrew Johnson may also use his influence in according to us that equally sacred right—the elective franchise.

12. *Resolved,* That we scorn and treat with contempt the allegation made against us that we understand Freedom to mean idleness and indolence; but we do understand Freedom to mean industry and the enjoyment of the legitimate fruits thereof; for he that works we believe has a right to eat, and any person or persons who believe otherwise do not rightly represent the colored people of Petersburg.

13. *Resolved,* That we have no feeling of resentment toward our former owners, but we are willing to let the past be buried with the past, and in the future treat all persons with kindness and respect who shall treat us likewise.

Petersburg, Va., *News,* June 9, 1865, quoted in the N.Y. *Daily Tribune,* June 15, 1865.

[d]

Resolutions of Vicksburg Negroes

Whereas, the President of the United States has, by proclamation, dated Washington, June 13, 1865, appointed a Provisional Governor for the State of Mississippi, Hon. W. L. Sharkey, and directs that a convention be called and an election held, allowing only such to vote at said election as were allowed to vote under the constitution and laws of the State of Mississippi as administered before the passage of the so-called ordinance of secession of January 9, 1861, excluding the loyal colored citizens, therefore

Resolved, That we regard such a policy as unjust to the colored citizens, paralyzing to the colored soldier, and most damaging to the early peaceful establishment of the Federal supremacy in rebellious territory.

Resolved, That in view of these facts, we will appeal to the people of the North, and will earnestly appeal to Congress, that the State of Mississippi be not restored to federal relations unless by her constitution she shall enfranchise her loyal colored citizens

Resolved, That the interests of our people in this State demand at an early day the establishment of a paper within the State that will fearlessly and faithfully defend the rights of the colored citizens.

N.Y. *Daily Tribune,* July 11, 1865.

[e]

Petition from Tennessee Negroes

The colored people of the State of Tennessee respectfully and solemnly protest against the congressional delegation from this State being admitted to seats in your honorable bodies until the Legislature of this State enacts such laws as shall secure to us our rights as freemen.

We cannot believe that the General Government will allow us to be left without such protection after knowing, as you do, what services we have rendered to the cause of the preservation of the Union and the maintenance of the laws. We have respectfully petitioned our Legislature upon the subject, and have failed to get them to do anything for us, saying that it was premature to legislate for the protection of our rights.

We think it premature to admit such delegation. It is true we have no vote, but we nevertheless desire and will do anything we can to support the Government.

We deem it unnecessary to attempt to make an argument in favor of our protest, believing as we do, the justice of our cause to be a far better argument than we could make; yet it may not be amiss to say that, inasmuch as the United States Constitution guarantees to every State in the Union a republican form of government, we are at a loss to understand that to be a republican government which does not protect the rights of all citizens, irrespective of color.

Being impressed with these convictions, we cannot refrain from appealing to your honorable and dignified assembly, entertaining the hope that we will be heard and our cause considered.

The Government did not forget to call for our help, and now we think that we have a right to call upon it.

Congressional Globe, Dec. 21, 1865, 39th Cong., 1st Sess., Pt. I, p. 107.

[f]

Complaint of Tobacco Workers

Dear Sirs We the Tobacco mechanicks of this city and Manchester is worked to great disadvantages. In 1858 and 1859 our masters hiered us to the Tobacconist at a prices ranging from $150 to 180. The Tobacconist furnished us lodging food and clothing. They gave us tasks to performe. all we made over this task they payed us for. We worked faithful and they paid us faithful. They Then gave us $2 to 2.50 cts, and we made double the amount we now make. The Tobacconist held a meeting, and resolved not give more than $1.50 cts per hundred, which is about one days work in a week we may make 600 pounds apece with a stemer. The weeks work then at $1.50 amounts to $9—the stemers wages is from $4 to $4.50 cents which leaves from $5 to 4.50 cents per week about one half what we made when slaves. Now to Rent two small rooms we have to pay from $18 to 20. We see $4.50 cents or $5 will not more then pay Rent say nothing about food clothing medicin Doctor Bills. Tax and Co. They say we will starve through laziness that is not so. But it is true we will starve at our present wages. They say we will steal we can say for ourselves we had rather work for our living. give us a chance. We are Compeled to work for them at low wages and pay high Rents and make $5 per week and sometimes les. And paying $18 or 20 per month Rent. It is impossible to feed ourselves and family—starvation is Cirten unles a change is brought about.

Tobacco Factory Mechanicks of Richmond and Manchester

J. T. Trowbridge, *A Picture of the Desolated States; and the work of restoration, 1865–1868* (Hartford, 1888), pp. 230–31.

[g]

Address from State Convention of North Carolina Negroes

Assembled as delegates from different portions of the State, and representing a large body of the colored population thereof, we most respectfully and humbly beg leave to represent to you, and through you to the people of North Carolina, something of our situation and wants as a people.

Earnestly disclaiming all wish to forestall your action, or to dictate in the solemn and important duties which have been intrusted to you in this most critical period; and confiding in your justice, wisdom and patriotism to guard the interests of all classes, and more particularly of that class which, being most helpless, will most need your just and kind consideration, they but exercise the rights guaranteed to the humblest citizen in this their petition.

It is with reverend and grateful acknowledgement of the divine favor and interposition that we accept the precious boon of freedom. Resulting as it has from a prolonged and bloody struggle of two great powers, and finally decreed by the national will—we look forward with confidence to see the decree ratified by the whole people of this State.

Though it was impossible to remain indifferent spectators of the struggle, you will do us the justice to admit that we have remained throughout obedient and passive, acting such part only as has been assigned to us, and calmly waiting upon Providence. Our brethren have fought on the side of the Union, while we have been compelled to serve in the camp, to build fortifications, and raise subsistence for the Confederate army. Do you blame us that we have meantime prayed for freedom to our race?

Just emerging from bondage, under which our race has groaned for 250 years, and suffering from its consequent degradation, we are fully conscious that we possess no power to control legislation in our behalf, and must depend wholly upon moral appeal to the hearts and consciences of the people of our State. Born upon the same soil, and raised in an intimacy of relationship with you, which is unknown in any other state of society, we have formed attachments for the white race which must be as enduring as life; and we can conceive of no reason that our God-bestowed freedom should now sever the kindly ties which have so long united us.

Filled with gratitude to God for his great blessings, we would bury in oblivion the wrongs of the past, and wish to become more united than ever, and more useful in all relations of life.

We are fully conscious that we cannot long expect the presence of Government agents, or of the troops to secure us against evil treatment from unreasonable, prejudiced, and unjust men. We have no desire to look abroad for protection and sympathy. We know we must find both at home, among the people of our own State, and merit them by our industry, sobriety and respectful demeanor, or suffer long and grievous evils.

We acknowledge with gratitude that there are those among the planters who have promptly conceded our freedom, and have manifested a just and humane disposition toward their former slaves. We think no such persons, or, very few, at least, have lost their working hands by desertion. At the same time, it must be known to you, that many planters have either kept the Freedman in doubt—have wholly denied his freedom, or have grudgingly conceded it, and while doing so, have expelled his family from the plantation which they may have cleared and enriched by their toil through long and weary years.

Some have withheld just compensation, or such pay as would not support the laborer and his family, while others have driven the hands away without any pay at all, or even a share of the crops they have raised. Women with families of children, whose husbands have been sold, have died, or have wrongfully deserted them, have in some cases been driven away from the homes where, under Slavery, they have spent a lifetime of hard service. Is it just or Christian thus to thrust out upon the cold world helpless families to perish?

These grosser forms of evil, we believe, will correct themselves under wise and humane legislation, but we do most respectfully and earnestly urge that some suitable measures may be adopted to prevent unscrupulous and avaricious masters from the practice of these and other similar acts of injustice and cruelty toward our people.

Our first and engrossing concern in our new relation is how we shall provide shelter and an honorable subsistence for ourselves and families. You will say, "Work." This we are willing and expect to do, but without the aid of just legislation, how shall we secure adequate compensation for our labor? If the kindly relations we so much desire shall prevail, must there not be mutual cooperation? As our longer degradation cannot add to your comfort, make us more obedient as servants, or more useful as citizens, will you not aid us by a wise and just legislation to elevate ourselves? We desire education for our children that they may be more useful in all the relations of life.

We most earnestly desire to have the disabilities under which we have formerly lived removed; to have all the oppressive laws which make unjust discriminations on account of race or color wiped from the statutes of the State. We invoke your protection for the sanctity of our family relations. Is this asking too much?

We most respectfully and urgently pray that some provision may be made for the care of the great number of orphan children, and the helpless and infirm who, by the new order of affairs, will be thrown upon the world without its protection. Also, that you will favor, by some timely and wise measures, the reunion of families which have been long broken up by war, or by the operation of Slavery.

Though associated with many memories of suffering as well as of enjoyment, we have always loved our homes, and dreaded, as the worst of evils, a forcible separation from them. Now that freedom and a new career are before us, we love this land and people more than ever before. Here we have toiled and suffered, our parents, wives and children are buried here, and in this land we will remain, unless forcibly driven away.

Finally, praying for such encouragement to our industry as the proper regulation of the hours of labor, and the providing the means of protection of our property and of our persons against rapacious and cruel employers, and for the collection of just claims, we commit our cause into your hands, invoking Heaven's choicest blessings upon your deliberations and upon the State.

N.Y. *Daily Tribune*, October 7, 1865.

[h]

Edisto Island Negroes Petition the President

Wee the freedmen of South Carolina wish to address you with a few lines conserning the sad feelings that is now resting upon our minds wee pray that god may guive you helth & good spirets that when you receive theas few notasis that you may receive them as the father did the prodical son wee have for the last four years ben studing with justis and the best of our ability what step wee should take to become a people: wee have lernt to respect all Just Causes that ever came from the union.

Mag genrl howard has paid the freedmen of South Carolinah a visit & caled a meating on Edisto Island South Carliner in the Centrel part of the island at the priskple Church thair hee beutifly addressed the freedmen of this island after his adress a grate many of the peple understanding what was said they got aroused & awoke to perfict sense to stody for them Selves what part of this law would rest against us, wee said in rafarence to what he said that nothing did apier at that time to bee very opressing upon us but the one thing that is wee freedmen should work for wages for our former oners or eny other man president Johnson of u st [United States] I do say . . . man that have stud upon the feal of battle & have shot there master & sons now Going to ask ether one for bread or for shelter or Comfortable for his wife & children sunch a thing the u st should not aught to expect a man [to do] . . . the King of south Carolina [i.e., one of the former slaveholders] ask the Privalage to have the stage that he might a Dress the ordenance [audience] of the freedman . . . [the] old master [claimed] such a fealing to Comply with the best order & also what was the best for the freedmen . . . [We said to him] Here is Plenty Whidow & Fatherles that have serve you as slave now losen a home . . . give Each one of them a acres & a one-half to a family as you has the labers & the Profet of there Yearly [early] Youth . . . [when] the Questin was asked him by General Howard, what would it sell your lan for a acres his anser that I would not take a hundred $100 of a acres that is a part of his union fealing so then we therefore lose fate [faith] in this southern Gentelman . . . [They beesech] the wise presidon

that sets on his seat [to give them] a chance to Recover out of this trubble
. . . these 3 Committee has Pleg the Trouth to you dis day.

Mary Ames, *From a New England Woman's Diary in Dixie in 1865* (Springfield, Mass., 1906). Copy in Boston Public Library.

[i]

Address of the State Convention to the White Inhabitants of South Carolina

Fellow-Citizens: We have here assembled as delegates representing the colored people of the State of South Carolina, in the capacity of a State Convention, to confer together and to deliberate upon our intellectual, moral, industrial, civil and political condition, and particularly our condition as affected by the great changes which have recently taken place in this State and throughout this whole country, to declare our sentiments, and to devise ways and means which may, through the blessing of God, tend to our improvement, elevation, and progress, fully believing that our cause is one which commends itself to the hearts of all good men throughout the civilized world; that it is the sacred cause of truth and righteousness; that it particularly appeals to those professing to be governed by that faith which teaches that "Whatsoever ye would that men should do unto you, do ye even so to them."

These principles we conceive to embody the great duty of man to his fellow man; and *as men* we only ask to be included in the practical application of this principle. We feel that the *justness* of our cause is a sufficient apology for our cause at this time.

Heretofore we have had no avenues opened to us or our children. We have had no firesides that we might call our own—none of those incentives to work for the development of our minds and the aggrandizement of our race in common with other people. The measures which have been devised for the development of white men, women and children have been denied to us. The laws which have made white men powerful have degraded us, because we were black and because we were reduced to the condition of chattels. But now that we are freemen—now that we are elevated, by the Providence of God, to manhood, we have resolved to stand up, and like men, speak and act for ourselves. We fully recognize the truth of the maxim. "The gods help those who help themselves."

In making this appeal to you, we adopt the language of the immortal Declaration of Independence: that "all men are created equal," and that "life, liberty, and the pursuit of happiness," are the right of all; that taxation and representation should go together; that governments are ordained to protect, and not to subvert, the rights of men, that the Constitution of the United States was framed to establish justice, to promote the general welfare, and to secure the blessing of liberty to all the people of the land; that resistance to tyrants is obedience to God, are all American principles and maxims, and, taken together, they form the constructive elements of the American Government.

We think we fully comprehend and duly appreciate the principles and measures which compose this platform; and all we desire or ask for is to be placed in a position that we could conscientiously and legitimately defend, with you, those principles against the surges of despotism to the last drop of our blood. We have not come together in battle array to assume a boastful attitude and to talk loudly of high-sounding principles, or of unmeaning platitudes; nor do we pretend to any great boldness; for we remember your former wealth, and greatness, and we know our poverty and weakness; and although we feel keenly our wrongs, still we come together, we trust, in a spirit of meekness and of patriotic good-will toward all the people of the State. But yet it is some consolation to know, (and it inspires us with hope when we reflect) that our cause is not alone the cause of four millions of black men in this country, but we are intensely alive to the fact that it is also the cause of millions of oppressed men in other "parts of God's beautiful earth," who are now struggling to be free in the fullest sense of the word and God and nature are pledged to their triumph. We are American by birth, and we assure you that we are Americans in feeling, and in spite of all the wrongs which we have so long and silently endured in this country, we can yet exclaim, with a full heart, "O, America, with all thy faults we love thee still! . . ."

Thus we would address you—not as Rebels and enemies, but as friends and fellow countrymen, who desire to dwell among you in peace, and whose destinies are interwoven and linked with those of the whole American people, and hence must be fulfilled in this country. As descendants of a race feeble and long-oppressed, we might with propriety appeal to a great and magnanimous people like the American for special favor and encouragement, on the principle that the strong should aid the weak, and that the learned should teach the unlearned. But it is for no such purpose that we raise our voices to the people of South Carolina on this occasion. We ask for no special privileges, or peculiar favors. We ask only for *even-handed justice*, for the removal of such positive obstructions and disabilities as past and recent legislation has thrown in our way and heaped upon us. Without any just cause or provocation on our part, we, by the action of your [Constitutional] Convention and Legislature, have, with few exceptions, been virtually excluded—

First: from the rights of citizenship, which you cheerfully accord to strangers, notwithstanding we have been born and reared in your midst, and were faithful while your greatest trials were upon you, and have done nothing since which could justly merit your disapprobation.

Second: We are denied the right of giving our testimony in the Courts of the State, in consequence of which our persons and property are subject, the former to every species of violence and insult, and the latter to fraud and spoliation without redress.

Third: We are also, by the present laws, not only denied the right of citizenship—the inestimable right of choosing who shall rule over us in the land of our birth, but by the so-called "Black Code" we are deprived of the rights which are vouch-safed to the lowest white profligate in the country—the right to engage in any legitimate business save under such unjust restraints as are imposed upon no other class of people in the State.

Fourth: You have, by legislative action, placed barriers in the way of our improvement in the arts and sciences. You have given us little or no encouragement to engage in agricultural pursuits, by refusing to sell us lands, while you are organizing societies to bring foreigners into the country, the clear intent of which is to thrust us out, or reduce us to a serfdom intolerable to us, and as you will find in the end, ruinous to your own prosperity.

Fifth: Your public journals wickedly charge us with destroying the products of the country since we have been made free, when they know that the country, and the products thereof, were destroyed by a desolating war of four years, in which we had no hand. How unjust to charge upon the innocent and helpless the very crimes which yourselves have committed, and which brought down ruin upon your own heads!

Sixth: We simply ask that we shall be recognized as *men;* that there be no obstructions placed in our way; that the same laws which govern *white men* shall govern *black men;* that we have the right of trial by a jury of our *peers;* that schools be established for the education of *colored children* as well as *white,* and that the advantages of both colors shall, in this respect, be *equal;* that no impediments be put in the way of our acquiring homesteads for ourselves and our people; that, in short, we be dealt with as others are—in equity and justice.

Seventh: We claim that we deserve the confidence and good will of all classes of men. We ask that the same opportunities be extended to us that freemen have a right to demand at the hands of their fellow-citizens. We desire the growth and prosperity of this State, and the well-being of *all* men, and we would be found ever struggling to elevate ourselves and add to the glory of the national character. We trust that the day is not far distant when you will acknowledge that our progress in social, intellectual, moral, and religious development entitles us to the highest commendation and respect, and that we shall be worthy to occupy with the best in the land, positions of trust and power; when we shall realize the great truth that "all men are endowed, by their Creator with certain inalienable rights" and that although complexions may differ, a "man's a man for a' that."

N.Y. *Daily Tribune*, November 29, 1865. The *Proceedings* of the Convention were published in pamphlet form in Charleston in 1865, and the language was somewhat moderated.

181

THE NORTHERN NEGRO, 1865

During the immediate post-Civil War months the Northern Negro increased the tempo of his battle for equality and exerted what pressure he could upon his general community and Congress for a progressively democratic reconstruction program in the South.

Below are published three documents illustrating these efforts. The first is the masterful speech made on May 10 by Frederick Douglass at the 32nd Annual Convention of the American Anti-Slavery Society, held in Boston. Douglass, together with Wendell Phillips, Charles L. Remond and Robert Purvis, led in the effort to maintain the Society's existence despite the passage of the Thirteenth Amendment, and his speech explains the reasons for this position.

The second document is an extract from an editorial in the *Colored Citizen* of Cincinnati expressing opposition to the colonization plans of the Ohio Congressman and quasi-Copperhead, Samuel S. Cox, then running, unsuccessfully, for Governor. The third document is the text of a petition submitted to Congress by the National Equal Rights League, meeting in Cleveland in October, calling for a constitutional amendment barring all Jim Crow legislation.

[a]

Frederick Douglass' Speech

Several gentlemen have been so kind as to refer to me in the course of this discussion, and my friend, Mr. [Samuel J.] May, referred to me as being opposed to the disbandment of this Society at any time during the present year. Having been thus referred to, I wish to put myself properly before the meeting. Almost the first work the American Anti-Slavery Society asked me to do, after employing me as an agent more than twenty years ago, was to accompany Stephen S. Foster and Abby Kelley (now Mrs. Foster) into the State of Rhode Island, to wage a most unrelenting war against what was called the "Dorr Constitution," because that Constitution contained the odious word "white" in it. That was regarded as legitimate anti-slavery work at that time; and that work was most effectively performed amid mobs and all sorts of violence. We succeeding in defeating that Dorr Constitution, and secured the adoption of a Constitution in which the word "white" did not appear. We thought it was a grand *anti-slavery* triumph, and it was; it was a good *anti-slavery* work. When I came North, and went to Massachusetts, I found that the leading work of the Abolitionists was to put the State of Massachusetts in harmony with the platform of the American Anti-Slavery Society. They said charity began at home. They looked over their statute-book, and whenever they found the word "white," there they recognized slavery, and they made war upon it. The anti-slavery ladies made themselves of no reputation by going about with petitions, asking the Legislature to blot out the hated word "white" from the marriage law. That was good anti-slavery work twenty years ago; I do not see why it is not good anti-slavery work now. It was a part of anti-slavery work then; it is a part now, I think.

I do not wish to appear here in any fault-finding spirit, or as an impugner of the motives of those who believe that the time has come for this Society to disband. I am conscious of no suspicion of the purity and excellence of the motives that animate the President of this Society [William Lloyd Garrison], and other gentlemen who are in favor of its disbandment. I take this ground; whether this Constitutional Amendment [the thirteenth] is law or not, whether it has been ratified by a sufficient number of States to make it law or not, I hold that the work of Abolitionists is not done. Even if every State in the Union had ratified that Amendment, while the black man is confronted in the legislation of the South by the word "white," our work as Abolitionists, as I conceive it, is not done. I took the ground, last night, that the South, by unfriendly legislation, could make our liberty, under that provision, a delusion, a mockery, and a snare, and I hold that ground now. What advantage is a provision like this Amendment to the black man, if the Legislature of any State can to-morrow declare that no black man's testimony shall be received in a court of law? Where are we then? Any wretch may enter the house of a black man, and commit any violence he pleases; if he happens to do it only in the presence of black persons, he goes unwhipt of justice. (Hear, hear.) And don't tell me that those people down there have become so just and honest all at once that they will not pass laws denying to black men the right to testify against white men in the courts of law. Why, our Northern States have done it. Illinois, Indiana and Ohio have done it. Here, in the midst of institutions that have gone forth from old Plymouth Rock, the black man has been excluded from testifying in the courts of law; and if the Legislature of every Southern State to-morrow pass a law, declaring that no Negro shall testify in any courts of law, they will not violate that provision of the Constitution. Such laws exist now at the South, and they might exist under this provision of the Constitution, that there shall be neither slavery nor involuntary servitude in any State of the Union.

Then another point. I have thought, for the last fifteen years, that we had an anti-slavery Constitution—a Constitution intended to secure "the blessings of liberty to ourselves and our posterity." But we have had slavery all along. We had a Constitution that declared that the citizens of Massachusetts should enjoy all the rights and immunities of citizens in South Carolina—but what of it? Let Mr. Hoar go down to South Carolina, and point to that provision in the Constitution, and they would kick him out of the State.* There is sometl ing down in South Carolina higher than Constitutional provisions.

Slavery is not abolished until the black man has the ballot. While the Legislatures of the South retain the right to pass laws making any discrimination between black and white, slavery still lives there. (Applause.) As Edmund Quincy once said, "While the word 'white' is on the statute-book of Massachusetts, Massachusetts is a slave State. While a black man can be turned out of a car in Massachusetts, Massachusetts is a slave State. While a slave can be taken from old Massachusetts, Massachusetts is a slave State." That is what I heard Edmund Quincy say twenty-three or twenty-four years ago. I never forget such a thing. Now, while the black man can be denied a vote, while the Legislatures of the South can take from him the right to keep and bear arms, as they can—they would not allow a Negro to walk with a cane where I came from, they would not allow five of them to assemble together—the work of the Abolitionists is not finished. Notwithstanding the provision in the Constitution of the United States, that the right to keep and bear arms shall not be abridged, the black man has never had the right either to keep or bear arms; and the Legislatures of the States will still have the power to forbid it, under this Amendment. They can carry on a system of unfriendly legislation, and will they not do it? Have they not got prejudice there to do it with? Think you, that because they are for the moment in the talons and beak of our glorious eagle, instead of the slave being there, as formerly, that they are converted? I hear of the loyalty at Wilmington, the loyalty at South Carolina—what is it worth?

Mr. MAY—Not a straw.

Mr. DOUGLASS—Not a straw. I thank my friend for admitting it. They are loyal while they see 200,000 sable soldiers, with glistening bayonets, walking in their midst. (Applause) But let the civil power of the South be restored, and the old prejudices and hostility to the Negro will revive. Aye, the very fact that the Negro has been used to defeat this rebellion and strike down

* In November, 1844, Samuel Hoar, a former Congressman, was sent by Gov. Briggs of Massachusetts to Charleston. His mission was to test the validity of a South Carolina law providing for the jailing of all free Negro seamen entering the state's ports. Mr. Hoar was forced to flee Charleston under threat of physical injury.

the standards of the Confederacy will be a stimulus to all their hatred, to all their malice, and lead them to legislate with greater stringency towards this class than ever before. (Applause.) The American people are bound—bound by their sense of honor (I hope by their sense of honor, at least, by a just sense of honor), to extend the franchise to the Negro; and I was going to say, that the Abolitionists of the American Anti-Slavery Society were bound to "stand still, and see the salvation of God," until that work is done. (Applause.) Where shall the black man look for support, my friends, if the American Anti-Slavery Society fails him? (Hear, hear.) From whence shall we expect a certain sound from the trumpet of freedom, when the old pioneer, when this Society that has survived mobs, and martyrdom, and the combined efforts of priest-craft and state-craft to suppress it, shall all at once subside, on the mere intimation that the Constitution has been amended, so that neither slavery nor involuntary servitude shall hereafter be allowed in this land? What did the slaveholders of Richmond say to those who objected to arming the Negro, on the ground that it would make him a freeman? Why, they said, "The argument is absurd. We may make these Negroes fight for us; but while we retain the political power of the South, we can keep them in their subordinate positions." That was the argument; and they were right. They might have employed the Negro to fight for them, and while they retained in their hands power to exclude him from political rights, they could have reduced him to a condition similar to slavery. They would not call it slavery, but some other name. Slavery has been fruitful in giving itself names. It has been called "the peculiar institution," "the social system," and the "impediment," as it was called by the General Conference of the Methodist Episcopal Church. It has been called by a great many names, and it will call itself by yet another name; and you and I and all of us had better wait and see what new form this old monster will assume, in what new skin this old snake will come forth. (Loud Applause.)

The Liberator, May 26, 1865.

[b]

Colored Citizen's *Editorial*

We have read the letter from General Cox with profound regret. It is a mistake in principle and in policy. This, we are persuaded, the General will live to see. The idea of colonizing our people, whether in another land or in this land, is, we would have the General understand, a product of slavery. Nobody proposes to colonize any other class. It is because we have been *enslaved;* it is because we have been a *subject* class; it is because the dominant races have for ages been unjustly disposing of our destinies, that such a thing is talked of. Who proposes to send the Germans, or the Irish, or the Swedes to some foreign land, or to set off several States for them in this country? Nobody; and why? Simply because they have not been chattels—have not for centuries been subject to masters. They have been in the habit of disposing of their own destiny; of deciding for *themselves* where they would live, and pursue their own happiness. This is the reason. . . . And now, as we have . . . ceased to be a *subject* class . . . we expect to be left with others and, like others, to decide where we will cast our lot. . . . This, we maintain, is our *purchased* right; for with our *blood* we have bought it. . . . The whole difficulty, as we conceive, of reconstruction springs from an unwillingness to carry out democratic principles. This causes the tug of war. Be simply *democratic*, gentlemen, and all is easy. . . .

The Cincinnati Colored Citizen, n.d., quoted in *The Liberator,* August 25, 1865.

[c]

Petition to Congress of National Equal Rights League

The undersigned officers and members of the National Equal Rights League call the attention of your honorable body to the 4th Article of the United States Constitution, Section 4th, in which we find that "the United States shall guarantee to every State in the Union a Republican form of government"; and seeing that in many States such a form of government does not exist, we therefore most respectfully ask the adoption of the following amendment to the Constitution of the United States:

That there shall be no legislation within the limits of the United States or Territories, against any civilized portion of the inhabitants, native-born or naturalized, on account of race or color, and that all such legislation now existing within said limits is anti-republican in character, and therefore void.

First Annual Meeting of the National Equal Rights League, held in Cleveland, Ohio, October 19th, 20th, & 21st, 1865 (Phila., 1865).

182

THE RULERS' FORCE AND VIOLENCE, 1866

As the organizational strength of the Negro people grew and as evidences of Negro-white unity accumulated, the Bourbons, whose power was threatened, turned more and more to the instrument of forcible repression. This resulted not only in a great many individual murders, but also in regularly recurring large-scale massacres.

Two typical mass slaughters of the year 1866 were those which occurred in Memphis, May 1–3, and in New Orleans, July 30. In each case the open connivance and active participation of the city officials and police, with important help from an abysmally chauvinistic press, were clear. And in each case only intervention by Federal troops—which came tardily—terminated the violence.

In the Memphis outbreak, forty-six Negroes (most of them Union veterans) and two white radicals were slaughtered, about seventy-five more were wounded, five Negro women were ravished, ninety homes, twelve schools and four churches were burned, and several radical whites, especially teachers, were driven out of the city. Evidence of anti-Jewish and anti-alien hatreds also appeared. In the New Orleans affair, the official casualties totaled thirty-five Negroes dead, three whites dead, one hundred and twenty-seven Negroes wounded, and nineteen whites (including ten policemen) wounded. The Army Surgeon at the scene expressed the belief, in his official report, that about ten more Negroes were killed and another twenty wounded, whose identities he never learned.

Documents illustrative of these occurrences are taken from the sworn testimony of Negro eyewitnesses given before Congressional investigating committees shortly after the events. The Memphis affair is seen through the eyes of two women, Mrs. Lucy Tibbs and Mrs. Sarah Song; the New Orleans outbreak, which centered at the Mechanics' Institute where a radical convention had assembled, is described by J. B. Jourdain, John Murral and John Sidney under the questioning of Congressman Thomas D. Eliot.

[a]

The Memphis Murders

Mrs. Lucy Tibbs questioned by the Chairman, Congressman Elihu B. Washburne of Illinois:

Where do you live? I have lived in Memphis very nearly three years.

How old are you? I do not know exactly. I suppose about twenty-four.

Have you a husband? Yes; my husband is on a steamboat. We came here from Jackson, Arkansas, when the rebellion broke out. . . .

I understand you to say, then, you saw four men killed under the circumstances stated, and that you know in addition of two others being killed, and that then you saw the dead body of this girl, Rachael? Yes, sir; and my brother got killed on Tuesday afternoon; who killed him I do not know.

What was his name? His name was Bob Taylor. He had been a member of the 59th Regiment, but was out of the service. On Tuesday afternoon when they were firing and going from house to house, I told him to try to get away if he could. He started to run away, but was found dead the next morning by the bayou just back of my house. He was older than I am. They robbed me that night of $300 of his money.

Did they come into your house? Yes; a crowd of men came in that night:

I do not know who they were. They just broke the door open and asked me where was my husband; I replied he was gone; they said I was a liar; I said, "Please do not do anything to me; I am just here with two little children."

Did they do anything to you? They done a very bad act.

Did they ravish you? Yes, sir.

How many of them? There was but one that did it. Another man said, "Let that woman alone—that she was not in any situation to be doing that." They went to my trunk, burst it open, and took this money that belonged to my brother.

Did they violate your person against your consent? Yes, sir; I had just to give up to them. They said they would kill me if I did not. They put me on the bed, and the other men were plundering the while this man was carrying on.

Were any of them policemen? I do not know; I was so scared I could not tell whether they were policemen or not; I think they were folks that knew all about me, who knew that my brother had not been long out of the army and had money.

Where were your children? In bed. . . .

How old are your children? One of them will soon be five, and the other will be two . . .

What did they mean by saying you was not in a condition to be doing that? I have been in the family way ever since Christmas. . . .

Mrs. Sarah Song questioned by the Chairman:

State your name and where you live. Sarah Song. I live about five miles from here.

Were you in Memphis at the time of the riots? Yes, sir; I was.

How old are you? I am between twenty and thirty.

Have you been a slave? I have been a slave.

What did you see of the rioting? I saw them kill my husband; it was on Tuesday night, between ten and eleven o'clock; he was shot in the head while he was in bed, sick.

Who shot him? I do not know; there were between twenty and thirty men who came to the house, when they first came, they halloed to us to open the doors; my husband was sick in bed and could not get up; he had been sick in bed two weeks; he had the jaundice; I lay there, I was so scared; we have two children who were with us. They broke the outside doors open; I staid in bed till they came in; the inside door was open; they came into the room and asked if we had any pistols or shot guns in the house; my husband said he had one, but it was only a rusty pistol, that his little boy had found; it was fit for nothing but the child to play with; then they told my husband to get up and get it; he got up and gave it to them. I then lighted a lamp after they got the pistol; they told my husband to get up and come out, that they were going to shoot him; they made him get up and go out of doors and told him if he had anything to say to say it quick, for they were going to kill him; if he said anything, I did not hear it. He stood outside, perhaps, a quarter of an hour; they asked him if he had been a soldier; he said he never had been. One of them said, "You are a damned liar; you have been in the government service for the last twelve or fourteen months." "Yes," said he, "I have been in the government service, but not as a soldier." Then another said, "Why did you not tell us that at first?" Then one stepped back and shot him as quick as he said that; he was not a yard from him; he put the pistol to his head and shot him three times; this was between ten and eleven o'clock; when my husband fell he scuffled about a little, and looked as if he tried to get back into the house; then they told him if he did not make haste and die, they would shoot him again. Then one of them kicked him, and another shot him again when he was down; they shot him through the head every time, as far as I could see. He never spoke after he fell. They then went running right off and did not come back again. . . .

"Memphis Riots and Massacres," *Report No. 101,* House of Representatives, 39th Cong., 1st Sess. (Serial #1274), pp. 160–61, 222–23.

[b]

The New Orleans Massacre

J. B. Jourdain:
  What is your age?
  I am thirty-four.
  How long have you lived in New Orleans?
  I was born here.
  Were you in this city on the thirtieth of July last?
  Yes, sir; I was here the whole month of July.
  Were you in the Mechanics' Institute on that day?
  Yes, sir; I was there about 12 o'clock. My attention was called to something going on outside; I heard a drum beating as if the military were coming, and I was much satisfied that it was so. As I looked up the street to where I heard the drum, I saw the United States flag flying, and I recognized a procession of colored persons with the flag. Then I went towards them, and as I got to the corner of Canal and Dryades the procession was coming up Dryades Street from below. When the tail part of the procession, which consisted of boys, came up, there was a pistol fired from a man who was standing on the corner of the banquette; it was fired by an officer with whom I am well

THE RULERS' FORCE AND VIOLENCE

acquainted; he is employed by the horse-car office; his name is Ellmore; he was then in the office, and I think is still; he was detailed by the police. He fired at the procession—at those colored boys; when he shot, the boys wheeled around. There were two or three shots fired by the same person; I believe it was by the same person. Then the police from the other side rushed and arrested one of these boys, and jerked him and took him to the cala-boose. The drum had kept on with the flag, and the boys all ran. I stood at the corner and did not go any further; I thought I would not go back to the Mechanics' Institute, and I remained there for perhaps ten minutes. On the corner where I was standing I saw the police from Dauphin Street turning up Canal Street, and running with pistols in their hands. I got on the side of the banquette and let them go by. As they passed Dryades Street they were firing in the street there, and the loafers that were there were throwing bricks at the Negroes, and the Negroes, too, were throwing bricks; and as the people came up they commenced firing. They fired to scare the people, but they fired with bullets. After firing some time the street got a little clear, so that they could go in. I followed them. When they got to the Mechanics' In-stitute they found the door fastened and they could not get in; then they backed out and fired several times through the windows.

Were the windows up or down? They were shut—some of them might have been open—and as they fired they broke the glass. Then the fire bells began to ring and the firemen began to come. The policemen then succeeded in bursting open the doors and went inside. What they did inside I do not know, but in about a quarter of an hour after there were a good many came out wounded, cut up, shot in the face and head; and there were police taking them to the calaboose; as they passed with them the crowd would knock them down and kill them, and some of the police were helping them kill them on the street. I spoke to the lieutenant of police, with whom I am acquainted—I am acquainted with them all somewhat—and I begged him "For God's sake, stop your men from killing these men so." He gave me no answer, but walked away to the Mechanics' Institute. After a while I spoke to him again; said I, "For God's sake, stop these men from this; I could arrest them all myself." His reply was, "Yes, God damn them; I'll set fire to the building and burn them all." I said no more, but went away. Afterwards I saw a man come out; he was led by a man at each arm; he had no hat on, and his face was all covered with blood. I was looking straight at him, and I said, "That's somebody I know"—I was speaking to myself. When he appeared the crowd cried out, "Kill him." "Kill the damned son of a bitch." I saw it was Dr. Dostie.* The officers had him, and were taking him towards Canal Street. The shots were fired while the police had hold of him, and some

* Dr. Dostie was a leading white radical.

of the police were wounded by their own men. It was a volley of shots; I saw he dropped, and he must have been more than half dead. I remarked, "There is one more." They then rushed back to the Mechanics' Institute, and every man that came out of the Institute was shot or knocked down with a loaded pistol, and when he was down they would shoot him.

Did you see this?

Yes, gentlemen, by my God, I saw it. What I tell you is the positive truth, and if I were to die, it would be with my conscience clean. I staid there for about three-quarters of an hour, for I thought my brother was in the hall. If I had not thought that, I should not have remained. I was too frightened to go into the hall, but I had to stay there, for I thought he would be brought out dead; but for this, I would have gone away long before. Many told me to go away, but I would not. . . .

John Murral:

What is your name and where do you live?

John Murral; 175 St. Charles Street.

How long have you lived in this city?

For twenty-seven years.

What is your business?

My business now is at the first district police station, at the calaboose.

What do you do there?

I am a porter there. . . .

What time in the morning of the 30th, which was Monday, did you go there?

I went there at 4 o'clock.

That is a little after daylight?

Yes, sir.

What did you see when you first got there?

I saw all the police, most of them sitting around, some out on the banquette, and some on the gallery, and a good many in the cap room, where they call the roll; I saw them all sitting down there, and I asked two or three of them I was intimate with what were they all doing there in the morning, because at 5 o'clock they are generally dismissed and have gone home. Two of them said to me, "We have been here ever since 12 o'clock last night; we were called in," they said; "we had orders." Said I, "What made you come in so soon?" He said, "We had orders to come here by the Mayor; the chief gave us orders to come in." I said, "What are you going to do?" One of them said, "I do not know what we are to do;" and when I went in the cap room I found lots of them asleep and some fixing their pistols. When I came down I said to Mr. Charter—he is turnkey, a white man—"What are all these policemen doing?" Charter said he "did not know exactly." I said, "There is something mighty funny." After a while he said, "The convention is going to meet to-day, and they expect there will be a riot." I said, "What kind of a riot?" He said, "There may be a fuss, and the policemen have come in here by order of the mayor, to go down to attend the convention." I said no more to him, but I went to cleaning out the three offices, swept them out, and went into the prison, and gave them all fresh water; then I came out and went over to the hall and got my ice. I met one of the colored boys that stays over at the City Hall; he was cleaning out the City Hall—the Mayor's office, and he said to me, "John, what are those men going to do?" I said, "Mr. Charter said they were going to attend the convention." At about 8 o'clock, when everything was fixed, water in the rooms, and all cleaned up, then all the day police came in (the night police were all there) and I said, "Have you all come off the beat?" and one of them said, "We will not be on the beat to-day." Said I, "What have you come in for?" They said, "We have orders to come in." About 9 o'clock I went to Mr. Charter and said to him, "What do they intend to do to-day? I heard just now," said I, "that these policemen intend to kill everybody at that convention." Said he, "Who said so?" I said, "Never mind, I heard it." I said, "They have pistols and clubs and bowie-knives, and I never saw that so before." "Well," said he, "I don't know about them having them pistols." He said, "I have not any;" and, said he, "you're not going." Then one of them came to me and said, "Are you going to that convention to-day?" I said, "No," and one said, "You had better stay here; if you go out you will be hurt." That was a little after 9 o'clock. It was a policeman that was talking to me; some of them know me, as I have been there a long while. Said I, "I am not going to the convention, I have no business there." Another said, "If you know what is good for you, you will stay here." Then I went home, and I said to my wife, "Don't you go out to-day; you stay in here." She said, "Why?" Said I, "Those policemen said we must keep very close; they have got pistols, bowie-knives, and clubs, and we had better keep close. . . ."

How long have you been in your present position?

Three years.

Have you ever seen the police assembled at the station in that way?

No, sir.

Did you ever see them armed in that way?

No, sir; never. . . .

John Sidney:

State where you live.

I have lived in New Orleans for twenty-two years. I was born in Nash-ville, Tennessee, and raised in Alabama.

Were you in New Orleans on the 30th of July last?

Yes, sir. I was one of the procession and marched at the head of the column. I had been in the 73d Regiment.

Were you in the procession on the 30th?

Yes, sir; and lost all of my musical instruments and got wounded besides.

Do you know who fired the first shot that was fired then?

Yes, sir. His name I cannot recollect. I know the young man whenever I see him; he is now on the police force down at the levee.

Who did he fire at?

At a colored man. The colored man he fired at is in the same building with me. . . .

When was that done?

At about ten o'clock. We marched up Dauphin Street; then marched up Burgundy to Canal Street, and then entered into Philippa Street. Just as we got across the corner of the street this Irishman fired a shot. The way it was done was this: A colored boy and a white boy got into a dispute. John McClernand hissed the white boy on. John McClernand used to be chief of police. He urged on the fight. Then one of our men went to part them. John McClernand shoved him off, and then the Irishman shot at the colored man.

Did he hit the colored man?

No, sir; he did not hit him with the shot. He struck him with a stick. Then we immediately rallied together, and our drummers beat the long roll. We marched on to the Mechanics' Institute and went up into the hall. After we got into the hall we thought everything would be quiet; but very soon afterwards the whole mob came up. They surrounded us. We rushed out. There was a pile of bricks lying in the street. We colored men gathered these bricks and defended ourselves as long as the bricks lasted, and then the mob closed in on us.

What was your procession going to do?

We just merely came there to see what could be seen and what was to be heard. We did not go there with any arms.

How many were there with you?

I suppose there were about one hundred in the procession. There were more when we got there. I suppose there were three or four hundred colored people in or about the building. I was standing close by Dr. Dostie when they shot him.

Who shot him?

I do not know. A man shot him out of a window on the corner of Philippa and Canal Streets. I saw him raise a gun and draw himself back, when he found out we saw him. Then our attention was turned to the mob going up the steps. I was standing at the right side of Dr. Dostie when the ball hit him on the arm. He just whirled around and said: "I am shot!"

Said I, "Where abouts?" He said: "In the arm; keep yourselves quiet."
Where was he when he was shot?

He was standing upon the platform in the hall upstairs.

Where did you get wounded?

In my side.

Who shot you?

A policeman.

Where were you when you were shot?

I was climbing out of a window in the back part of the building. The police told us that if we came out and delivered ourselves up, we would not be disturbed. One of them said: "John, come down; I will not hurt you." But there were other policemen standing there, and one of them shot me.

"New Orleans Riots," *Report No. 16,* House of Representatives, 39th Cong., 2d Sess. (Serial #1304).

183

THE FIRST YEAR OF RADICAL RECONSTRUCTION IN THE SOUTH, 1867

The brazenness of the Bourbons' reactionary policies and actions so soon after the end of fighting, the fact that the industrial bourgeoisie through the Republican Party desired to consolidate its hold over the national government, the protests of the old Abolitionists, and the militant resistance of the Negro people aided by many radical southern whites combined to produce the defeat of the restoration governments. Late in 1866 and early in 1867 these governments were replaced in most of the South by Radical Reconstruction administrations.

Four documents are published below in an attempt to depict conditions and trends in various parts of the South during 1867. The first document records the remarks made by Francis Cardozo of South Carolina at a mass meeting of Charleston Negroes and whites, held March 21. Mr. Cardozo spoke as one of a committee of thirteen Negroes appointed at a previous meeting to draft a platform for a South Carolina Union Party. This platform, which called for, among other things, uniform free compulsory education, a vast internal improvements program of railroad and canal building, the ending of imprisonment for debt and of corporal punishment, the division and sale on easy terms of all unoccupied land, and a broad state-supported social welfare program was defended by Mr. Cardozo prior to his making the remarks printed below.

The second document is a petition to Congress drawn up in July and signed by fifty-four Negro men of Owensboro, Kentucky, protesting against taxation which hit Negroes harder than whites, and against inadequate educational provisions by the state.

The third and fourth documents come from editorials appearing in *The New Orleans Tribune,* the first Negro daily newspaper (published each day, but Monday, in French and English), and an organ of the Republican Party of Louisiana. These editorials deal with the relations between planters and field workers, and with the origins and purposes of the Radical Reconstruction movement.

[a]

Cardozo's Remarks

In the North, there are two divisions of political parties—the Copperheads and the Republicans. The former have acted, and do now act, in perfect harmony with the Southern Whites, while our Northern Republican friends, from the day Lincoln was elected until the passage of the bill by Congress a month ago, have been fighting for our rights. Is it not then the part of wisdom for us to unite with this latter party? They who have been our friends in all seasons of adversity and have shown their friendship by the sacrifice of their lives and their treasure. Surely that man is foolish indeed who would not. But then it may be said, perhaps, after all, that the Southerners are now going to meet with us, and we can be friends. That may be so, but if so, let them come and adopt our platform and join the Republican Party.

We are not opposed to united action. We will gladly welcome union with all our Southern friends, but let them join the party which is true and has been tried, and then there will be united action. But if any advise you to leave that party, whose principles are so clearly those of justice and right, depend upon it that man is your enemy. If he is your friend let him act with you. We bear no enmity to any, but we are determined to secure our rights, and by the eternal vigilance that is the price of liberty, with God's blessing, we hope we shall. By every principle of gratitude, by every desire of security, it behooves you to act with the Republican Party. The noble men of that party have battled for your rights, and have been triumphant over foes and pretended friends. Do you not owe them a debt of gratitude? (Cries of "Yes, yes.")

The N.Y. *Daily Tribune,* March 26, 1867.

[b]

Petition from Kentucky Negroes

To the honorable Senate & House of Representatives of the United States:
We, the undersigned, colored citizens of Daviess county, Kentucky, knowing the high regard Kentucky holds for the Constitution of the United States; as a majority of at least forty thousand of her citizens have proclaimed in platforms and creeds that they wish, in every particular, to be governed

by that sacred instrument, the Constitution of the United States; as we would not have our native State (by mistaken legislation, we suppose) violate that sacred instrument and impose upon one portion of citizens a greater amount of taxes for a specified purpose than on another portion, living in and citizens of the same locality, for no other reason than that our skins are dark.

An act of the Kentucky legislature approved March 9, 1867, provides that there shall be, in addition to the capitation tax of two dollars already levied, an additional tax of two dollars ($2). The white citizens are taxed two dollars under the same head. Again, the act above alluded to reads that the trustees of each common school district *may* cause a school to be taught for the education of Negro and mulatto children. Now, the word "may" leaves it *optional* with the trustees whether they will have the school taught or not; and we presume that all persons who are acquainted with Kentucky proclivities will at once come to the conclusion that the trustees will say that "Negroe schools" are calculated to breed strife and unfit the mind of the freedman to perform that domestic duty so indispensable to the citizens of Kentucky. Again, [the law] says: "The sheriff may notify any person indebted to a Negro or mulatto, and stop from the money due the said Negro or mulatto the amount of his taxes" &c. &c. Now, without any notification whatever, the sheriff of the county will call on the man for whom we are working and draw from our wages the amount of this tax. We ask, is this in accordance with any principle of free government, to not even ask us for our taxes, but garnishee our money in the hands of our employers? And, again, we have no idea that one dollar of this money will ever benefit the persons from whom it is collected, or their children of color.

These oppressive laws are made without our help, and we are rendered powerless. Will our great and only friend, the Congress of the United States, look to this matter?

Executive Document No. 7, House of Representatives, 40th Cong., 2d Sess.

[c]

Editorial from the New Orleans Tribune *

EMPLOYERS AND EMPLOYEES

On the 4th of the present month [November], a "great Convention of planters," of the parishes of Rapides and Avoyelles met at Cheneyville, and

---

* Below the masthead on the editorial page, this paper stated: "To every Citizen His Rights—Universal Suffrage—Equality Before the Law—To Every Laborer His Dues—An Equitable Salary and Weekly Payments—Eight Hours A Day A Legal Day's Work."

adopted resolutions which we find printed in the Marksville *Villager* of the 9th instant. They will show to any impartial reader the true spirit of the planters of that place. It will be sufficient here to say that they deprecate the working on shares of the laborers; they oppose the payment of wages at the end of every month, so as to give the planter a better chance of cheating the laborer of his due—"a small advance for clothing, medicine, etc., is all that can reasonably be demanded, or safely made." They set forth that the price of labor has not to be regulated by the great law of demand and supply, or by the more equitable law of the wants of the laborer, but by "the value of the staple production"; so that should cotton be depreciated on the market the laborer will have to starve, while the planter will keep the little money he may make by selling it. They agree together for exacting from laborers a "certificate of good conduct," which, of course, will always be refused to those who claim their full right, so that none but servile tools may have work, while *men* will be rejected and reduced to starvation. They enter into an agreement not to employ any laborer who belongs to a political club, so as to prevent the workingmen becoming acquainted with their duties and their rights as citizens, with the evident object of keeping them in the dark and using them as their tools at the ballot box. This proscription of men for belonging to a political organization whatever, is one of the grossest insults ever done to our Republican institutions: They will not only refuse to give work to members of clubs, but "will not rent them lands on ANY TERMS." It is an undisguised proscription.

This proscription is extended by the 6th resolution to white persons friendly to the blacks. Not only land will be refused them on lease, but those planters will "PURGE THE COUNTRY" of such as "by their conduct exhibit a hostile purpose to our (planters') interest," whereby we see that this incorrigible class of despots threatens with unlawful expulsion and even death the citizens who will not be found acting in the planters' interest. What society is this where a man has no security and no right to remain unless he be subservient to a given class? Who will call that by any other name than base and shameless despotism? Is not this the case for the threatened white man to say "let us have liberty or death"?

[To this, the paper points out, Negroes have replied as indicated by the following example:]

Resolutions Adopted At A Meeting of the Mansura Club of Avoyelles

Whereas at a meeting of planters of Avoyelles and Rapides, held at Cheneyville, in the parish of Rapides, resolutions have been passed and adopted calculated to pervert by prejudice the minds of our friends North and South, to induce them to believe that our conduct is of such a nature as to endanger the peace of society, and

Whereas in the face of such false accusation it becomes our duty to destroy the erroneous impression they may have made upon the public mind: Therefore,

Resolved, 1st. That we deplore the condition of those men who have not as yet evinced that the teachings of humanity had softened their hard nature (the natural effect of the evils of slavery), and that we think it is time they should begin to repent for all the crimes they have committed upon the innocent and unprotected under their domination during the existence of barbarism.

2d. *Resolved*, That if we have organized ourselves in political clubs, it was for the purpose of becoming acquainted with our rights and duties as citizens, and to support the policies of our political friends North and South, and that our demeanor on the plantation and at the ballot-box manifest no opposition to the peace of society and the quiet enjoyment of the right of property, that we have never advocated the confiscation of the lands of the leaders in the late rebellion and if there is anything inimical in our conduct it partakes of a political character only.

3d. *Resolved*, That the organization of the Radical or Union Republican Party in this parish, is entirely friendly to the interests, peace and agricultural prosperity of the country, that its object is to promote the elevation of the colored race to the broad principles of the Declaration of our Independence, and to destroy the deep seated evils engendered by the barbarous institution of slavery.

4th. *Resolved*, That we most categorically deny all the assertions made against the colored population as fake and uncalled for.

5th. *Resolved*, That we consider ourselves, although poor and houseless, as much a part of the nation and society as they, and that we have at heart the tranquility of the country and that we will zealously work for Reconstruction, the establishment of common schools, opposition to slavery, universal suffrage, protection to all in the enjoyment of equal rights before the law, the perpetual maintenance of the Union and for the party which has rendered to man his manhood.

Paulin Guigonet,
President, Manusra Club

Joseph Laurent, Secretary.

[d]

Editorial from the New Orleans Tribune (2)

THE FIRST GOVERNMENT OF THE PEOPLE

After three years' hesitation and delay the National Government concluded at last to take the right step for reconstruction. Every way was first tried except the sound and logical one. The first attempt at reconstruction was through military power. Provisional officers, taken from the army, were appointed as governors and mayors; provost marshals and freedmen's bureau agents were intrusted with the supervision of affairs in the country parishes. They understood very little of the political situation. Governor Shepley discarded the propositions of the Free State Committee. Provost marshals showed the rebels more courtesy and granted them more favors than they did to poor but devoted Union men. Agents of the Freedmen's Bureau might have been designated better as planters' agents. They took more trouble to procure hands for the owners of large plantations than to protect the freed people and defend their rights. We still recollect Gen. Banks' order on "small-pox passes," by which, under the absurd plea of preventing the spreading of small-pox, the colored people were placed under a law of exception as far as their movements were concerned. They were not allowed to change plantations, they could not leave a place and hunt for work—which is the natural right of all free laborers—unless they first obtained a pass from their former employer, who, of course, refused to give them any. The hypocritical "small-pox passes" remain on Gen. Banks' record, as one of the most flagrant failures to understand and to establish freedom.

The pro-slavery spirit inspired the act of the military administration. The military was not the power to understand civil liberty; generals used to arbitrary command, felt better disposed in favor of the chiefs of the plantations than in favor of the common laborers. They were, moreover, unwilling to take the responsibility of any important change. And after Butler—who was an exception to the rule—had left us, they did, perhaps unconsciously, as much as they could for the slave power, and as little as they could for the cause of liberty and the rights of men.

At last, however, the military government relinquished its hold. The Convention of 1864 assembled, and under the Constitution they framed, a civil government having its legislative, its executive, and judicial officers, was inaugurated. The attempt was made under the inspiration of the military, and could be, of course, but a continuance of the same errors already made. A very small number of the people of a small number of parishes was called upon to vote. The representatives of the old Union minority of white men met at the City Hall, and ignoring the change of the times, believing themselves the legitimate successors of King Cotton, they made an oligarchical Constitution, nearly as bad, for it was as partial as that of 1852. They forgot through pride and presumption, that they had no power by themselves to uphold the white union oligarchy thus created. The fact is that the very day when military rule came to an end, and the qualified voters—the white voters—under the Constitution of 1864 went to the polls, the Union oligarchs were put aside and rebel oligarchs reinstated in their stead. It did not take great power of intellect to foresee that result. The UNION and subsequently the *Tribune* warned our white friends, at the time, of the evident fate in store for them. Still they kept up their illusions; for could they listen to a black organ? The dullest among them believed himself smarter than any colored man in the land; and down they went, having consummated their own ruin. Gov. Wells vindicated our forebodings. He promptly turned them out of office; and then they could see whether the black organ had seen things correctly or not. From that day they began to call again at our office; they said they were ready to retrieve their faults, and to proclaim universal suffrage. But the golden opportunity had passed away, they had been blind at the opportune time; they had played in their enemies' hands. And rebels showed at the Mechanics' Institute how they intended to treat them.

This was the end of the Union white man's government. Since the eventful day of the 30th of July, 1866, we have lived under the grasp of the rebel oligarchy, restored to power. But Congress has finally given us the means of relief. After governments of minorities, we are at last enabled to organize a government of the people. Let us hope that the Convention of 1867 will have more foresight, a sounder judgment and more liberalism than had the Convention of 1864. They have to work in the interest of the whole people and secure the rights of all classes of citizens, of whatever race or color, unless they want to see the fabric they will attempt to build up crumble to pieces, and partake of the fate of the government erected in 1864.

New Orleans *Tribune*, Nov. 22, Nov. 24, 1867. Copies in the Boston Athenaeum.

184

UNDERMINING RECONSTRUCTION: 1) UNCLE TOMISM, 1868–1872

Radical Reconstruction had attacked Jim Crow, enfranchised the Negro people, established a free public school system, and instituted a broad social welfare program. It had democratized the administrative and judicial apparatus, encouraged manufacturing, enhanced the rights of women, eliminated legal reflections of anti-Semitism and brought about the beginnings of a wider distribution of the land.

The Bourbons therefore detested it and to combat it they resorted to legal trickery, fraud, a taxpayers' strike, the buying up of renegades—Negro and white —and above all, violence. Illustrative of the role of the handful of Negroes willing to participate in anti-Radical activity are the two documents that follow. The first is the speech made by one Sydenham Porter of Livingston, Alabama, on July 18, 1868, urging Negroes to abstain from political activity; the second consists of the resolutions of the Colored Democratic Club of Montgomery, Alabama, adopted August 1, 1872, and calling for Negro support of the Democratic Party in the current Presidential campaign. The leader of this Montgomery club was Caesar Shorter who had been a slave of Governor Shorter of Alabama. Neither appeal, of course, was successful.

[a]

Sydenham Porter's Speech

Ladies, Gentlemen, and Fellow-Citizens: Our country is what I propose to talk about at this time. If we think a moment, and look around us, we see our gin-houses and screws and fences and barns destroyed, and nobody to build them up. Ruin and decay is on every hand.

We must admit something is wrong. Why is all this? Because we have been called from our regular duties to follow after scalawags and carpet-bag politicians to the injury of ourselves and families. They tell us they are our friends. Have they ever done anything for us? Nothing. On the other hand, have we ever done anything for them? We elected them to office. And did you ever see one of them that didn't want office? . . . We have turned our backs on those that we have been raised with, and who support us, and followed after strangers who done nothing for us. This is the reason we are no better off to-day, and there is such a bad state of things.

The only way for us to get along and do well is to let politics alone and go to work to gather crops that are now growing, and have something to live on. Politics is a thing we know nothing about; and if we did, it is a mighty unprofitable business. We are encouraged by a certain class of people to go ahead with politics, because they want to use us to get our votes. If we take any part in politics, let us do it like men, and not have so much parade and "to do" about it. Let us respect everybody's opinion, and have harmony and good feeling between all, especially with those who have known us since childhood till the present hour. They are the ones that have helped and assisted us, and all the money I have made since I have been free come from them. We must continue to live together, and unless there is good feeling between us, it is impossible for us to prosper, make money or a living. If we desire peace and prosperity, let us say or do nothing that will stir bad feeling. He who looks back at the past and talks about our bondage does not love peace and harmony. We must look ahead and do our duty in the future. We must also recollect if anybody is to blame for our bondage, it is all the people of the United States, and not the southern people alone.

Then let us let politics alone, go to work, and cherish good and kind feeling toward our old friends, and they will continue our friends; we will thrive and prosper. But if we do not work and attend to our business and do our duty, but go to public meetings all the time, and stir up bad feelings, ourselves, our families, and our country will be ruined. I know many that I have talked with agree with me, and I hope all of us will strive to do for the best, influenced by a desire for peace and harmony, and a good will to all mankind.

Testimony Taken by the Joint Committee to Inquire into the Condition of Affairs in the Late Insurrectionary States. (The K.K.K. Conspiracy Investigation), Washington, 1872, Government Printing Office), *Alabama*, III, pp. 1665–66. (Hereafter cited as *K.K.K. Investigation*.)

[b]

Resolutions of the Montgomery Club

Whereas, The creation and perpetuation of a friendly and peaceful relation between the white and colored people of the South is absolutely essential to the prosperity of the latter and can only be effected by the defeat of the administration candidates, therefore

Be it Resolved, That we, a portion of the colored people of this city and county of Montgomery do heartily endorse the nomination of Greeley and Brown * and will use all honorable means to secure their election.

Be it further Resolved, That it is our honest conviction that the adoption of the Liberal Republican platform by the Democratic Party throws around the colored people every guarantee necessary for the protection of their rights under the Constitution of the United States.

Be it further Resolved, That to support the Grant Administration in the face of the favorable political auspices would be detrimental to our interests, both local and national.

Be it further Resolved, That we recognize no other place but the South as our home, and that the interests of the white and colored people here are one and in common and should be regarded by both in order to secure a peaceable settlement of existing prejudices.

* Horace Greeley, editor of the N.Y. *Tribune* and Benjamin Gratz-Brown, Governor of Missouri, were the candidates for President and Vice-President on the combined Liberal Republican-Democratic Party ticket in 1872.

Be it further Resolved, That we oppose all secret organizations for political purposes, or any party that slanders or proscribes men because of their party principles.

Montgomery, Ala., *Daily Advertiser*, Aug. 8, 1872.

185

UNDERMINING RECONSTRUCTION: 2) LEGAL TACTICS, 1868

A prime example of an attempt to defeat Reconstruction, by legal means, comes from Georgia. There, in 1868, a considerable number of Radicals was elected to the state legislature, but reactionaries still held control of that body. This majority declared that two Senators and twenty-five Representatives were ineligible since they were Negroes, and these men were expelled. Through mass meetings, demonstrations and delegations to Washington, these expelled members were readmitted in 1869, but the next year the Democrats forcibly regained power. Below are printed the formal protests of the two ousted Senators, George Wallace and Tunis G. Campbell, and the speech delivered in the House by Henry M. Turner, Negro representative of Bibb County, on September 3, 1868.

[a]

Protest of the expelled Senators

Mr. President, and gentlemen of the Senate:

You have this day decided by your vote, that we are not eligible to seats on the floor of the senate.

Sirs, by a very large majority of the votes cast in our several districts, and by the right guaranteed us both in the Constitution of the United States and of the State of Georgia, as well as in the reconstruction-laws of Congress, we claim to be the legal elected representatives of a very large portion of— and nearly one-half of the legal electors of the State of Georgia. Sirs, the Constitution and laws of Georgia strictly provide that no laws shall be made or enforced which shall abridge the privileges or immunities of citizens of the United States, or of this State, or deny to any person within its jurisdiction the equal protection of its laws.

Therefore, in behalf of ourselves, our constituents, and also in behalf of nearly five hundred thousand loyal citizens of this State, we do enter our solemn protest against the illegal, unconstitutional, unjust and oppressive action of this body, based upon the resolution of the Senators from the 35th Senatorial District, declaring us ineligible on account of color.

[b]

Henry M. Turner's Speech

Mr. Speaker:

Before proceeding to argue this question upon its intrinsic merits, I wish the members of this House to understand the position that I take. I hold that I am a member of this body. Therefore, sir, I shall neither fawn or cringe before any party, nor stoop to beg them for my rights. Some of my colored fellow members, in the course of their remarks, took occasion to appeal to the sympathies of Members on the opposite side, and to eulogize their character for magnanimity. It reminds me very much, sir, of slaves begging under the lash. I am here to demand my rights, and to hurl thunderbolts at the men who would dare to cross the threshold of my manhood. There is an old aphorism which says, "Fight the Devil with fire," and if I should observe the rule in this instance, I wish gentlemen to understand that it is but fighting them with their own weapon.

The scene presented in this House, to-day, is one unparalleled in the history of the world. From this day, back to the day when God breathed the breath of life into Adam, no analogy for it can be found. Never, in the history of the world, has a man been arraigned before a body clothed with legislative, judicial or executive functions, charged with the offence of being of a darker hue than his fellowmen. I know that questions have been before the Courts of this country, and of other countries, involving topics not altogether dissimilar to that which is being discussed here to-day. But, sir, never in all the history of the great nations of this world—never before—has a man been arraigned, charged with an offence committed by the God of Heaven Himself. Cases may be found where men have been deprived of their rights for crimes and misdemeanors; but it has remained for the State of Georgia, in the very heart of the nineteenth century, to call a man before the bar, and there charge him with an act for which he is no more responsible than for the head which he carries upon his shoulders. The Anglo-Saxon race, sir, is a most surprising one. No man has ever been more deceived in that race than I have been for the last three weeks. I was not aware that there was in the character of that race so much cowardice, or so much pusillanimity. The treachery which has been exhibited in it by gentlemen belonging to that race has shaken my confidence in it more than anything that has come under my observation from the day of my birth.

What is the question at issue? Why, sir, this Assembly, to-day, is discussing and deliberating on a judgment; there is not a Cherubim that sits around God's eternal Throne, to-day, that would not tremble—even were an order issued by the Supreme God Himself—to come down here and sit in judgment on my manhood. Gentlemen may look at this question in whatever light they choose, and with just as much indifference as they may think proper to assume, but I tell you, sir, that this is a question which will not die to-day. This event shall be remembered by posterity for ages yet to come, and while the sun shall continue to climb the hills of heaven.

Whose Legislature is this? Is it a white man's Legislature, or is it a black man's Legislature? Who voted for a Constitutional Convention, in obedience to the mandate of the Congress of the United States? Who first rallied around the standard of Reconstruction? Who set the ball of loyalty rolling in the State of Georgia? And whose voice was heard on the hills and in the valleys of this State? It was the voice of the brawny-armed Negro, with the few humanitarian-hearted white men who came to our assistance. I claim the honor, sir, of having been the instrument of convincing hundreds—yea, thousands—of white men, that to reconstruct under the measures of the United States Congress was the safest and the best course for the interest of the State.

Let us look at some facts in connection with this matter. Did half the white men of Georgia vote for this Legislature? Did not the great bulk of them fight, with all their strength, the Constitution under which we are acting? And did they not fight against the organization of this Legislature? And further, sir, did they not vote against it? Yes, sir! And there are persons in this Legislature to-day, who are ready to spit their poison in my face, while they themselves opposed, with all their power, the ratification of this Constitution. They question my right to a seat in this body, to represent the people whose legal votes elected me. This objection, sir, is an unheard of monopoly of power. No analogy can be found for it, except it be the case of a man who should go into my house, take possession of my wife and children, and then tell me to walk out. I stand very much in the position of a criminal before your bar, because I dare to be the exponent of the views of those who sent me here. Or, in other words, we are told that if black men want to speak, they must speak through white trumpets; if black men want their sentiments expressed, they must be adulterated and sent through white messengers, who will quibble, and equivocate, and evade, as rapidly as the pendulum of a clock. If this be not done, then the black men have committed an outrage, and their Representatives must be denied the right to represent their constituents.

The great question, sir, is this: Am I a man? If I am such, I claim the rights of a man. Am I not a man because I happen to be of a darker hue than honorable gentlemen around me? . . .

But Mr. Speaker, I do not regard this movement as a thrust at me, it is a thrust at the Bible—a thrust at the God of the Universe, for making a man and not finishing him; it is simply calling the Great Jehovah a fool. Why, sir, though we are not white, we have accomplished much. We have pioneered civilization here; we have built up your country; we have worked in your fields, and garnered your harvests, for two hundred and fifty years! And what do we ask of you in return? Do we ask you for compensation for the sweat our fathers bore for you—for the tears you have caused, and the hearts you have broken, and the lives you have curtailed, and the blood you have spilled? Do we ask retaliation? We ask it not. We are willing to let the dead past bury its dead; but we ask you now for our RIGHTS. You have all the elements of superiority upon your side; you have our money and your own; you have our education and your own; and you have your land and our own, too. We, who number hundreds of thousands in Georgia, including our wives and families, with not a foot of land to call our own—strangers in the land of our birth; without money, without education, without aid, without a roof to cover us while we live, nor sufficient clay to cover us when we die! It is extraordinary that a race such as yours, professing gallantry, and chivalry, and education, and superiority, living in a land where ringing chimes call child and sire to the Church of God—a land where Bibles are read and Gospels truths are spoken, and where courts of justice are presumed to exist; it is extraordinary to say, that, with all these advantages on your side, you can make war upon the poor defenseless black man. . . .

You may expel us, gentlemen, but I firmly believe that you will someday repent it. The black man cannot protect a country, if the country doesn't protect him; and if, tomorrow, a war should arise, I would not raise a musket to defend a country where my manhood is denied. The fashionable way in Georgia when hard work is to be done, is, for the white man to sit at his ease, while the black man does the work; but, sir, I will say this much to the colored men of Georgia, as if I should be killed in this campaign, I may have no opportunity of telling them at any other time: Never lift a finger nor raise a hand in defense of Georgia, unless Georgia acknowledges that you are men, and invests you with the rights pertaining to manhood. Pay your taxes, however, obey all orders from your employers, take good counsel from friends, work faithfully, earn an honest living, and show, by your conduct, that you can be good citizens. . . .

You may expel us, gentlemen, by your votes, today; but, while you do it, remember that there is a just God in Heaven, whose All-Seeing Eye beholds alike the acts of the oppressor and the oppressed, and who, despite the machinations of the wicked, never fails to vindicate the cause of Justice, and the sanctity of His own handiwork.

Ethel M. Christler, "Participation of Negroes in the Government of Georgia 1867–1870," unpublished master's thesis, Atlanta University, 1932, pp. 34–35 and appendix B.

186

UNDERMINING RECONSTRUCTION: 3) VIOLENCE AND FRAUD, 1871–1876

A] INDIVIDUAL TESTIMONY

The basic means for destroying Radical Reconstruction, as has already been stated, were violence and fraud. From a tremendous mass of available material demonstrating this point, there are published below a few documents which are quite typical and which cover the entire South and the entire period. This material has been divided into two groups—letters or sworn statements from individual Negroes, and resolutions or petitions from Negro mass meetings.

Of the material from individuals the earliest is dated July, 1871 while the latest is June, 1876. Nine Negro men and women offer evidence here—in every case of things they, themselves, witnessed, did, or suffered—and represented are the states of South Carolina, Florida, Alabama, Mississippi, Louisiana and Texas.

These documents illuminate not only the bestiality of the reactionaries and the torment of the Negro, but also the Negro's persistence and courage. They demonstrate, too, the basic significance of the land question, show the Negro's struggle for political and civil rights, and demonstrate in several instances the existence of Negro-white unity within the South in the midst of terror.

The 1871 material comes from the printed *Testimony Taken by the Joint Select Committee to Inquire into the Condition of Affairs in the Late Insurrectionary States*. This Joint Congressional Committee, consisting of five Senators and eight Representatives, was appointed on April 20, 1871 as the result of a message from President Grant, the previous month, informing Congress that life and property were insecure in the South, and that the collection of revenue and the delivery of mail were impeded there. The 1875 and 1876 material comes from the reports of two Congressional Committees which were appointed to investigate reports of fraud and violence in Mississippi and Louisiana elections.

[a]

Columbia, South Carolina, July 3, 1871

Willis Johnson (colored) sworn and examined.

Where do you live?

At Leonidas Sims's, in Newberry County.

How long have you lived there?

This year. I lived there one year since I have been free before this year.

What is he?

A planter.

Are you a laborer?

Yes, sir.

Can you read and write?

No, sir.

Were you taught any before you were free?

No, sir.

Have you been taught any since?

No, sir.

Have you been at any time visited by men masked and disguised—Ku-Klux?

Yes, sir.

When?

Last night two weeks ago.

Go on and tell what you saw and what they said and did, telling it in your own way.

When I awoke, as near as I can tell, it was between 12 and 1 o'clock. I heard some one call "Sims." I held still and listened, and heard them walk from his door to my door. I was up-stairs, and I got up and came down-stairs. They walked back to his house again and asked him to put his head out. He did not answer, but his wife asked them who they were. They said they were friends. They walked back to my door again, and just as they got to the door they blew a whistle. Another whistle off a piece answered, and then men seemed to surround the house and all parts of the yard. Then they hallooed, "Open the door." I said nothing. I went to the head of the bed and got my pistol, and leaned forward on the table with the pistol just at the door. They tried with several surges to get the door open, but it did not come open. They went to the wood-pile and got the axe, and struck the front-door some licks, bursted it open, and then went to the back door and burst it open. Nobody had yet come into the house; they had not come in. They said, "Strike a light." Then I dropped down on my knees back of the table, and they struck some matches and threw them in the house, and two of them stepped in the front door, and that brought them within arm's length of me as they stood there. As soon as they did that, I raised my pistol quickly, right up to one's back, and shot, and he fell and hallooed, and the other tried to pull him out. As he pulled him I shot again. As they were pulling, others ran up and pulled him out in the yard, and when the whole party was out in the yard I stepped to the door and shot again, and then jumped to the back door and ran. I got off. I staid away until the next morning; then I came back and tracked them half a mile where they had toted this man and laid him down. I was afraid to go further. Mr. Sims and I were together, and I would not go any further, and he told me to go away; that I ought not to stay there; that he saw the men and saw the wounded man, and was satisfied that he was dead or mortally wounded, and I must leave. Mr. John Calmes, the candidate of the democrats for the legislature, advised me to take a paper and go around the settlement to the white people, stating that I would never vote the radical ticket, and he said he did not think they would interfere with me then. He said that all they had against me was that on election day I took the tickets around among the black people; and he said: "You knocked me out of a good many votes, but you are a good fellow and a good laborer, and we want labor in this country." I told him I would not do that. . . .

Spartanburgh, South Carolina, July 6, 1871

Charlotte Fowler (colored) sworn and examined.

Where do you live?

On Mr. Moore's premises.

Do you know in what township?

No, sir; my son does.

Is it in this county?

No, sir; I did live in Spartanburgh County with my husband, before the old man was killed; but now I live with my son.

How long ago is it since your husband was killed?

It was the 1st of May.

What was his name?

Wallace Fowler.

Tell how he was killed.

The night he was killed—I was taken sick on Wednesday morning, and I laid on my bed Wednesday and Thursday. I didn't eat a mouthful; I couldn't do it, I was so sick; so he went out working on his farm. We still had a little grandchild living with me—my daughter's child. He had two little children living with him on the farm, but still that little child staid with me. He kept coming backward and forward to the house to see how I got on and what he could do for me. I never ate nothing until Thursday night. When he came home he cooked something for me to eat, and said: "Old woman, if you don't eat something you will die." Says I: "I can't eat." Says he: "Then I will eat, and feed the little baby." That is the grandchild he meant. I says: "You take that little child and sleep in the bed; I think I have got the fever, and I don't want you to get it." He said, "No, I don't want to get the fever, for I have got too much to do." He got up and pulled off his clothes, and got in bed. He came and called to the grandchild, Tody—she is Sophia—and he says: "Tody, when you are ready to come to bed, come, and grandmother will open your frock, and you can go to bed." So he laid there for about a half an hour, and then I heard the dogs. I was only by myself now, for the children was all abed. Then I got up and went into my room to my bed. I reckon I did not lay in bed a half an hour, before I heard somebody by the door; it was not one person, but two—ram! ram! ram! at the door. Immediately I was going to call him to open the door; but he heard it as quick as lightning, and he said to them: "Gentlemen, do not break the door down; I will open the door"; and just as he said that they said: "God damn you, I have got you now." I was awake and I started and got out of bed, and fell down on the floor. I was very much scared. The little child followed its grandfather to the door—you know in the night it is hard to direct a child. When he said, "God damn you, I have got you now," and he said, "Don't you run," and just then I heard the report of a pistol, and they shot him down; and this little child ran back to me before I could get out, and says, "Oh, grandma, they have killed my poor grandpappy." He was such an old gentleman that I thought they just shot over him to scare him; but sure enough, as quick as I got to the door, I raised my right hand and said, "Gentlemen, you have killed a poor, innocent man." My poor old man! Says he, "Shut up." I never saw but two of them, for, by that time, the others had vanished.

How did you know there were any others there?

The little boy that was there when they shot his grandpappy ran into the house; he was there, and when they started I heard the horses' feet going from the gate. I was then a hallooing and screaming. After they shot the old man, they came back in the house—"Chup! Chup! Chup! make up a light." I said, "I am not able to make up a light; I have been sick two days." I called to the little girl, "Is there any light there?" She says, "No." But the mantel was there, where I could reach it, where they put the splinters, and I said, "Light that splinter"; and she lit the splinter. He said, "Hand it here"; and she handed it to him; and then he says, "March before me, march before me." That was done in the middle of my room. He says, "Hand me up your arms"—that is, the guns. Says I, "There isn't any here, sir." Says he, "Hand me up that pistol." I says, "There is none here; the old man had none in slavery, and had none in all his freedom, and everybody on the settlement knows it." When he told me about the light he put that pistol up to my face—so—and says, "If you don't come here I will get you light out of this." He did that when I was a poor woman by myself. . . .

Did these men have masks on?

Only the one that shot him.

What kind of a mask?

It was all around the eyes. It was black; and the other part was white and red; and he had horns on his head. He came in the house after he killed the old man and told me about the light, and I made the little girl make a light; he took the light from her and looked over the old man. Another man came out of the gate, and looked down at the old man and dropped a chip of fire on him, and burnt through his shirt—burnt his breast. They had shot him through the head, and every time he breathed his brains would come out. . . .

Was the old man dead when the fire was thrown on him?

He did not die until Friday between 1 and 2 o'clock; but he couldn't speak a word. He was just bleeding, and his brains and blood came out over his eyes . . .

Did your old man * belong to any party?

Yes, sir.

What party?

The radicals.

How long did he belong to them?

Ever since they started the voting.

Was he a pretty strong radical?

Yes, sir; a pretty strong radical.

Did he work for that party?

Yes, sir. . . .

Did he vote at the last election?

Yes, sir.

Livingston, Alabama, Nov. 1, 1871

John Childers (colored) sworn and examined.

. . . She (a daughter of mine) was awfully badly whipped. I was not here. I was in Mississippi. I came here the day after she was whipped. I got back the next day. She lived seven days after I got home. My wife hired her out to a man while I was gone, and he awfully abused her. It was done the Wednesday before the last 4th of July. You can count back from the last 4th of July and see what time it came on.

Was there more than one person concerned in whipping her?

No, sir; Mr. Jones, who had her employed from my wife, he was the one that did it. I aimed to prosecute him at the last gone court, but the witnesses, by some means or other, was run away. I don't know; I could not tell how they got them out of the way. There was no case made of them.

Did she die because of the whipping?

I am satisfied that she did. I can't say that, but I am satisfied that she did.

Did you see her body after she had been whipped?

I did; I examined her myself; I buried her with scars on her that long (illustrating;) a finger-length.

How long after the whipping did she die?

In eight days.

How old was she?

---

* He was about seventy years old.

She would have been ten years old the 26th of next August.

What was she whipped for?

She was hired out as a nurse to see to the baby; she had taken the baby out to the front yard among a parcel of arbor vitae; and, being out there, the baby and she together, she was neglectful, so as to leave the baby's cap out where it was not in place when the mother of the child called for the cap, and it could not be found. That is what she told me when I came home that she was whipped for. When I came home on Friday night, I think, to the best of my recollection, in July, before the 4th of July, I wrote to my wife I would be home on the 4th of July; I think this last 4th of July was on Saturday. You know better than I do. Anyhow, I came home the day before the 4th of July. I found my little daughter at home. She had run away from the place where she was abused; but I saw the rest of the children playing in the yard, and she was in the door sitting there, and I thought that was strange, because she was a mighty playful chap, and I asked, "What are you sitting here for?" And she says, "Pap, Mr. Jones has beat me nearly to death." (The witness weeping.) . . .

Did you ever hear any threats made by democrats against Negroes of what would be done if they voted the radical ticket?

I have had threats on myself. I can tell them.

What kind of threats were made to you?

I have had threats if we all would vote the democratic ticket we would be well thought of, and the white men of the country—the old citizens of the country—would protect us; and every struggle or trouble we got into we could apply to them for protection, and they would assist us.

Where did you hear that said?

I have heard it often. At the last election it was given to me. There was a man standing here in the court-house door; when he started to the ballot-box he told me he had a coffin already made for me, because he thought I was going to vote the radical ticket.

Who was that man?

Well, I am afraid to tell his name, sir.

That was the last election—the last presidential election?

No, sir; the last governor's election—last fall.

Did you hear any other Negroes threatened?

Well, there was so many of them threatened, I could not say. It was just as drinking is for such things as that to be; but then I could not name any particular one that had that threat on him, because it was on all.

Were the colored folks generally alarmed by these threats, and afraid to vote their true sentiments?

Yes, sir, they were.

I have heard that a great many colored people voted the democratic ticket at the last governor's election.

Yes, sir.

What made them do it?

For fear. I voted it myself. I voted the democratic ticket.

Were you afraid if you voted the radical ticket you would be harmed?

I was, sir; because, as I just stated to you, there was a man told me he had a coffin already made for me.

If the colored people were not interfered with; if they were allowed to vote their own sentiments freely, and without any molestation, how would they generally vote?

Radical, sir.

Do you know this Sydenham Porter?

Yes, sir; I am well acquainted with him. I have known him for fifteen years.

He votes the democratic ticket, does he not?

Yes, sir.

They think a good deal of him?

Yes, sir.

Put him up to speak in their political meetings, do they not?

Yes, sir; they do.* He is something superior to the balance of the colored people in the community.

By whom is he employed; what does he follow for a living?

Well, sir, he isn't employed particularly by no one; he was so well helped up that he works his own scales; he has a little shebang of his own running.

What is that?

Selling whiskey and other things.

Do the white democrats patronize—go there and drink his whiskey?

I don't know whether they do. He is out in the out edge of town; I never go to his house.

Does he seem to have plenty of money and dress well?

Yes, sir, he does.

You think he makes it profitable to be a democrat?

In his way of acting he seems to be a little above the general run of the race.

Is he well thought of by the colored people?

No, sir. In other words, the general part. The leading parties of our radical party has gone over that way.

What do you think has induced them to go over?

Promises and influences.

* For an example of his speeches see document No. 184[a].

So far as your acquaintance with your people goes, how many of them do you think would vote the democratic ticket, if left to themselves?

Not one, sir. Not a single one.

Where a colored man is known as a democrat, and votes the democratic ticket, is he ever whipped or interfered with?

Not at all, sir.

So, it is only the radicals that are whipped, and their children killed?

Yes, sir; these men that contends for their equal rights for person and property with the white men.

They are the men that are singled out and punished, are they?

Yes, sir.

How many of your people in this county do you think have been whipped, or otherwise outraged because of their political sentiments?

O, hundreds. I could not number them to you, sir.

Can you name any other colored men that voted the democratic ticket for the same reason you did—prominent colored men?

I never questioned them, sir, what was their reasons for voting it, but I heard of all such threats and inducements that were given to influence them to vote the democratic ticket. I could not say that any other man besides myself did it for the same reason I did?

But that is your belief?

Yes, sir, that is it. I voted it, and I don't pretend to deny it before nobody. When I was going to the polls there was a man standing in the door and says, "Here comes you, God damn your soul, I have got a coffin already made for you." I had two tickets in my pocket then; a democratic ticket and a radical ticket; I pulled out the democratic ticket and showed it to him, and he says, "You are all right, go on."

Jacksonville, Florida, November 10, 1871.
Hannah Tutson (colored) sworn and examined.

State your age, where you were born, and where you now live?

As near as I can tell I am about forty-two or forty-three years old. I was born in Gadsden, Florida, and I now live in Clay County, near Waldo, on old Number Eleven Pond.

Are you the wife of Samuel Tutson?

Yes, sir.

Were you at home when he was whipped last spring?

Yes, sir; I was at home.

Tell us what took place then, what was done, and how it was done.

When they came to my house that night the dog barked twice, and the old man got up and went out of doors and then came back and lay down; she flew out again, and I got up and went out of doors; I knew the slut barked more than usual, but I could see nothing; I went back into the house, and just as I got into bed five men bulged right against the door, and it fell right in the middle of the floor, and they fell down. George McRae was the first to get up. I had no chimney in the house, but a board floor, and he went where I had left all the children; went circling around toward the children's bed, and I said "Who's that?" The old man had not spoke. George McRae ran right to me and gathered me by the arm. As I saw him coming I took up the child— the baby—and held to him. The old man threw his arms around my neck and held on to me. Cabell Winn catched hold of my foot, and then there were so many hold of me I cannot tell who they were. George McRae and Cabell Winn were the first to take hold of me. He said, "Come in, True-Klux." I started to scream, and George McRae catched me right by the throat and choked me. I worried around and around, and he catched the little child by the foot and slinged it out of my arms. I screamed again, and he gathered me again. Then there were so many hold of me that they got me out of doors. After they got me out, I looked up and I saw Jim Phillips, George McRae, and Henry Baxter. I looked ahead of me and they had the old man; and they tore down the fence the same as if you saw people dragging hogs from the butcher-pen. And they went to another corner of the fence and jerked me over, just as if they were jerking a dumb beast. The old man was ahead of me, and I saw Dave Donley stamp on him. I said, "Sam, give up; it is not worth while to try to do anything; they will try to kill us here." They said, "O, God damn you, we will kill you." I said, "I will go with you." George McRae said, "Come right along." I said, "Yes, I am coming; I will come right along." After they carried me about a quarter of a mile from the house—may be a little more; I cannot tell exactly how far it was; it was a good distance from the house—they took me through a path to a field, and down to the lower end of the field. When they got there he said, "Come here, True-Klux." The True-Klux came there and stopped and whispered about as far from here to this gentleman [pointing to a member of the committee sitting at the table]. Then he said, "Now, old lady, you pretend to be a good Christian; you had better pray right off." I cast my eye up to the elements and begged God to help me. George McRae struck me over the head with a pistol, and said, "God damn you, what are you making this fuss for?" I said, "No." He said, "Where is the ropes?" They said they had lost the ropes. Now, I never saw any horses; I did not see any that night. They went off next to my field and came back with a handful of saddle-girths, with the buckles on them. They took and carried me to a pine, just as large as I could get my arms around, and then they tied my hands there. They pulled off all my linen, tore it up so that I did not have a piece of rag on me as big as my hand.

They tied me, and I said, "Men, what are you going to do with me?" They said, "God damn you, we will show you; you are living on another man's premises." I said, "No; I am living on my own premises; I gave $150 for it and Captain Buddington and Mr. Mundy told me to stay here." He said, "God damn you, we will give them the same as we are going to give you." I quit talking to them, only as they asked me anything. They tied me to a tree and whipped me for awhile. Then George McRae would say, "Come here, True-Klux." Then the True-Klux would come, and they would step off about as far as that gentleman and whisper; and then they would say that they would go off to where the saddles were. They would go, and then when they came back they would whip me again. Every time they would go off, George McRae would act scandalously and ridiculously toward me and treat me shamefully. When he saw them coming again he would make me get up. He would make me squat down by the pine, and say, "What are you trembling for?" I would say that I was cold, and was afraid that I would freeze. He would get his knees between my legs and say, "God damn you, open your legs." I tell you, men, that he did act ridiculously and shamefully, that same George McRae. He sat down there and said, "Old lady, if you don't let me have to do with you, I will kill you." I said, "No; do just what you are going to do." He said, "God damn you, I am going to kill you." They whipped me, and went off again to the horses, and got liquor of some kind and poured it on my head, and I smelled it for three weeks, so that it made me sick. They went off and whispered, and then he told them to go to my house and tear it down. He asked me where was my ox. It was in the field, but I would not tell him; I said that my son-in-law had got my cart. He said, "Where is your son-in-law?" I said, "He has gone to Palatka." He said, "Where is your ox?" I would not tell him. He would whisper to them, and tell them to go and get the ox, and to get my things and to start them off to-night. He said, "Let's start them right off to-night." They would go and hunt, and then come back. He would make me sit down while they were gone. Understand me, men, while they were going to hunt for that ox, George McRae would make me sit down there, and try to have me do with him right there. They came back and whipped me. I said, "Yes, men, if you will stop whipping me, I will give way to you." Gentlemen, you do not know what expressions Cabell Winn made out of his mouth. It was all smutty on their faces, only right from the ear down, and their hands were smutty. Some were in their shirt-sleeves, and some had their coats on. I had been working with them very nearly three years. You know that when any person gets half drunk, he cannot alter his voice but what you can tell him. I have been working and washing for them; I had not been two weeks from his mother's house, where I had been washing; I washed there every week. That is the way they did me;

they came back and whipped me. George McRae said, "I came to dispossess you of this place once before." There were four men whipping me at once.

With what?

With saddle-girths, as I told you; with surcingles off the saddles. George McRae said, "We came to dispossess you once before, and you said you did not care if we did whip you." I said, "Stop, men, and let me see." One of them said, "Stop, and let her get her breath." Mr. Winn talked all kind of nasty talk to me. I got so I did not count Mr. Winn more than he counted me. I told Mr. Winn just exactly three weeks before they whipped me that I did not care what they did for me just so I saved my land. Said I, "In the red times,* how many times have they took me and turned my clothes over my head and whipped me? I do not care what they do to me now if I can only save my land." He again asked me if I said that, and I said, "Stop; I will see." After a minute I said, "Yes, I did say so." Cabell Winn says, "Yes, you damned bitch, you did say so." I did not tell anybody but Cabell Winn and his daddy, for my husband was gone. The night they came to whip me they did not expect to find the old man there, and when they found he had hold of me as they were carrying me to the door, he says, "O, God damn you, are you here?" And the time they were whipping me they said, "Now, listen, God damn you, at that poor old man; you were a God damned old bitch to get the poor old man in this fix; listen at him, you damned old bitch." I would have this just the way you hear me tell it now before the others, but they stopped me.

How many lashes did they give you in all?

I cannot tell you, for they whipped me from the crown of my head to the soles of my feet. I was just raw. The blood oozed out through my frock all around my waist, clean through, when I got to Captain Buddington's. After I got away from them that night I ran to my house. My house was torn down. I went in and felt where my bed was. It was along in the middle of the floor. I went to the other corner of the house and felt for my little children. I could not see one, and the bed was hoisted up in the corner of the house and hitched there, and is there now. I could not feel my little children and I could not see them. I said, "Lord, my little children are dead." I went to the box of my things and I picked up a dress I had there, but I went five miles before I put it on my back. When I got near one of my neighbor's house I hollered "murder," and they heard me, and they said they heard horses' feet go by. I did hear horses myself, and I hollered, for I was afraid. I cannot read, and I have got no clock, but as near as I can get to it, I got away from them an hour to day, and I went twelve miles by sunrise after I got away from them. I went through to Mr. Montgomery's house. I could not bear my clothes

* That is, during slavery.

fastened on me. I told them to give me a light as quick as they could so that I might go back and hunt up my children. I have two grown sons and a daughter, who are married and gone off. I said, "Give me a light; I expect my husband is dead, and I want to go back and find my children." I went back again, and I heard him holler, but I could hear nothing of my children. They said, "Go by Mr. Ashley's and get him to ride up there." I went by Mr. Ashley's, and went in there. I turned up my clothes and let Mr. Ashley see how I was whipped. I had on nothing but a frock, and I could not fasten it. He said, "Woman, go back home and hunt for your husband and children. If he is dead, don't stand to bury him, but go right on to Whitesville." I told him I did not know how to go there. He said, "If you have not been it is right enough to hunt up your boys, and let them go with you; if your husband is dead don't stand to bury him."

Did you find your children?

I did next day at 12 o'clock.

Where were they?

They were there at my house, where the true-klux had whipped me. Their father lay out to the middle of the night, and my children lay out there too. They said that when they got away from me they went out into the field, and my little daughter said that as the baby cried she would reach out and pick some gooseberries and put them into its little mouth. When she could hear none of them any more she went up into the field to a log heap and staid there with her brother and the baby. At daylight the old man came by a little house I had been living in, and which I used to keep some corn and things in, and they had torn it down, and the hogs had been in there eating up what corn and little stuff I had there.

How old were your children?

One was about five years old, another betwixt nine and ten, and the other was not quite a year old, lacking two months.

That was the one you had in your arms when they jerked it away?

Yes, sir.

Did the baby get hurt?

Yes, sir; in one of its hips. When it began to walk one of its hips was very bad, and every time you would stand it up it would scream. But I rubbed it and rubbed it, and it looks like it was outgrowing it now.

How soon did you see your husband?

Only when I saw my children. He was whipped so bad he could not travel as I did; he staid at home. When I got back there Mr. Chestnut, a white gentleman, had him there, and he and Mr. Chesnut were sitting there talking.

Did you see where he had been whipped?

Yes, sir; he could not sit up.

Where had he been whipped, on what part of his body?

All over it; his legs were whipped more than anywhere else. They did not begin to whip me as they did him. When I came Mr. Chesnut was there, and unfastening my frock, my daughter gave me some linen to put on, and Mr. Chesnut looked at me where I was whipped. I went by Mr. Rohan Wall's and let them look at me once. But they stand to it to-day, until yet, that that land is not mine; they say it is Tire's. Mr. Winn coaxed me and begged me to give it up before they whipped me.

He wanted to make you give up the land?

Yes, sir; they came there about three weeks before they whipped me to dispossess me of the place.

Who came there before?

George McRae, and old Mr. Sullivan, and Dave Donley, and Mr. Hagan, and Jake Winn. Mr. Byrd Sullivan came on Saturday. I spoke to them very rash, and I was sort of sorry I spoke to them in that way. Mr. Hagan came back and wanted to give me some advice. He told me it was Judge Buddington and Barney Crocker. I said I did not believe it, because they told me that this was my land, and not Tire's land. Tire was the first one who made out that he entered my land. I said, "I am going to die on this land." Hagan said, "You better give it up." Mrs. Lane sent for me to come and wash for her one day in a week, to scour and wash, any day in the week I felt like it. They made me mad Saturday about driving me from my place, and I would not go to Mrs. Lane's the first of the week. I had to go through Jake Winn's yard to go to her house. My son was working there, and I went in and saw Mrs. Winn and told her good morning. She says, "Hannah, I thought you were gone." I said, "Gone where?" She said, "Off the place." I said, "No, I am not going off the place; didn't Captain Buddington tell me to stay here? I am not going; no law is going to move me from here except Tallahassee law." I said, "What are they going to do to me, Mrs. Hagan?" She said, "They are going to whip you." I said, "I wish they would whip me," and then I went off. I told Mrs. Lane about it, and she said, "I have nothing to do with it; it is your land; you ought to have your land." She went and told Mr. Byrd Sullivan. He pretended to be courting of her then; she told him what I had to say. That was on Wednesday. On Friday while I was eating my breakfast, with nobody there but me and my little children, Byrd Sullivan came to my house with Jake Winn and Dave Donley and George McRae. They went into the field and let down the fence; the old man was gone to the hammock. Old Byrd Sullivan came up to the house and said: "Aunty, these people are devilish people; they are determined to put you off this land. Now, pay good attention to what I say. When you get your hand into a lion's mouth you pull it out just as easy as you can. Pay good attention to me. I would like to see your old man this morning, but he is not at home. You can tell your old man to give it up, or in a month's time, or such matter, they will come here, and the lot will push him out of doors and let you eat this green grass." I began to cry, and he said, "You will stop this grieving and crying; tell your old man to keep on writing; I know what you paid for this land; you gave cotton for it." I said, "Yes; I gave cotton enough to come to $150." He said, "Tell your old man to keep on writing, and when he gets the papers for his land let him come to me and he will have his land back." I said, "Mr. Ashley, Mr. Rohan and Mr. Swindell told me not to give it up; that if I let anybody else come on the land I could not get it back."

How long had you been living there?

Nearly three years.

How many crops had you made?

Two crops.

And this crop would have been the last?

Yes, sir.

You spoke about some of them "wanting to do with you," as you expressed it.

Yes, sir.

What one was that?

George McRae.

Did you give way to him?

No, sir; George McRae acted so bad, and I was stark naked. I tell you, men, he pulled my womb down so that sometimes now I can hardly walk.*

K.K.K. *Investigation*, South Carolina, I, pp. 326–27, 386–92; Alabama, III, pp. 1722–26; Florida, pp. 59–62.

[b]

Affidavit from John Walker

Gregg County, Texas, July 26, 1875

Myself and Steven Jones, Pinkney Jones, Jacob Hall, and Henry Raglam went to the town of Gladewater and Gregg County, Texas. All of us got a job of work to do at Mr. Cooper's saw-mill, at or near the same place; and we had only been there two days; we was attacked by an armed crowd of white men, about thirty some odd in number; and I made an alarm, and told the other men that we all had better get out, for I see whole parcel of white

* Several of the white men were tried—and quickly acquitted—in this instance. Mr. and Mrs. Tutson were held in prison over a week-end for their pains in insisting upon court action.

men coming toward us; and they hailed us to stop; if we did not, God damn us, they would kill us; and they all escaped except Henry Ragley [sic] ; and they fired four shots upon him and killed him dead in the house, and then set the house on fire and burned the body up in there; and we fled to Jefferson, Texas, for a safe place, and reported to Charles Horn and A. J. Malloy, and they told us that nothing could be done about it. All this on or about the 4th day of July, 1875.

Joint Affidavit from George Underwood, Ben Harris and Isiah Fuller
Caddo Parish, La., August 3, 1875

We worked, or made a contract to work, and make a crop on shares on Mr. McMoring's place, and worked for one-third (⅓) of the crop, and he (McMoring) was to find us all of our provisions; and in July, 1875, we was working alone in the field, and Mr. McMoring and McBounton came to us and says, "Well, boys, you all got to get away from here; and that they had gone as far as they could go, and you all must live agreeable, or you shall take what follows"; and the two white men went and got sticks and guns, and told us that we must leave the place; and we told them that we would not leave it, because we don't want to give up our crop for nothing; and they told us that we had better leave, or we would not get anything; and we wanted to justice, but he would not let us have justice; and we told them that we would get judges to judge the crop, to say what it is worth; and the white men told us that no judge should come on his place; and we did not want to leave the place, but they beat Isiah Fuller, and whipped him, and then we got afraid, and we left the place; and we got about thirty acres in cotton, and the best cotton crop in that part of the parish; and we have about twenty-nine acres of corn, and about the best corn in the parish, and it is ripe, and the fodder ready to pull, and our cotton laid by; and runned us off from the place, and told us not to come back any more; and we were due McMoring the sum of one hundred and eighty dollars ($180) and they told us that if they ever heard of it any more that they would fix us; and all the time that we were living and working on the place they would not half feed us; and we had to pay for all, or half of our rashings, or what we had to eat, and that is all that was due them for; and we worked for them as though we were slaves, and then treated like dogs all the time.

Executive Document No. 30, 44th Cong., 2nd Sess. (Serial No. 1755), pp. 166, 169.

Jackson, Miss.—June 20, 1876.
Mrs. Margaret Ann Caldwell (colored) sworn and examined.
What is your name?
Margaret Ann Caldwell.
Where do you live?

In Clinton, Hinds County.

Was Mr. Caldwell, formerly [state] senator, your husband? *

Yes, sir.

What was his first name?

Charles.

When did he die?

Thursday night, in the Christmas [1875]. Him and his brother was killed.

You may state to the committee what you know of his death.

I know when he left the house on the Thursday evening, in the Christmas, between dark and sundown. In the beginning of the day he was out on his fox-chase all day. The first commencement was an insult passed on his nephew, and he came out home.

Who was that?

David Washington; he is in Washington City now. He is there in business; watchman in the Treasury Department now; has been ever since October, I think. So they picked a fuss; Waddy Rice, in George Washington's blacksmith shop, in Clinton. They commenced talking this way: I think David said they asked, "How many did he kill on the day of the Moss Hill riot? † Who did he shoot?" David said that he did not know as he shot anybody; said he didn't know that he shot anybody. They told him, he said, "he came there to kill the white people, and if he did, to do his work in the day, and not to be seeking their lives at night?" David came immediately back to my house. His uncle was at the fox-chase. I said, "Don't go out any more. Probably they are trying to get up a fuss here."

His uncle sent him downtown for something. He staid in the house until he came.

That was about four o'clock in the evening, and some one had told about the fuss picked with his nephew, and he walked down town a half hour, and came back and eat his dinner, and just between dark and sundown he goes back down town again. He went down town knocking about down there. I do not know what he was doing down there, until just nearly dusk, and a man, Madison Bell, a colored man, came and says, "Mrs. Caldwell you had better go down and see about Mr. Caldwell, I think the white folks will kill him; they are getting their guns and pistols, and you had better go and get your husband away from town."

I did not go myself; I did not want to go myself, but went to Professor

* For details on Mississippi Reconstruction and the career of Charles Caldwell, see H. Aptheker, *To Be Free* (N.Y., 1948), pp. 163–87.

† The "Moss Hill riot" occurred near Clinton, Miss., in Sept., 1875 and was part of the Bourbons' calculated policy of violence and terror. At the "riot" itself two whites were killed and four wounded, while two Negroes died and five were injured. For several days thereafter an unbridled, systematic slaughter of Negro and white radicals occurred, the total murdered exceeding thirty-five.

Bell and said would he go and get him. Mr. Bell went, and he never came back at all until he came back under arrest.

I was at my room until just nearly dark.

The moon was quite young, and the chapel bell rang.

We live right by it. I knew the minute the bell tolled what it all meant.

And the young men that lived right across the street, when the bell tolled, they rushed right out; they went through the door and some slid down the window and over they sprang; some went over the fence. They all ran to the chapel and got their guns. There was 150 guns there to my own knowing; had been there since the riot, at the Baptist Chapel. They all got their guns.

I went down town, and then all got ahead everywhere I went; and some of them wanted to know who I was, but I hid my face as well as I could. I just said "woman" and did not tell who I was.

As I got to town I went to go into Mr. Chilton's store and every store was closed just that quick, for it was early, about 6 o'clock. All the other stores were closed. Chilton's was lit by a big chandelier, and as I went over the lumber-yard I saw a dead man. I stumbled over him, and I looked at him, but I did not know who it was, and I went into Chilton's, as I put my foot up on the store steps, standing as close, maybe a few feet, (everything was engaged in it that day,) there was Judge Cabinis [E. W. Cabaniss], who was a particular friend of my husband; a particular friend to him. He was standing in the center with a gun with a blue strap, in the center of the jam; and as I went to go in they cussed me and threatened to hurt me, and "make it damned hot for me," and the judge among the balance; but he said he didn't know me afterward. And they all stood; nobody would let me go in; they all stood there with their guns.

I know there was two dead men there, but I did not think it was my husband at the time.

I stood right there, and as I stood there they said to me, "If you don't go away they would make it very damned hot for me"; and I did not say anything, and walked off, and walked right over the dead man. He was right in my path where I found the body. He was lying broadside on the street. I did not know who he was. I then stooped and tried to see who he was, and they were cursing at me to get out of the town, to get out.

Then I went up, and there was Mrs. Bates across the street, my next-door neighbor. I seed her little girl come up by us and she said, "Aunt Ann, did you see my uncle here?" I said, "I did not." "I saw a dead body on the street. I did not know who he was." She said, "What in the world is going on down town?" Says I, "I don't know, only killing people there." She says, "Aaron Bates's hand is shot all to pieces, and Dr. Bangs is killed." He was not killed, but was shot in the leg; nobody killed but my husband and brother.

I went over to the house, and went upstairs and back to my room and laid down a widow.

After I had been home I reckon three-quarters of an hour, nearly an hour, Parson Nelson came up—Preacher Nelson and he called me. I was away upstairs. He called several times, and I heard him call each time. He called three or four times, and says, "Answer, don't be afraid; nobody will hurt you." He says, "Don't be afraid; answer me"; and after I had made up my mind to answer, I answered him what he wanted, and he said, "I have come to tell you the news, and it is sad news to you. Nobody told me to come, but I come up to tell you." I didn't say anything. "Your husband is dead." He said, "he is killed, and your brother, too, Sam."

I never said anything for a good while. He told me nobody would hurt me then; and when I did speak, says I, "Mr. Nelson, why did they kill him?" He says, "I don't know anything about it." He said just those words, "I don't know anything about it." He says, after that, "Have you any men folks about the place?" I says, "No." He says: "You shan't be hurt; don't be afraid of us; you shan't be hurt."

I never said anything whatever. He went off.

Sam's wife was there at the same time with three little children. Of course it raised great excitement.

After a length of time, Professor Hillman, of the Institute, the young ladies' school or college, he brought the bodies to the house; brought up my husband, him and Frank Martin. Professor Hillman and Mr. Nelson had charge of the dead bodies, and they brought them to the house; and when they brought them, they carried them in the bedroom, both of them, and put them there; they seed to having them laid out, and fixed up, and all that.

Mr. Nelson said in my presence, I listened to him, he said, "A braver life never had died than Charly Caldwell. He never saw a man died with a manlier spirit in his life."

He told me he had brought him out of the cellar.

You see when they had shot Sam, his brother, it was him who was lying there on the street. They shot him right through his head, off his horse, when he was coming in from the country, and he fell on the street. He was the man I stumbled over twice. I did not know who he was. When they shot him, they said they shot him for fear he would go out of town and bring in other people and raise a fuss. He found out, I suppose, that they had his brother in the cellar, so he just lay there dead; he that was never known to shoot a gun or pistol in his life—never knew how.

Mr. Nelson said that Buck Cabell carried him into the cellar; persuaded him to go out and drink; insisted upon his taking a drink with him, and him and Buck Cabell never knowed anything against each other in his life; never had no hard words. My husband told him no, he didn't want any Christmas. He said, "You must take a drink with me" and entreated him, and said, "You must take a drink." He then took him by the arm and told him to drink for a Christmas treat; that he must drink, and carried him into Chilton's cellar, and they jingled the glasses, and at the tap of the glasses, and while each one held the glass, while they were taking the glasses, somebody shot right through the back from the outside of the gate window, and he fell to the ground.

As they struck their glasses, that was the signal to shoot. They had him in the cellar, and shot him right there, and he fell on the ground.

When he was first shot, he called for Judge Cabinis, and called for Mr. Chilton; I don't know who else. They were all around, and nobody went to his relief; all of them men standing around with their guns. Nobody went to the cellar, and he called for Preacher Nelson, called for him, and Preacher Nelson said that when he went to the cellar door he was afraid to go in, and called to him two or three times, "Don't shoot me," and Charles said, "Come in" he wouldn't hurt him and "take me out of the cellar," that he wanted to die in the open air, and did not want to die like a dog closed up.

When they taken him out, he was in a manner dead, just from that one shot; and they brings him out then, and he only asked one question, so Parson Nelson told me—to take him home and let him see his wife before he died; that he could not live long.

It was only a few steps to my house, and they would not do it, and some said this.

Nelson carried him to the middle of the street, and the men all hallooed, "we will save him while we've got him; dead men tell no talkes." Preacher Nelson told me so. That is what they all cried, "We'll save him while we got him; dead men tell no talkes."

Whether he stood up right there in the street while they riddled him with thirty or forty of their loads, of course, I do not know, but they shot him all that many times when he was in a manner dead. All those balls went in him.

I understood that a young gentleman told that they shot him as he lay on the ground until they turned him over. He said so. I did not hear him.

Mr. Nelson said when he asked them to let him see me they told him no, and he then said, taking both sides of his coat and bringing them up so, he said, "Remember when you kill me you kill a gentleman and a brave man. Never say you killed a coward. I want you to remember it when I am gone."

Nelson told me that, and he said that he never begged them, and that he never told them, but to see how a brave man could die.

They can find no cause; but some said they killed him because he carried the militia to Edwards, and they meant to kill him for that. The time the guns were sent there, he was Captain under Governor Ames, and they said they killed him for that; for obeying Governor Ames.

After the bodies were brought to my house, Professor Hillman and Martin all staid until one o'clock, and then at one o'clock the train came from Vicksburgh with the "Murdocs." * They all marched up to my house and went into where the two dead bodies laid, and they cursed them, those dead bodies, there, and they danced and threw open the window, and sung all their songs, and challenged the dead body to get up and meet them, and they carried on there like a parcel of wild Indians over those dead bodies, these Vicksburgh "Murdocs." Just one or two colored folks were sitting up in the room, and they carried on all that in my presence, danced and sung and done anything they could. Some said they even struck them; but I heard them curse and challenge them to get up and fight. The Vicksburgh Murdocs done that that night. Then they said they could not stay any longer.

Then the day after that Judge Cabannis asked me was there anything he could do, and I told him, I said, "Judge, you have already done too much for me." I told him he had murdered my husband, and I didn't want any of his friendship. Those were the words I told him the next day, and he swore he did not know me at that time; but I saw Judge Cabinis with this crowd that killed my husband. I saw him right in the midst, and then he made his excuse. He said he did everything he could for Charles, and that he was crazy. Well, they could not tell anything he had done.

They said Aaron Page was shot during the fuss. In the league that was held here in that town, that day my husband was buried, they all said that he did not shoot him. They said that Aaron Page was shot accidentally; that my husband did not kill him. All started up from picking a fuss with my nephew.

As for any other cause I never knew; but only they intended to kill him because for carrying the militia to Edwards; for obeying Governor Ames,† and that was all they had against him.

At the same time, when they had the Moss Hill riot, the day of the dinner in September, when they came over that day, they telegraphed for the Vicksburgh "Murdocs" to come out, and they came out at dark, and when they did come, about fifty came out to my house that night; and they were breaking the locks open on doors and trunks; whenever they would find it closed they would break the locks. And they taken from the house what guns they could find, and plundered and robbed the house. The captain of the Vicksburgh "Murdocs" his name is Tinney.

What day was that?

---

* The strong-arm men carried the name of the Modoc Indians against whom the U.S. Army had recently waged war.
† Caldwell, as a militia captain, had attempted to prevent violence during the 1875 election.

The day of the Moss Hill riot, in September.

When; the Clinton riot?

The 4th day of September. They came out, and Tinney staid there, and at daybreak they commenced to go, and he, among others, told me to tell my husband that the Clinton people sent for him to kill him, and he named them who they were to kill—all the leaders especially, and he says, "Tell him when I saw him"—he was gone that night; he fled to Jackson that evening with all the rest—"we are going to kill him if it is two years, or one year, or six; no difference; we are going to kill him anyhow. We have orders to kill him, and we are going to do it, because he belongs to this republican party, and sticks up for these Negroes." Says he, "We are going to have the South back in our own charge, and no man that sticks by the republican party, and is a leader, he has got to die." He told me that; and that the southern people are going to have the South back to ourselves, and no damned northern people and no republican party; and if your husband don't join us he has got to die. Tell him I said so. I told him what he said. I did not know Tinney at the time; and when I saw my husband enter, I told him, and he knew him from what I said, and he saw him afterward and told him what I said. He just said that he said it for devilment. They carried on there until the next morning, one crowd after another. I had two wounded men. I brought them off the Moss Hill battle-field, and these men treated me very cruelly, and threatened to kill them, but they did not happen to kill them.

Next morning, before sun up, they went to a house where there was an old black man, a feeble old man, named Bob Beasly, and they shot him all to pieces. And they went to Mr. Willis's and took out a man, named Gamaliel Brown, and shot him all to pieces. It was early in the morning; and they goes out to Sam Jackson's, president of the club and they shot him all to pieces. He hadn't even time to put on his clothes. And they went out to Alfred Hastings; Alfred saw them coming. And this was before sun up.

This morning after the Clinton riot?

On the morning of the 5th, and they shot Alfred Hastings all to pieces, another man named Ben. Jackson, and then they goes out and shoots one or two further up on the Madison road; I don't know exactly; the name of one was Lewis Russell. He was shot, and Moses Hill. They were around that morning killing people before breakfast. I saw a young man from Vicksburgh that I knew, and I asked him what it all meant.

Who was he?

Dr. Hardesty's son; and I asked him what did it mean, their killing black people that day? He says, "You all had a big dinner yesterday, and paraded around with your drums and flags. That was impudence to the white people. You have no right to do it. You have got to leave these damned Negroes;

leave them and come on to our side. You have got to join the democratic party. We are going to kill all the Negroes. The Negro men shall not live." And they didn't live; for every man they found they killed that morning, and did not allow any one to escape them, so he said. So he told me all they intended to do about the colored people for having their dinner and parading there, and having their banners; and intended to kill the white republicans the same. Didn't intend to leave any one alive they could catch, and they did try to get hold of them, and went down on Monday morning to kill the school-teacher down there, Haffa, but he escaped.* Jo Stevens and his son Albert Stevens, I believe, was his name—they just murdered them right on through. These people staid there at the store and plundered it, and talked that they intended to kill them until they got satisfaction for three white people that was killed in that battle. I can show who was the first white man that started the riot; and I can show you I have got his coat and pants, and I can show you how they shot him. They blamed all on my husband, and I asked what they killed Sam for; asked Dr. Alexander. They said they killed him because they were afraid he would tell about killing his brother. They killed my husband for obeying Governor Ames's orders, and they cannot find anything he did. He didn't do anything to be killed for. Then they have got his pistols there and they won't give them to me. I have asked for them I don't know how many times.

Report of the Select Committee to Inquire into the Mississippi Election of 1875 . . . Report No. 527, 44th Cong., 1st Sess., Vol. I (Serial No. 1669), pp. 435–40.

187

UNDERMINING RECONSTRUCTION: 3) VIOLENCE AND FRAUD, 1871–1876

B] GROUP TESTIMONY

Negroes not only individually but also collectively cried out against reactionary terror. As typical examples of this type of activity there are printed below three documents.

The first is a petition from Kentucky Negroes to Congress dated March 25, 1871, and including as an appendix a detailed listing of over one hundred instances of violence against Radicals beginning late in 1867. The second document is a memorial to Congress dated Montgomery, December 2, 1874. It came from a State Convention of Alabama Negroes meeting one month after the planters, with the active assistance of Northern industrialists, had swept back into political domination. The memorial presents the facts to Congress, prays for the enforce-

---

* On Sept. 6, 1875, William P. Haffa, a white teacher and a radical Justice of the Peace, was murdered and his wife forced to flee.

ment of the Constitution and broaches the possibility of a mass exodus of Negroes from the State. The third document, also a petition to Congress, issued from a committee appointed by the State Convention of the Negroes of Georgia held in Atlanta late in November, 1874. After stating the facts concerning terror and corruption, the petition went on to urge passage of civil rights legislation and amendment of the judicial process in Georgia.

[a]

Petition from Kentucky Negroes

To the senate and house of Representatives in Congress assembled: We the Colored Citizens of Frankfort and vicinity do this day memorialize your honorable bodies upon the condition of affairs now existing in this the state of Kentucky.

We would respectfully state that life, liberty and property are unprotected among the colored race of this state. Organized Bands of desperate and lawless men mainly composed of soldiers of the late Rebel Armies Armed disciplined and disguised and bound by Oath and secret obligations have by force terror and violence subverted all civil society among Colored people, thus utterly rendering insecure the safety of persons and property, overthrowing all those rights which are the primary basis and objects of the Government which are expressly guaranteed to us by the Constitution of the United States as amended; We believe you are not familiar with the description of the Ku Klux Klans riding nightly over the country going from County to County and in the County towns spreading terror wherever they go, by robbing whipping ravishing and killing our people without provocation, compelling Colored people to brake the ice and bathe in the Chilly waters of the Kentucky River.

The Legislature has adjourned they refused to enact any laws to suppress Ku Klux disorder. We regard them as now being licensed to continue their dark and bloody deeds under cover of the dark night. They refuse to allow us to testify in the state Courts where a white man is concerned. We find their deeds are perpetrated only upon Colored men and white Republicans. We also find that for our services to the Government and our race we have become the special object of hatred and persecution at the hands of the Democratic party. Our people are driven from their homes in great numbers having no redress only the U.S. Courts which is in many cases unable to reach them. We would state that we have been law abiding citizens, pay our tax and in many parts of the state our people have been driven from the poles, refused the right to vote. Many have been slaughtered while attempting to vote, we ask how long is this state of things to last.

We appeal to you as law abiding citizens to enact some laws that will protect us. And that will enable us to exercise the rights of citizens. We see that the senators from this state denies there being organized Bands of desperaders in the state, for information we lay before you an number of violent acts occured during his Administration. Although he Stevenson * says half Dozen instances of violence did occur these are not more than one half the acts that have occured. They Democratic party has here a political organization composed only of Democrats not a single Republican can join them where many of these acts have been committed it has been proven that they were the men, don with Armies from the State Arsenal. We pray you will take some steps to remedy these evils.

Don by a Committee of Grievances appointed at a meeting of all the Colored Citizens of Frankfort & vicinity.

Mar. 25th, 1871

Henry Marrs, Teacher colored school
Henry Lynn, Livery stable keeper
N. N. Trumbo, Grocer
Samuel Damsey, B. Smith [Blacksmith]
B. T. Crampton, Barber

Committee

1. A mob visited Harrodsburg in Mercer County to take from jail a man name Robertson, Nov. 14, 1867.

2. Smith attacked and whipped by regulation in Zelun County Nov. 1867.

3. Colored school house burned by incendiaries in Breckinridge Dec. 24, 1867.

4. A Negro Jim Macklin taken from jail in Frankfort and hung by mob January 28, 1868.

5. Sam Davis hung by mob in Harrodsburg May 28, 1868.

6. Wm. Pierce hung by a mob in Christian July 12, 1868.

7. Geo. Roger hung by a mob in Bradsfordsville Martin County July 11, 1868.

8. Colored school Exhibition at Midway attacked by a mob July 31, 1868.

9. Seven person ordered to leave their homes at Standford, Ky. Aug. 7, 1868.

10. Silas Woodford age sixty badly beaten by disguised mob. Mary Smith Curtis and Margaret Mosby also badly beaten, near Keene Jessemine County Aug. 1868.

* Governor—later, Senator—John W. Stevenson.

11. Cabe Fields shot—and killed by disguise men near Keene Jessamine County Aug. 3, 1868.

12. James Gaines expelled from Anderson by Ku Klux Aug. 1868.

13. James Parker killed by Ku Klux Pulaski, Aug. 1868.

14. Noah Blankenship whipped by a mob in Pulaski County Aug. 1868.

15. Negroes attacked robbed and driven from Summerville in Green County Aug. 21, 1868.

16. William Gibson and John Gibson hung by a mob in Washington County Aug. 1868.

17. F. H. Montford hung by an mob near Cogers landing in Jessamine County Aug. 28, 1868.

18. Wm. Glassgow killed by a mob in Warren County Sep. 5, 1868.

19. Negro hung by a mob Sep. 1868.

20. Two Negros beaten by Ku Klux in Anderson County Sept. 11, 1868.

21. Mob attacked house of Oliver Stone in Fayette County Sept. 11, 1868.

22. Mob attacked Cumins house in Pulaski County. Cumins his daughter and a man name Adams killed in the attack Sept. 18, 1868.

23. U.S. Marshall Meriwether attacked captured and beatened with death in Larue County by mob Sept. 1868.

24. Richardson house attacked in Conishville by mob and Crasban killed Sept. 28, 1868.

25. Mob attacks Negro cabin at hanging forks in Lincoln County. John Mosteran killed & Cash & Coffey killed Sept. 1869.

26. Terry Laws & James Ryan hung by mob at Nicholasville Oct. 26, 1868.

27. Attack on Negro cabin in Spencer County—a woman outraged Dec. 1868.

28. Two Negroes shot by Ku Klux at Sulphur Springs in Union County, Dec. 1868.

29. Negro shot at Morganfield Union County, Dec. 1868.

30. Mob visited Edwin Burris house in Mercer County, January, 1869.

31. William Parker whipped by Ku Klux in Lincoln County Jan. 20/69.

32. Mob attacked and fired into house of Jesse Davises in Lincoln County Jan. 20, 1868.

33. Spears taken from his room at Harrodsburg by disguise men Jan. 19, 1869.

34. Albert Bradford killed by disguise men in Scott County, Jan. 20, 1869.

35. Ku Klux whipped boy at Standford March 12, 1869.

36. Mob attacked Frank Bournes house in Jessamine County. Roberts killed March 1869.

37. Geo Bratcher hung by mob on sugar creek in Garrard County March 30, 1869.

38. John Penny hung by a mob at Nevada Mercer county May 29, 1869.

39. Ku Klux whipped Lucien Green in Lincoln county June 1869.

40. Miller whipped by Ku Klux in madison county July 2d, 1869.

41. Chas Henderson shot & his wife killed by mob on silver creek Madison county July 1869.

42. Mob decoy from Harrodsburg and hangs Geo Bolling July 17, 1869.

43. Disguise band visited home of I. C. Vanarsdall and T. J. Vanarsdall in Mercer county July 18/69.

44. Mob attack Ronsey's house in Casey county three men and one woman Killed July 1869.

45. James Crowders hung by mob near Lebanon Merion county Augt 9, 1869.

46. Mob tar and feather a citizen of Cynthiana in Harrison county Aug. 1869.

47. Mob whipped and bruised a Negro in Davis county Sept. 1869.

48. Ku Klux burn colored meeting-house in Carrol county Sept. 1869.

49. Ku Klux whipped a Negro at John Carmins's farm in Fayette county Sept. 1869.

50. Wiley Gevens killed by Ku Klux at Dixon Webster county Oct. 1869.

51. Geo Rose killed by Klu Klux near Kirkville in Madison county Oct. 18, 1869.

52. Ku Klux ordered Wallace Sinkhorn to leave his home near Parkville Boyle county Oct. 1869.

53. Man named Shepherd shot by mob near Parksville Oct. 1869.

54. Regulator killed Geo Tanhely in Lincoln county Nov. 2d, 1869.

55. Ku Klux attacked Frank Searcy house in madison county one man shot Nov. 1869.

56. Searcy hung by mob madison county at Richmond Nov. 4th, 1869.

57. Ku Klux killed Robt Mershon daughter shot Nov. 1869.

58. Mob whipped Pope Hall and Willett in Washington county Nov. 1869.

59. Regulators whipped Cooper in Palaski County Nov. 1869.

60. Ku Klux ruffians outraged Negroes in Hickman county Nov. 20, 1869.

61. Mob take two Negroes from jail Richmond Madison county one hung one whipped Dec. 12, 1869.

62. Two Negroes killed by mob while in civil custody near mayfield Graves county Dec. 1869.

63. Allen Cooper killed by Ku Klux in Adair county Dec. 24th, 1869.

64. Negroes whipped while on Scott's farm in Franklin county Dec. 1869.

65. Mob hung Chas Fields in Fayette county Jan. 20, 1870.

66. Mob take two men from Springfield jail and hung them Jan. 31, 1870.

67. Ku Klux whipped two Negros in Madison county Feb. 1870.

68. Simms hung by mob near Kingston Madison county Feb. 1870.

69. Mob hung up, then whipped Douglass Rodes near Kingston Madison County February 1870.

70. Mob takes Fielding Waller from jail at Winchester Feb. 19th, 1870.

71. R. L. Byrom hung by mob at Richmond Feb. 18th, 1870.

72. Perry hung by mob near Lancaster Garrard County April 5th, 70.

73. Negro hung by mob at Crab-orchard Lincoln county Apr. 6th, 1870.

74. Mob rescue prisoner from Summerset jail Apr. 5, 1870.

75. Mob attacked A. Owen's house in Lincoln county Hyatt killed and Saunders shot Apr. 1870.

76. Mob releases five prisoners from Federal Officers in Bullitt county Apr. 11th, 1870.

77. Sam Lambert shot & hung by mob in Mercer county Apr. 11th, 1870.

78. Mob attacks William Palmer house in Clark County William Hart killed Apr. 1870.

79. Three men hung by mob near Gloscow Warren county May 1870.

80. John Redman killed by Ku Klux in Adair county May 1870.

81. William Sheldon Pleasanton Parker Daniel Parker Willis Parker hung by mob in Laurel county May 14th, 1870.

82. Ku Klux visited Negro cabins at Deak's Mill Franklin county robbed and maltreated inmates May 14th, 1870.

83. Negro's school house burned by incendiaries in Christain county May 1870.

84. Negro hung by mob at Greenville Muhlenburgh county May 1870.

85. Colored school house on Glen creek in Woodford county burned by incendiaries June 4th, 1870.

86. Ku Klux visited Negro cabin robbing and maltreating inmates on Sand Riffle in Hay county June 10, 1870.

87. Mob attacked Jail in Whitley County two men shot June 1870.

88. Election riot at Harrodsburg four person killed Aug. 4, 1870.

89. Property burned by incendiaries in Woodford county Augt. 8, 1870.

90. Turpin & Parker killed by mob at Versailled Augt. 10, 1870.

91. Richard Brown's house attacked by Ku Klux, in Hay.

92. Simpson Grubbs killed by a band of men in Montgomery county Augt. 1870.

93. Jacob See rescued from Mt. Sterling jail by mob Sept. 1870.

94. Frank Timberlake hung by a mob at Flemingburg Fleming county Sept. 1870.

95. John Simes shot & his wife murdered by Ku Klux in Hay county Sept. 1870.

96. Oliver Williams hung by Ku Klux in Madison county Sept. 1870.

97. Ku Klux visited cabins of colored people robbed and maltreated inmates at Havey Mill Franklin county.

98. A mob abducted Hicks from Lancaster Oct. 1870.

99. Howard Gilbert shot by Ku Klux in Madison county Oct 9th, 1870.

100. Ku Klux drive colored people Bald-Knob Franklin county Oct. 1870.

101. Two Negroes shot on Harrison Blanton's farm near Frankfort Dec. 6th, 1870.

102. Two Negroes killed in Fayette county while in civil custody Dec. 18, 1870.

103. Howard Million murdered by Ku Klux in Fayette county Dec. 1870.

104. John Dickerson driven from his home in Hay county and his daughter ravished Dec. 12, 1870.

105. A Negro named George hung by a mob at Cynthiana Harrison county Dec. 1870.

106. Negro killed by Ku Klux near Ashland Fayette county January 7th, 1871.

107. A Negro named Hall whipped and shot near Shelbyville Shelby county Jan. 17, 1871.

108. Ku Klux visited Negro cabin at Stamping Ground in Scott county force (White) & Ku Klux killed two Negroes killed in self defence.

109. Negro killed by Ku Klux in Hay county January 14, 1871.

110. Negro church & school house in Scott county [burned?] Jan. 13, 1871.

111. Ku Klux maltreated Demar his two sons and Joseph Allen in Franklin Jan. 1871.

112. Dr Johnson whipped by Ku Klux in Magoffin county Dec. 1871.

113. Property burned by incendiaries in Fayette county Jan. 21, 1871.

114. Attack on mail agent—North Benson Jan. 26, 1871.

115. Winston Hawkins fence burned and notice over his door not come home any more April 2d, 1871.

116. Ku Klux to the number of two hundred in February came into Frankfort and rescued from jail one Scroggins that was in civil custody for shooting and killing one colored man named Steader Trumbo.

MS. in The National Archives, Washington, D.C., Records of the U.S. Senate, 42d Cong., 1st Sess.

[b]

Memorial from Alabama Negroes

To His Excellency the President of the United States, and the honorable the Congress of the United States:

The colored people of the State of Alabama, who by virtue of the three latest amendments to the Constitution of the United States became emancipated, and also became citizens of the United States, feeling anxiously and solemnly impressed by their past and present condition in the State of Alabama, and by the grave and menacing dangers that now surround and threaten them and their constitutional rights, have as a race and as a people assembled together in convention to consider their situation, and to take solemn counsel together as to what it becomes them to do for their self-preservation.

We, therefore, for your better information upon the subject, do humbly present for your consideration and action the following memorial:

That as a race, and as citizens, we never have enjoyed, except partially, imperfectly, and locally, our political and civil rights in this State. Our right to vote in elections has been, in a large portion of this State, denied, abridged, and rendered difficult and dangerous ever since we became voters. The means used by our political opponents to destroy or impair their right have been various; but have chiefly consisted of violence in the form of secret assassination, lynching, intimidation, malicious and frivolous prosecutions and arrests, and by depriving or threatening to deprive us of employment and the renting of lands, which many of us, in our poverty and distress, were unable to disregard. These acts of lawlessness have been repeated and continued since our first vote in 1868, and their effect has been such that from ten to fifteen thousand of the votes of our race have in each election been either repressed or been given under compulsion to our political opponents.

It is true that in some counties, and in parts of other counties, we have been exempt from these acts of lawlessness, but yet they have been committed to such an extent as greatly to diminish our votes, and once at least, in 1870, and probably on the third of November, A.D. 1874, was this lawlessness so great as to give (without the other frauds perpetrated) the election and all its fruits to our political opponents. . . .*

The investigation made in the years 1870–'71 by a committee of Congress known as the Ku-Klux committee, developed and established the fact of the organized existence, in many parts of this State since the year 1868, of a

---

* Many detailed statistics follow to prove this assertion.

secret, powerful, vindictive, and dangerous organization composed exclusively of white men belonging to the democratic party in this State, and whose objects were to control the labor and repress or control the votes of colored citizens of this State. That organization, or a substitute and successor to it, under a changed name and a somewhat changed wardrobe and personal manifestation, still exists in all its hideous and fearful proportions.

It is composed chiefly of ex-soldiers of the late confederate army accustomed to military movements and the use of arms, and it is, essentially a military organization. This organization we solemnly believe pervades all of the late rebellious States, and contains more than a hundred thousand arms-bearing men, most of whom are experienced and skilled in war. The definite political object of this organization is, by terror and violence, to make the citizenship and franchises of the colored race, as established by the Constitution of the U.S. practically and substantially a nullity. Nothing but fear restrains them from making open war upon the Government and the flag of the United States. We pray you not to be deceived by their professions, for they are "wise as serpents," and they profess respect for the United States and obedience to its laws, while in their secret conclaves they curse them.

They have only changed their tactics. Defeated in their scheme of secession, they have fallen back upon the old South Carolina plan of nullification. Being unable to defeat or nullify the constitutional amendments by their votes while the republican party is in power, or by open war, they have resolved to nullify them by secret war, violence and terror.

Nor have we fared better in our civil rights of life, liberty, and property which have come for adjudication before the State courts. It is true that republican judges have generally presided over the superior courts of this State, and have generally shown a disposition to do us justice, but even these have been to some extent, warped by local pressure. But the main reasons for this failure of justice are that the sheriffs, probate judges and clerks of courts have almost universally, throughout the State, in plain violation of State laws, failed or refused to put men of our race on grand and petit juries in most of the counties in Alabama, and it has followed, as a consequence, that the lives, liberties, and property of black men have been decided by grand and petit juries composed exclusively of white men who are their political opponents. In controversies between our race and white men, and in criminal trials where the accused or the injured is a black man, it is almost if not quite impossible for a black man to obtain justice. . . . Our lives, liberties, and properties are made to hang upon the capricious, perilous, and prejudiced judgments of juries composed of a hostile community of ex-slaveholders who disdain to recognize the colored race as their peers in anything, who look upon us as being *by nature an inferior race*, and by right their chattel property. . . .

For three or four months past especially, our lives, and the lives of nearly all republicans in this State, have had no protection except the fear of the authority and laws of the United States. But for the presence of United States troops, and civil officers of the United States, hundreds of the active and earnest republicans of this State would have been assassinated. But even with the protection of these agencies, many of our race were shot down and killed at the polls on the 3d day of November last only because they chose to exercise their right to vote, as in the cases of Mobile and Barbour Counties, where Norman Freeman, Bill Jackson, and William Kinney, (in Mobile) and Alfred Butler, George Walker, W. C. Keils, white, and others (in Barbour) whose names are at present unknown, were killed, and a large number wounded. Many of the victims of the White League in Barbour County were found dead in the woods and partially eaten by vultures; and these crimes will go utterly unnoticed and unpunished by the State courts. . . .

Desiring to do full justice to all, and to misrepresent nothing, we admit with pleasure, and with hopeful encouragement, that about fifteen per cent of the white citizens of Alabama are faithful and loyal to the government and laws of the United States; that at least fifteen thousand of these citizens, at the recent election on the 3d day of November, voted with us for "tolerance, peace, and charity," though in doing so they were compelled to pass through an ordeal "that tried men's souls." Nothing has ever been witnessed in the United States that approaches in kind or quality the scenes through which these heroic men have passed. . . .

The election just past bears palpable fraud on its face. The census of 1870 shows in this State 202,046 citizens of this State over the age of 21 years. This number has certainly not increased since the census, for the emigration from the State has largely exceeded the immigration to it. And yet, at the November election the actual vote, officially counted, was 201,046, while 3,000 other votes actually cast were destroyed, or not counted, making 204,-046 votes actually cast. As a physical or moral fact, this vote is simply impossible. Many counties doubled their possible voting population on the 3d of November, 1874, and these excesses have been confined exclusively to democratic counties and democratic majorities and gains.

In three previous elections, two of them presidential elections, and which may be taken as a fair exponent of the voting capacity of the State, the largest vote cast, only two years ago, was only 170,000, while the November election of 1874 shows more than 200,000, or a gain of more than 30,000.

As a result of that election the democratic party, which made the canvass confessedly on "the race issue," white against black, and which, discarding its designation of democratic, called itself "the white man's party," has just come into possession of all the departments of the State government. Its inauguration was accompanied with a display of physical and military power and of terror that were never before witnessed in this State as an accompaniment of such event.

The legislature, now in session, has in its procedures displayed toward the colored race a spirit of marked bitterness, injustice, and vindictiveness which justly adds to our apprehensions of the future. With every department of the State government hostile to us, how may we expect or hope for justice or even for mercy?

Pressed around with these wrongs, misfortunes, and dangers, and solemnly impressed with their gravity, no resource or hope suggests itself to us but an earnest, prayerful, and we hope not unavailing, appeal to the President and the Congress of the United States, who still have the power and the agencies that may, in some measure, right our wrongs and diminish our misfortunes.

The question which our case and condition presents to you is simply this: whether our constitutional rights as citizens are to be a reality or a mockery, a protection and a boon or a danger and a curse; whether we are to be freemen in fact or only in name; and whether the late amendments to the Constitution are to be practically enforced or to become a nullity and stand only "as dead letters on the statute-book." . . .

It is absolutely essential to our protection in our civil and political rights that the laws of the United States shall be so enforced as to compel respect for and obedience to them. Before the State laws and State courts we are utterly helpless. If the laws of the United States, upon which alone we can rely, are not enforced, we hold all of our rights at the mere mercy of wrongdoers and criminals. If these laws are not enforced, both the laws and the government which enacts them fall into contempt.

Our race have now met in convention to consider solemnly the question of their future destiny in this State and in this country. We have no reason to expect from our political opponents, now dominant in this State, the exercise of justice, mercy, or wise policy. Not recognizing the value of our labor, their leaders declare our presence as a curse to the State, and profess to look with pleasure upon our *exodus* from the State. The solemn question with us is, Shall we be compelled to repeat the history of the Israelites and go into exile from the land of our nativity and our homes, to seek new homes and fields of enterprise, beyond the reign and rule of Pharaoh?

The question presses upon us for an early solution. We linger yet a while to learn what will be done to avert these evils by the power that made us free men and citizens, and whose honor and good faith stand pledged to make that emancipation and citizenship something more than a delusion and a mockery.

We present these facts for the consideration of the government of the United States, and ask its immediate interference in the terrible situation that it has left us after solemnly promising to guard us in the enjoyment of the privileges that it has given to us—namely, all the rights of citizenship.

PHILIP JOSEPH,
President of the Convention.

Executive Document No. 64, House of Representatives, 43rd Cong., 2nd Sess., transmitted to Congress by the President, Dec. 22, 1874.

[c]

Memorial from Georgia Negroes

To the Senate and House of Representatives

The undersigned designated as a Committee of the Colored Convention assembled in the city of Atlanta Georgia November 30th 1874 to memorialize the Congress of the United States—through you would most respectfully submit the following.

It will be seen by reference to the proceedings of the Convention that universal disquietude and alarm exists among our people based upon undeniable facts, that the rights vouchsafed to them under and by the constitution of the United States and the Amendments thereto, have not been accorded to them in the dispensation and enforcement of the Laws of Georgia and of the United States. That we regard with reasonable alarm the manifest disposition of the Democratic party of this State to deprive us of the Exercise of the Elective franchise. Which disposition was made patent and unmistakable at the last Election in this State for Members to Congress. We can refer to the many and various localities throughout Georgia where the rights of our people at the ballot box were held in utter abeyance and contempt, and the election precincts in many places were taken possession of by bullies and desperadoes, who aided by accomplices, so wrought upon the fears of our people by threats and intimidation and by open handed violence as to prevent them from the exercise of the ballot, and as a natural consequence our people are discouraged and crestfallen. And as a last cherished hope would humbly come before the Congress of the United States through their chosen delegate C. Wimbish Esq. of this State and appeal to your wisdom to rescue them from the perils which so evidently and so ruthlessly threaten by the adoption of such measures as will remedy the hardships so justly complained of by a loyal population numbering five hundred and forty-five thousand souls in this State. We are aware that the laws as passed by the Successive Sessions of Congress since emancipation are complete in spirit, yet the trouble is that these laws so salutary and just in their provisions have not been enforced as a rule in this State but have remained upon the statute books only as a dead letter.

We cannot point to any locality in Georgia where we can in truth say that our lives and our liberties are perfectly secure. Emerging from a state of bondage to the stature of freemen as a result of the late War, we can to some extent account for the opposition and cruelty imposed upon our race by our former Secession rebel masters . . . Our race have even within the last twelve months been wantonly and cruelly murdered and many others outrageously maltreated by bands of men who [one word illegible] the country in disguise as well as in open defiance of law and order and in the face of all this, which is undeniably true.

And further recognizing the fact as we do that the laws of Georgia guarantee to all persons irrespective of race color or previous condition, who are reputed as intelligent and upright, an equal participation in the jury box and equal accomodations in public thoroughfares together with other rights and privilidges and immunities as mentioned in the civil rights bill now pending before Congress, our people are painfully aware of the fact, that by a partial and unjust administration of the laws of this State that our people have been practically denied said rights and privilidges, and for remedy whereof they do earnestly request the Congress of the *United States* to pass the pending civil rights bill,* thus giving the colored people a speady and ample means of vindicating said rights and privilidges under the laws, and we would further most respectfully ask that in order to properly enforce the rights guaranteed to our race by certain laws passed by Congress in 1866 and since that time that Congress will pass a law authorizing the removal of all civil or criminal causes in which colored persons are parties already commenced or pending or hereafter to be commenced in the State Courts to the United States Circuit Courts. When it shall be made to appear that said Colored Citizens cannot get justice in said State Courts by reason of race color or previous condition or by reason of pregisdice or other local causes. Said causes to be transfered from the State to the Federal courts upon the sworn affidavits of the defendant or the plaintiff as the case may be.

We could even weary your patience with a long and tedious itemized statement of the wrongs imposed upon our people but will desist, indulging the hope as we do, that enough is known to satisfy you that our complaints are

---

* A Civil Rights Law, illegalizing discrimination in hotels, theatres and public carriers, was signed by President Grant on March 1, 1875, but was declared unconstitutional by the Supreme Court in October, 1883.

true and the demand made by our people reasonable and in full accord with the genious and spirit of liberty.

And recommend our people never cease in their adoration and love for a government that protects the weak as well as the strong, dispensing equal blessings to all.

We have the honor to be with distinguished regard

Your obedient servants.

Rev Romulus Moore, Chairman

Dr. H. E. Baldwin

Rev. Geo. W. Pitts

W. H. Groves

MS. in The National Archives, Washington, D.C., Records of the U.S. Senate, 43rd Congress, 2nd Session.

188

THE NEGRO IN CONGRESS DURING RECONSTRUCTION, 1871–1876

From the 41st Congress through the 44th (1869–1877) a total of fourteen different Negroes were at various times members of the House of Representatives (from South Carolina, Georgia, Mississippi, Florida, Alabama, North Carolina and Louisiana) and two Negroes—Hiram R. Revels and Blanche K. Bruce, both of Mississippi—were members of the Senate. They made, on the whole, a commendable record, and actively fought for progressive legislation.

Three documents are offered below as indicative of the congressional work of these men. The first is a speech by Jefferson Franklin Long, up to the present the only Negro Congressman from Georgia. Born in Knoxville, Georgia, in 1836, Long was self-educated and earned his living as a tailor. Prominent in Radical efforts from the beginning of Reconstruction, he was elected to Congress for the short term, 1870–71. For several years thereafter he remained a political leader, and he died in Macon in 1900. Reprinted is a brief speech he delivered in the House on February 1, 1871, in opposition to the granting of the suffrage to those who had played leading roles in the secession effort—a measure passed in 1872.

The second document is part of a long speech delivered in Congress on January 10, 1874, by Richard Harvey Cain of South Carolina. Here Cain appeals for the passage of a Civil Rights Bill, which, in emasculated form, became law a year later. Cain had been born free in Virginia in 1825. As a child and a young man he lived and studied in Ohio, and then, as a minister in the African Methodist Episcopal Church, labored in Missouri, Iowa and New York. With the close of the Civil War he went to South Carolina and became prominent in religious and political affairs. After serving as an alderman of Charleston and a member of the state legislature, he was a member of Congress, 1873–75 and 1877–79. In 1880 he became a Bishop and later served as President of Paul Quinn College in Waco, Texas. He died in 1887.

The third document concerns the massacre of Negroes which occurred on July 8, 1876 in Hamburgh, South Carolina. This appears in the context of an attempt made one week later by Robert Smalls, Congressman from South Carolina, to get the Federal government to employ troops in order to prevent such outrages. Robert Smalls served in Congress from 1875 to 1887, a longer period than any other Negro. He had been born a slave in Beaufort in 1839 and catapulted into national fame in May, 1862, when he led fifteen other slaves in bringing a Confederate gunboat, *The Planter*, out of Charleston to the blockading Union fleet. He served throughout the remainder of the war as a Union pilot, and led in Radical activity following the War. After service in the state legislature he was elected to Congress and, following his defeat in the 1887 campaign, he served as Collector of the Port of Beaufort until 1913. Two years later Robert Smalls died.

[a]

Jefferson F. Long

Mr. Speaker: The object of the bill before the House is to modify the test-oath. As a citizen of the South, living in Georgia, born and raised in that State, having been there during the war and up to the present time, I know the condition of affairs in that State. Now, sir, we propose here today to modify the test-oath, and to give to those men in the rebel States who are disloyal today to the government this favor. We propose, sir, to remove political disabilities from the very men who were the leaders of the Ku Klux and who have committed midnight outrages in that State.

What do those men say? Before their disabilities are removed they say, "We will remain quiet until all of our disabilities are removed, and then we shall again take the lead." Why, Mr. Speaker, in my State since emancipation there have been over five hundred loyal men shot down by the disloyal men there, and not one of those who took part in committing those outrages has ever been brought to justice. Do we, then, really propose here today, when the country is not ready for it, when those disloyal people still hate this Government, when loyal men dare not carry the "stars and stripes" through our streets, for if they do they will be turned out of employment, to relieve from political disability the very men who have committed these Ku Klux outrages? I think that I am doing my duty to my constituents and my duty to my country when I vote against any such proposition.

Yes, sir; I do mean that murders and outrages are being committed there. I received no longer ago than this morning a letter from a man in my State, a loyal man who was appointed postmaster by the President, stating that he was beaten in the streets a few days ago. I have also received information from the lower part of Georgia that disloyal men went in the midnight disguised and took a loyal man out and shot him; and not one of them has been brought to justice. Loyal men are constantly being cruelly beaten. When we take the men who commit these outrages before judges and juries we find that they are in the hands of the very Ku Klux themselves who protect them.

Mr. Speaker, I propose, as a man raised as a slave, my mother a slave before me, and my ancestry slaves as far back as I can trace them, yet holding no animosity to the law-abiding people of my State, and those who are willing to stand by the Government, while I am willing to remove the disabilities of all such who will support the Government, still I propose for one, knowing the conditions of things there in Georgia, not to vote for any modification of the test-oath in favor of disloyal men.

Gentlemen on the other side of the House have complimented men on this side. I hope the blood of the Ku Klux has not got upon this side; I hope not. If this House removes the disabilities of disloyal men by modifying the test-oath, I venture to prophesy you will again have trouble from the very same men who gave you trouble before.

Congressional Globe, 41st Congress, 3rd Session, p. 881.

[b]

Richard H. Cain

But, says the gentleman from North Carolina, some ambitious colored man will, when this law is passed, enter a hotel or railroad car, and thus create disturbance. If it be his right, then there is no vaulting ambition in his enjoying that right. And if he can pay for his seat in a first-class car or his room in a hotel, I see no objection to his enjoying it. But the gentleman says more. He cited, on the school question, the evidence of South Carolina, and says the South Carolina University has been destroyed by virtue of bringing into contact the white students with the colored. I think not. It is true that a small number of students left the institution, but the institution still remains. The buildings are there as erect as ever; the faculty are there as attentive to their duties as ever they were; the students are coming in as they did before. It is true, sir, that there is a mixture of students now; that there are colored and white students of law and medicine sitting side by side; it is true, sir, that the prejudice of some of the professors was so strong that it drove them out of the institution; but the philanthropy and good sense of others were such that they remained; and thus we have still the institution going on, and because some students have left, it cannot be reasonably argued that the usefulness of the institution has been destroyed. The University of South Carolina has not been destroyed. . . .

A word now as to the question of education. Sir, I know that, indeed, some of our Republican friends are even a little weak on the school clause of this bill; * but, sir, the education of the race, the education of the nation, is paramount to all other considerations. I regard it important, therefore, that the colored people should take place in the educational march of this nation, and I would suggest that there should be no discrimination. It is against discrimination in this particular that we complain.

Sir, if you look over the reports of superintendents of schools in the several States, you will find, I think, evidences sufficient to warrant Congress in passing the civil-rights bill as it now stands. The report of the commissioner of education of California shows that, under the operation of law and of prejudice, the colored children of that State are practically excluded from schooling. Here is a case where a large class of children are growing up in our midst in a state of ignorance and semi-barbarism. Take the report of the superintendent of education of Indiana, and you will find that while efforts have been made in some places to educate the colored children, yet the prejudice is so great that it debars the colored children from enjoying all the rights which they ought to enjoy under the law. In Illinois, too, the superintendent of education makes this statement: that, while the law guarantees education to every child, yet such are the operations among the school trustees that they almost ignore, in some places, the education of colored children.

All we ask is that you, the legislators of the nation, shall pass a law so strong and so powerful that no one shall be able to elude it and destroy our rights under the Constitution and laws of our country. That is all we ask. . . .

We do not want any discriminations to be made. If discriminations are made in regard to schools, then there will be accomplished just what we are fighting against. If you say that the schools in the State of Georgia, for instance, shall be allowed to discriminate against colored people, then you will have discriminations made against us. We do not want any discriminations. I do not ask any legislation for the colored people of this country that is not applied to the white people. All that we ask is equal laws, equal legislation, and equal rights throughout the length and breadth of this land.

The gentleman from North Carolina (Mr. Vance) also says that the colored men should not come here begging at the doors of Congress for their rights. I agree with him. I want to say that we do not come here begging for

---

* A clause in the original Civil Rights Bill illegalizing Jim-Crow education was in fact deleted from its final version.

our rights. We come here clothed in the garb of American citizenship. We come demanding our rights in the name of justice. We come, with no arrogance on our part, asking that this great nation, which laid the foundations of civilization and progress more deeply and more securely than any other nation on the face of the earth, guarantee us protection from outrage. We come here, five millions of people—more than composed this whole nation when it had its great tea-party in Boston Harbor, and demanded its rights at the point of the bayonet—asking that unjust discriminations against us be forbidden. We come here in the name of justice, equity, and law, in the name of our children, in the name of our country, petitioning for our rights.

Congressional Record, 43rd Cong., 1st Sess., vol. II, pt. 1, pp. 565–67.

[c]

Robert Smalls

I offer the amendment which I send to the desk. The clerk read as follows:
Add to the first section * the following:
Provided, That no troops for the purposes named in this section shall be drawn from the State of South Carolina so long as the militia of that State peaceably assembled are assaulted, disarmed, and taken prisoners, and then massacred in cold blood by lawless bands of men invading that State from the State of Georgia.

I hope the House will adopt that proviso as an amendment to the bill. As I have only five minutes I send to the desk a letter published in one of the newspapers here from an eye-witness of the massacre at Hamburgh, and I ask the Clerk to read it.

The Clerk read as follows:

The origin of the difficulty, as I learn from the best and most reliable authority, is as follows: On the Fourth of July the colored people of the town were engaged in celebrating the day, and part of the celebration consisted in the parade of the colored militia company. After marching through the principal streets of the town, the company came to a halt across one of the roads leading out of the town. While resting there two white men drove up in a buggy, and with curses ordered the company to break ranks and let them pass through. The captain of the company replied that there was plenty of room on either side of the company, and they could pass that way. The white men continued cursing and refused to turn out. So the cap-

* Of a joint resolution to provide for the protection of the Texas frontier on the Lower Rio Grande during the so-called Texas Border Troubles.

tain of the militia, to avoid difficulty, ordered his men to break ranks and permit the buggy to pass through.

[An attempt to interrupt reading fails.]

The order was obeyed, and the white men went on their way uttering threats. The next day a colored trial justice issued processes against the officers of the company, based on the complaint of the two white men, citing the officers to appear and answer to a charge of obstructing the public highway. They obeyed the writs, and after a slight examination the justice adjourned the trial until Saturday, the 8th instant. On that day, at an early hour, the town commenced to fill up with white men, armed to the teeth with repeating rifles and revolvers. The colored people had no idea of the bloody tragedy which was soon to take place, and consequently made no preparations to resist an attack, and were almost defenseless.

Late in the afternoon General M. C. Butler, one of the most malignant of the unreconstructed rebels, rode into the town, accompanied by a score of well-armed white men, and stated to the leading colored men that he came for the purpose of prosecuting the case on the part of the two white men, and he demanded that the militia company should give up their arms and also surrender their officers. This demand the militia was ready to comply with for the purpose of avoiding a difficulty if General Butler would guarantee them entire safety from molestation by the crowd of white desperadoes. This Butler refused to do, and persisted in his demand for the surrender of the guns and officers, and threatened that if the surrender was not immediately made he would take the guns and officers by force of arms. This threat aroused the militia company to a realizing sense of their impending danger, and they at once repaired to a large brick building, some two hundred yards from the river, used by them as an armory, and there took refuge. They numbered in all about forty men and had a very small quantity of ammunition. During this time, while the militia were taking refuge in their armory the white desperadoes were coming into the town in large numbers, not only from the adjacent county of Edgefield, but also from the city of Augusta, Georgia, until they numbered over fifteen hundred well-armed and ruffianly men, who were under the immediate command and direction of the ex-rebel chief, M. C. Butler. After the entire force had arrived, the building where the militia had taken refuge was entirely surrounded and a brisk fire opened upon it. This fire was kept up for some two hours, when, finding that the militia could not be dislodged by small arms, a messenger was sent to Augusta for artillery. During all this time not a shot had been fired by the militiamen. The artillery arrived and was posted on the bank of the river and opened fire on the building with grape and canister.

[An attempt to interrupt reading fails.]

The militia now realized that it was necessary to evacuate the armory at once. They proceeded to do so, getting out of a back window into a corn-field. They were soon discovered by the ruffians, and a rush was made for them. Fortunately, by hiding and hard fighting, a portion of the command escaped, but twenty-one were captured by the bushwhackers and taken im-mediately to a place near the railroad station.

Here a quasi-drumhead court-martial was organized by the blood-hunters, and the last scene of the horrible drama began. It must now be remembered that not one of the twenty-one colored men had a pistol or gun about them. The moment they were captured their arms were taken from them, and they were absolutely defenseless. The orderly sergeant of the militia company was ordered to call the roll, and the first name called out to be shot in cold blood was Allan T. Attaway, the first lieutenant of the company, and holding the position of county commissioner of Aiken County, in which county Ham-burgh is situated. He pleaded for his life, as only one in his position could plead, but his pleading were met with curses and blows, and he was taken from the sight of his comrades and a file of twelve men fired upon him. He was penetrated by four balls, one entering his brain, and the other three the lower portion of his body. He was instantly killed and after he was dead the brutes in human shape struck him over the head with their guns and stabbed him in the face with their bayonets. Three other men were treated in the same brutal manner. The fifth man when taken out made a dash for his life, and luckily escaped with only a slight wound in his leg.

In another portion of the town the chief of police, a colored man named James Cook, was taken from his house and while begging for his life brutally murdered. Not satisfied with this, the inhuman fiends beat him over the head with their muskets and cut out his tongue.

Another colored man, one of the marshals of the town, surrendered and was immediately shot through the body and mortally wounded. He has since died. So far as I * have been able to learn only one white man was killed. It will thus be seen that six colored men were brutally murdered and one wounded, while on the side of the whites only one white man was killed. After this holocaust of blood was over the desperadoes in large bodies entered the houses of most of the prominent colored men of the town and completely gutted them. They stole all they possibly could, and what they could not steal they destroyed. Furniture was smashed, books torn to pieces, pictures cut from their frames, and everything that could be destroyed was given up to the demon of destruction. Such scenes my eyes have never before witnessed

---

* When a Democrat, Mr. Cochrane of Pennsylvania, demanded that Smalls name the correspondent, he replied: "I will say to the gentleman that if he is desirous that the name shall be given in order to have another Negro killed, he will not get it from me."

and the distress and suffering among the poor colored people were heart-rending to behold. The town is desolate and the inhabitants have taken refuge in Aiken, Columbia, and other points. The civil authorities are powerless or too negligent to do anything, and peace and order cannot be preserved unless United States troops are sent to this point at once.

The scenes during the massacre were fearful to behold—the moon shining down upon the horrid scene lighting up the whole with a ghastly light; the popping of the small arms; the screams of frightened women and terrified children; the loud reports from the artillery, all tended to make a scene terrible and more fearful to behold. And now what was the provocation given for this hellish slaughter? The answer is, nothing. Legally the militia had the right of way over the public road. The day was the nation's holiday. The militia had a perfect right to parade, and vehicles of all kinds were required to keep out of their way, and not interfere with their marching. Again, General Butler had not the shadow of a right to demand the arms of the militia. They were organized under the constitution and laws of the State, and were part and parcel of the armed force of the Commonwealth. No private citizen had the slightest right to molest them. Such molestation was a direct blow at the power and authority of the State. It was a revolutionary step, and should be thus punished.

[Reading interrupted, but resumed.]

Are the southern colored citizens to be protected or are they to be left at the mercy of such ruffians as massacred the poor men of Hamburgh? Murdered Attaway was a man of considerable prominence in the republican party of the county. He was a law-abiding citizen, held a responsible office, and was well thought of by very many people. The other murdered men were good citizens and have never been known to infringe the law. The whole affair was a well and secretly planned scheme to destroy all the leading republicans of the county of Aiken living in Hamburgh. M. C. Butler, who lost a leg while fighting in the ranks of the rebels, and who is to-day the bitterest of Ku-Klux democrats, was the instigator of the whole affair and the blood-thirsty leader of the massacre. He boasted in Hamburgh during the fight that that was only the beginning; that the end should not be until after the elections in November. Such a man should be dealt with without pity or without hesitation. The United States Government is not powerless, and surely she will not be silent in an emergency like this, the parallel of which pen cannot describe. In this centennial year will she stand idly by and see her soil stained with the blood of defenseless citizens, and witness the bitter tears of women and children falling upon the murdered bodies of their loved ones? God forbid that such an attitude will be assumed toward the colored people of the South by the "best Government the world ever saw." Something must be done, and that quickly, or South Carolina will shed tears of blood and her limbs be shackled by democratic chains.

What I have written in this letter are facts which I vouch for entirely, and are not distorted in any degree. It's a "plain, unvarnished" narration of painful and horrible truths.

Congressional Record, 44th Cong., 1st Sess., vol. IV, pt. 5, pp. 4641–42.

189

THE NEGRO IN THE NORTH AND WEST DURING RECONSTRUCTION, 1866–1874

Of the approximately five million Negroes in the United States in 1870 some half a million lived outside the South. To convey some idea of their varied activities in the post-Civil War decade eight documents are presented below.

The first two documents [a, b] are extracts from the proceedings of two Negro State Conventions, one held in Galesburg, Illinois in 1866, the other in Utica, New York three years later. In each case some sixty delegates expressed the determina· tion of themselves and their constituency to struggle unremittingly for full equality, and specifically for the elimination of all distinctions in voting, in jury-selection and in education.

The third document [c] tells the story of the founding, in 1870, of the National Medical Society of the District of Columbia—the antecedent of the oldest Negro medical society, the Medico-Chirurgical Society—in protest against the Jim-Crow practices of the Medical Society of the District. The leaders in this effort were, among others, Dr. Robert Reyburn, Dr. C. Adams Gray, Dr. John G. Stephenson and Dr. Alexander T. Augusta, the last of whom had risen to the rank of Lieutenant-Colonel in the Union Army—the highest rank achieved by a Negro during the Civil War.

The fourth document [d] is a memorial from a convention of the Negroes of Indian Territory (later Oklahoma) held in January, 1870, and explains quite fully the special and peculiar disabilities suffered by these Negroes.

The fifth document [e] consists of an extract from an article on Negro working people of New York—particularly seamen—written for a Negro newspaper early in 1870 by William P. Powell. This piece is of particular interest because of its references to early organizational activities among New York Negro workers—something mentioned with tantalizing incompleteness in other sources.

The sixth document [f] is an editorial from a California Negro newspaper in 1872 relative to the struggle going on there to eliminate Jim Crow schools. The seventh document [g] is a memorial from a New York Negro organization, the Citizens' Civil Rights Committee, to a governmental body of New York City in 1873 demanding the employment of Negroes in public capacities.

The final document [h] in this group is an extract from a speech by William Still of Philadelphia (whom we previously met as an Underground Railroad leader) explaining why he, and many other leading Negroes of that city, including Robert

Purvis, had opposed the local Republican machine and supported the "People's Party" candidate for Mayor, Col. A. K. McClure, in 1874. The document itself is indicative of a developing political independence which marked the practice of many Negroes, and culminated in considerable Negro support of later regional and national third party movements, notably the Populist movement of the '90's.

[a]

Convention of Illinois Negroes

Report of the Committee on Resolutions

Whereas, Taxation without representation is contrary to the genius and spirit of our republican institutions, and

Whereas, The colored people of the State of Illinois are taxed for the support of the public schools, and denied, by the laws of the State, the right of sending their children to said schools,* therefore,

Resolved, That we regard it as a gross usurpation, unjustly shown toward the colored citizens of Illinois, and that this Convention do hereby recommend to the colored people of the State to send their petitions to our legislature, asking for the repeal of said law.

Resolved, That our State legislature, having ratified the amendment to the Constitution of the United States, abolishing slavery, and repealing a part of her black code, giving the colored men the right to *testify in the courts of justice,* must be regarded as still remiss in her duty, until she educates the children of three thousand colored men who helped to fill the quota of the State.

Resolved, That to deprive us and our children of this invaluable right (honorably and patriotically defended by the blood of our fathers, brothers and sons), is treating us with wrong and cruel injustice, unheard of in any civilized land or country whose government, national or State, have received the services of black soldiers in defending the liberties of the entire people.

Resolved, That in view of the services rendered by the loyal and patriotic black men of the State of Illinois, during the war which has just ended, wiping from our national escutcheon the foul stain of slavery, that we ask the legislature to give us the free exercise of our inherent right, namely, the elective franchise.

Resolved, That the constitutional disability under which colored men labor in this State, calls loudly for redress; it insults our manhood, and disgraces the name of our great State.

Resolved, That in spite of every opposition, we recommend to our people the propriety of getting an interest in the soil, believing that there is power in

* Fewer than 100 Negro children then attended Illinois public schools.

so doing; moreover, to cultivate and improve the same is one of the great means of elevating ourselves and every disfranchised American.

Resolved, That we believe the times require an earnest co-operation of the colored citizens throughout the State in securing a recognition of our rights as man and citizens, by the next legislature, and that we will unite our efforts with those of our brethren elsewhere in securing the aforesaid end. . . .

Resolved, That our efforts for the achievement of the suffrage question, the admission of our children into public schools, the acquirement of lands, and the raising of stock shall be unceasing; that we feel our manhood, and must exercise it on every occasion, until we are satisfied that the prejudice which now exists against us is done away, and that we shall be treated as men and brethren throughout the State.

Resolved, That as a people whose characteristics are religious, we will continue to preach and pray, and, if necessary, fight against all laws making a difference on account of color, either in Church or State.

Resolved, That we do not ask our white friends to elevate us, but only desire them to give us the same opportunities of elevating ourselves, by admitting us to the right of franchise, and an equal chance for educating ourselves, by opening the doors of their free schools and colleges.

Bryan Smith, Gallatin County
D. Fletcher, Knox County
H. Hicklin, Sangamon County
S. D. Williams, Knox County

J. Stanley, Cook County
E. R. Williams, Cook County
C. S. Jacobs, Mercer County
George T. Fountain, Adams County

Proceedings of the Illinois State Convention of Colored Men, Assembled at Galesburg, . . . (Chicago, 1867).

[b]

Convention of New York Negroes

A large minority of the citizens of the United States are denied those rights which were given them by their Creator. They are taxed without being represented; they are subject to trials by juries which are not their peers; they are murdered without having redress; they are taxed to support common schools while their children are denied the privilege of attending those in their respective wards; they are called upon for the military service of their country without receiving proper protection from the country, and without any incentives whatever of being commissioned officers.

These grievances belie the Declaration of Independence by which the American people profess to be governed. We have been laboring for the last two and a half centuries to enrich the country without having received a particle of remuneration. We have been promised our rights but have not yet received them. And we do not now counsel any other means than thoughts, words, and the integrity of the Republican party.

We demand all the rights and prerogatives enjoyed by our white fellow-citizens. We have lived here two and a half centuries, and know only this country as our home. Here we have a few cherished memories, and many sad ones; yet our country is dear to us with all her faults. We demand these rights as natives of this country. We demand them for our long unrequited toil; we demand them from our part in the recent Rebellion, without which, millions more of dollars and thousands more previous lives would have been spared; we demand them for the protection of our wives and children; we demand them as a large minority of the entire population of the country; we demand them for the safety of the Republican party with which we shall ally ourselves so long as it continued to battle for righteousness and justice; we demand them as *men*, children of a common Father.

N.Y. *Daily Tribune*, August 20, 1869.

[c]

Memorial of the National Medical Society of the District of Columbia

To the Senate and House of Representatives of the United States:

Whereas it has been stated in a published circular, that the persons endeavoring to form a medical society on the basis of "equality before the law," have maliciously and falsely attacked the Medical Society of the District of Columbia, we deem it but just to the public, as well as ourselves, to make the following statement of facts:

Within the past few years some colored physicians, regular graduates of medical colleges, and of untarnished character and reputation, having held positions as surgeons in the Union army during the rebellion, have settled in this city, and secured to themselves a large professional practice.

There being only one medical society in the District where all licenses to practice must be obtained, and all advantages flowing from medical and professional discussions were to be enjoyed, it became the duty of these colored physicians to obtain license and membership, in order to keep up their medical education, and derive all the advantages from weekly professional discussion.

The Medical Society of the District of Columbia has, on two different occasions, refused to elect these colored physicians to membership, acknowledging that the color of the candidates was the reason for so doing; and some of its members have refused to consult with them, because they were not members of the Society.

This was in June, 1869. Hoping that discussion of the subject would aid in securing justice, we were content to await the result.

January 3, 1870, by a vote of 26 to 10, the Society refused to consider a resolution offered by Dr. Reyburn, which read as follows, viz:

"*Resolved,* That no physician (who is otherwise eligible) should be excluded from membership in this Society on account of his race or color."

Some of the present officers of the Society have refused to consult with the colored physicians, but instead thereof, have taken care of patients who were under their care, without giving them the customary notice of their dismissal, in direct violation of the ethics of the profession.

These colored physicians have applied to the Society for membership, but were rejected by a large majority, although the Board of Examiners reported favorably on them. At the last election of officers in the Society, held January 3, 1870, the chairman of this Board was removed, and a gentleman, late of the Confederate army, well known for his opposition to the admission of colored physicians, was elevated in his place, thus insuring their future defeat. Other gentlemen who served during the war in the Confederate army are now prominent in the control of its affairs.

At the same meeting, a white candidate, a gentleman of high professional standing, and occupying an important position, was objected to solely on the ground that he was believed to be in favor of colored members.

Again, the circular published by the committee of the Society, states that their weekly meetings are "social reunions." These meetings are conducted under strict parliamentary rules, from the opening to the adjournment, and only professional questions, essays, and papers are brought forward for discussions, and gentlemen are even required to obtain permission from the President to retire from the meeting. If these meetings, held in compliance with the charter of the Society, are social reunions, then the meetings of all bodies not strictly parliamentary are social reunions.

Other colored men will soon graduate from medical colleges in the United States and throughout the world, and their rights should be protected and guaranteed within this District.

It is a fact worthy of note, that this is the only country and the only profession in which such a distinction is now made. Science knows no race, color, or condition; and we protest against the Medical Society of the District of Columbia maintaining such a relic of barbarism.

We, for the reasons stated, and in accordance with the spirit of the times, ask Congress to grant a charter to a new Society, which will give all rights, privileges and immunities to all physicians, making only the presentation of a diploma from some college recognized by the American Medical Association, and good standing in the profession, the qualifications necessary for membership.

The New Era (Washington), January 27, 1870.

[d]

Memorial from Negroes of Indian Territory

To the Senate and House of Representatives in Congress assembled:

The undersigned, a committee on behalf of the colored people of the Choctaw and Cherokee tribes of Indians, appointed at a convention held by said colored people near Scullyville, Indian Territory, on the 15th of January, 1870, would respectfully represent to your honorable bodies—

That, although freed from slavery by the result of the late war, we enjoy few, if any, of the benefits of freedom.

Being deprived as yet of every political right, we are still wholly in the power of our late masters, who were almost a unit on the side of the rebellion against the government, and who, from having been compelled to relinquish their ownership in us, regard our presence among them with no favorable eye.

That we, under these circumstances and in our helpless condition, have suffered, and still do suffer, many ills and outrages, even to the loss of many a life, may be readily surmised, and is a notorious fact.

By the treaty held at Fort Smith, Ark., in September, 1865, the following stipulations were enacted in our behalf, viz:

Art. 3. The Choctaws and Chickasaws, in consideration of the sum of $300,000, hereby cede to the United States the territory west of the 98° west longitude, known as the leased district, provided that the said sum shall be invested and held by the United States, at an interest not less than 5%, in trust for said nations, until the legislatures of the Choctaw and Chickasaw nations respectively shall have made such laws, rules, and regulations as may be necessary to give all persons of African descent, resident in the said nations at the date of the treaty of Fort Smith, and their descendants, heretofore held in slavery among said nations, all the rights, privileges, and immunities, including the right of suffrage, of citizens of said nations, except in the annuities, moneys, and public domain claimed by, or belonging to, said nations respectfully; and also to give to such persons who were residents as aforesaid, and their descendants, 40 acres each of the land of said nations on the same terms as the Choctaws and Chickasaws, to be selected on the survey of said land, after the Choctaws and Chickasaws and

Kansas Indians have made their selections as herein provided; and immediately on the enactment of such laws, rules, and regulations, the said sum of $300,000 shall be paid to the said Choctaw and Chickasaw nations in the proportion of ¾ to the former and ¼ to the latter, less such sum, at the rate of $100 *per capita*, as shall be sufficient to pay such persons of African descent before referred to as within 90 days after the passage of such laws, rules, and regulations shall elect to remove from the said nations respectively. And should the said laws, rules, and regulations not be made by the legislatures of the said nations respectively within two years from the ratification of this treaty, then the said sum of $300,000 shall cease to be held in trust for the said Choctaw and Chickasaw nations, and be held for the use and benefit of such of said persons of African descent as the United States shall remove from the said territory in such manner as the United States shall deem proper, the United States agreeing, within 90 days from the expiration of the said two years, to remove from said nations all such persons of African descent as may be willing to remove; those remaining or returning after having been removed from said nations to have no benefit of said sum of $300,000, or any part thereof, but shall be upon the same footing as other citizens of the United States in the said nations.

Art. 4. The said nations further agree that all Negroes, not otherwise disqualified or disabled, shall be competent witnesses in all civil and criminal suits and proceedings in the Choctaw and Chickasaw courts, any law to the contrary notwithstanding; and they fully recognize the right of the freedmen to a fair remuneration on reasonable and equitable contracts for their labor, which the law should aid them to enforce. And they agree, on the part of their respective nations, that all laws shall be equal in their operation upon Choctaws, Chickasaws, and Negroes, and that no distinction affecting the latter shall at any time be made, and that they shall be treated with kindness and be protected against injury; and they further agree, that while the said freedmen now in the Choctaw and Chickasaw nations remain in said nations, respectively, they shall be entitled to as much land as they may cultivate for the support of themselves and families, in cases where they do not support themselves and families by hiring, not interfering with existing improvements without the consent of the occupant, it being understood that in the event of the making of the laws, rules, and regulations aforesaid, the 40 acres aforesaid shall stand in place of the land cultivated as last aforesaid.

But thus far none of the conditions contained in the above articles has been fulfilled, and the time set for their fulfillment has long since expired. We sought to bring our grievances to the notice of your honorable bodies at the last session of Congress, and for this purpose held a mass meeting on the 16th of February, 1869, but before we could perfect arrangements to send our petition by a trusty messenger, Congress had adjourned.

On the 25th of September, 1869, the colored people residing in the eastern portion of the Choctaw and Chickasaw country held a convention at Scullyville, near the western boundary of Arkansas, to take in consideration of their condition, and there passed the following resolutions:

Whereas, the Choctaws and Chickasaws utterly failed and wilfully neglected to fulfill the stipulations of the treaty made with the government of the United States, and approved July, 1866, in regard to the colored people of said nations: therefore be it

Resolved, That we do no longer consider those stipulations in relation to us as of any force whatever.

Resolved, That we consider ourselves full citizens of those nations, and fully entitled to all the rights, privileges, and benefits as such, the same as any citizen of Indian extraction.

Resolved, That as we can claim no other country as ours except this Territory, we desire to continue to live in it in peace and harmony with all others living therein.

Resolved, That we are in favor of having this Indian country sectionized and a certain amount of land allotted to each inhabitant as his own.

Resolved, That we are in favor of opening this territory to white immigration, and of selling to them, for the benefit of the whole people of these nations, our surplus lands.

Resolved, That this convention elect three trusty men to act for us as delegates, whenever our interest demands it.

A convention to be held by the colored people of the western portion of the Territory, to take similar action in relation to their condition, was frustrated by the Indians, who threatened the life of any colored man attempting to meet at the appointed place and time, tore down and destroyed the printed posters giving notice of the proposed convention, and had a leading colored man, on his way to the place of meeting, arrested through the United States agent.

Upon this, another meeting of the colored people was held on the 15th of January last, at Scullyville, Indian Territory, at which they reaffirmed the resolutions of September 26, 1869, and passed the following additional resolutions, viz:

Whereas, the colored people of the Choctaw and Chickasaw nations were, by force, intimidation and threats against their lives, prevented from holding a peaceable convention in which to deliberate upon an amelioration of their deplorable condition, and bring it to the notice of the government;

Resolved, That we regard the action of those engaged in preventing us from exercising the right of assemblying peaceably as unwarranted, unjust and tyrannical.

Resolved, That we regard the arrest of Richard Brashears, while on his way to the proposed Armstrong Academy convention, at the instigation of the United States agent and by the United States marshal, as a most outrageous and flagrant violation of our rights as freemen, and a disgrace to the government.

Resolved, That we are less than ever inclined to leave our native country, and more than ever claim protection from the government, equal rights with the Indians, and a speedy throwing open of the Territory to white settlement.

And whereas not a single stipulation of the treaty of Fort Smith concerning us has been kept by our late masters; and whereas, by a most insidious clause in said treaty, a large number of our brethren, who at the time were either still in the Union army or had not ventured to return to their country, are debarred from again becoming residents of their native country;

Resolved, That we earnestly entreat the national government not to permit so cruel an outrage to be inflicted on its own defenders, and not to allow rebels to punish loyal men for their loyalty;

Resolved, That James Ladd, Richard Brashears, and N. C. Coleman be, and are hereby, authorized to act as delegates for us, the colored people of the Choctaw and Chickasaws nations, to lay this our petition for relief before Congress, and in case they are unable to proceed thither, to authorize Hon. V. Dell,* of Fort Smith, Ark., to be our representative at Washington.

Believing, as we do, that your honorable bodies have the power and the will to redress our grievances as well as the *right,* notwithstanding all "treaties," so called, of which so much only is kept by our late masters as suits their convenience, we trustfully turn to you to afford us the desired relief, and to secure to us those rights to which we claim to be entitled as men, as citizens of these United States, and as natives of the Indian Territory. And as in duty bound we will ever pray,

James Ladd
Richard Brashears
N. C. Coleman
*Committee on the part of the Colored People
of the Choctaw and Chickasaw Nations*

Senate Miscellaneous Documents No. 106, 41st Cong., 2nd Sess., (1870).
* A white Republican leader in Arkansas, state senator and editor of the Fort Smith newspaper, *New Era.*

[e]

Negro Workers in New York

On behalf of the working classes of the city, county and state of New York, I desire to state that, among the various branches of diversified labor, there are 3500 colored seamen engaged in the mercantile marine service, sailing to and from the port of New York. The aggregate amount of wages earned by these men is $1,260,000 per annum . . . There is now no invidious discrimination as to color, wages or grade of service, as there was in the days of slavery. They are amenable to the same laws which alike govern all who are engaged in the mercantile-marine service. They are self-supporting. The avenues to promotion are open to all who are qualified, for the highest position. As navigators, all other things being equal, they can command first class ships. One colored seaman (Captain George Brooks,) received his certificate as ship master in the spring of 1868, and sailed from the port of New York in command of a vessel manned entirely by colored seamen, bound to the coast of Africa, and to one or more ports in Europe, and back to the United States, and gave entire satisfaction to the owners.

There is also an organization in the port of New York, incorporated April 15th, 1863, known as the "American Seamen's Protective Union Association," with an accumulating capital.

There are several benevolent societies, and also several workingmen and women's protective unions, organized for mutual relief and protection. The oldest and most prominent is the "New York African Society for Mutual Relief," founded in 1808, and chartered by the State of New York March 23d, 1810. This Society has kept up its organization for near 62 years without intermission. All branches of skilled and unskilled laborers are members viz: Master builders, tailors, shoemakers, machinists, and blacksmiths, printers, farmers, notary public and commissioner, seamen, longshoremen and common laborers. This society owns real estate valued at $40,000, and supports its sick and infirm members.

The colored population of the State of New York is estimated at 60,000, viz: New York, King's, Queen's, Suffolk, and Richmond counties, 27,000; in the other counties of the State, 33,000, one-fifth of which would give us, adding 3,500 colored seamen, 15,500 voters.

There are in the city of New York fifty engineers, four hundred waiters, seven basketmakers, thirty-two tobacco twisters, fifty barbers, twenty-two cabinetmakers and carpenters, fourteen masons and bricklayers, fifteen smelters and refiners, two rollers, six moulders, five hundred longshoremen, and twenty-four printers. . . . What we most need, next to a plenty of work, in New York, as well as in other Northern States, is the elective franchise. . . .

The New Era (Washington), February 17, 1870.

[f]

California Negroes Fight Jim Crow Schools

The assertion that colored children would be insulted and abused if admitted to the public schools is refuted wherever the experiment is tried. That is often alleged as a reason for excluding them from those institutions, and so great has been the solicitude of some for the welfare of our children that they would sooner deprive them of all means of education than subject them to insult from white children, by admitting them in the same schools. This we have always denied, and have said the antagonism would soon wear away by the irresistible power of attraction, and recent events have proven that our opinion was correct. . . .

The experiments work so well in Brooklyn, that the Board of Education of Oakland have decided to admit colored children into the public schools of that city. A committee of colored citizens waited on the Board at their last meeting, and presented a petition to that effect, which after considerable discussion was granted. The public schools in Oakland will shortly close for vacation; when they open again in July, colored children will be admitted.

The Elevator (San Francisco), May 4, 1872. Copy in the Bancroft Library, University of California, Berkeley. The publisher of this newspaper was Philip A. Bell.

[g]

New York Civil Rights Committee

To the President and Members of the Board of Commissioners of Parks:

Gentlemen, Heretofore we have been denationalized and brutalized into chattels personal, and denied the rights of freedom and American citizenship for no color of crime, but for the crime of color.

But now, thanks to an overruling Providence, we are living in a period of the history of the Republic in the education and elevation of the two races to a higher sphere of universal freedom, and of intellectual culture of national greatness and grandeur, and in a government of the people and by the people.

Standing, as we do now, on the comprehensive platform of Republican liberty—to wit—equal rights to all: Therefore, under these assurances a number of our citizens, who are also members of the Citizens' Civil Rights Committee, have organized and appointed the undersigned a Committee on Patronage, for the purpose of presenting the claims of our people to their share of public employment, and to ask your honors to appoint colored men to places of profit and trust in your department, as it may be in your power to confer.

It may not be out of place to inform your honors that the Honorable Board of Police Commissioners, through this Committee, have already given employment to forty-four colored men, and are making arrangements to enroll more colored men in the service of their department. With sentiments of high esteem and awaiting your early compliance, we have the honor to be, very respectfully yours,

William P. Powell, Chairman,
Louis V. Williams,
Edward V. C. Eato,
John S. Freeman

N.Y. *Herald*, October 11, 1873.

[h]

William Still on Independent Voting

The slavery issues on which the two parties have so long been contending are all, except Senator Sumner's Civil Rights Bill, settled, and the way is now prepared for new issues; such as Tariff, Currency, Specie Payments, Railroads, Government bonds, the United States Debt, the Granges Movement, &c. It needs but half an eye to see that these issues are soon to bring about many political changes. It is deeply interesting to mark how the signs are portending the near approach of these events.

Landless and without capital, even with the Civil Rights Bill secured by the Congress of the Nation, the condition of the colored man would still be pitiable, unless he is wise. Of course he cannot vote the Democratic ticket when the Democratic party is arrayed against him; but it would not be unwise to carefully watch the changes in parties and movements, as there are many Democrats, doubtless, who still adhere to the party of their Fathers, who are no longer in sympathy with old pro-slavery doctrines and ideas; and while they still hold on to their party they are anxious for a general change, in which the civil and political rights of the colored man shall be recognized. Now which would be just the best way on the part of the colored man to help bring about this desirable change, I may not be able to point out, but I am sure the counsel that favors the wholesale denunciation of every Democrat and every colored man who might be disposed to vote a Democratic ticket, will never hasten that long-looked for day of peace which should be desired by every American citizen.

William Still, *An Address on Voting and Laboring, delivered at Concert Hall, March 10th, 1874* (Phila., 1874).

190

THE NEGRO ON THE NATIONAL SCENE DURING RECONSTRUCTION, 1868–1880

In addition to work within the North and the South during the years of Reconstruction there were, on many issues and occasions, opinions expressed and actions taken by the Negro people on a national scale.

Of particular importance were the issues of women's suffrage, the organization of labor and the Negroes' civil rights, and printed below are eight documents illustrative of these matters. A salient event of the period, too, was the founding by the federal government in April, 1865, of the Freedmen's Savings and Trust Company, whose business was confined to Negroes. This bank failed in June, 1874, in the midst of a general depression, after many thousands of Negroes had deposited almost $3,300,000 in the bank's approximately forty branches. The calamity that this represented for many Negroes plus the fact that its last president was Frederick Douglass made the event an outstanding one, and a document concerning it is published below. A final document in this group is devoted to the first national convention of Negro newspapermen, illustrating the emergence on a nationwide scale of a burgeoning Negro press, as well as the beginnings, on the same scale, of a significant professional and middle-class element among the Negro people.

The first two documents [a, b] deal with the question of woman suffrage. In the earlier of these, Frederick Douglass, writing from Rochester, N.Y., September 27, 1868, is explaining to a former Abolitionist and suffragette, Mrs. Josephine White Griffing of Washington, why he feels the question of Negro suffrage to be of greater urgency, at the time, than that of woman suffrage though he reiterates his support of the latter. The second document consists of a letter written to Douglass as the editor of the *New National Era* by a Negro woman, Mrs. Mary Olney Brown, urging that the paper use the Fourteenth Amendment as a wedge to bring about the enfranchisement of Negro women.

Documents three through six relate to the Negro's activity within the labor movement shortly after the Civil War. The third document [c] consists of an extract from the speech delivered by Isaac Myers of Baltimore, representing the Colored Caulkers' Trades Union Society, at the third annual convention of the National Labor Union, held in Philadelphia in August, 1869. As one of nine Negro delegates to this convention Myers made an historic appeal—unfortunately, not heeded—for unity between Negro and white workers.

Though lip service was paid to Myers' call by the National Labor Union, real action did not follow. As a result there was formed in Washington in December, 1869, a Negro National Labor Union. Its constitution forms the fourth document [d] printed below, while the fifth document [e] consists of an address, apparently the work of John Mercer Langston, adopted by the over two hundred delegates at the founding convention of this Union as indicative of their motives. The sixth document [f] consists of a memorial to Congress submitted by the same December, 1869 convention calling for the distribution of land to "the colored laborers of the southern States."

Documents seven and eight deal with civil rights. The seventh [g] is a news story from the *New National Era* telling of a national delegation of Negroes pressing these demands upon President Grant in January, 1872. The eighth document [h] is a memorial to Congress praying for civil and political equality from the National Civil Rights Convention meeting in December, 1873.

The ninth document [i] comes from Frederick Douglass and deals with the Freedmen's Bank. This consists of testimony by Douglass given February 14, 1880, before a Senate Committee, under the chairmanship of Blanche K. Bruce, investigating the Bank's failure in line with Senator Bruce's successful efforts to reimburse its depositors.

The tenth document [j] consists of the speech made by P. B. S. Pinchback, formerly Acting-Governor of Louisiana, as chairman of the Convention of Colored Newspaper Men held in Cincinnati in August, 1875. To this convention may be traced the origins of the present Associated Negro Press.

[a]

Frederick Douglass' Letter

My dear Friend: I am impelled by no lack of generosity in refusing to come to Washington to speak in behalf of woman's suffrage. The right of woman to vote is as sacred in my judgment as that of man, and I am quite willing at anytime to hold up both my hands in favor of this right. It does not however follow that I can come to Washington or go elsewhere to deliver lectures upon this special subject. I am now devoting myself to a cause not more sacred, certainly more urgent, because it is life and death to the long-enslaved people of this country; and this is: Negro suffrage. While the Negro is mobbed, beaten, shot, stabbed, hanged, burnt, and is the target of all that is malignant in the North and all that is murderous in the South, his claims may be preferred by me without exposing in any wise myself to the imputation of narrowness or meanness towards the cause of woman. As you very well know, woman has a thousand ways to attach herself to the governing power of the land and already exerts an honorable influence on the course of legislation. She is the victim of abuses, to be sure, but it cannot be pretended I think that her cause is as urgent as that of ours. I never suspected you of sympathizing with Miss Anthony and Mrs. Stanton in their course. Their principle is: that no Negro shall be enfranchised while woman is not. Now, considering that white men have been enfranchised always, and colored men have not, the conduct of these white women, whose husbands, fathers and brothers are voters, does not seem generous.

"Griffing Papers," Columbia Univ. Library; published by Joseph Borome in *The Journal of Negro History* (1948), XXXIII, pp. 469–70.

[b]

Letter to Frederick Douglass

I have been for a long time wondering why you do not insist on the trying out of the provisions of the Fourteenth and Fifteenth Amendments to the Constitution of the United States, as regards the right of colored citizens to vote. Do you say that colored citizens do vote? I answer, yes. A part of them vote. But did it ever occur to you that colored women citizens have the same right to vote that colored men citizens have? That the same amendments that gave citizenship, with all rights, privileges and immunities to the colored man, gave also the same citizenship with its rights, privileges, and immunities to the colored woman. . . .

Now, what I want to urge upon the colored class of our citizens is, that as the Fourteenth and Fifteenth Amendments to the Constitution give the colored women the unmistakable right to vote, that they see to it that their mothers, wives, sisters, and daughters are as fully protected in the exercise of that right as they themselves are. It is a gross injustice that the colored women have so long been defrauded of their right to vote. Somebody must take the lead in this matter, and I see no better way to bring the subject before the people than for the New National Era (the paper above all others devoted to the elevation of the colored race) to take the question up, and insist on the full enforcement of the Fourteenth and Fifteenth Amendments to the Constitution of the United States.

MARY OLNEY BROWN.

New National Era (Washington), October 24, 1872.

[c]

Isaac Myers' Speech

. . . Gentlemen, silent but powerful and far-reaching is the revolution inaugurated by your act in taking the colored laborer by the hand and telling him that his interest is common with yours, and that he should have an equal chance in the race for life . . . I speak today for the colored men of the whole country, from the lakes to the Gulf—from the Atlantic to the

Pacific—from every hill-top, valley and plain throughout our vast domain, when I tell you that all they ask for themselves is a fair chance; that you shall be no worse off by giving them that chance; that you and they will dwell in peace and harmony together; that you and they may make one steady and strong pull until the laboring men of this country shall receive such pay for time made as will secure them a comfortable living for their families, educate their children and leave a dollar for a rainy day and old age. Slavery, or slave labor, the main cause of the degradation of white labor, is no more. And it is the proud boast of my life that the slave himself had a large share in the work of striking off the fetters that bound him by the ankle, while the other end bound you by the neck.

The New York Times, August 19, 1869.

[d]

Constitution of the [Negro] National Labor Union

Article I

Section 1. This organization shall be known as the National Labor Union, and its jurisdiction shall be confined to the United States.

Article II

Section 1. The National Labor Union shall be composed of such organizations as may now or hereafter exist, having for their object the amelioration and advancement of those who labor for a living.

Section 2. Each organization shall be entitled to one representative, and each State Labor Union to three for the State at large in the National Labor Union, provided that representatives derive their election direct from the organizations they claim to represent.

Article III

Section 1. The officers of the National Labor Union shall be elected annually on the third day of the session, and shall hold their offices until their successors are duly elected. They shall consist of a President, Vice-President, Recording and Assistant Secretary, Treasurer, and an Executive Committee of nine members.

Section 2. The above named officers shall constitute a Bureau of Labor.

Section 3. There shall be one Vice-President for each State, Territory, and the District of Columbia to be chosen by the State Labor Unions where they exist. Where there are no State Labor Unions, by the State Labor Conventions, at their next meeting preceding the annual meeting of the National Labor Union. If neither elect a Vice-President, then the National Labor Union shall have power to appoint at their regular annual meeting.

Section 4. The Bureau of Labor shall be located in the City of Washington, D.C.

Article IV

Section 1. The President shall preside at all meetings of the National Labor Union and "the Bureau of Labor" and preserve order and enforce the laws. He shall sign all orders for money drawn on the Treasurer by the Secretary, and be the Custodian of the Seal, which shall be affixed to all documents emanating from his office, and perform such other duties as may be required of him by the Bureau of Labor, and the interest of the various organizations in the several states demand.

Section 2. The Vice-President shall, in the absence or disabilities of the President, perform the duties of his office.

Article V

Section 1. The Recording Secretary shall keep a correct account of the proceedings of the National Labor Union and the Bureau of Labor. He shall fill all blanks and write all orders for money on the Treasurer. He shall keep a debit and credit account, and shall report the condition of the finances at each meeting of the Bureau of Labor, and perform such other service as may be required by the National Labor Union and the Bureau of Labor. In his absence, the Assistant Secretary shall perform the duties of his office.

Article VI

Section 1. The Treasurer shall secure all money, pay all bills and orders that may be drawn on him, and properly attested. He shall keep a debit and credit account, and report at each meeting of the Bureau of Labor. He may be required to give such bonds with such security as the Bureau may require.

Article VII

Section 1. The Bureau of Labor shall meet at least once in each month, at such time and places as the interest of the Union may require. They shall fill all vacancies in said Bureau. They shall have the power to grant charters to the various organizations in the different states. In connection with the President they shall advise and superintend to organization of Labor Unions, land, loan, building and co-operative associations generally, in the different states. They shall inquire into and inform the various organizations as to when, where, and how money can be obtained, in what sums, and at what rate of interest, and what security will be required. They shall give especial attention to protecting the rights of workingmen of the various organizations chartered by the National Labor Union by bringing to justice those who rob them of their wages, and by bringing about such legislation in the several states as may be necessary for the interest and advancement of the condition of the laboring classes.

Section 2. They shall regulate the salary of the President, Secretary, and such other officers as may be necessary to accomplish the objects of the National Labor Union.

Section 3. They shall report annually to the National Labor Union the condition of the various organizations, also the general condition of colored labor in the United States, with recommendations as they may think necessary.

Section 4. They shall, in connection with the President, act as agent for the securing of employment, to labor of all kinds, and its transfer from one state to another.

Section 5. All communications in relation to business pertaining to the Labor Union or Bureau of Labor must be marked on the envelope "official," and addressed to the President, Post Office Box 191, Washington, D.C.

Article VIII

Section 1. Seven members, in any organization, shall be sufficient to apply for a charter, which shall be granted on the payment of five dollars.

Section 2. It shall be the duty of each organization to prepare an annual statement of the condition of said organization, with such other information as may be to the interest of workingmen, and forward it to the Bureau at least one month before the meeting of the National Labor Union, that the reports may be printed for the use and benefit of the National Labor Union at its annual meetings.

Article IX

Section 1. Each local organization or representative shall pay a tax of ten cents annually per member. The tax of an organization shall be paid on the presentation of the credentials of the delegate; and no delegate shall be allowed to take part in the deliberations of the Union until the tax is paid.

Article X

Section 1. The meeting of the National Labor Union shall be held on the second Monday of December in each year; and shall commence its session at 12 M.

Section 2. Special meetings of the National Labor Union may be called by the President, upon the request of the Bureau of Labor.

Article XI

Order of Business

1. Report of Committee on Credentials.
2. Roll of Members.
3. Reading of Minutes.

4. Report of Bureau of Labor.
5. Report of Standing and Special Committees.
6. Report of Local Organizations.
7. Unfinished Business.
8. New Business.
9. Adjournment.

Article XII

Section 1. This Constitution shall only be altered or amended at the regular annual meetings of the National Labor Union by a two-thirds vote of all members present.

> Isaac Myers, President,
> George T. Downing, Vice-President,
> Lewis H. Douglass, Secretary,
> Calvin Cruser, Treasurer

The New Era (Washington), April 21, 1870.

[e]

Address Adopted by the Negro National Labor Union

In our organization we make no discrimination as to nationality, sex, or color. Any labor movement based upon such discrimination and embracing a small part of the great working masses of the country, while repelling others because of its partial and sectional character, will prove to be of very little value. Indeed, such a movement, narrow and divisional, will be suicidal, for it arrays against the classes represented by it all other laboring classes which ought to be rather allied in the closest union, and avoid these dissensions and divisions which in the past have given wealth the advantage over labor.

We would have "the poor white man" of the South born to a heritage of poverty and degradation like his black compeer in social life, feel that labor in our organization seeks the elevation of all its sons and daughters; pledges its united strength not to advance the interests of a special class; but in its spirit of reasonableness and generous catholicity would promote the welfare, and happiness of all who "earn their bread in the sweat of their brow."

With us, too, numbers count, and we know the maxim, "in union there is strength," has its significance in the affairs of labor no less than in politics. Hence our industrial movement, emancipating itself from every national and partial sentiment, broadens and deepens its foundations so as to rear thereon a superstructure capacious enough to accommodate at the altar of common interest the Irish, the Negro and the German laborer; to which, so far from being excluded, the "poor white" native of the South, struggling out of moral and pecuniary death into life "real and earnest," the white mechanic and laborer of the North, so long ill taught and advised that his true interest is gained by hatred and abuse of the laborer of African descent, as well as the Chinaman, whom designing persons, partially enslaving, would make in the plantation service of the South the rival and competitor of the former slave class of the country, having with us one and the same interest, are all invited, earnestly urged, to join us in our movement, and thus aid in the protection and conservation of their and our interests.

In the cultivation of such spirit of generosity on our part, and the magnanimous conduct which it prompts, we hope, by argument and appeal addressed to the white mechanics, laborers and trades unions of our country, to our legislators and countrymen at large, to overcome the prejudices now existing against us so far as to secure a fair opportunity for the display and remuneration of our industrial capabilities.

We launch our organization, then, in the fullest confidence, knowing that, if wisely and judiciously managed, it must bring to all concerned, strength and advantage, and especially to the colored American as its earliest fruits that power which comes from competence and wealth, education and the ballot, made strong through a union whose fundamental principles are just, impartial and catholic.

The New Era, January 13, 1870. (This was the first number of the newspaper, edited then by J. Sella Martin with Frederick Douglass as corresponding editor.)

[f]

Memorial from Negro National Labor Union

To the honorable the Senate and House of Representatives of the United States of America:

The memorial of the laboring men of the United States in convention assembled respectfully showeth, that the condition of the colored laborers of the southern States appeals most forcibly to Congress to intervene in their behalf, by such just and timely measures as properly fall within the scope of the national authority.

Abundant evidence has been laid before this convention showing that the average rate of wages received by the colored agricultural laborer of the South does not exceed sixty dollars ($60) per annum. Out of this small sum he is required to clothe himself and purchase necessary articles for subsistence, for, as a general thing, the only allowance that he receives from his employer consists of one peck of corn or meal per week.

Recent returns at the National Bureau of Statistics show that this unrequited labor furnished to the exports of the country during the fiscal year ending June 30, 1869, the enormous amount of one hundred and sixty-eight millions of dollars ($168,000,000) in gold, in the single article of cotton alone. Reliable testimony exhibits the fact that the net profits to the employer from this cotton product, making due allowance for the market value of the land, and deducting every item that enters into cost of production, and allowing each planter at the rate of two thousand dollars ($2,000) per annum for his personal services in superintending his laborers, amount to about fifty (50) per cent on the capital invested, while the laborers who produced it have not only been left penniless, but are nearly two millions of dollars ($2,000,000) in debt, despite the utmost thrift and economy on their part.

Your memorialists are aware of the so-called axiom of political economy which declares that "the price of labor, like that of any other commodity, is regulated by the law of supply and demand." But this proposition, while true in its application to a normal condition of society, where the ordinary laws of trade and production alone control prices, it is *not* true as regards the planters and their colored employes in the southern States, for the landowners there can and *do* absolutely regulate the price of labor by combining against the laborer. These combinations would ordinarily be controlled by prudent considerations of profit and loss, which usually govern the investment of capital, and the fear of counter-organizations on the part of the employes would in some measure restrain the oppressive spirit of the employer. But in this case resistance by organized effort is impossible, for the earnings of the laborer leave him no surplus, and when he ceases to labor he begins to starve.

These combinations are very largely inspired and sustained by political causes, as well as by the certainty of ultimate success in securing from the laborer the largest possible amount of work for the smallest possible amount of pay. The political causes above referred to, as stimulating combinations on the part of the landed proprietors against the colored laborers, spring from the well-attested fact that the one class, with but a few exceptions, exhibits an implacable hostility to our system of free government, while the other sustains with unwavering devotion and uncompromising loyalty to the principles upon which it rests. Hence the possession of civil rights by the colored laborer, conferred upon him not only as an act of justice, but as a national safeguard, and for his self-protection, invites aggression which he cannot repel, and his political privileges become to him the source of personal peril. The freedom of the ballot is thus sought to be subdued by the necessity for bread, and, with the loyal colored laborer of the South, duty to his country involves danger to himself. Your memorialists believe that this great wrong is not without a feasible remedy, and that the true and immediately practicable remedy lies in making a fair proportion of the laborers themselves land-owners. This will place colored agricultural labor beyond the absolute control of artificial or political causes, by lessening the amount of labor *for hire,* and increasing at the same time the demand for that class of laborers. To this end your memorialists pray that the surveyed public lands in the southern States may be subdivided into tracts of forty (40) acres each, and that any freedman who shall settle on one of these subdivisions, and cultivate the same for the space of one year, shall receive a patent for the same, the title to such land to vest in the settler and his heirs, and to be inalienable for the period of ten years from the date of entry.

Your memorialists beg leave to invite the attention of your honorable body to the following exhibit of the public domain now in the southern States, as shown by the records of the General Land Office:

	Acres
Alabama	6,496,421
Arkansas	11,307,278
Florida	17,328,344
Louisiana	6,493,499
Mississippi	4,718,517
Total	46,344,059

It will thus be seen that there are in the South, in the round numbers, forty-six millions three hundred and forty-four thousand acres of public land.

Estimating the number of freedmen who would probably avail themselves of the right of settlement on the terms proposed at two hundred thousand, (200,000), or about one-fourth ($\frac{1}{4}$) of the ablebodied colored males in the southern States, the government could give each colored settler forty (40) acres, and still have a residue of over thirty-eight millions of acres of public land in the South, the value of which residue would be greatly enhanced by the contiguity of numerous settlements to it, the opening of roads, &c; while the population thus endowed would add proportionately to the sources of national taxation, and would thereby not only swell the aggregate products of American industry, but would add greatly to the list of consumers or purchasers of many of those products which they cannot now enjoy.

Your memorialists are assured and believe that the existing homestead and pre-emption laws will with some modifications and extensions, accomplish the result herein desired.

And your memorialists further pray that your honorable body will enact a law authorizing the President to appoint a land commission, to consist of suitable persons, whose duty it shall be to purchase lands in those southern States in which there are no public lands, and have the same divided into tracts of forty (40) acres each, and sold to freedmen in five (5) years, the whole sum to be thus used in the purchase of homesteads for freedmen not to exceed two million ($2,000,000) of dollars.

And your memorialists further pray that the railroad grants of public land, made by the government to several of the railway corporations in the southern States, and by them forfeited by reason of their non-compliance with the conditions annexed to the same, be not revived, but that the lands embraced in such lapsed grants be brought within the operations of the Homestead Act, as herein prayed for.

And your memorialists will ever pray, &c.

We hereby certify that the above memorial was unanimously adopted in the national labor convention begun to beholden in the city of Washington, D.C., on Monday, the 6th day of December, A.D. 1869.

J. H. Harris, North Carolina

President National Labor Convention

T. J. Mackey, S.C., Sella Martin, Mass.,

John P. Sampson, O., W. L. J. Hayes, N.C.; William J. Wilson, N.J., George T. Downing, R.I., A. Ward Handy, Pa., J. H. Rainey, S.C., James T. Rapier, Ala., Charles H. Peters, District of Col., William Perkins, Md., J. W. Loguen, N.Y., Caleb Milburn, Del.

Vice-Presidents National Labor Convention

Attest: Louis [sic] H. Douglass,
Secretary.

Senate Miscellaneous Document No. 3, 41st Cong., 2nd Sess.

[g]

A Civil Rights Delegation

A delegation, composed of the following named prominent colored men of Washington: John F. Cook, District register; John T. Johnson, District treasurer; Hons. John A. Gray, Jas. A. Handy, and Lewis H. Douglass, members of the District Legislature; Prof. John M. Langston, Howard University; Dr. Charles P. Purvis, Henry Johnson, John H. Brooks, Wm. Syphax, Perry Ryder, Chas. R. Douglass, Walker Lewis, and Wm. H. Smith, accompanied by the delegates from Philadelphia, headed by Professor Richard T. Greener, James Whipper Purnell, Levi Cromwell, and James F. Needham, who brought from that city a petition, bearing over 2,000 signatures, in favor of the civil rights bill; also, a delegation from Richmond, Va., consisting of John Oliver, Esq., Hon. P. J. Carter, Henry Cox, and A. C. Coleman, members of the Virginia Legislature, and Hon. W. H. Gray, of Arkansas, called, by appointment, at the Executive Mansion on the 10th inst., for the purpose of paying their respects to the President, and to request that he would give the weight of his influence in favor of the bill pending in the Senate, known as the supplementary civil rights bill.

Mr. John F. Cook, after severally introducing the gentlemen, addressed the President, as follows:

Mr. President, we are here to-day to see you in the interest of the bill now being considered in Congress, which proposes to secure to the colored citizens of the United States the enjoyment of the usual accommodations, advantages, facilities, and privileges furnished by common carriers by land and water, many of which received and are receiving enormous land grants and subsidies from the General Government, the common heritage of all, by inn keepers and by managers of public and licensed institutions, supported wholly or in part by moneys derived from general taxation, and enjoying other than ordinary immunities.

We are deprived of the privileges of these public arrangements, denied the enjoyment of these advantages. These discriminations against us are extremely unjust, unreasonable, and detrimental, founded and sustained in a state of political circumstances existing prior to the war of the rebellion, hoary in a long continued exercise of this abuse, and fortified by customs long existing . . . As American citizens enjoying the elective franchise and other privileges that citizenship, the title-deed of manhood, affords, we feel sensitively the denial of these rights and privileges; we feel strongly the degradation enforced on us by those distinctions founded on color merely; under this system of discrimination we see the very growth of caste, hatred, and prejudice; we see equally the dwarfing and degrading effect on ourselves. . . .

New National Era, January 18, 1872.

[h]

Memorial from Civil Rights Convention, 1873

Honorable Senate and House of Representatives in Congress assembled:

We regret the necessity which compels us to again come before you and say "we are aggrieved." We are authorized to say to those in authority, to Congress, to the people whom it represents, that there are nearly five millions of American citizens who are shamefully outraged; who are thus treated without cause. The recognitions made within a few years respecting in part our rights, make us more sensitive as to the denials of the rest.

Late declarations recognizing our entitlement to all of our rights, with essential ones withheld, render the grievances even more intolerable. Our grievances are many; our inconveniences through the denial of rights are great; but we shall refer only to those that may be expected through the action of Congress, by statutes forbidding them under penalties. We shall take it for granted that action will be had by Congress, protecting us from invidious distinctions in the enjoyment of common carriers, hotels and other public places of convenience, and refreshment in public places of amusement, and in enjoying other civil rights; but there are indications that there may be some objection made to Federal action against discrimination as to race and color in the management of public instruction; and in empanelling juries, the objections alleging that it is unconstitutional for Congress to legislate to effect these cases. We propose to notice these objections briefly. They come from lawyers, who, like men in other callings, have their thoughts circumscribed by their training and habits of reflection. We do not feel bound, in a matter involving rights, to be circumscribed thereby. Language should be used whenever it may without outraging it, to best subserve equity and justice. A decision of the supreme judiciary is binding and irrevocable, as affecting the particular case adjudicated, but is to be regarded only as a light which may be used, nay, should be, in any other case before that Judiciary, to assist in finding a proper solution of the case. It has no imperative binding force upon any subsequent case.

The force of recorded decisions as to the powers of Congress is somewhat impaired, because they were rendered under a bias or influence differing from the present.

The interest of slavery, a State institution, was so great and overshadowing as to subjugate church as well as state, morality as well as the laws of the land; decisions were rendered in its interests; it was ever keen, active, resolute, extremely suspicious. The State-Rights theory, one essential to slavery, was persistently urged. How it was adhered to may be seen in its producing the late rebellion, its grave-yard. Therefore the learnings of legal minds through decisions and opinions made popular by this State-Rights theory, must not be permitted to have the controlling sway some lawyers are disposed to give them; hence we are emboldened to take exceptions to the theory that Congress may not interpose except in the United States courts to secure unto a citizen an impartial jury. We affirm there is no prohibitory clause of the Constitution denying this right. On the other hand, we affirm that it ranges itself among the powers delegated to Congress, at least by implication; that it is a power inherent in the Government from its character, one supported by the principles of common law. It is in maintenance of a national right. We are at a loss to find the part of the Constitution which admits Congress to go as far as it has gone in protecting the civil rights of citizens in the several States, assented to by objecting Senators, but which forbids its going far enough to effectually protect the civil rights of a citizen wherever the stars and stripes have sway.

If Congress may throw the protecting arm of the law around any citizen of the United States, in every State, so as to forbid any denial or discrimination in hotels and public conveyances on account of race and color, it certainly may do in protecting him from invidious rules impairing the right of property; it may say the common school, paid for and owned by all citizens in common, shall not be made to serve to the degradation and humiliation of any class thereof; that a branch of the Government maintained to train the child as to his proper relation to his Government and his fellow citizens, must not therein be trained in opposition to the government's fundamental principles. The reasonableness of this view is most apparent when it is considered that the State taxes in common to educate, and when it assumes to educate, it must be under certain defined and admitted principles, one of which is that there shall not be a privileged class; that citizens are to be educated with the idea that we are a nation, one of many, with a common identity and interest; that all are equal before the law; that citizens are called on, regardless of race or color, to bear the duties and responsibilities of citizenship; they must ignore any invidious distinction; the States must not foster distinctions based on race and color.

A distinction must be made between the private school maintained at the private expense of individuals, and those of public schools maintained by moneys taken from the pockets of all; let private schools be maintained by parties willing to pay for them; but let the public or common school be opened for all, and if the associations therein be not altogether agreeable, set it down to the character of our Government and institutions and avoid the disagreeable fact, not by outraging the rights of others, but by paying for a private school. This view is independent of the fact that the Constitution says that no State shall make or enforce any law which shall abridge the privileges or immunities of citizens of the United States, and that no State shall deprive any person of life, liberty, or property without due process of law, nor deny to any person within its jurisdiction the equal protection of the law; and that Congress shall have power to enforce the same by appropriate legislation.

It is an abridgement of the privileges of a citizen to say he shall not, because of his race and color, elect as to the common school he shall attend, subject, of course, to such general regulations as are not invidious in their character, and are made to apply alike to all citizens. It is depriving the citizen of his property to say he shall not enjoy, unless under humiliating conditions, the right of ownership, in common, of the public schools, he owning and maintaining them in common, but denied the common use. This, then, is the conclusion: the citizen is entitled to whatever belongs to him, and is not bound to accept an equivalent. It is not an equal protection of the laws to keep a person from the full enjoyment of his property, or to force him to accept what a party may regard as an equivalent.

This same argument applies to constituting of juries, and we shall apply it in considering whether Congress has the right to secure to any citizen the benefit of an impartial jury of his peers.

Article 1st, Section 8th, of the Constitution, says: "Congress shall have power to make all laws which shall be necessary and proper for carrying into execution the powers vested by the Constitution in the Government of the United States." The Constitution further says: "The Constitution and the laws of the United States which shall be made in pursuance thereof, are the supreme law of the land, and the judges in every State shall be bound thereby." The Constitution, by implication as well as by direct words, affirms an impartial jury to be a constitutional right, of course to be maintained as such, to be a supreme law of the land, anything in the Constitution and laws of any State to the contrary notwithstanding; which amounts to a prohibition on a State from repressing an impartial jury. From all of which it is evident, as well as from the binding force of the common law in securing an impartial jury, that Congress has power to protect, by law, the citizen in this great national and common right under civilized government.

The fact that Federal legislation has been had and acquiesced in, and judicial decisions have enforced the same, establishing the theory that the National Government may interpose and regulate the judiciary of the States, restraining them from proscribing citizens because of their race or color; as, for instance, actions had under the present existing civil rights laws, which regulate the receiving of testimony in the several States, show that the power exists to protect us from the injustice of which we complain. Senator Thurman has said, on the Senate floor: "If a State violated one of the prohibitions imposed upon it by the Constitution, it was competent for Congress to afford a remedy." It consequently ranges itself among the powers delegated to the United States, and if Senators see their way clear to pass a bill protecting citizens from denial and proscription in enjoying common carriers and hotels, public places of convenience and refreshment, amusement, and the like, it may protect us in our common school and jury rights. This view is indorsed by the republican party, and this is their platform on which our worthy President was elected. "Complete liberty and exact equality in the enjoyment of all civil, political, and public rights should be established and effectually maintained throughout the Union by efficient and appropriate State and Federal legislation."

It is not complete liberty and exact equality to be compelled to go to a proscribed school; to be tried by a jury from which every individual of the class to which the party tried belongs is excluded because he is of that class. The republican party, now in power, said there should be efficient and appropriate State and Federal legislation against the same. It is quite significant that the opponents of the republicans in the presidential canvass went into it with a platform which, as to civil rights, was not opposed to this position of the republicans; and in all subsequent elections, in which the democrats have alluded to everything they could think of to represent the republican party in the most odious light . . . they did not think it would be politic and effectual in arousing indignation against the party to make the platform of the party as to civil rights, committing it to Federal action, a subject of condemnation.

In making this appeal, we confidently expect at the hands of our own party a favorable response which expectation is increased by manifestations exhibited by parties who have hitherto bitterly opposed us. May we not beseech such to fully fraternize with our friends?

Very respectfully, your memorialist,

GEO. T. DOWNING,
Acting President.

House Miscellaneous Document No. 44, 43rd Cong., 1st Sess.

[i]

Douglass on Freedmen's Bank

Washington, D.C., *February* 14, 1880
FREDERICK DOUGLASS sworn and examined.
By the CHAIRMAN [Sen. B. K. Bruce]:

Question. Mr. Douglass, will you state your connection with the Freedman's Bank; what position you held in that institution, when you were elected to that position, and how long you remained in it?

Answer. I was for a short time president of the Freedman's Bank. I was elected to the position about the middle of March, 1874, but hesitated about taking the office until about the first of April. I then, under persuasion of different members of the board of trustees, accepted the office, as they said it would help to inspire confidence in the soundness of the bank. I remained in that position until the bank was handed over or the institution was put in the hands of the present commissioners. All told, I was in the institution about three months. . . .

Q. Did you not write and publish one or more circulars expressing your belief in the soundness of the bank?   *A*. Well, I wrote two circulars almost immediately upon going into the bank, upon representations that were made to me by those that I supposed knew the true condition of the bank, asking depositors and others to hold on, and expressing the belief that we could weather the crisis and pay dollar for dollar in the end. Nevertheless, I expressed myself in some parts of these circulars so doubtfully that I was charged before the trustees with having destroyed the credit of the bank by these very circulars. . . .

Q. What caused you, Mr. Douglass, to doubt the solvency of the bank, at last?

A. I found that it was in want of money, for one thing—very much in want of money; and on one occasion the actuary came into the bank and stated that we must have ten thousand dollars that day, or the bank would have to close . . . So I loaned the bank ten thousand dollars; and as week after week went on and I found it impossible to get back my ten thousand dollars, I naturally enough began to doubt the soundness of the bank; most people would under such circumstances (smiling); though I did at last obtain my ten thousand dollars.

Another reason induced me to disbelieve in the bank. I found that I was the only trustee of the bank that deposited any money in it. I went up before this Banking Committee, at the other end of the Capitol, and stated my belief in the insolvency of the bank, and forthwith a number of trustees were brought together—they came before that committee—and they contradicted all that I had said concerning the insolvency of the bank. They said that we could go on. Well, I was left out in the cold. However, it was very soon believed by the committee that we were insolvent, and legislation was enacted which finally brought us, or very speedily brought us, to a close. . . . But at the same time I was a depositor there. I had two thousand dollars in the bank at the time, and when I found it was to be closed up, since I had been partly instrumental, through my circulars, in inspiring confidence in the institution, I thought I would not make myself a preferred creditor and left my money in there, although I had the same chance of taking it out that others had.

Senate Report No. 440, 46th Cong., 2nd Sess., pp. 236–39.

[j]

P. B. S. Pinchback at First Convention of Negro Newspapermen, 1875

A year and a half ago a paragraph went around proposing a National organization of colored editors. A call was issued, and we * have met here to-day in pursuance of that object. Our first object is to make colored people's newspapers self-sustaining—not that we expect to make money out of them. Our people, as a class, are not largely a reading class, but it is on them that we must rely for patronage. Of the four millions who were recently in slavery we cannot expect any large portion of them to be readers; but we must look to their children as they grow up. We can not expect, for sometime, to derive much income from advertising, not until our people become active and enterprising in business matters.

In making the call for this organization we included the ministers, for they can do more than any other class to induce the colored people to become readers of newspapers. The fact was, said the speaker, warming up and becoming truly eloquent, the colored people must learn to rely more upon themselves than heretofore. Even in Congress, the white people, the dominant race, are beginning to throw in our teeth that enough has been done for us, and we must now take care of ourselves. I do not object to this. We are numerous enough, and all we need is to be intelligent enough to take care of ourselves. We are four millions, out of thirty millions who inhabit this country and we have rights as well as privileges to maintain and we must assert our manhood in their vindication.

The black people of this country can furnish in time of need, for its defense, over 800,000 soldiers to march under the glorious banner of universal liberty. With this force as a political element, and as laborers, producers and consumers, we are an element of strength and wealth too powerful to be ignored by the American people. All we need is a just appreciation of our own power and our own manhood. This rolling in the dust—this truckling to power, whether wrapped up in an individual or a party, I have long since abandoned. I strike out boldly, as if born in a desert, and looking for civilization. I am groping about through this American forest of prejudice and proscription, determined to find some form of civilization where all men will be accepted for what they are worth. I demand nothing for our race because

* Representatives were present from the Lexington, Ky., *American Citizen,* the Memphis *Planet,* the San Francisco *Elevator,* the New Orleans *Louisianian,* the Carroll Parish, La., *True Republican,* the Baton Rouge *Grand Era,* the Los Angeles *Pacific Appeal,* the Galveston *Spectator,* the Concordia, La., *Eagle,* the Philadelphia *Christian Recorder,* the Cincinnati *Colored Citizen,* the New York *Progressive American* and the Terre Bonne, La., *Republican.*

they are black. Even the wrongs of two hundred years I will overlook, although they entitle us to some consideration. Still I hope the future will present no necessity for frequent reference to this matter.

The speaker said he would not advise any separate political organization; but as the Irish and German citizens of this country had their organizations for the promotion of their mutual interests, they must consolidate their efforts and work together harmoniously to a common purpose.

Convention of Colored Newspaper Men, Cincinnati, Aug. 4, 1875 (n.p., n.d.).

VI

Early Post-Reconstruction Era

191

THE POST-RECONSTRUCTION GENERATION,
1870–1890

One of the several "unknown" large areas in the history of the American Negro is the post-Reconstruction generation. The impression is widespread that with the crushing of Reconstruction a state of torpor descended upon the Negro people, broken only, perhaps, with the rise of Booker T. Washington and the ensuing Washington-Du Bois controversy.

This impression is the result of a failing of American historiography and not of a sudden state of passivity among the Negro people. The fact is that after the restoration of Bourbon power in the South the struggles of the Negro people continued and, in many respects, advanced. Reaction's economic and political power was frequently and seriously challenged, numerous proposals and programs for activity were brought forward and weighed, mass migrations occurred, many Negro organizations were formed, and Negroes joined in the urban and rural battles waged by the American common people against maturing monopoly capitalism.

To give some picture of the rich content of this era reaching from the end of Reconstruction to the beginning of the Populist movement, we have divided the documentary material into six main categories. The first is concerned with the various proposals and programs enunciated by Negroes from the 70's to 1890. The second deals with the separate Negro organizations founded during these years in order to implement the proposals. The third category includes material illustrative of mass migrations which marked the period, particularly, though not exclusively, the Great Exodus of 1879. The fourth grouping offers material on the Negroes' participation in general mass organizations, especially political parties and labor unions, while the fifth section deals with the continued use by the Bourbon of violence for political ends. The sixth section is concerned with miscellaneous matters of this period exemplifying experiences unique to the Negro people.

I.
PROPOSALS AND PROGRAMS:

A myriad of proposals and programs came from Negro individuals, newspapers, magazines and organizations during the years now being considered. To illustrate the most important of these there follow fifteen documents dealing with various proposals for migration, plans for industrial education, evaluations of socialism, trade unions and schemes for achieving land-ownership, proposals for armed resistance to reactionary terror, suggestions in the struggle for civil liberties, and overall strategies for conducting the battle against oppression.

The first document [a] is a memorial to Congress dated Topeka, Kansas, March 27, 1886 and is signed by George Charles of that city in his capacity as president of the African Emigration Association, established in 1881. This proposal for migration to Africa is indicative of a persistent idea among some Negroes and, characteristically, is marked by a sense of Negro nationality. The second document [b] is from an article, published in 1890, entitled "Is The Negro Capable of Self-Government?" by a Negro minister of Milledgeville, Georgia, the Rev. A. B. Gibson, and concerns proposals for erecting a Negro State in the West. Such ideas were common after Reconstruction. This also, quite typically, is expressive of a somewhat rudimentary sense of Negro nationality.

The third document [c] is an early speech by Booker T. Washington in behalf of his educational program. This, entitled "The Educational Outlook in the South," was delivered before the National Educational Association in Madison, Wisconsin on July 16, 1884, three years after the founding of Tuskegee Institute. The fourth document [d] is a call signed by Negro leaders throughout the country for a conference on industrial education which was held in New Orleans in January, 1885.

The fifth document [e] is an early example of the consideration of socialism in the Negro press. This is in the form of an article, "Socialism" published in 1886 in *The A.M.E. Church Review*, a quarterly issued in Philadelphia. The author, hostile to and manifestly uninformed about his subject, was Alexander Clark, a Negro lawyer of Chicago. In the sixth document [f], taken from the same quarterly of the same year, John R. Lynch—born a slave, Speaker, in 1872, of the Mississippi House of Representatives, a member of Congress, 1873–77, 1882–83, temporary national chairman of the Republican National Convention, 1884—answers affirmatively the question "Should Colored Men Join Labor Organizations?"

In the seventh document [g] the question "Shall Negroes Become Land-Owners?" is answered positively and in detail in 1887 by a Negro publicist, William Hannibal Thomas, later author of a viciously anti-Negro book, *The American Negro*, published in 1901 by Macmillan.

Documents eight through ten are examples of expressions of a very militant attitude present among a considerable number of Negroes during this period. Document eight [h], an editorial from the Chicago *Conservator* of 1880, hails the work of Negroes who burned part of Clarksville, Tennessee in retaliation for a lynching. Document nine [i] is an editorial from the Cleveland *Gazette* of 1889 indicating somewhat similar feelings on its part and quoting an Alabama paper to the same effect. The tenth document [j] consists of a speech made by John E. Bruce, a leading Negro journalist, in October, 1889, calling for "a resort to force under wise and discreet leaders."

A strategy in the civil rights struggle is outlined in the eleventh document [k]. This consists of the resolutions adopted by a mass meeting held in Washington in 1883 after the Supreme Court had found the Civil Rights Act to be unconstitutional.

The last four documents in this section illustrate general strategies in the developing resistance efforts of the Negro people. Document twelve [l] consists of extracts from the speech delivered by Frederick Douglass, as president of the National Convention of Colored Men held in Louisville, Kentucky, in September, 1883. Listening to Douglass were Negro leaders from twenty-four states plus the District of Columbia, including men like W. A. Pledger of Georgia, J. E. O'Hara of North Carolina and G. H. Ruffin of Massachusetts.

The thirteenth document [m] is made up of excerpts from the volume, *Black and White: Land, Labor and Politics* in the South, by T. Thomas Fortune, published in New York in 1884. Fortune, born a slave in Florida, was an editor of the New York *Age,* and a leading orator and organizer. The influence of Marx and Henry George upon his thinking is clear in this volume, though some years later he became quite conservative and closed his career as a supporter of and propagandist for Booker T. Washington's Tuskegee machine.

The fourteenth document [n] consists of the text of an address delivered in January, 1888, in Selma, Alabama, by the Rev. M. Edward Bryant, an editor and minister of that city. It is noteworthy for its militant and forthright stand on such basic issues as labor unions, resistance to violence, and the building of Negro organizations.

The final document [o] in this group is a Negro's reply to Henry W. Grady's significant speech on "The New South" delivered at the Boston Merchants' Association in December, 1889. This speech, in various forms and for several years, was delivered by Grady, editor of the Atlanta, Ga., *Constitution,* before industrial and financial organizations throughout the North as part of the Bourbons' efforts to cement their alliance, in the role of junior partners, with the actual owners of the South's wealth.

The reply, expressing an awareness of this motive and the Negro people's will to resist the pawning of the South-land of their blood and labor, came from the Reverend Joshua A. Brockett, minister of St. Paul's A.M.E. Church in Cambridge, Massachusetts. It was widely reprinted in the Negro—not the white—press.

[a]

African Emigration Association, 1886

To the members of the Senate & House of Representatives of Congress:
Whereas we, the Negroes of the United States, were brought from Africa and sold as slaves in this country and served as such from 1620 to 1865; and

Whereas we were set free without a penny and left at the mercy of our late masters and their brothers, who owned all this country from the Atlantic to the Pacific; and who for over two hundred years had regarded us as inferiors and slaves; and

Whereas there are sixteen thousand of us who have already returned to Africa; and

Whereas there are thousands of us in humble circumstances who yet wish to return to Africa, and there try to build up a United States in Africa, modeled after this Government, and under the protecting care of the same, for the elevation of the African and for the perpetuity of our race, which is here losing its identity by intermixture with the white races, and other troubles, &c.: Therefore,

We, the members of the African Emigration Association, and such citizens as are willing to aid and encourage us, ask you for an appropriation, to be disbursed through such a channel as in your judgment you may direct.

It is the purpose of this petition to help only those who wish to go to Africa, in whatever parts of the United States they may be found.

Congressional Record, April 6, 1886, 49th Cong., 1st Sess., p. 3138.

[b]

"Is The Negro Capable of Self-Government?"

In reading newspapers we have a mixture of joy and sorrow. We were glad to pick up our morning paper during the agitation of the Blair Educational Bill * in Congress. We opened our paper the next morning and found it had been defeated; we were sorry.

We read again that McCabe's † friends intended petitioning the President to appoint him governor of the territory of Oklahoma and thousands of our people were pouring into the same and that the Negroes would soon be in the majority in the territory, and that steps would be taken asking that it be made a Negro State, ruled and governed entirely by Negroes.‡ This

---

* Senator Henry W. Blair (Republican of New Hampshire) several times, in the 1880's and early '90's, introduced a bill providing for the distribution of surplus Federal revenues to state schools in proportion to the prevalence of illiteracy, but this was never passed.

† Edwin P. McCabe, formerly State Auditor of Kansas, led a movement to make of Oklahoma a Negro state. He edited a newspaper, *The Herald,* devoted to this cause, from his residence in Langston, Okla., one of the twenty-five self-governing all-Negro communities of Oklahoma which had their beginnings in this agitation of the '90's and still exist.

‡ The concept of a Negro state had been projected by Negroes, including leaders like Martin Delany and Sojourner Truth, for many years. Its significance in terms of a budding consciousness of Negro nationality is clear. Typical editorial statements on this idea within the time range of this volume follow:

" 'What do you think of making a great Negro state under this government, as a way out of the race trouble?' We think nothing of it; if the two classes cannot live in this country as they are, they certainly cannot live in such relations as must necessarily result from any such plan."—*Christian Recorder,* March 13, 1890.

Under the title, "A Negro State," the *Indianapolis Freeman* editorialized, July 29, 1905: "The more we think about this subject the more we are convinced that it is not only possible, but that it would be an easy matter for the colored people to make Oklahoma

we regarded as good news and were so eager for our paper to come, for we were so glad. Alas! One day I opened my papers—I commenced seeing the tide changing. The people were ordered to stop going into the territory—it was not made a Negro State; McCabe was not appointed governor. Oh, we were sorry. He must still remain where he does not desire to stay. . . .

Could he live in a country ruled and governed entirely by Negro judges, lawyers, doctors, jurors, sheriffs, deputies, mayors, councilmen, legislators, governors? Could he live under Negro bankers, merchants, manufacturers? Could he live under the Negro operating every plant of industry? Having asked those questions, I will now ask another. Would he be as successful under Negro rule and government as he is under the white man's? . . .

This is a white man's country, and government and he is proving it North, South, East and West, democrats and republicans. For my part, I am tired of both parties; the Negro's back is sleek where they have rode him so much. . . .

Christian Recorder, June 26, 1890.

[c]

Booker T. Washington, 1884

Any movement for the elevation of the Southern Negro, in order to be successful must have to a certain extent the cooperation of the Southern whites. They control government and own the property—whatever benefits the black man benefits the white man. The proper education of all the whites will benefit the Negro as much as the education of the Negro will benefit the whites. The Governor of Alabama would probably count it no disgrace to ride in the same railroad coach with a colored man, but the ignorant white man who curries the Governor's horse would turn up his nose in disgust . . . Brains, property, and character for the Negro will settle the question of civil rights. The best course to pursue in regard to the civil rights bill in the South is to let it alone; let it alone and it will settle itself. Good school-teachers and plenty of money to pay them will be more potent in settling the race question than many civil rights bills and investigating committees.

Now, in regard to what I have said about the relations of the two races, there should be no unmanly cowering or stooping to satisfy unreasonable whims of Southern white men, but it is charity and wisdom to keep in mind the two hundred years' schooling in prejudice against the Negro which the ex-slave holders are called upon to conquer. A certain class of whites in the

and Indian Territory a State under their own control and management; where all the opportunities of any other American would be theirs." The same influential paper, August 12, 1905, reiterated its support of this idea.

South object to the general education of the colored man on the ground that when he is educated he ceases to do manual labor, and there is no evading the fact that much aid is withheld from Negro education in the South by the states on these grounds. Just here the great mission of INDUSTRIAL EDUCATION coupled with the mental comes in. It "kills two birds with one stone," viz: secures the cooperation of the whites, and does the best possible thing for the black man. An old colored man in a cotton field in the middle of July lifted his eyes toward heaven and said, "De cotton is so grassy de work is so hard, and de sun am so hot, I believe this darky am called to preach." This old man, no doubt, stated the true reason why not a few enter school.* Educate the black man, mentally and industrially, and there will be no doubt of his prosperity; for a race who has lived at all, and paid, for the last twenty years, twenty-five and thirty per cent interest on the dollar advanced for food, with almost no education, can certainly take care of itself when educated mentally and industrially . . .

E. Davidson Washington, ed., *Selected Speeches of Booker T. Washington* (Garden City, 1932, Doubleday), pp. 6–7.

[d]

Call for a Conference on Industrial Schools, 1885

Emancipated, turned loose, poor, ignorant and houseless, continually surrounded by difficulties and embarrassments sufficient to apall and retard, by commendable effort on their part, sustained by the generous aid of philanthropists friendly to education, our race in the South has made gratifying advance, mentally and morally. But with this progress of mind and morals, we are confronted with the need of opportunity to qualify ourselves for those activities and industries necessary to make a people prosperous and happy. Our great want now is "cunning hands" to accompany cultured brains. After obtaining the benefit of our public schools our boys should be fitted for some useful and profitable means of livelihood. The restrictions engendered by trades unions, and the obstacles of race prejudice concur to make it impossible for them to obtain trades in the workshops of the country. Therefore, we need industrial schools where our youth can qualify in the various mechanical pursuits and thereby ennoble themselves, and add value to the State. For the establishment of these "schools of trade" we require a united effort and should make earnest appeal to the philanthropy of the nation.

* The story Mr. Washington tells and the manner in which he chose to tell it were not atypical of his speeches before white audiences. This provoked very caustic comment from many Negro newspapers and leaders.

In view of this vital necessity the undersigned * do hereby call a conference, without distinction, of delegates appointed by mass meetings in cities and counties; presiding officers of colleges, principals of schools, bishops, and leading ministers; editors and publishers friendly to the movement are also invited to meet at New Orleans, La., January 15, 1885, for expression on this subject.

M. W. Gibbs, *Shadow and Light* (Washington, 1902), pp. 202–03.

[e]

Alexander Clark on Socialism, 1886

To no portion of the American public does the subject of Socialism address itself with the interest it possesses for 7,000,000 Afro-American citizens. They have cause, transcending the grievances of the vaunted Commune, for revenging themselves upon the cruelties of old systems. They might be excused for listening to the siren voices of the Socialists. But under stress of burning wrongs and the opportunity of retributive justice, they demonstrate their ability to "stand still and see the salvation of God." To the alluring spirit of the Commune they will not the less maintain their souls against temptation. In grand harmony with the beneficent spirit to whose hands I so confidently commit the future, this century has been glorified with the magistracy of Abraham Lincoln and the Emancipation Proclamation. What brighter augury can the Afro-American desire of a future to which he looks for his emancipation from ignorance, from poverty and from the lingering inequalities of race?

That we may not be confounded and misled by the ambiguity of terms and possibly become involved in the plots of anarchists and other evil designing men, is it not well, that, as Afro-Americans, we remain standing face to face, and in faith with Providence who is the great counsel and help of nations as well as individuals, and continue our trust in that genius of American liberty, which struck the shackles from four millions of our people and lifted legislation to the summit of Sumner's magna charta of our Civil Rights? We want nothing of socialism or the Commune, the strike or the boycott, the mob or the riot. For us be it sufficient that we emulate the spirit and faith of Lincoln, Grant, Sumner and their noble compeers, men devoted to liberty and justice, but equally the friends and champions of law and order as the benign agencies of man's highest good. Let us be beguiled

---

* There were thirty-eight signers, including M. W. Gibbs of Little Rock, J. C. Napier of Nashville, Bishop B. F. Tanner of Philadelphia, P. H. Clarke of Cincinnati, B. K. Bruce of Washington, P. A. Bell of San Francisco, F. L. Barnett of Chicago, G. T. Downing of Newport, P. B. S. Pinchback of New Orleans, and Frederick Douglass.

into following no flag of murky hues, or strange device, but stand, unbound by any complications, with free consciences, in the simple dignity and loyalty of American citizens, and giving our heart's whole allegiance to God and country.

The A.M.E. Church Review (Phila.), July, 1886, III, pp. 53–54.

[f]

John R. Lynch On Trade Unions, 1886

Colored men should not identify themselves with any organization that seeks the accomplishment of its purposes through a resort to lawlessness and violence. They should maintain their reputation of being a law-abiding and law-observing people, except so far.as may be necessary for the protection of themselves and their families. They should discountenance, discourage and condemn lawlessness, violence, communism, socialism and anarchy. . . .

The laboring people in this country can secure all the rights to which they are justly entitled without violating law, and there is no better way to bring about this result than through organization. The legitimate object and purpose of labor organizations should be to call public attention to the condition and wants of the laboring people with a view to creating a sentiment that will enforce a recognition of their just and reasonable demands— to unite their efforts and labors in an intelligent direction for their mutual aid, protection and advancement. Such organizations, created and organized for such purposes, are entitled to and should receive the assistance and support of laboring colored people. It is understood, of course, that I refer to such organizations as do not discriminate on account of race or color in the admission of persons to membership. I hope it is not necessary to advise the laboring colored people to strongly oppose and antagonize every organization that will exclude persons of color from the organization without regard to merit. . . . It is the duty of the colored people of the present generation to give their sons and daughters an industrial education and have them contend for recognition by, and admission into, reputable and intelligent labor organizations, and take their chances in the race of life upon terms of equality with the whites.

The A.M.E. Church Review, October, 1886, III, pp. 165–67.

[g]

William H. Thomas on Land-Owning, 1887

Life at best is a serious problem with the Negro. Throughout the land he is the football of caste, the servant of mercenary capital. Whatever, therefore, lifts him above his present level is to be eagerly embraced and fostered. Every true man in the race should bestir himself and organize land purchase associations; the cry should be heard from one end of the country to the other, "Land for the landless Negroes." . . . The heart of the nation has not awakened to the real needs of the Negro. The financial world has no conception of the wealth which would grow out of such an enterprise. Both are dumb with indifference, but humanitarian measures of universal application seldom originate outside of great crises. Meanwhile, the General Government is under moral obligation to devise such measures of relief for the freed people as will ameliorate their material condition. Specious pleading and sophistical ingenuity may interpose legal objections, hedged about with inane constitutional inhibition, but the statement of fact remains unchallenged, and whose only answer lies in the equity of justice between man and man, and government and citizen. The Negroes were held as slaves by the mandate of national and constitutional law—they were emancipated by the same authority. In both instances national jurisdiction was held to be supreme. If slavery was right, emancipation was wrong. If the reverse is true, the Negroes were illegally held to service; some measure of compensation, therefore, is due them, not only from individuals who were the nominal owners, but from the National Government which was the prime factor in their enslavement and maintenance in bondage. No measure of compensation would work such beneficial results to the freed people as the ownership of land. A legislative measure which secured its acquisition by these people would be exalted to the dignity of sound statesmanship. In furtherance of this principle I suggest that the General Government should purchase a quantity of land in each Southern State for the benefit of the Freedmen, on the same principle that it has granted subsidies to railroads and other corporations for the promotion of the general welfare. In those States like Alabama, Arkansas and Florida, where public lands already exist, they should be utilized for this purpose and in pursuance of this object. I submit a feasible plan: the Federal Government should buy or appropriate in each South Atlantic and Gulf State 2000 square miles of territory, or 1,280,000 acres of land, allotting 40 acres to each homestead. This would give to each State 30,000 farms, the original cost of which should not exceed $6,000,000; to erect suitable houses would cost $3,000,000 more, while mules, farming implements, seeds and subsistence would require an additional $6,000,000, making a total outlay of $15,000,000 for 30,000 farms, or a grand total expenditure in eight States of $120,000,000 for 240,000 well-equipped homesteads. The purchase and supervision of this matter should be under the direction of the department of agriculture. This estimate is made at the maximum rate, and will include all necessary expenditure for first cost; the estimate for mules, farm implements and subsistence will show a decided decrease in a practical application of this method, since many of the small planters will supply themselves. The saving made in this direction should be used for the erection of school-houses, for normal training and industrial education, and made self-supporting through manual labor. The unexpended balance of 80,000 acres of land in each State should be devoted to such educational purposes. Each farm should be leased for a period of two years, at an annual rental of five bales of cotton, with the privilege of purchase at the expiration of the lease; the two years of probation will test the fitness and integrity of the tenant and secure *bona fide* purchasers. Other safeguards that will readily suggest themselves should be thrown around both the tenant and government interest, not to hamper either, but to ensure exact fulfillment of all conditions stipulated by the contract on the part of each. The total rent for two years will reach 2,400,000 bales of cotton, and at a low valuation would yield $101,000,000, or $19,000,000 less than the original purchase money. At the termination of the probationary period, let these farms be sold on a credit of five years, on the basis of five annual payments, to be made at the rate of three bales of cotton per annum, the government to retain an equitable title until all liabilities are discharged by the purchaser, when a deed will issue to him.

No apology is needed for this proposition; it has the merit of utility. There is no measure within the range of probabilities that the South could or would endorse which would so assuredly recoup its financial forces as the practical exemplification of this proposition, and, at the same time, partially condone its offensive crimes against the Freedmen.

I herewith submit a brief estimate of the monetary advantage that will accrue to the General Government by the adoption of my proposition. 240,-000 farms, with an annual return of three bales of cotton from each farm, will amount to 720,000 bales per year, or a total of 3,600,000 bales for five years, which, at $42 per bale, will yield $151,200,000; add to this the $101,-000,000 received as rent, and the government has in seven years the enormous return of $252,200,000 on an outlay of $120,000,000, an excess over all expenditure of $132,200,000, to say nothing of the vast increase in the general wealth of the people. This surplus revenue could be returned to the national treasury, or used in the purchase of additional land for distribution and occupation on the same basis. . . . I am confident, no matter how stubbornly and selfishly resisted, the Southern land problem will be eliminated either by aggressive race action, or a revolution of silent forces in social economics. When this change is effected it will give the colored race their opportunity, which, I apprehend, they will not be slow to accept, for substantial improvement and permanent development in material gain.

The A.M.E. Church Review, July, 1887, III, pp. 485–91.

[h]

Chicago Conservator *Editorial, 1880*

BLOOD, BRAND, OR LIBERTY

Clarksville, Tennessee, was visited last week by a terrible fire. The business portion of the town was burned, leaving a mere shell of suburban residence in place of the great tobacco mart of Tennessee. It is supposed to be the work of incendiaries and the colored people bear the blame. When the city was burning, they gathered in little knots and crowds; discussed the situation, witnessed with a good deal of manifest satisfaction the strenuous efforts to suppress the fire, but would not lend a helping hand, for love or money. We are loath to advocate lawlessness. We deplore the necessity of resorting to arson and rapine but if such things must come, let them come. If the colored people of Clarksville did fire the town, we regret the necessity but not the act. If they had been denied the rights and privileges of men; if, by studied persecution, their hearts have been hardened; if goaded by oppression to desperation they have lost all their interest in and love for their homes; we are proud to see them have the manhood to be the willing witnesses of its destruction.

The colored people of Clarksville were incensed over a multitude of wrongs. Not long ago, a colored man was lynched upon the charge of an attempt at outrage. An attempt, mind you. This is a comprehensive term in the South. It embraces a wink by a colored man at a white girl a half mile off. Such a crime is worthy of lynching, but a beastly attack upon a colored girl by a white man is only a wayward indiscretion. The colored people have stood such discriminations long enough.

The people of Clarksville have broken the ice, God grant it may extend from Virginia to Texas. Still later, a colored man was brutally killed by a policeman, and ever since, the people have given forth mutterings, not loud, but deep. . . . [President] Hayes has plainly told the colored people they must make peace at any price. We repeat it, but with a different signification—they must make peace at any price. It may cost treasure, it may cost blood, it may cost lives, but make it, be the cost what it may. . . . The trying scenes of a presidential contest will soon be upon us. We claim no prophetic vision, but we warn the southern whites that they need not expect such one-sided scenes of butchery in future. They will have to make a choice between Blood, the Brand, and Political Liberty.

Ralph N. Davis, "The Negro Newspaper in Chicago," unpublished master's thesis, University of Chicago, 1939, pp. 11–12.

[i]

Cleveland Gazette *Editorial, 1889*

Editor Bryant, of the *Southern Christian Recorder,* is an exile from home, family and business because of an article published in the Selma (Ala.) *Independent* of August 17. Messrs. S. H. Clark and E. C. Jones are editors and proprietors of the paper, and Mr. Bryant avers that he "had nothing to do with it" (the article). The portion which has riled the chivalrous(?) whites of Selma reads as follows:

"Were you (the whites) to leave this South land, in twenty years it would be one of the grandest sections of the globe. We would show you mossback crackers how to run a country. You would never see convicts half starved, depriving honest workmen of an honest living. It is only a matter of time when this whole State's affairs will be changed, and I hope to your sorrow. We were never destined always to be servants, but like all other races will and must have our day; you now have yours. You have predicted that at no very distant day we will have our race war, and we hope, as God intends, that we will be strong enough to wipe you out of existence and hardly leave enough of you to tell the story. It is bound to come, and just such hot-headed cranks as the editors of some of our Democratic journals are just the right set to hasten it. It is fate."

This is a chunk of truth and of course made the "mossback crackers" and friends murderously angry. Truth always does.

Some satisfaction can be extracted from the knowledge that Messrs. Clark and Jones have reached Pittsburgh safely. How it will be with Editor Bryant remains to be learned. This, indeed, is a sad commentary upon the boasted freedom of the press and of American citizens.

The Cleveland Gazette, August 31, 1889. The editor was H. C. Smith.

[j]

John E. Bruce's Speech, 1889

I fully realize the delicacy of the position I occupy in this discussion and know too well that those who are to follow me will largely benefit by what I shall have to say in respect to the application of force as one of the means to the solution of the problem known as the Negro problem. I am not unmindful of the fact that there are those living who have faith in the efficacy of submission, who are still impregnated with the slavish fear which had its origin in oppression and the peculiar environments of the slave period. Those who are thus minded will advise a pacific policy in order as they believe to affect a settlement of this question, with which the statesmanship of a century has grappled without any particularly gratifying results. Agitation is a good thing, organization is a better thing. The million Negro voters of Georgia, and the undiscovered millions in other southern states—undiscovered so far as our knowledge of their number exists—could with proper organization and intelligent leadership meet force with force with most beneficial results. The issue upon us cannot be misunderstood by those who are watching current events . . . The man who will not fight for the protection of his wife and children is a *coward* and deserves to be ill treated. The man who takes his life in his hand and stands up for what he knows to be right will always command the respect of his enemy.

Submission to the *dicta* of southern bulldozers is the basest cowardice, and there is no just reason why manly men of any race should allow themselves to be continually outraged and oppressed by their equals before the law. . . .

Under the present condition of affairs the only hope, the only salvation for the Negro is to be found in a resort to force under wise and discreet leaders. He must sooner or later come to this in order to set at rest for all time to come the charge that he is a moral coward. . . .

The Negro must not be rash and indiscreet either in action or in words but he must be very determined and terribly in earnest, and of one mind to bring order out of chaos and to convince southern rowdies and cutthroats that more than two can play at the game with which they have amused their fellow conspirators in crime for nearly a quarter of a century. Under the Mosaic dispensation it was the custom to require an eye for an eye and a tooth for a tooth under a no less barbarous civilization than that which existed at that period of the world's history; let the Negro require at the hands of every white murderer in the south or elsewhere a life for a life. If they burn our houses, burn theirs, if they kill our wives and children kill theirs, pursue them relentlessly, meet force with force everywhere it is offered. If they demand blood exchange it with them, until they are satiated. By a vigorous adherence to this course the shedding of human blood by white men will soon become a thing of the past. Wherever and whenever the Negro shows himself to be a man he can always command the respect even of a cutthroat. Organized resistance to organized resistance is the best remedy for the solution of the vexed problem of the century which to me seems practicable and feasible and I submit this view of the question, ladies and gentlemen, for your careful consideration.

MS. in John E. Bruce Collection, Folder #7, Shomburg Collection, N.Y. Public Library. The MS. is dated October 5, 1889, but the occasion and place where the speech was delivered are not known by the editor.

[k]

Resolutions of Civil Rights Congress, 1883

Whereas, The Supreme Court of the United States has solemnly declared its opinion that the Congressional Enactment known as the Civil Rights Law, of February 27, 1875, is not in accordance with the United States Constitution, and is consequently inoperative as a measure for the protection of the Negro in his manhood rights; and whereas, the customs and traditions of many of the States in the Union are inimical to the Negro as a man and a citizen, and he finds neither in the common law nor in the sentiments of his white fellow citizen that full protection which he has earned by his loyalty and devotion to the Nation in its hour of extreme peril; and whereas, it is our duty as good, law abiding citizens, to respect the decisions of the Courts as to the validity of the laws upon which they are called to pass judgment, therefore, be it

Resolved, That words of indignation or disrespect aimed at the Supreme Court of the United States would not only be useless as a means for securing our main object—namely, the protection due to our manhood and citizenship—but, on the contrary, would tend to alienate our friends and all who have faith in the honesty and integrity of that august and learned tribunal.

Resolved, That it is the primal duty of all lovers of their country, all friends of justice, without respect to party lines, to see to it that the full and equal protection of the laws are afforded every citizen, without respect to race, color, or previous condition of servitude.

Resolved, That we hold the Republican party to the enforcement of this demand: "That complete liberty and exact equality in the enjoyment of all civil, political, and public rights should be established and effectually maintained throughout the Union by efficient and appropriate State and Federal legislation, and that neither the law nor its administration should admit any discrimination in respect to citizens by reason of race, creed, color or previous condition of servitude."

Resolved, That we would remind the Democratic party of its declaratives in the National Convention of 1872, "that we recognize the equality of all men before the law, and hold that it is the duty of government in its dealings with the people to mete out equal and exact justice to all, of whatever nativity, race, color, or persuasion, religious or political."

Resolved, That it is the paramount duty of the colored voter to give his aid and support to that party or coalition of parties that will give force and meaning to the utterances, pledges, and demands of the Republican and of the Democratic parties in their respective platforms of 1872 in respect to the protection of colored citizens in their manhood rights.

Resolved, That no more conclusive evidence of the sincerity of the utterances of the two great political parties of the land can be afforded than the adoption in the several States under their control of a measure guaranteeing that protection sought to be established by the Civil Rights Act of 1872.

Resolved, That the progress of the colored American citizen in morals, education, frugality, industry, and general usefulness, as a man and as a citizen, makes it the part of sound policy and wisdom to maintain and protect him in the enjoyment of the fullest and most complete rights of citizenship.

Resolved, That we invite the co-operation of all good men and women in securing such legislation as may be necessary to complete our freedom, and that we advise the immediate organization of civil rights associations throughout the country, through which proper agitation and earnest work for our cause may be inaugurated and carried out.

Proceedings of the Civil Rights Mass Meeting held at Lincoln Hall [Washington], *Oct. 22, 1883* (Washington, 1883).

[1]

Douglass' Speech at 1883 National Convention

. . . With apparent surprise, astonishment and impatience we have been asked: "What more can the colored people of this country want than they now have, and what more is possible to them?" It is said they were once slaves, they are now free; they were once subjects, they are now sovereigns; they were once outside of all American institutions, they are now inside of all and are a recognized part of the whole American people. Why, then, do they hold Colored National Conventions and thus insist upon keeping up the color line between themselves and their white fellow countrymen? We do not deny the pertinence and plausibility of these questions, nor do we shrink from a candid answer to the argument which they are supposed to contain. For we do not forget that they are not only put to us by those who have no sympathy with us, but by many who wish us well, and that in any case they deserve an answer.

Before, however, we proceed to answer them, we digress here to say that there is only one element associated with them which excites the least bitterness of feeling in us or that calls for special rebuke, and that is when they fall from the lips and pens of colored men who suffer with us and ought to know better. A few such men, well known to us and the country, happening to be more fortunate in the possession of wealth, education and position than their humbler brethren, have found it convenient to chime in with the popular cry against our assembling, on the ground that we have no valid reason for this measure or for any other separate from the whites; that we ought to be satisfied with things as they are. With white men who thus object the case is different and less painful. For them there is a chance for charity. Educated as they are and have been for centuries, taught to look upon colored people as a lower order of humanity than themselves and as having few rights, if any, above domestic animals, regarding them also through the medium of their beneficient religious creeds and just laws—as if law and practice were identical—some allowance can, and perhaps ought to, be made when they misapprehend our real situation and deny our wants and assume a virtue they do not possess. But no such excuse or apology can be properly framed for men who are in any way identified with us. What may be erroneous in others implies either baseness or imbecility in them. Such men, it seems to us, are either deficient in self-respect or too mean, servile and cowardly to assert the true dignity of their manhood and that of their race. To admit that there are such men among us is a disagreeable and humiliating confession. But in this respect, as in others, we are not without the consolation of company: we are neither alone nor singular in the production of just such characters. All oppressed people have been thus afflicted.

It is one of the most conspicuous evils of caste and oppression, that they inevitably tend to make cowards and serviles of their victims, men ever ready to bend the knee to pride and power that thrift may follow fawning, willing to betray the cause of the many to serve the ends of the few; men who never hesitate to sell a friend when they think they can thereby purchase an enemy. Specimens of this sort may be found everywhere and at all times. There were Northern men with Southern principles in the time of slavery, and Tories in the revolution for independence. There are betrayers and informers today in Ireland, ready to kiss the hand that smites them and strike down the arm reached out to save them. Considering our long subjection to servitude and caste, and the many temptations to which we are exposed to betray our race into the hands of their enemies, the wonder is not that we have so many traitors among us as that we have so few.

The most of our people, to their honor be it said, are remarkably sound and true to each other. . . .

If liberty, with us, is yet but a name, our citizenship is but a sham, and our suffrage thus far only a cruel mockery, we may yet congratulate ourselves upon the fact, that the laws and institutions of the country are sound, just and liberal. There is hope for a people when their laws are righteous, whether for the moment they conform to their requirements or not. But until this nation shall make its practice accord with its Constitution and its righteous laws, it will not do to reproach the colored people of this country with keeping up the color line—for that people would prove themselves scarcely worthy of even theoretical freedom, to say nothing of practical freedom, if they settled down in silent, servile and cowardly submission to their wrongs, from fear of making their color visible. They are bound by every element of manhood to hold conventions, in their own name, and on their own behalf, to keep their grievances before the people and make every organized protest against the wrongs inflicted upon them within their power. They should scorn the counsels of cowards, and hang their banner on the outer wall.

Who would be free, themselves must strike the blow. We do not believe, as we are often told, that the Negro is the ugly child of the National family, and the more he is kept out of sight the better it will be for him. You know that liberty given is never so precious as liberty sought for and fought for. The man outraged is the man to make the outcry. Depend upon it, men will not care much for a people who do not care for themselves. Our meeting here was opposed by some of our members, because it would disturb the peace of the Republican party. The suggestion came from coward lips and misapprehended the character of that party. If the Republican party cannot stand a demand for justice and fair play, it ought to go down. We were men before that party was born, and our manhood is more sacred than any party can be. Parties were made for men, not men for parties.

If the six millions of colored people of this country, armed with the Constitution of the United States, with a million votes of their own to lean upon, and millions of white men at their back, whose hearts are responsive to the claims of humanity, have not sufficient spirit and wisdom to organize and combine to defend themselves from outrage, discrimination and oppression, it will be idle for them to expect that the Republican party or any other political party will organize and combine for them or care what becomes of them. Men may combine to prevent cruelty to animals, for they are dumb and cannot speak for themselves; but we are men and must speak for ourselves, or we shall not be spoken for at all. We have conventions in America for Ireland, but we should have none if Ireland did not speak for herself. It is because she makes a noise and keeps her cause before the people that other people go to her help. It was the sword of Washington that gave Independence the sword of Lafayette. In conclusion upon this color objection, we have to say that we meet here in open daylight. There is nothing sinister about us. The eyes of the nation are upon us. Ten thousand newspapers may tell if they choose of whatever is said and done here. They may commend our wisdom or condemn our folly, precisely as we shall be wise or foolish.

We put ourselves before them as honest men, and ask their judgment upon our work.

THE LABOR QUESTION

Not the least important among the subjects to which we invite your earnest attention is the condition of the laboring class at the South. Their cause is one with the laboring classes all over the world. The labor unions of the country should not throw away this colored element of strength. Everywhere there is dissatisfaction with the present relation of labor and capital, and today no subject wears an aspect more threatening to civilization than the respective claims of capital and labor, landlords and tenants. In what we have to say for our laboring class we expect to have and ought to have the sympathy and support of laboring men everywhere and of every color.

It is a great mistake for any class of laborers to isolate itself and thus weaken the bond of brotherhood between those on whom the burden and hardships of labor fall. The fortunate ones of the earth, who are abundant in land and money and know nothing of the anxious care and pinching poverty of the laboring classes, may be indifferent to the appeal for justice at this point, but the laboring classes cannot afford to be indifferent. What labor everywhere wants, what it ought to have and will some day demand and receive, is an honest day's pay for an honest day's work. As the laborer becomes more intelligent he will develop what capital already possess— that is the power to organize and combine for its own protection. Experience demonstrates that there may be a wages of slavery only a little less galling and crushing in its effects than chattel slavery, and that this slavery of wages must go down with the other. . . .

THE ORDER SYSTEM

No more crafty and effective device for defrauding the Southern laborer could be adopted than the one that substitutes orders upon shop-keepers for currency in payment of wages. It has the merit of a show of honesty, while it puts the laborer completely at the mercy of the land-owner and the shop-keeper. He is between the upper and the nether millstones and is hence ground to dust. It gives the shop-keeper a customer who can trade with no other storekeeper, and thus leaves the latter no motive for fair dealing except his own moral sense, which is never too strong. While the laborer holding the orders is tempted by their worthlessness as a circulating medium, to get rid of them at any sacrifice, and hence is led into extravagance and consequent destitution.

The merchant puts him off with his poorest commodities at highest prices, and can say to him take those or nothing. Worse still. By this means the laborer is brought into debt, and hence is kept always in the power of the land-owner. When this system is not pursued and land is rented to the freedman, he is charged more for the use of an acre of land for a single year than the land would bring in the market if offered for sale. On such a system of fraud and wrong one might well invoke a bolt from heaven—red with uncommon wrath.

It is said if the colored people do not like the conditions upon which their labor is demanded and secured, let them leave and go elsewhere. A more heartless suggestion never emanated from an oppressor. Having for years paid them in shop orders, utterly worthless outside the shop to which they are directed, without a dollar in their pockets, brought by this crafty process into bondage to the land-owners, who can and would arrest them if they should attempt to leave them when they are told to go.

We commend the whole subject to the Senate Committee of Labor and Education, and urge upon that Committee the duty to call before it not only the land-owners, but the landless laborers of the South, and thus get at the whole truth concerning the labor question of that section.

EDUCATION

On the subject of equal education and educational facilities, mentioned in the call for this convention, we expect little resistance from any quarter. It is everywhere an accepted truth, that in a country governed by the people, like ours, education of the youth of all classes is vital to its welfare, prosperity, and to its existence.

In the light of this unquestioned proposition, the patriot cannot but view with a shudder the widespread and truly alarming illiteracy as revealed by the census of 1880.*

The question as to how this evil is to be remedied is an important one. Certain it is that it will not do to trust to the philanthropy of wealthy individuals or benevolent societies to remove it. The States in which this illiteracy prevails either cannot or will not provide adequate systems of education for their own youth. But however this may be, the fact remains that the whole country is directly interested in the education of every child that lives within its borders. The ignorance of any part of the American people so deeply concerns all the rest that there can be no doubt of the right to pass laws compelling the attendance of every child at school. Believing that such is now required and ought to be enacted, we hereby put ourselves on record in favor of stringent laws to this end.

* The 1880 census listed 70% of the Negro population as illiterate.

In the presence of this appalling picture presented by the last census, we hold it to be the imperative duty of Congress to take hold of this important subject, and, without waiting for the States to adopt liberal school systems within their respective jurisdictions, to enter vigorously upon the work of universal education.

The National Government, with its immense resources, can carry the benefits of a sound common-school education to the door of every poor man from Maine to Texas, and to withhold this boon is to neglect the greatest assurance it has of its own perpetuity. As a part of the American people we unite most emphatically with others who have already spoken on this subject, in urging Congress to lay the foundation for a great national system of aid to education at its next session. . . .

POLITICAL EQUALITY

Flagrant as have been the outrages committed upon colored citizens in respect to their civil rights, more flagrant, shocking and scandalous still have been the outrages committed upon our political rights, by means of bull-dozing and Kukluxing, Mississippi plans, fraudulent counts, tissue ballots and the like devices. Three States in which the colored people outnumber the white population are without colored representation and their political voice suppressed. The colored citizens in those States are virtually disfranchised, the Constitution held in utter contempt and its provisions nullified. This has been done in the face of the Republican party and successive Republican Administrations.

It was once said by the great O'Connell that the history of Ireland might be traced like a wounded man through a crowd by the blood, and the same may be truly said of the history of the colored voters of the South.

They have marched to the ballot-box in face of gleaming weapons, wounds and death. They have been abandoned by the Government and left to the laws of nature. So far as they are concerned, there is no Government or Constitution of the United States.

They are under control of a foul, haggard and damning conspiracy against reason, law and constitution. How you can be indifferent, how any leading colored men can allow themselves to be silent in presence of this state of things, we cannot see.

"Should tongues be mute while deeds are wrought which well might shame extremest hell?" And yet they are mute, and condemn our assembling here to speak out in manly tones against the continuance of this infernal reign of terror.

This is no question of party. It is a question of law and government. It is a question whether men shall be protected by law or be left to the mercy of cyclones of anarchy and bloodshed. It is whether the Government or the mob shall rule this land; whether the promises solemnly made to us in the Constitution be manfully kept or meanly and flagrantly broken. Upon this vital point we ask the whole people of the United States to take notice that whatever of political power we have shall be exerted for no man of any party who will not in advance of election promise to use every power given him by the Government, State or National, to make the black man's path to the ballot-box as straight, smooth and safe as that of any other American citizen.

POLITICAL AMBITION

We are as a people often reproached with ambition for political offices and honors. We are not ashamed of this alleged ambition. Our destitution of such ambition would be our real shame. If the six millions and a half of people whom we represent could develop no aspirants to political office and honor under this Government, their mental indifference, barrenness and stolidity might well enough be taken as proof of their unfitness for American citizenship.

It is no crime to seek or hold office. If it were it would take a larger space than that of Noah's Ark to hold the white criminals.

One of the charges against this convention is that it seeks for the colored people a larger share than they now possess in the offices and emoluments of the Government.

We are now significantly reminded by even one of our own members that we are only twenty years out of slavery, and we ought therefore to be modest in our aspirations. Such leaders should remember that men will not be religious when the devil turns preacher . . .

We are far from affirming that there may not be too much zeal among colored men in pursuit of political preferment; but the fault is not wholly theirs. They have young men among them noble and true, who are educated and intelligent—fit to engage in enterprise of "pith and moment"—who find themselves shut out from nearly all the avenues of wealth and respectability, and hence they turn their attention to politics. They do so because they can find nothing else. The best cure for the evil is to throw open other avenues and activities to them.

We shall never cease to be a despised and persecuted class while we are known to be excluded by our color from all important positions under the Government.

While we do not make office the one thing important, nor the one condition of our alliance with any party, and hold that the welfare, prosperity and happiness of our whole country is the true criterion of political action for ourselves and for all men, we cannot disguise from ourselves the fact that our persistent exclusion from office as a class is a great wrong, fraught with injury, and ought to be resented and opposed by all reasonable and effective means in our power.

We hold it to be self-evident that no class or color should be the exclusive rulers of this country. If there is such a ruling class, there must of course be a subject class, and when this condition is once established this Government of the people, by the people and for the people, will have perished from the earth.

National Convention of Colored Men at Louisville, Ky., September 24, 1883 (Louisville, 1883). Copy in the library of Dr. W. E. B. Du Bois.

[m]

T. Thomas Fortune's *Black and White*, 1884

In discussing the political and industrial problems of the South, I base my conclusions upon a personal knowledge of the condition of classes in the South, as well as upon the ample data furnished by writers who have pursued, in their way, the question before me. That the colored people of the country will yet achieve an honorable status in the national industries of thought and activity, I believe, and try to make plain.

In the discussion of the land and labor problem I but pursue the theories advocated by more able and experienced men, in the attempt to show that the laboring classes of any country pay all the taxes, in the last analysis, and that they are systematically victimized by legislators, corporations and syndicates.

Wealth, unduly centralized, endangers the efficient workings of the machinery of government. Land monopoly—in the hands of individuals, corporations or syndicates—is at bottom the prime cause of the inequalities which obtain; which desolate fertile acres turned over to vast ranches and into bonanza farms of a thousand acres, where not one family finds a habitation, where muscle and brain are supplanted by machinery, and the small farmer is swallowed up and turned into a tenant or slave. While in large cities thousands upon thousands of human beings are crowded into narrow quarters where vice festers, where crime flourishes undeterred, and where death is the most welcome of all visitors.

The primal purpose in publishing this work is to show that the social problems in the South are, in the main, the same as those which afflict every civilized country on the globe; and that the future conflict in that section will not be racial or political in character, but between capital on the one hand, and labor on the other, with the odds largely in favor of non-productive wealth because of the undue advantage given the latter by the pernicious monopoly in land which limits production and forces population disastrously upon subsistence. My purpose is to show that poverty and misfortune make no invidious distinctions of "race, color, or previous condition," but that wealth unduly centralized oppresses all alike; therefore, that the labor elements of the whole United States should sympathize with the same elements in the South, and in some favorable contingency effect some unity of organization and action, which shall subserve the common interest of the common class. . . .

The great newspapers, which should plead the cause of the oppressed and the down-trodden, which should be the palladiums of the people's rights, are all on the side of the oppressor, or by silence preserve a dignified but ignominious neutrality. Day after day they weave a false picture of facts—facts which must measurably influence the future historian of the times in the composition of impartial history. The wrongs of the masses are referred to sneeringly or apologetically.

The vast army of laborers—men, women, and even tender children—find no favor in the eyes of these Knights of the Quill. The Negro and the Indian, the footballs of slippery politicians and the helpless victims of sharpers and thieves, are wantonly misrepresented—held up to the eyes of the world as beings incapable of imbibing the distorted civilization in the midst of which they live and have their being. They are placed in the attic, only to be aired when somebody wants an "issue" or an "appropriation."

There are no "Liberators" today, and the William Lloyd Garrisons have nearly all of them gone the way of all the world.

The part played by the ministry of Christ in the early conflict against human slavery in this country would be enigmatical in the extreme, utterly beyond apprehension, if it were not matter of history that the representatives of the Christian Church, in conflicts with every giant wrong, have always been the strongest supporters, the most obsequious tools of money power and the political sharpers who have imposed their vile tyrannies upon mankind. . . .

I do not indulge in the luxury of prophecy when I declare that the American people are fostering in their bosoms a spirit of rebellion which will yet shake the pillars of popular government as they have never before been shaken, unless a wiser policy is inaugurated and honestly enforced. All the indications point to the fulfilment of such declaration.

The Czar of Russia squirms upon his throne, not because he is necessarily a bad man, but because he is the head and center of a condition of things which squeezes the life out of the people. His subjects hurl infernal machines at the tyrant because he represents the system which oppresses them. But the evil is far deeper than the throne, and cannot be remedied by striking the occupant of it—*the throne itself must be rooted out and demolished.* So the Irish question has a more powerful motive to foment agitation and murder than the landlord and landlordism. The landlord simply stands out as the representative of the real grievance. To remove *him* would not remove the evil; agitation would not cease; murder would still stalk abroad at noonday. *The real grievance is the false system which makes the landlord possible.* The appropriation of the fertile acres of the soil of Ireland, which created and maintains a privileged class, a class that while performing no labor, wrings from the toiler, in the shape of rents, so much of the produce of his labor that he cannot on the residue support himself and those dependent upon him aggravates the situation. It is this system which constitutes the real grievance and makes the landlord an odious loafer with abundant cash and the laborer a constant toiler always upon the verge of starvation. Evidently, therefore, to remove the landlord and leave the system of land monopoly would not remove the evil. Destroy the latter and the former would be compelled to go. . . .

When the American Government conferred upon the black man the boon of freedom and the burden of the franchise, it added four million men to the already vast army of men who appear to be specially created to labor for the enrichment of vast corporations, which have no souls, and for individuals, whom our government have made a privileged class, by permitting them to usurp or monopolize, through the accepted channel of barter and trade, the soil, from which the masses, the laboring masses, must obtain a subsistence, and without the privilege of cultivating which they must faint and die. It also added four millions of souls to what have been termed, in the refinement of sarcasm, "the dangerous classes"—meaning by which the vast army of men and women who, while willing and anxious to make an honest living by the labor of their hands, and who—when speculators cry "over-production," "glutted market," and other claptrap—threaten to take by force from society that which society prevents them from making honestly.

When a society fosters as much crime and destitution as ours, with ample resources to meet the actual necessities of every one, there must be something radically wrong, not in the society but in the foundation upon which society is reared. Where is this ulcer located? Is it to be found in the dead · weight of illiteracy which we carry? The masses of few countries are more intelligent than ours. Is it to be found in burdensome taxation or ill-adjusted tariff regulations? Few countries are burdened with less debt, and many have far worse tariff laws than curse our country. Is it to be found in an unjust pension list? We hardly miss the small compensation which we grant to the men (or their heirs) who, in the hour of National peril, gave their lives freely to perpetuate the Union of our States. Where, then, is secreted the parasite which is eating away the energies of the people, making paupers and criminals in the midst of plenty and the grandest of civilizations? Is it not to be found in the powerful monopolies we have created? Monopoly in land, in railroads, telegraphs, fostered manufactures, etc.,—the gigantic forces in our civilization which are, in their very nature, agents of public convenience, comfort and absolute necessity? . . .

It is almost as hard for an educated black man to obtain a position of trust and profit as it is for a camel to go through the eye of a needle. The missionaries, the preachers, and the educators, assisted by the newspapers and the magazines, have educated the people into the false opinion that it is safer to "donate" a thousand dollars to a colored college than it is to give one black man a chance to make an honest living. . . .

Indeed, the multiplication of colleges and academies for the "higher education of colored youth" is one of the most striking phenomena of the times: as if theology and the classic were the things best suited to and most urgently needed by a class of persons unprepared in rudimentary education, and whose immediate aim must be that of the mechanic and the farmer—to whom the classics, theology and the sciences, in their extremely impecunious state, are unequivocable abstractions. There will be those who will denounce me for taking this view of collegiate and professional preparation; but I maintain that any education is false which is unsuited to the condition and the prospects of the student. To educate him for a lawyer when there are no clients, for medicine when the patients, although numerous, are too poor to give him a living income, to fill his head with Latin and Greek as a teacher when the people he is to teach are to be instructed in the *a b c's*—such education is a waste of time and a senseless expenditure of money.

I do not inveigh against higher education; I simply maintain that the sort of education the colored people of the South stand most in need of is *elementary and industrial*. They should be instructed for the work to be done. Many a colored farmer boy or mechanic has been spoiled to make a foppish gambler or loafer, a swaggering pedagogue or a cranky homiletician. Men may be spoiled by education, even as they are spoiled by illiteracy. Education is the preparation for a future work; hence men should be educated with special reference to that work. . . .

The "party of great moral ideas," having emancipated the slave, and enfranchised disorganized ignorance and poverty, finally finished its mission, relinquished its right to the respect and confidence of mankind when, in 1876, it abandoned all effort to enforce the provisions of the war amendments.

That party stands today for organized corruption, while its opponent stands for organized brigandage. The black man, who was betrayed by his party and murdered by the opponents of his party, is absolved from all allegiance which *gratitude* may have dictated, and is today free to make conditions the best possible with any faction which will insure him in his right to "life, liberty and the pursuit of happiness." . . .

The Republican party has degenerated into an ignoble scramble for place and power. It has forgotten the principles for which Sumner contended, and for which Lincoln died. It betrayed the cause for which Douglass, Garrison and others labored, in the blind policy it pursued in reconstructing the rebellious States. It made slaves freemen and freemen slaves in the same breath by conferring the franchise and withholding the guarantees to insure its exercise; it betrayed its trust in permitting thousands of innocent men to be slaughtered without declaring the South in rebellion, and in pardoning murderers, whom tardy justice had consigned to a felon's dungeon. It is even now powerless to insure an honest expression of the vote of the colored citizen. For these things, I do not deem it binding upon colored men further to support the Republican party when other more advantageous affiliations can be formed. And what of the Bourbon Democratic party? There has not been, there is not now, nor will there ever be, any good thing in it for the colored man. Bourbon Democracy is a curse to our land. Any party is a curse which arrays itself in opposition to human freedom, to the universal brotherhood of man. No colored man can ever claim truthfully to be a Bourbon Democrat. It is a fundamental impossibility. But he can be an independent, a progressive Democrat. . . .

The colored man is in the South to stay there. He will not leave it voluntarily and he cannot be driven out. He had no voice in being carried into the South, but he will have a very loud voice in any attempt to put him out. The expatriation of 5,000,000 to 6,000,000 people to an alien country needs only to be suggested to create mirth and ridicule. The white men of the South had better make up their minds that the black man will remain in the South just as long as corn will tassel and cotton will bloom into whiteness. The talk about the black people being brought to this country to prepare themselves to evangelize Africa is so much religious nonsense boiled down to a sycophantic platitude. The Lord, who is eminently just, had no hand in their forcible coming here; it was preëminently the work of the devil. Africa will have to be evangelized *from within,* not *from without.* The Colonization society has spent mints of money and tons of human blood in the selfish attempt to plant an Anglo-African colony on the West Coast of Africa. The money has been thrown away and the human lives have been sacrificed in vain. The black people of this country are Americans, not Africans; and any wholesale expatriation of them is altogether out of the question. . . .

In every quarter of the globe the cry of depressed and defrauded labor is heard. The enormous drain upon the producing agents necessary to maintain in idleness and luxury the great capitalists of the world who accumulated their ill-gotten wealth by fraud, perjury and "conquest," so called, grinds the producing agent down to the lowest possible point at which he can live and still produce. The millionaires of the world, so called "aristocracies," and the taxes imposed by sovereign states to liquidate obligations more frequently contracted to enslave than to ameliorate the condition of mankind, are a constant drain which comes ultimately out of the laboring classes in every state.

What are millionaires, any way, but the most dangerous enemies of society, always eating away its entrails, like the vultures that preyed upon the chained Prometheus? Take our own breed of these parasites; note how they grind down the stipend they are compelled to bestow upon the human tools they must use to still further swell their ungodly gains! . . .

I have walked through the tenement wards of New York, and I have seen enough want and crime and blasted virtue to condemn the civilization which produced them and which fosters them in its bosom.

I have looked upon the vast army of police which New York City maintains to protect life and so-called "vested rights," and I have concluded that there is something wrong in the social system which can only be kept intact by the expenditure of so much productive force, for this vast army, which stands on the street corners and lurks in the alley ways, "spotting" suspicious persons, "keeping an eye" on strangers who look "smart," this vast army contributes nothing to the production of wealth. It is, essentially, a parasite. And yet, without this army of idlers, life would be in constant danger and property would fall a prey not only to the vicious and the desperate, but to the hungry men and women who have neither a place to shelter them from the storms of heaven, nor food to sustain nature's cravings from finding an eternal resting place in the Potter's Field. And, even after every precaution which selfishness can devise, courts of law and police officers are powerless to stay the hand of the pariahs whom society has outlawed—the men and women who are doomed to starve to death and be buried at the expense of society. The streets of every city in the Union are full of people who have been made desperate by social adjustments which prophets laud to the skies and which philosophers commend as "ideal," as far as they go. . . . Men talk daily of "over production," of "glutted markets," and the like; but such is not a true statement of the case. There can be no over production of anything as long as there are hungry mouths to be fed. It does not matter if the possessor of these hungry mouths are too poor to buy the bread; if they are hungry, there is no overproduction. With a balance of $150,000,000 of trade; with plethoric granaries and elevators all over the land; with millions of swine, sheep and cattle on a thousand hills; with millions of surplus revenue in the vaults of the National treasury, diverted from the regular channels of trade by an ignorant set of legislators who have not gumption enough to reduce unnecessary and burdensome taxation without upsetting the industries of the country,—with all its grandiloquent exhibition of happiness and prosperity, the laboring classes of the country starve to death, or eke out an existence still more horrible.

The factories of the land run on half time, and the men, women and children who operate them grow pinch-faced, lean and haggard, from insufficient nutriment, and are old and decrepit while yet in the bud of youth; the tenements are crowded to suffocation, breeding pestilence and death; while the wages paid to labor hardly serve to satisfy the exactions of the landlord—a monstrosity in the midst of civilization, whose very existence is a crying protest against our pretentions to civilization. . . .

Let us turn to the South and see if a black skin has anything to do with the tyranny of capital; let us see if the cause of the laboring man is not the same in all sections, in all States, in all governments, in the Union, as it is in all the world. If this can be shown; if I can incontestibly demonstrate that *the condition of the black and the white laborer is the same, and that consequently their cause is common;* that they should unite under the one banner and work upon the same platform of principles for the uplifting of labor, the more equal distribution of the products of labor and capital, I shall not have written this book in vain, and the patient reader will not have read after me without profit to himself and the common cause of a common humanity. . . .

As I have said elsewhere, the future struggle in the South will be, not between white men and black men, but between capital and labor, landlord and tenant. Already the cohorts are marshalling to the fray; already the forces are mustering to the field at the sound of the slogan.

The same battle will be fought upon Southern soil that is in preparation in other states where the conditions are older in development but no more deep-seated, no more pernicious, no more blighting upon the industries of the country and the growth of the people. . . .

The hour is approaching when the laboring classes of our country, North, East, West and South, will recognize that they have a *common cause,* a *common humanity,* and a *common enemy;* and that, therefore, if they would triumph over wrong and place the laurel wreath upon triumphant justice, without distinction of race or of previous condition *they must unite!* And unite they will, for "a fellow feeling makes us wond'rous kind." When the issue is properly joined, the rich, be they black or be they white, will be found upon the same side; and the poor, be they black or be they white, will be found on the same side.

Necessity knows no law and discriminates in favor of no man or race.

T. Thomas Fortune, *Black and White: Land, Labor and Politics in the South* (N.Y., 1884).

[n]

M. Edward Bryant of Alabama, 1887

. . . We see around us thousands of blessings . . . They call upon us to . . . swear never to rest contented night nor day until the tyrannical spirit of oppression which yet lingers in this land as the sprouts of the deadly upas tree of slavery shall be plucked up root and branch, and a man and a woman shall be known by the way they conduct themselves, without regard to color.

Let the world know that we prefer death . . . to such liberty as we have today. The white fathers died that their children might be free. Does the Negro love HIS children less?

Against that honest class of whites who are in favor of giving us our rights, I have nothing to say but praise. Neither do I plead for war or resort to force but a fixed, unyielding, unalterable determination to defend ourselves when attacked and to petition, persuade and demand our rights whatever may be the consequences. Simply imitate the whites themselves. They would die before they would endure what we are enduring. History proves this.

This is a day of great rejoicing and thanksgiving with us and rightly so. But the Negro is yet to create his own national thanksgiving and celebration day by some mighty achievements of his own. He is yet to march his own army across the Red Sea and erect his own monuments, and his own poets are to compose and sing his own triumphal songs. . . .

What kind of government is this under which we live today . . . these descendants [of slaveholders] are still trying to perpetuate a system worse than slavery upon the colored and poor whites of this country which threatens the curse of God again upon this land. The laborers of this country are oppressed and trodden down. In the North, the Goulds, and Vanderbilts, are the oppressors and tyrants.

In the South, the legislatures, social system, land owners, advance houses and in fact two-thirds of whites are the usurpers, tyrants, oppressors.

Above Broad street dominates below Broad, whether they be Negroes or poor whites. It was just such a state of things which bursted to splinters every ancient empire and is making European and American governments tremble today. The Negro is so treated today in regard to his civil, political and social rights in many parts that any condition would be preferable to his present condition. That in this country and under this government all men are created equal is, especially in the South, a lie. . . .

We are robbed, swindled, cheated, assassinated, falsely imprisoned, lynched, told to stand back and every indignity heaped upon us. The future will tell a sad story if this is continued. . . .

Social equality can never arise except by the consent of the parties themselves. We want civil and political rights . . . what should the Negro be advised to do under the circumstances?

1. Join the Knights of Labor and every other organization which promises to struggle to bring about a revolution and reformation in our affairs.

2. Organize leagues to raise money to prosecute railroads, steamboats, stores, hotels and every one who tries to abridge our rights.

3. Organize leagues, not to create confusion, but to defend ourselves when attacked, just as the whites have always done.

4. Trade with your own business houses and those white men only who treat us right.

5. Never work any man's land who in any way abridges or helps to abridge our rights.

6. Support your own newspapers and never those who seek every opportunity to throw mud at us. No one can tell what and how much good our newspapers are doing to uplift the race.

7. Build schools everywhere, controlled and taught by yourselves, where true manhood and womanhood are taught. You need never expect a Negro child to be properly taught in a school which Southern white people control. His education and training and avarice disqualify him for this work. . . .

The colored people are waking up. Has the Negro the power to carry out the above measures? The Negro has great latent power. He only needs to learn how to use this power wisely . . . We want to live in peace with all mankind, and especially with the whites of the South. Our interests are identical. But we do not want the peace of the lamb with the lion . . . Give us all our rights, not social equality, and we will die by you, for you and with you . . . Will you do this or force us away from you? Let us unite to break the chains of prejudice, ostracism, deprivation of civil, political and social rights and the sins that are worse than physical slavery . . .

The Christian Recorder (Phila.), January 19, 1888.

[o]

Brockett Answers Grady, 1890

Henry W. Grady, of Atlanta, Ga., delivered an address before the Boston Merchants' Association at their annual banquet, on Thursday evening, December 13 [1889]. That speech, because of its eloquence and significance, has aroused an unusual amount of earnest discussion in all circles and in all grades of society. All just minds of all classes and of all races will freely acknowledge that it was an eloquent address, by which fact the power of the individual mind is hindered for a moment in passing an accurate opinion upon its veracity, justice and motive. But, upon reflection, judgment returns, and notwithstanding that Mr. Grady is the exponent of the doctrine of a so-called "new South," finds nothing new presented by him as the solution of the Negro problem. In that address, beneath the glamour of eloquence, the old rebel spirit, and the old South is seen throughout. In every expression of every line in which the Negro is mentioned the old spirit of Negro hatred is manifest. The beautifully phrased compliments so charmingly paid the North are but a disguise to conceal the hand which once strove to stab it. That hand still holds the knife, kept bright and keen by disappointed hopes of twenty years and more. This is readily seen through the crafty thrusts it deals to New England's deserted or artificially made farms. In that man's veins courses the blood of generations of trafficers in human slavery. . . . Mr. Grady declares his love for the blacks! . . .

The gentleman asks the question when will the black cast a free ballot? His reply is, when ignorance anywhere is not dominated by the will of the intelligent; when the laborer casts his vote unhindered by his boss; when the strong and steadfast do not everywhere control the suffrage of the weak and shiftless. Then and not till then will the Negro be free. He also says that the Negro vote can never again control in the South. He asks of the North, "Can we solve this question?" and answers, "God knows."

Consistency, thou art a jewel! It is declared that the Negro is peaceful and industrious on the one hand, weak and shiftless on the other. If he is peaceful surely the South has small need to fear an uprising. Politics, then, is the only source whence danger can come to the whites. If the black vote is never to control again, why should Mr. Grady state that the condition of the people is fraught with danger from the presence of a shiftless people? Whence the need of that wail for sympathy, if, as Mr. Grady says, the colored man must down, and the white partisan might as well understand it? If the colored man is never to rise, why waste so much eloquence upon a unless subject? The problem is already solved.

Mr. Grady asserts that nearly one-half of the school fund is used to educate the Negro. If the South is leagued together to maintain itself against this beleaguring black host, why educate it?

Has Mr. Grady to learn that education and power are inseparable? I will give Mr. Grady fair warning if they continue to give one-half or thereabouts to the school fund to educate a black man, then he will rise against the greatest odds that the South can oppose; not God alone, but even I know when the black man will be free.

Mr. Grady says that the Negro has not a basis upon which to rest his political conviction, and that of 300,000 voters, not one in a hundred can read his ballot. That is a splendid compliment to the educational system which costs the South so dear. Either the South is amazingly stupid to pay so dearly for such meagre results, or the Negro is incapable of learning, or the money is not paid.

Mr. Grady states that the Negro, by every species of villainy and folly, has wasted his substance and exhausted his credit. By the side of that statement I will place another of Mr. Grady's statements, namely, that from the Negroes' willing hands comes $1,000,000,000 of farm crops. If the latter statement is true, then the character of the Negro in the former statement has been falsified. Does Mr. Grady desire to make a strong case against this villainous race at the expense of the truth? And if the former statement is true, that the Negro is villainously wasteful, the $1,000,000,000 crops are but a creation of fancy, and the Northern sons with their modest patrimony would do well to remain standing in their doors, or turn their gaze in any direction but southward.

Again, with childlike innocence, Mr. Grady asks, can it be seriously maintained that we are terrorizing the people from whose willing hands comes every year $1,000,000,000 in crops? Or that we have robbed a people who, 25 years from unrewarded slavery, have amassed in one State $20,000,000 worth of property?

In Georgia, Mr. Grady's own state, the Negro's real wealth accumulated since the war, is $20,000,000. Its population of Negroes is 725,132. Twenty millions of dollars divided among that number will give to each person $27.58. Upon the same basis of calculation the total wealth of the Negro in the 15 Southern States, including the District of Columbia, is $146,-189,834. The colored population of these states is 5,305,149. It seems an enormous sum. In those 15 states the Negro has, by the exceedingly friendly aid of their best friends, amassed a fortune of one dollar a year.

Should they not because of this rapid accumulation of wealth balance their little account, clutch to the mule, jog down the furrow and let the world wag on?

Look now for a moment at those billion dollar yearly crops accumulating for 27 years, giving us the almost inconceivable sum of 27 billions of dollars which, divided between a number of whites equal to that of blacks, each one would from this 27 billions of dollars, receive $5,089.39. Thus the blacks receive for their willing toil through 27 years $27.58, while the whites receive $5,089.39. These are both sides of the Grady picture of Negro wealth which was intended to deceive the North. Gaze upon it.

Mr. Grady manifested the love he bears us by arousing the public sentiment to riot in Atlanta because the postmaster had appointed a colored man to a clerkship in the postoffice.

Why if the blacks are contented and happy in their cabin homes did New Bedford look upon the pitiful sight, but three winters ago, of a black man with barefooted and ragged wife and children trudging along its streets in the dead of winter?

The man who thus led his family had in the South worked while daylight lasted, yet had received but 40 cents in money the year before. His wife, a cook, received $2 a month for her labor.

Brought from that land in childhood by loyal white friends . . . reared and trained here, I little dreamed that in after years I should be returned at the command of my parents. Such, however, was the case. Then I learned that though cotton may whiten beneath the stars, horny handed and slavish toil has most to do with its growth and whitening. The wheat may lack the sunshine in its bearded sheaf, but if it listens to the prayers of the oppressed it shrinks within its sheaf and turns black with horror of great grief. . . .

Again Mr. Grady says of the three essentials, iron, cotton, wood, that region has easy control. Make the list of essentials four, and add unpaid colored labor. He also says in cotton they have a fixed monopoly. In iron a proven supremacy. In timber, the reserved supply of the republic. They have also the Negro, the foundation of their institutions.

Upon that land there rests a curse, which can only be removed by and through the redemption of the Negro.

Again Mr. Grady describes a scene of his old black mammy as she held him in her black arms and led him smilingly to sleep. I can easily conjure up a scene of those old white aproned nurses as they in the long watches of the night, led those fractious young ones in to sleep. In helplessness that black mammy was compelled to nurse the young vulture whose wings of thought would soon bear him with crooked beak and whetted talons from the milk of the mother to the blood of her children.

From your loins, my people, a race shall spring that shall possess the land in which their fathers' bones repose; a race which for manliness no race shall surpass; a race that shall know no fear but that of wrong; that shall laugh scornful defiance in the rebel face, and demand restitution for the centuries of their fathers' unrequited toil. In peace and justice we will work out our own redemption, and in that redemption present to the world the solution of the Negro problem. If peace and justice be denied we will suffer on and multiply until God's own time will have fully come; then we shall stand forth as terrible as an army with banners, and the South shall shake with the power of the Negro's tread.

The Christian Recorder (Phila.), January 16, 1890.

II.
NEGRO ORGANIZATIONAL ACTIVITY

With the defeat of Reconstruction, the Negro people regrouped their forces and advanced again to challenge the enemy. One of the ways they did this was through the formation of their own instruments, institutions and organizations. This period is marked by the establishment of such Negro schools as Selma University (1878) and Tuskegee Institute (1881) in Alabama, Allen University in South Carolina (1880), Lane College in Tennessee (1882), and Livingstone College in North Carolina (1886); and of such Negro newspapers as the Savannah *Tribune* (1875), Chicago *Conservator* (1878), Los Angeles *California Eagle* (1879), Washington *Bee* (1882), Cleveland *Gazette* (1883), Richmond *Planet* (1884) and the New York *Age* (1885). In addition, numerous political, economic, social and professional organizations were founded on a local, regional and national scale to conduct the liberation fight on varying levels and in different fields.

To illustrate this multi-faceted activity thirteen documents are published below. The first [a] is the Declaration of Objects of the Colored Men's Progressive and Co-Operative Union founded in Baltimore in 1875 under the leadership of Isaac Myers. This lasted but a short time and its influence was confined largely to Maryland. The next document [b] consists of the militant public address adopted in December, 1878 by the Young Men's Progressive Association of New Orleans. The leaders of this organization included Thomas J. Boswell, Edward Jackson and J. Madison Vance, Jr.

The third document [c] consists of an appeal to Governor Wiltz of Louisiana, made in 1880, by Albert Demas, a Negro State Senator. Senator Demas was acting on behalf of several Negro plantation workers who had been jailed for leading a strike of fellow workers in the parishes of St. James, St. John the Baptist and St. Charles. The plantation owners, assisted by the Governor's proclamation of a state of emergency and the subsequent use of the state militia, succeeded in breaking the strike. As part of the strikebreaking came the imprisonment of the strike-leaders for whom Senator Demas appealed.

The fourth document [d] is the formal address made to president-elect Garfield in January, 1881, by a delegation of eleven persons representing Negro Republicans of the Carolinas, Virginia, Georgia, Florida and Texas. The spokesman for this group was Robert B. Elliott of South Carolina, a member of Congress from 1871 to 1875.

The fifth document [e] is a memorial to Congress from a convention of Kansas Negroes which met in April, 1882. Present, as representatives of the approximately

60,000 Negroes then in Kansas, were forty-five delegates from fifteen counties under the leadership of the Rev. A. Fairfax, Edward W. Dorsey and Richard Stafford. The main import of the petition was a request for the distribution of public lands in Oklahoma to the Negro people.

In October, 1882 a State Convention of Rhode Island Negroes met in Newport with George T. Downing as the leading figure. The fifty delegates representing the approximately seven thousand Negroes of that state expressed a very critical attitude towards the Republican party and this significant indication of political independence forms the sixth document [f] in this group.

The seventh document [g] consists of the report of the committee on grievances of the 1883 State Convention of Colored Men of Texas, held in the hall of the House of Representatives in Austin. Over one hundred and twenty delegates and alternates from about twenty counties, led by the Rev. A. Grant, I. G. Scott and Mack Henson, were present. The report is a very forthright document taking up such questions as miscegenation, education, convict labor, discrimination in public places and in jury-selection.

Document eight [h] is made up of the proceedings of a meeting of the North Carolina (Negro) State Teachers' Association held in Raleigh in November, 1886. Here these Negro men and women, under the chairmanship of J. C. Price, raised the demand for Negro higher education, for federal support of education, and the establishment of uniform requirements and salaries for Negro and white teachers. The ninth document [i] is from the pen of E. J. Waring, a Negro lawyer of Baltimore. It describes the formation and activity of the Mutual United Brotherhood of Liberty in the United States, an organization dedicated to fighting in the courts any infringement of the legal rights of Negroes.

The tenth document [j] consists of extracts from the minutes of a Consultation Convention held in Macon in January, 1888. Three hundred Negroes from all parts of Georgia were present with the Rev. W. J. White, editor of the *Georgia Baptist*, presiding. The militance of this very representative gathering will surprise those who have believed that Booker T. Washington's program of acquiescence enjoyed near-unanimous support from the Negro people. The convention considered lynching, education, jim-crowism in the militia, the jury system and on railroads, and led to the establishment of the Union Brotherhood of Georgia. This Brotherhood was analogous to the organization described by Mr. Waring in the preceding document, though its purposes were somewhat broader.

In 1887, T. Thomas Fortune suggested the formation of a National Afro-American League. In November, 1889 a call went out for the holding of a founding convention of such a League to meet in Chicago in January, 1890. This call was signed by men like Bishop Alexander Walters of New York, Edward E. Cooper, editor of the Indianapolis *Freeman*, and H. C. Smith, editor of the Cleveland *Gazette*. As a result there assembled in Chicago at the appointed time, 147 delegates from 21 states and the District of Columbia who proceeded to elect W. A. Pledger of Georgia chairman of the meeting, to found the Afro-American National League and to select as its first president and secretary J. C. Price of North Carolina and T. Thomas Fortune, respectively. For about a decade the League and its local branches led a fairly vigorous life as a center for the expression of a considerable body of Negro opinion. Published below, as the eleventh document [k], are the speeches by Fortune (at the founding convention), and by W. A. Pledger, an ironic petition to Congress "unanimously adopted" by the delegates, and Article II of the League's constitution defining its objects.

The twelfth document [l] consists of an address to the people of the United States adopted by a "Convention of Colored Americans" meeting in Washington in February, 1890. This address was submitted to the United States Senate by a committee representing the Citizens' Equal Rights Association made up of P. B. S. Pinchback of Louisiana, P. H. Carson of Washington, James Hill of Mississippi, J. A. Taylor of Virginia, Thomas E. Miller of South Carolina and P. H. Murray of Missouri.

The last document [m] in this group consists of a description of Tuskegee Institute as seen by the very sympathetic T. Thomas Fortune in 1890. This school was founded nine years before in fulfillment of a promise made in 1880 by a white Democratic candidate for the state legislature to Lewis Adams, a prominent Negro Republican politician of Macon County, in return for Adams' backing. Adams, himself, was an early trustee of the institution and after Washington was put in charge of it, Tuskegee became the center of Northern big-business "philanthropy" among Negroes.

[a]

Progressive and Co-Operative Union, 1875

Whereas, it is an undeniable fact that a strong and powerfully organized opposition exists in this country to the colored man's full and complete enjoyment of all the rights and privileges of American citizenship; and

Whereas, we believe that the full enjoyment of said rights is to be obtained and preserved only by combination, organization and perseverance by colored men; therefore

Resolved, That we organize for the following objects under the name of the "Colored Men's Progressive and Co-Operative Union":

1. To secure equal advantages in schools of all grades, from the primary school to the university.

2. To secure a full and complete recognition of our civil rights, and to defend by all proper means any abridgement of the same.

3. To use all justifiable means to obtain for our children admission into the workshops of our country, that they may obtain a practical knowledge of all mechanical branches of business.

4. To labor for the moral and social elevation of our people.

John M. Langston, *Freedom and Citizenship* (Washington, 1883), p. 259.

[b]

Young Men's Progressive Association of New Orleans, 1878

It would be unnecessary, not to say tedious, to go over the period of fifteen years, during which time our people were made to suffer the bitterest trials; their grievances, if well collected, would cover thousands of pages, every line of which would move the heart of any man except a Southern bulldozer. We can conceive how difficult it is for the civilized and refined people of the North to give credence to any statements concerning these horrible deeds, which belong properly to the dark ages of barbarity and crime. Yet they are facts which stand forth as plain as the noonday sun.

When President Hayes inaugurated his "Southern policy," which gave the long-coveted "local self-government" to the South, we had hoped that the prejudicial feeling in regard to the black man's suffrage had subsided forever; we had hoped that there would have been no more assassinations, whippings, or intimidations; we had hoped that the good citizens of the South, without regard to race, color or previous condition, would have been allowed on election day to go to the polls, and in the language of President Hayes, "cast one unintimidated ballot and have that ballot honestly counted." Illusory, fallacious hopes at the first election after the inauguration of that policy, the outrages inflicted upon defenceless colored citizens— Republicans in politics and convictions—by the lawless bands of nightriders, styling themselves "Regulators" or White Leaguers, in the larger Republican parishes of the IVth, Vth, and VIth Congressional Districts, may well evoke the earnest consideration and hearty condemnation of every loyal American throughout the country—such cases as that of Daniel Hill, of Quachita Parish, who was riddled with bullets, and his assassination completed whilst upon his dying bed trying to make peace with his God; Herman Bell, of the same parish, taken from his home in the dead of night, dragged to the woods and massacred, his body left to feed the vultures and the prowling beasts of the forest; Commodore Smallwood, Charles Carroll, John Higgins and Washington Hill, of Concordia Parish; Charles Bethel, Robert Williams, Munday Hill, James Stafford, Louis Posttewart, William Henry, and others, of Tensas parish, who were ruthlessly murdered in their different parishes for no other reason than that of being Republicans, and for attempting to exercise their rights as American citizens. Whole parishes were run over, and victims of "local self-government" were left by scores hanging to trees; all this even during the awful time when God was pouring his wrath upon the State as a seeming chastisement for these hellish deeds.* These are facts, patent facts, no matter how incredible they may seem.

The above summary is enough to show beyond controversy that the corner-stone of Southern creed consists in the gradual but relentless extermination of the Negro race. Upon the successful operation of that barbarous doctrine hang the hopes of these irreconcilable enemies of the Constitution to get full control of the Government. No item in the history of the darkest ages of barbarism offers a parallel, either as to the character of the con-

* The reference is to the severe yellow fever epidemic which hit Louisiana in 1878.

trivance, or the manner of execution. Pacific appeals and virtuous examples will never solve the problem of American suffrage in the South; experience has abundantly demonstrated that all experiments founded on policy and sentimentalism looking to this end have signally failed. Such is the condition of our State today, and these are the reasons for the inauguration of this association. If we are citizens of this great and free country, we demand our rights as such. We appeal first to President Hayes, and we are proud to hail with pleasure his message in relation to his "Southern policy"; we see in it the honest sentiments of an honorable statesman; we see in it the humanitarian, the Christian and the President, and we look to him to rectify these unparalleled outrages upon American citizens.

We protest that "local self-government" South means political outrages under which the rights of citizens need the protecting arm of the National Government. We appeal to Congress to enact such laws as will remedy the present outrages upon the civil and political rights of Republican citizens of the South. We appeal to the judiciary to punish without distinction of position, wealth or pedigree, these lawless men who dye their hands in innocent bood, or those who aid and abet the same. We appeal to the religious and moral sentiment of the whole country to lend their aid in suppressing these great wrongs. We are uncompromisingly opposed to any scheme looking to the disfranchisement of our race. We indulge the conviction that the offences committed against, and all assaults made upon American citizenship, can be checked in the South as they are in the North, if the laws are properly enforced. We are proud to acknowledge our adhesion to the National Republican party, but we stand ready to cooperate with the good citizens of any section of the State in the interest of reform, wherever such cooperation does not interfere with our cardinal principles. We shall always consider it a special cause for gratification whenever our assistance can be instrumental in promoting the commercial interests of this Commonwealth. Ever mindful of the fact that we are vitally interested in the welfare of the State, we shall always strive for its prosperity. In fact, the record of our race in that direction is a flattering memento to our remembrance.

We favor the calling of a convention at the earliest practical moment, for the purpose of devising means by which we can secure the enjoyment of that protection which so far has been simply a taunt to our suffering people. We want freedom of ballot for all citizens alike. We want safety in life and property, freedom in the pursuit of happiness, and in the acquiring of education. We find these blessings in the Constitution, and we hope to find the solution of the means of enjoying them in the hearts of the American people.

The Young Men's Progressive Association propose that the grievances of our race in the South shall be made known to the world. We advise the colored men to set aside their personal differences in this solemn hour of our existence, and turn over a clean leaf in salutation of the dawn of a new era which pleads for harmony, unity and cordialty. Our motto is, "The Constitution; order, and good government."

N.Y. *Daily Tribune*, January 1, 1879.

[c]

Appeal for Imprisoned Negro Strikers

New Orleans, March, 23, 1880

To His Excellency Governor Wiltz, of the State of Louisiana,

The undersigned, having pleaded guilty to trespas before Judge Augustin, holding court at St. Charles Court-House on Saturday, March 20th, and having been brought to New Orleans to serve out their sentence, ask you for a remission of the same on the following grounds:

We, as well as the majority of our people, were misled as to our rights when we acted as we did in the recent strike; and when we were guilty of trespass, we did not know we were exceeding our rights; we really thought we had a right to go where other laborers were working, even though it was on the property of an individual, and induce these laborers to join us.

We now understand we have no such rights; we understand we have no right to go on the property of other people against their will, and we propose to obey this law hereafter.

We feel sure the laborers in our parish will respect the law, as we intend to hereafter, and believe quietness and peace will continue from this time, and that when laborers differ with their employers hereafter about the price of their labor, it will be in a peaceable manner, and with law always on their side.

For these reasons, your Excellency, we would ask a remission of our sentence, and allow us to return to our wives, our children, and our work.*

Appleton's Annual Cyclopedia for 1880 (N.Y. 1888), p. 417.

[d]

Negro Republicans Visit the President-Elect, 1881

As representatives of the colored Republicans of the States of Virginia, North Carolina, South Carolina, Georgia, Florida, and Texas, we have come in their behalf and in our names to congratulate you on your triumphant election . . . pray that you may be girded by the Divine wisdom in securing

* The sentences were remitted.

to all American citizens the blessing of equal laws and just administration . . . Although clothed with the rights of citizenship by the provisions of the Constitution of the United States . . . yet still in all the Southern States we are but citizens in name and not in fact. Our right to participate in elections for the choice of public officers is not only questioned, but, in many localities, absolutely denied us by means of armed violence, fraud and intimidation . . .

We are powerless, Sir, to redress these wrongs through the machinery of the State Courts, for to all intents and purposes they are organized against us . . . This condition of affairs, added to the unfair and unjust treatment of our people at the hands of those who constitute the class of employers, has created a spirit of unrest among them . . .

Another difficulty under which we labor is the want of proper educational facilities for our children . . . we would respectfully urge the importance of creating a national system of education for the toiling masses, under the supervision and control of the Federal Government. . . .

N.Y. *Daily Tribune*, January 15, 1881.

[e]

Negroes of Kansas Memorialize Congress, 1882

At a delegate convention of the colored people of Southern Kansas assembled in the city of Parsons on this 27th day of April, A.D. 1882, in accordance with a printed call . . . after prior deliberation and thorough consultation upon the important object of our coming together at this time: We, the delegates of said convention, are united in the opinion, that our race may be greatly benefitted without any actual loss, possibly gain, to the United States government, by a compliance with the following requests.

1st. That Congress appropriate every third section of land in the Oklahoma territory for the occupancy of colored emigrants from the south, leaving the two intermediate sections open for settlement as may be thought best.

2nd. That Congress appoint a government agent for each district in the territory.

3rd. Authorize said agents to given written permits to colored families to locate upon eighty acres of land each. Requiring each family to cultivate portions of said land for their own benefit and free of rent, during five successive years under written contract.

4th. Empower the agent to loan to each family suitable materials for erecting a comfortable dwelling house and stable, six months rations for team and families, a cook stove, needed seeds, a team, a wagon, a plow, and other necessary farming implements. Said family contracting to pay for the same in annual payments within five years; and in case of failure to do so, the property to revert to the agent. All of the previously described property (real or personal) shall be under the supervision and control of the agent.

5th. Every family that complies with the terms of the contract and who within five years returns or pays the agent for all the loaned articles will be entitled to receive from the agent a government deed for the property at the time of final payment.

6th. That Congress donate a sufficient number of school houses and lots, and employ teachers therein for one year, under a compulsory educational law.

7th. Prohibit the sale of all intoxicating liquors as a beverage.

"LAST BUT NOT LEAST," Earnestly desiring that one great God and Father of all races of mankind, may mercifully fill your hearts with true Christian sympathy, and your mind with pure wisdom, in remembrance of the great "golden rule," while you are engaged in discussing the merits of this our first appeal to you, we will anxiously await a wise and favorable decision by you.

Proceedings of the Convention of Colored Men, held in . . . Parsons, Kansas . . . April 27–28, 1882 (Parsons, 1882). Copy in Library of Congress. The petition was printed also in the *Congressional Record*, June 7, 1882, 47th Cong., 1st Sess., p. 4656.

[f]

Rhode Island Negroes on Republican Party, 1882

Resolved, That the Republican party of our State has failed to properly recognize the worthiness and faithful devotion of its colored adherents; that it continues to do so in the face of earnest but respectful remonstrances.

Resolved, That while we cling to those principles which have made the party acceptable to the people, and would adhere steadfastly to its nominations, we affirm our determination to support that person let him be allied to whatever party he may be, if he shall convince us that he has the most regard for our rights and feelings as citizens of the State.

Resolved, That we demand common respect, and a fair representation in the apportionment of prominent and other offices; not simply because of the money considerations that usually accompany office, but that it may be seen that our class is respected and deferred to as are other citizens.

Resolved, That we hold in contempt, as a traitor to manhood and his race, that man who will permit his vote to be influenced by a tender of money or any other corrupting influence.

Appleton's Annual Cyclopaedia . . . 1882 (N.Y. 1889), p. 721.

[g]

Texas State Convention of Negroes, 1883

We, your Committee on Grievances, beg leave to make the following report:

We find that the denial to the colored people of the free exercise of many of the rights of citizenship, is due to the fact of there being such great prejudice against them as a race. This prejudice was engendered from the belief which underlay the institution of slavery, and which kept that institution alive, and built it to the enormous proportions which it has attained; that is, the belief that the Negro was intended by the Divine Creator as servants and menials for the more favored races; hence, was not to be accorded the rights and privileges exercised by other races. Very naturally, then, was it thought fitting and proper, and in keeping with Divine intention, to keep the Negro bowed down in slavery. The sudden change from a status wherein we were slaves to one in which we were made freemen; and then, further, to that in which we became citizens equal before the law, was so unexpected and contrary, both to the training and teaching of our former owners, that they have never fully accepted said changes, though they have affected to accept them, because their acceptance was made the only condition upon which they could regain their former position in the Union. We submit, that it is contrary to the natural order of things for them to have surrendered their belief in the matter simply because they were physically overpowered. And, not only is the belief in the Negro's inferiority and creation for servants deeply rooted in the minds of its advocates, but it has culminated in what seems to be a bitter hatred and fixed prejudice. This culmination was brought about by the Negro being taken from the position of a slave and forcibly placed equal to his former master; also, by his being subsequently utilized in carrying on the war against the unfortunates of the lost cause after the battle had been transferred from the field to the ballot-box; and in doing this he adhered to a political party which he kept up by his support, and which was nearly identical with the triumphant party which had caused their former owners' defeat on the bloody field of battle. This is the outcome of a train of circumstances naturally liable to produce just such a result.

The reason given by our debasers, when attempting to justify themselves in regarding us socially so grossly inferior is, that it always has been their policy to do so, and hence it always will be. This remark refers to the fact that they regarded us thus during slavery as a ground upon which they justified slavery, and as they have experienced no change of mind they will continue thus to regard us. Your committee arrived at this conclusion: that if our former owners deny our social equality, they cannot be expected to be swift in respecting our legal equality or equality before the law; for it is the social regard one has for another as a member of society, which impels him to protect and accord unto such a one his legal rights. Hence, if there be a class who socially regard us less favorably than they do other races, to an extent that they are prejudiced, such a class certainly are indifferent as to whether we obtain our legal rights or not. Accordingly, social disregard may well imply absolute indifference as to another's legal rights, but never that *mutual* regard which is supposed to possess citizens of a common country. It is a true rule that the degree to which any right is enjoyed as a citizen, is measured by the willingness of the whole body of citizens to protect such a right; if there is lack of regard there is, therefore, lack of the will to protect. We find, therefore, that this social disregard is the sole cause of all the infringements upon our rights as a race, as we shall specify:

MISCEGENATION LAW

Prominent among the enactments in furtherance of this social disregard, is a law of this State punishing as felons all persons who intermarry when one is a descendant of the Negro race and the other is not. The same series of laws impose an insignificant fine only for the same persons to live together in unlawful wedlock, or have carnal intercourse with each other without being married. In most cases, say ninety-nine cases in one hundred, parties of the two races thus unlawfully cohabiting are not even reported, or if reported not punished. And, sad to remark in many cases officers of the law are disqualified to try such cases; in many others, those who would in good faith testify against offenders of this class, would do so at the risk of their lives.

The result of this series of crimes, tolerated and encouraged by our criminal Code, which makes pretensions to preserving public morals, common decency and chastity, is to increase immorality in the lower classes of both races to an alarming extent. The law should never imply that a thing otherwise lawful is a felony, and that a thing of the same nature unlawful in itself is less than a felony. Colored females, victims of this well-laid plan, called a law to protect public morals, and common decency and chastity, are severely censured, and our whole race indiscriminately described as a race without morals. A careful consideration of the operation of the law convinces all fair-minded persons, that the law was intended to gratify the basest passions of certain classes of men who do not seek such gratification by means of lawful wedlock. We are pained to announce that the law bears its evil fruits. The Committee dismiss the consideration of this dark subject with the recommendation that the Convention urge upon our next Legislature the necessity of an amendment to this law that will punish as rigidly for all carnal intercourse between the two races, unlawfully carried on, as it punishes them for intermarrying. If the Legislature do this, they will show a willingness to stop the tide of immorality that now makes such inroads upon the morals of some of our most promising females.

FREE SCHOOLS

The Constitution, and laws made in pursuance thereof, make provision for the education of the youth of the State, without regard to race or previous condition. Further, they make provision that cities may assume the control of school affairs within their limits, on condition that they make a special taxation upon their property in order to lengthen the school term to ten months. What we complain of is, that notwithstanding the Constitution, laws, courts, and the Board of Education have decided that provision for each race must be equal and impartial, many cities make shameful discrimination because the colored people do not own as much property on which to pay taxes as the white people do, in proportion to the number of children in each race. They utterly refuse to give colored schools the same provision as to character of buildings, furniture, number and grade of teachers as required by law. The result of this discrimination is, that the white schools of such cities show good fruit, while the colored show poor fruit or none at all. We here say that this charge of discrimination is not made against all cities, but against only such as really discriminate. And again, there are many colored teachers appointed mainly on account of their personal relations with the individuals composing the Boards, and not with reference to the peculiar needs of the pupils to be benefitted, neither the fitness of the teacher nor the wishes of patrons.

We are glad to say, however, that many school boards, exclusively white, do their full duty towards colored schools. Still we deem it proper and just, in recognition of our rights, to assist in supervising and controlling, to have some colored man or men appointed on school boards in cities where there is a large number of colored pupils and patrons—especially where suitable men can be found. We make no complaint against the provision made by the Legislature of our State for the education of our children, but against the partial manner in which those provisions are executed by some of the local authorities.

TREATMENT OF CONVICTS

Another sore grievance that calls for the consideration of this Convention is the treatment of convicts, a large proportion of whom are colored. It is inhuman and cruel in the extreme. We do not refer to those that are kept within the walls. They are under the immediate care and supervision of the management, and we believe considerately treated. But most of the convicts are scattered over the State on farms, having no one to administer to their physical, moral or spiritual needs but a host of inhuman, brutal convict guards. When a fresh convict is carried to the farms, he is taken down by the other convicts and beaten, at the command of the guard, and that, too, with a large piece of cowhide. The guard takes this method of taming the new-comer. Of course this lays him up, but in a few days he is hauled out of his sick quarters and put to work, whether he is physically able to do it or not. The law provides that a convict physically unable to work shall not be required to do so, such inability to be ascertained by the examination of the penitentiary physician. But, convicts on farms, who are mostly colored, have no physician to determine such inability, and even when sick and dying have none, unless the hiring planter, who has no particular interest in saving his life, sees fit to employ one. In many cases sick convicts are made to toil until they drop dead in their tracks. Many again, driven to desperation by inhuman treatment, seek to relieve themselves by attempting to escape when the chances are against them, thus inducing the guards to shoot them, which they are ready to do on the slightest pretext. Others are maltreated by being placed in the pillory or stocks until they are dead or nearly so.

When convicts are brutally murdered, nothing is done with their slayers unless the indignant citizens are prompt in insisting upon their punishment. In nine cases out of ten, parties sent to investigate these occurrences report the killing justifiable, because guards and their friends find it convenient to make it appear so. When legislative committees visit one of these convict camps, they always find the convicts ready to report that they are well treated, because all of them, both white and black, are previously warned by their guards to report thus or accept the consequences which will surely follow. Again we will state, although the law justifies the killing of a convict escaping from the penitentiary, when his escape can be prevented in no other way, still we fail to see wherein it can be justified when the convict is carried on a farm, away from the penitentiary, and given a chance to escape only to be deliberately shot down in attempting to do so. We believe such to be deliberate murder, and should be punished as such.

Believing that most of the evils can be remedied by the appointment of a colored inspector who is a humane man, having power to investigate the affairs of convict camps and the management of convict labor on private farms, therefore, we recommend to the Governor and Board such an appointment at the earliest possible moment. We recommend also, that as most of the State convicts are colored, that there be appointed at least one colored commissioner of penitentiaries. Though our men and youths are sent to the penitentiary to be reformed, in most cases they are made worse by the inhumanities and immoral habits of their guards, who, in many cases, are worse morally than the convicts themselves. We think that this Convention should pass a resolution condemning, in strongest terms, the practice of yoking or chaining male and female convicts together. This is an act of officials done only for the purpose of further demoralizing those persons, especially so where they are only county convicts.

RAILWAYS, INNS AND TAVERNS *

The criticisms and censures of many, that colored persons in demanding admission to first class are forcing social intercourse, are unjust and unwarranted. For those who censure know that if the companies were to furnish accommodations for colored passengers holding first class tickets, equal to the accommodations furnished white passengers holding the same, though such accommodations be in separate cars, no complaint will be made. But selling two classes of passengers the same kind of tickets, at the same time and price, certainly sell to them the same accommodations and privileges. The colored people, like any other class of citizens, will contend for the right in this matter so long as our [State] Constitution reads, "all men when they form a social compact have equal rights," and even longer.

We would also state that we do not contend for the privilege of riding in the car with whites, but for the right of riding in cars equally as good, and for the mutual right of riding in their car if they have a separate one, whenever they are permitted to ride in ours if we have a separate one. We believe that the State laws to be adequate to protect us in every right, and that there is no necessity of appealing to a law of Congress unless the laws and government of our own State refuse to recognize and protect these rights.

As for accommodations at public inns, taverns and hotels, we have the same right as other races to be accommodated on equal terms and conditions, though we cannot compel them to accommodate us in the same room, at the same table or even in the same building, but the proprietor can be compelled to make provision as good. We recognize the fact that our State law is as adequate to protect a colored man in the exercise of his rights as it is to protect a white man. While not encouraging the contention for our rights at hotels when we can make other provision, we urge our people to invoke the aid of the courts when their rights with reference to railroads are violated, and ask that they assert our rights thereon by such damages as are sufficient to assert them.

JURIES

The prevailing practice among sheriffs and jury commissioners of summoning jurors exclusively white or nearly so, is in direct violation of the

* Some delegates objected to this section, but it was sustained by the convention as a whole.

laws of this State, for no person is disqualified as a juror on account of his color. If the sheriff and commissioners exclude any one by practice on account of color, it is such an exclusion as is not contemplated by law, for the parties summoning cannot excuse themselves by saying they knew of none who could read and write, for that is a qualification they are to assume and let the court test jurors' qualifications after they are summoned. A juror who sits in judgment on a case involving the rights of a man whom he regards with less consideration than he does members of his own class, is in law an incompetent juror, and should by law be excluded on evidence of such lack of regard. We deem it to be the duty of all judges to, at all times, specially instruct sheriffs and commissioners with reference to correcting these abuses, so as to secure to every individual, white or black, a fair and impartial trial by a jury composed of men acknowledging themselves to be his peers.

In furtherance of a desire to effectually and legitimately prescribe a remedy for the evils and wrongs complained of, we recommend the formation of an organization to be known and called "The Colored People's Progressive Union." It shall have for its object the protection of the rights of the colored people of Texas, by giving aid and direction in the prosecution of suits in support of every right guaranteed to colored people as citizens. We recommend that our delegates to the National Convention [held in Louisville, Ky., later that year] be instructed to urge upon said Convention the necessity of organizing a national convention of the same name and for the same object, under which, if organized, this State Association shall act as a branch.

Proceedings of the State Convention of Colored Men of Texas, held at the City of Austin, July 10–12, 1883 (Houston, 1883). Copy in library of the University of Michigan at Ann Arbor.

[h]

North Carolina Teachers' Association, 1886

Reports of Committees

RESOLUTIONS ON NORMAL AND COLLEGIATE INSTITUTE AND REPORT NO. 1

It has been well said that education is the "cheap defense of nations." History and experience have proved that this is true philosophy; whether it has been realized in the ability to defend one's self against the rash incursions of foreign foes or in divesting a government of internal corruption and disunity—the sure precursors of public decadence and subsequent public death. Ignorance has ever been one of the greatest of impediments, if not obstacles, to the progress of peoples, races, States and Nations. It is an internal cancer which continually eats out the vitals of its possessor; the great fosterer of jealousies, the harbinger of crime. We cannot then wonder at the spirit of the genius of our government when it is instituted "for the common defense" and "to promote the general welfare."

All the States of the Union catching the spirit of the national constitution, seek by education to provide "for the common defense." Indeed before there was a national constitution the States exemplified this spirit.

Our own "Old North State" put herself on record in behalf of public education in her constitution of 1776, adopted at Halifax a dozen years before the ratification of the national constitution. But the language of the present constitution is unmistakable when it says: "Schools and the means of education shall forever be encouraged," and the present school law of the State in harmony with the contemplated sentiment of the organic law is even more explicit and definitive. To the end that education may be thus encouraged it is the common verdict of these times that special preparation on the part of the teacher is necessary. The teacher must give tone to the public school system of the State; but this tone necessarily involves the progress of education among the masses—hence normal and training schools are an urgent necessity, a reasonable demand of the day.

But can we forget that there is a peculiar condition of things in the South, that there are racial lines which sometimes mark our unfortunate limits for one or the other of the races subject to them. These "limits" however, seem to work out at length to the especial misfortunes of the Negro. How unnecessary! How unjust! How unwise! when even a heathen reasoning would argue that all the citizens of the State, regardless of color, should be educated in order to evince the spirit of our constitutions as well as insure the perpetuity of our institutions.

Therefore, as a matter of wisdom, the State should make ample provisions for the education of its coming generations. But more especially as a matter of duty—because it involves justice and conserves the high behests of Heaven—the State should make haste to secure to itself the safest and cheapest of defenses. And this is pre-eminently necessary and just as it pertains to the education of the freedmen constituting a part of the citizenship of the State.

To have separate schools seems to be a part of the political organism of the South; and we would not have it otherwise, but there should not be any wide disparagement in favor of or against either race. This would be out of harmony with the genius of American institutions, a subversion of the principles which have made the government of Washington, Hamilton and Jefferson, one of the greatest governments of modern times. Therefore, be it,

Resolved, 1st. That we, the colored educators and friends of Negro education in North Carolina, do hereby express our opinion that it is the duty of our State to make reasonable and just provisions for the training of the colored teachers of the State and for the high school training of the colored youth.

Resolved, 2nd. That we do hereby give to our committee appointed to memorialize the Legislature our hearty endorsement in every effort and request they shall make that the State may be induced to do its duty to the colored teachers and youth of the State.

Resolved, 3rd. That the present Normal School provisions are inadequate and do not justify the educational boast of the State.

Resolved, 4th. That the State should make appropriations for the establishment and management of a State Normal and High School Institute for its colored citizens which would be a reasonable offset for the University, largely encouraged and supported by public patronage and State money, and used exclusively in the interest of its white citizens.

Resolved, 5th. That we offer these resolutions in all candor and prompted by a consciousness that there is not at present adequate provisions for the demands which the importance of the profession among the colored citizens of the State justifies.

Respectfully submitted,

S. G. Atkins,	Mrs. Annie J. Cooper,
R. H. W. Leak,	D. A. Lane,
Ed. A. Johnson,	E. E. Smith,
Jas. B. Dudley,	Miss Fannie O'Kelly,
Jno. R. Hawkins,	Miss Oleonora Pegram,
	Mrs. Geo. T. Wassom.

RESOLUTIONS ON THE BLAIR BILL AND REPORT NO. 2

WHEREAS, Through the persevering and untiring efforts of Senator Henry W. Blair, of New Hampshire, the attention of the whole country has been directed to the importance of an appropriation by the National Government, of a sum of money sufficient to guarantee better facilities for the education of the illiterate youths of the country;

AND WHEREAS, The Senate of the United States has given said measure its hearty and emphatic endorsement, by providing for the appropriation of $77,000,000 to meet such an urgent need, although defeated in the House of Representatives, because of not having been allowed to be reported. Therefore, be it

Resolved, By the North Carolina State Teachers' Association in convention assembled, that the thanks of the teachers and people of the State are due and are hereby tendered Hon. Henry W. Blair, for his persistent and unremitting efforts to provide such a measure as the Blair Educational Bill for the relief of our educational disabilities, and as a further means of promoting the condition of all the unfortunate classes of our people. . . .

Resolved, That we unanimously petition the Congress urging that the bill be passed at once, as the best means of preparing the masses for the patriotic exercise of an intelligent citizenship.

J. C. Dancy,   S. H. Vick,
E. L. Thornton,   Mrs. E. E. Smith,
G. S. Smith,   Mrs. G. T. Wassom,
                                         Miss Lucilla Smith.

RESOLUTIONS ON UNIFORM STANDARD OF EXAMINATIONS AND UNIFORM SALARIES, REPORT NO. 3

We, your committee on Uniform Standard of Examination and fixed Salaries, have carefully considered this matter and make the following recommendations:

1. That a State Board of Examiners be appointed, whose duty it shall be to examine all applicants for certificates to teach in the free public schools of the State, and that said certificate shall be good in any county for a term of five years.

2. We recommend that the present method of county examinations be continued with a provisor, that the State Board of Education prepare a number of questions for each examination fixed by law, which shall be the same throughout the State. An examination upon these questions shall be the minimum and shall not exclude any auxiliary or collateral questions by the county examiner to test the applicant's ability to answer any question, nor shall it exclude such other additional questions as may be necessary to add where the school for which the applicant is examined, shall require a teacher of superior grade.

Resolved, We recommend that the pay of teachers be fixed by law, and that in cities and towns where there are graded schools supported entirely or in part by an extra tax, the pay of white and colored teachers shall be the same for the same quality of work.

Respectfully submitted,

                                         Miss Maggie E. Whiteman,
N. F. Roberts,   E. H. Hunter,
Jas. L. Battle,   Miss Leonora T. Jackson,
W. C. Coleman,   J. O. Crosby.

Negro Sentiment in North Carolina, on the Duty and Necessity of the State's Establishing a Normal and Collegiate Institute for the Benefit of its Colored Citizens . . . (Raleigh, 1886). Copy in library of Dr. W. E. B. Du Bois.

[i]

Mutual United Brotherhood of Liberty, 1887

They tell us we are free; that we are citizens; that we are under the protection of the law. It's a lie! They tell us Justice is blind. It's a lie, for the Blind Goddess raises her bandage from the eyes to ascertain the race and color of those kneeling at her shrine before she dispenses law . . . And when we murmur, complain, cry aloud and demand our constitutional rights and privileges, they tell us we are drawing the color line. It is false. The white man draws the color line. . . .

My theme is the colored man before the law, and we have set forth the injustice done us, and this address would be wanting in practical value did I not at least *attempt* to give some remedy. I said there is law enough for us. We ask not special legislation, but impartial enforcement of law. One powerful method is wise utilization of our political forces—but I am now to speak of another.

I have the honor to be the counsel of an organization in my adopted city and State known as the United Brotherhood of Liberty. The purpose of the organization is to test in the courts infringement of the rights of colored people, whether as a race or as individuals, and I had the honor to prosecute the first case undertaken by that body. And this is the plan I shall now elaborate. I said that we have law enough. It remains for us to exact our rights and privileges from the law. Our difficulty is our individual inability to meet the expense of a legal contest. Thus, when a colored man is denied some right or privilege he must needs suffer the wrong, because he cannot afford to vindicate himself in the courts. I cannot, in a more concise manner, indicate the purpose and method of resorting to law to secure our rights than by quoting an interview had with me recently by a Baltimore paper:

"The Mutual United Brotherhood of Liberty of the United States," said E. J. Waring, the first colored lawyer in Baltimore, to a *News* reporter to-day, "is composed of some of the most prominent colored men in the United States. Its organization grew out of the decision of the Supreme Court of the United States in 1883, that the Civil Rights Bill was unconstitutional. This left the colored man and white man on exactly the same plane, so far as the Constitution of the United States, the Constitution of Maryland and the laws framed under them are concerned.

"The next step made necessary," continued Mr. Waring, "was to exact those rights and make them as beneficial to the colored as to the white race. We have for many years gone into politics and supported one or the other party, believing that its success meant our protection, but we have been disappointed, and hereafter we shall try the peaceful but powerful aid of the courts.

"The consideration of the bastardy act," further said Mr. Waring, "will probably be taken up by the Court of Appeals before the end of January next, and if the decision be adverse to us the Brotherhood of Liberty will carry the case to the Supreme Court of the United States.

"As soon as that case is disposed of we shall take up the subject of the employment of colored teachers in colored schools, and increase of facilities for colored boys and girls obtaining an education. Wherever in the whole country a colored man is denied his just rights the Brotherhood will furnish the means for him to obtain redress in the courts."

Thus the plan is clear. We should organize the country over. Raise funds and employ counsel. Then, if an individual is denied some right or privilege, let the race make his wrong their wrong and test the cause in law. If in any county colored men are excluded from the jury panel, take up the case of some colored man convicted by such a jury, raise the high constitutional question involved and test the validity of the conviction. Some may say that this is futile—that we shall fail. Suppose we do at first, do we not know that in the end, phoenix-like, there will emerge from a sea of failures glorious success. Agitation in a good cause must eventually win the day, as long as the God of angels and of men occupies His throne of love and power.

That there is efficacy in an appeal to law for justification and vindication may be exemplified by reference to three cases occurring in Maryland within a year. 1st. Three Baltimore ladies were denied accommodations on a steamer, sued the company and won. 2d. A young colored girl was terribly beaten by a white man who refused to pay her wages due, and drove her from his house. The young girl sued and recovered heavy damages. 3rd. In Baltimore City I had the pleasure of winning a suit against a white dry goods merchant for striking a colored lady with a yardstick. And finally, through the efforts of your humble servant as counsel for the Brotherhood of Liberty, the obnoxious Bastardy Law * has been declared unconstitutional. . . .

I cite these cases to illustrate in a practical way what can be accomplished in the courts, by way of establishing our equality before the law. Let similar efforts be made everywhere, and when white men deny us our rights let us call them into court and compel them to defend the wrong.

The A.M.E. Church Review (Phila., July, 1887), III, pp. 497–505.

---

* The law provided that legal proceedings could be instituted only if the mother was a white woman.

[j]

Georgia Consultation Convention, 1888

To the Colored Citizens of Georgia:—

The matter of having a Consultation meeting of the leading colored men of the State has been under discussion for some time. On the 24th day of November, 1887, a number of gentlemen met in the city of Macon, Ga., to discuss the advisability of making a call. After fully considering the matter, it was unanimously decided to invite the leading colored men of Georgia, to meet in the city of Macon, on Wednesday morning, January 25th, 1888, at 10 o'clock. The Chairman of that meeting, Rev. W. J. White, was appointed to prepare and issue a call for this meeting.

It is not deemed necessary to enter into details in this call, beyond stating that we believe the time has come when the colored men of Georgia should meet, consult and agree upon some wise course of future action, for the promotion of the race's welfare. After more than 20 years of freedom and its benefits, with thousands of our people greatly advanced from the degradation of slavery days, the colored men of Georgia find a predominating sentiment among their white fellow-citizens, to keep them in a condition largely assimilating to their condition when held in bondage. But as the darkest cloud has its silver lining, so the colored men of Georgia see some rays of hope in the fact that a large number of the best white people of the state are ready and willing to give them a fair chance in the race of life.

The present chain-gang and penitentiary system of Georgia, is simply barbarous, and yet no past legislature has removed this foul blot. Every attempt at improvement has failed, and as a matter of fact, the helpless convicts of the state are being made the subjects of cruelty far beyond the limit authorized by the statutes, even in providing for the enforcement of the most rigid discipline. The educational facilities afforded by the state are totally inadequate to the needs of the people and yet the colored people are deprived of a just share of the small amount provided for this purpose. Under the influence of a senseless and unrelenting prejudice, the legislature at its last session has connected with the continuance of the annual appropriation of the *Eight Thousand Dollars* to the Atlanta University, conditions which amount to a virtual withdrawal of this money from that school. This action was taken in the face of the fact that appropriations to white institutions of learning were larger than in former years. The colored men of Georgia owe it to themselves and their children to organize and unite their strength with the good white people of the state for the removal of existing evils, and the securement of more of the benefits to which their citizenship entitles them. This call is addressed to all classes of our people and we trust the people will interest themselves in raising money to assist their leaders to attend.

Ministers of the gospel, school teachers, professional men, the farmer, the merchant, the mechanic, the artizan, and the wage worker are invited to attend. A people who will not try to help themselves cannot expect others to help them. Let us help ourselves and ask the Lord to turn the hearts of others to our help. . . .

Col. W. A. Pledger offered the following resolution:

Resolved, That while we deplore the necessity, we commend the courage of the colored people of Charleston and Greenville, S.C., in raising money to defend the colored men who lynched the white man who had outraged the colored woman near Greenville, S.C., thus carrying out the idea of imitation of our white brothers.

This resolution was adopted, but after some further discussion . . . the resolution was reconsidered and referred to a committee of three, consisting of Capt. J. W. Lyons, Col. W. A. Pledger and Rev. E. K. Love, to be remodeled. . . .

The second committee on Pledger resolution reported as follows:

We utterly repudiate and condemn lynch law, but commend the course of the colored men of Charleston and Greenville, S.C., who are trying to raise funds to secure a fair trial for the colored men who are charged with lynching the white man who committed an outrage upon a colored woman near Greenville, S.C.

The report was unanimously adopted.

Rev. S. A. McNeal submitted the report of committee on

LYNCH LAW

which was adopted as follows:

WHEREAS, We are surrounded with such a condition of circumstances, known as Lynch law, and

WHEREAS, The Negro is the victim of nearly all the lynchings in this state, and all other states in this country; and

WHEREAS, It has come to your committee's notice through public print, that 123 persons were lynched in the United States last year, and

WHEREAS, This unlawful and inhuman practice is becoming so alarmingly great, that we, the colored men of Georgia, in Convention have assembled, denounce the same, and offer the following:

Resolved, That it is a fundamental idea of our theory of government, that no man shall be deprived of life, liberty or property, without due process of law. It is therefore barbarous, cruel and an alarming outrage of law, that what is known as lynch law, should, under any circumstances, be tolerated, suffered or endured.

Resolved, further, That it is the duty of every true citizen to do all in his power to break up this infamous practice and outrage of law. . . .

Committee on state organization submitted their report through J. T. White, Esq., which was unanimously adopted.

COMMITTEE ON STATE ORGANIZATION

Mr. President, and Gentlemen of the Convention:

We, your committee on State Organization, after due deliberation, a free interchange of ideas and opinions, have concluded our work, and ask that while we come to you, to give an account of our stewardship, you give us your earnest attention. We have gone into the discharge of our duty, deeply sensible, we trust, of the solemn responsibility placed upon us, and sincerely anxious to so work, as to have the approval of our own consciences first; your plaudits after. The paramount consideration with your committee has been, "How can we best unite our people, so as to secure concert of action upon those things which vitally affect our highest interest as citizens of this grand old commonwealth?" Realizing as we did, that the action of our committee must bear the crucial test of your criticism, we tried, so far as the power in us rested, to present that plan which would best accomplish the end desired and at the same time, meet your approval.

Our people are now in an interesting, but not necessarily embarrassing, position. True, perplexing problems continually present themselves, but it is with no small degree of race pride, that I stand in my place as a member of this Convention, and declare in the most emphatic terms at my command, that there is no phase of the Negro Problem, as it presents itself in this country, which Negro wisdom cannot properly comprehend and *ably* solve, if given a fair opportunity to work out our own salvation. Work it out in "fear and trembling," it may be, but work it out; demonstrate it so plainly that "he who runs may read." From this Convention, there must go no uncertain sound. The eyes of the country are upon us, and accordingly, as we perform our duty, will the verdict upon us be; well or illy done. All of the remedies provided by the highest civilization must have been applied and failed to effect a cure; statesmanship must have confessedly exhausted itself, ere my race in this State, will accept as a fact, the statement of the white people, that there is no balm in Gilead. We took it, Mr. President, that from this Convention, there would be demanded some tangible evidence that we are here for the people. Something must be done to show that we know the situation; sympathize with existing conditions; recognize the fact that desperate diseases demand desperate remedies; know our duty in the premises, and knowing it, dare to perform it, let the consequences be what they may. Momentous times are upon us. Upon our shoulders as leaders are fearful responsibilities. *Now,* if ever, in the history of our people, "He who dallies is a dastard, and he who doubts is damned."

To the following plan of organization, we invite your attention:

UNION BROTHERHOOD OF GEORGIA—STATE COUNCIL

WHEREAS, It has been found necessary in all ages of the world's progress for men engaged in a common cause, and aiming to accomplish purposes beneficial to all alike, to form some sort of compact; and

WHEREAS, There are a number of objects that pertain to the best interest of the people of Georgia, and in which the colored people of the State are specially interested, because of the fact that some of the matters bear specially upon them, and

WHEREAS, We, the colored people of Georgia in Convention assembled, realize the importance of more unity of action in the use of the ballot, and

WHEREAS, We believe that such an organization will tend, not only to prevent the prostitution of the ballot which is so largely prevalent in our state at the present time, but will elevate the franchise to that higher use which will make the voice of the people the voice of God; and

WHEREAS, We regard such consummation as most desirable to all classes of our state; therefore be it

Resolved, That we do here agree to form an organization, the objects, aims and purposes of which shall be as follows:

OBJECT AND NAME

1st. The object of this organization shall be to so unite the colored voters of Georgia through local organizations, that they may so cast their ballots as to effect the best interests of the state, and of all classes without regard to race or creed.

2nd. To this end each member of the organization will be held in duty bound to vote in state, county and municipal elections, for such men or measures as shall be endorsed by the state or local councils of this organization. It being distinctly understood that this organization has to do, only with state, and not national affairs.

3rd. This organization shall be known as the Union Brotherhood of Georgia.

4th. It shall have a State Executive Council, a State Council, and local organizations as hereinafter provided.

MEMBERSHIP

The membership of this Union Brotherhood shall comprise the members of all local organizations in the state, organized under this Constitution.

STATE COUNCIL

The State Council of this Union Brotherhood shall consist of the President, 13 Vice-Presidents, Recording Secretary, Corresponding Secretary and Treasurer, the Chairman of each Senatorial District Council, and the Chairman of each County and City Council as hereinafter provided.

OFFICERS AND EXECUTIVE COUNCIL

The officers of the State Council of the Union Brotherhood shall be a President, 3 Vice-Presidents from the State at large, 10 Vice-Presidents to be chosen, one each from the ten Congressional districts of Georgia, a Recording Secretary, Corresponding Secretary, Treasurer and Chaplain. These officers shall constitute the State Executive Council. They shall have the general oversight and management of the Union Brotherhood, when the State Council is not in session. They shall be elected annually at the regular meeting of the State Council of the Union Brotherhood, and shall hold their office one year, or until their successors are elected, and take their seats. Provided, that the officers elected at the organization of this Union Brotherhood shall hold their seats until the annual meeting in 1889.

MEETINGS

The meetings of the State Council of this Union Brotherhood shall be held annually at such time and place as may be fixed by the State Executive Council.

SENATORIAL DISTRICT COUNCIL

In each of the Senatorial Districts of Georgia, the Vice-President in whose Congressional District said Senatorial District is located, shall call a meeting of delegates, to be elected by the people in each district, who, when assembled, shall constitute a Senatorial District Council of the Union Brotherhood of Georgia. The officers of this Senatorial District Council shall be a Chairman, Secretary, and Treasurer. The Chairman of each Senatorial District shall be *ex-officio* a member of the State Council of the Union Brotherhood of Georgia. Should any Senatorial District be located in two Congressional Districts the Vice-President in whose district two counties are located, shall have jurisdiction over the whole.

COUNTY AND CITY CHAIRMAN

In each county of the state, and in the cities of Atlanta, Augusta, Savannah, Macon, Athens, Rome, Columbus and Brunswick, the Vice-President in whose district said county and city is located, shall call a mass meeting for the purpose of choosing a county and city chairman who shall be *ex-officio* members of the State Council of the Union Brotherhood of Georgia. Provided, that the county chairman in counties where above cities are located, shall not have jurisdiction within the corporate limits of said cities, nor shall a city Chairman have jurisdiction outside of said city.

SUB-ORGANIZATIONS

The State Executive Council shall provide for the organization of as many sub-councils of the Union Brotherhood in counties and cities, as they may from time to time deem advisable. The State Executive Council shall have power to make all necessary by-laws, rules and regulations for the carrying out of the objects of this Brotherhood. The President shall, by the concurrence of any four members of the State Executive Council, call extra or special meetings of the State Council. The Executive Council shall have power to fill any vacancies that may occur in its own body. . . .

REPORT OF COMMITTEE ON RESOLUTIONS

Your committee on resolutions respectfully submit the following report:

We, the representatives of the colored citizens of Georgia, in Convention assembled, do hereby issue the following statement to the people of the state, bearing upon questions which we regard as being of vital interest to the glory and prosperity of the commonwealth.

1st. It is a right of the people, irrespective of race, color, or previous condition, to be called upon to perform the high duty of jurors, therefore we view with alarm and remonstrate against the failure of the authorities in more than 130 counties of this state to call colored men to the discharge of this high function of citizenship. We recommend that the people in all the counties of Georgia, where this deprivation of their rights is practiced, by petition and resolution respectfully and properly drawn, press the consideration of this question to the end, that it may be remedied.

2nd. Common carriers are endowed with certain franchises given by the state for the compassing of the convenience of the people at large; they are the creatures of the state and are as amenable to the law as the humblest citizen. We therefore denounce, in unmeasured terms, the practice of railroads in charging colored citizens of the state first-class fare for passage on their trains, and then, in defiance of their plighted faith, coercing them into the acceptance of inferior accommodations.

3rd. The action of the General Assembly of Georgia, in coupling with the continuance of the appropriation to the Atlanta University, conditions that amounted to its withdrawal, for causes frivolous and insufficient, was unjust, unfair and illegal. We therefore recommend that the people throughout the state take steps to secure in the next Legislature representatives pledged to the removal of these conditions and the restoration of this appropriation to that school, unfettered and untrammeled by these conditions, our equitable share of the landscript fund—the nation's bounty.

4th. The present penitentiary system of Georgia is a foul blot upon our civilization; a stain upon the escutcheon of the state; a means by which speculators enrich themselves at the expense of, and on the miseries of the criminal classes of the state, with but slight regard to the requirements of law or the obligations of humanity that one creature holds to another. We do not condemn the proper punishment of transgressors of the law, but we deny the right of the state to entrust or delegate this high function of administering punitive justice to persons or corporations, as it exercises under the penitentiary system of Georgia. We recommend that the people in each county of Georgia organize themselves for the purpose of securing legislative representation pledged to the abolition of this system in our state, and the erection of one more in consonance with the enlightened judgment of the present day.

5th. The ballot in all Republican or Democratic forms of government is the only means by which the citizen in the last resort, can express his will or wishes, hence it is a question of the greatest magnitude that any suspicion should be entertained, that after depositing the ballot, it has been by any unlawful or illegitimate means, tampered with. We, therefore, recommend to the people, that they vote to elevate no man to office or power who is not fully committed to the inviolability of a free ballot and a fair count.

6th. Legislative representations and taxation are traditionally and historically the inseparable rights of every American citizen. We, therefore recommend that the colored citizens in all of the counties of Georgia organize for the purpose of securing their proper voice in the Legislature of the state.

7th. Intelligence being the basis and foundation around which clusters the hope for the perpetuity of every form of government; therefore it is the duty of the state to provide for the education of the masses, and to justly and equitably apply the money raised for this purpose.

8th. A well regulated militia being the defense and safe-guard of our form of government, it is the duty of the state to properly provide for this institution, and to impartially distribute official recognition of all classes of citizens who are voluntarily connected with this service.

Minutes of Consultation Convention, Macon, Ga., Jan. 25, 1888 (n.p., n.d.). Copy in library of Dr. W. E. B. Du Bois.

[k]

Founding Convention of Afro-American League, 1890

1. *Fortune's Speech:*

We are here to-day, as representatives of 8,000,000 freemen, who know our rights and have the courage to defend them. We have met here to-day to emphasize the fact that the past condition of dependence and helplessness upon men who have used us for selfish and unholy purposes, who have murdered and robbed and outraged us, must be reversed. . . . Ladies and gentlemen, we have been robbed of the honest wages of our toil, we have been robbed of the substance of our citizenship by murder and intimidation; we have been outraged by enemies and deserted by friends; and because in a society governed by law, we have been true to the law, true to treacherous friends, and as true in distrust of our enemies, it has been charged upon us that we are not made of the stern stuff which makes the Anglo-Saxon race the most consummate masters of hypocrisy, of roguery, of insolence, of arrogance, and of cowardice, in the history of races.

Was ever race more unjustly maligned than ours? Was ever race more shamelessly robbed than ours? Was ever race used to advance the political and pecuniary fortunes of others as ours? Was ever race so patient, so law abiding, so uncomplaining as ours?

Ladies and gentlemen, it is time to call a halt. It is time to begin to fight fire with fire. It is time to stand shoulder to shoulder as men. It is time to rebuke the treachery of friends in the only way that treachery should be rebuked. It is time to face the enemy and fight him inch by inch for every right he denies us. . . . For the constitutional opponents of our rights we have no faith, no confidence, and no support, and of professed friends we here demand that they perform their part of the contract, which alone can justify the sacrifices we have been called upon to make. If it cannot do this, then it has ceased to be the party of Lincoln . . . and deserves to die, and will die, that another party may rise to finish the uncompleted work, even as the whig party died that the republican party might triumph in the nation . . . I am now and I have always been a race man and not a party man. Let this League be a race league. To make it anything else is to sow the seed of discord, disunion, and disaster at the very beginning of our important work. We stand for the race, and not for this party or that party, and we should know a friend from a foe when we see him. . . .

I now give in consecutive order the reasons which, in my opinion, justify the organization of the National Afro-American League, to wit:

1. The almost universal suppression of our ballot in the South . . .

2. The universal and lamentable reign of lynch and mob law, of which we are made the victims . . .

3. The unequal distribution of school funds . . .

4. The odious and demoralizing penitentiary system of the South, with its chain gangs, convict leases and indiscriminate mixing of males and females.

5. The almost universal tyranny of common carrier corporations in the South—railroad, steamboat and other—in which the common rights of men

and women are outraged and denied by the minions of these corporations.

6. The discrimination practiced of those who conduct places of public accommodation, and are granted a license for this purpose, such as keepers of inns, hotels and conductors of theaters and kindred places of amusement.

7. The serious question of wages, caused in the main by the vicious industrial system in the South, by the general contempt employers feel for employes, and by the overcrowded nature of the labor market . . .

I have pondered long and seriously on the evils which beset us, and I have sought, as light was given me, for an antidote to them, if such there be. I lay them before you, and you are here to adopt or reject them.* I propose, then,

1. The adoption by this league of an Afro-American Bank, with central offices in some one of the great commercial centres of the republic and branches all over the country. We need to concentrate our earnings . . .

I propose (2) the establishment of a Bureau of Emigration. We need to scatter ourselves more generously throughout the republic.

I propose (3) the establishment of a committee on legislation. We need to have a sharp eye upon the measures annually proposed in the federal and state legislatures affecting us and our interests, and there are laws everywhere in the republic the repeal of which must engage our best thought and effort.

I propose (4) the establishment of a bureau of technical industrial education. We need trained artisans, educated farmers and laborers more than we need educated lawyers, doctors, and loafers on the street corners. The learned professions are overcrowded. There is not near so much room at the top as there was in the days of Daniel Webster.

And I propose (5) lastly the establishment of a bureau of co-operative industry. We need to buy the necessaries of life cheaper than we can command them in many states. We need to stimulate the business instinct, the commercial predisposition of the race. We not only want a market for the products of our industry, but we want and must have a fair, and a living return for them. . . .

As the agitation which culminated in the Abolition of African slavery in this country covered a period of fifty years, so may we expect that before the rights conferred upon us by the war amendments are fully conceded, a full century will have passed away. We have undertaken no child's play. We have undertaken a serious work which will tax and exhaust the best intelligence and energy of the race for the next century. . . .

* These proposals were not adopted by the Convention.

2. *Pledger's Speech:*

Within the past few months two distinguished gentlemen from Georgia have spoken in this city and in Boston; * and the mere fact that they sought to mislead and confuse the Northern mind on the disloyal condition of the dominant classes of the South was a tacit, if not incriminating admission, the forced confession of a "guilty conscience," that the Southern situation needed apology, explanation and defense. To concede that there is a "Southern Question," or a "Race Problem," is to admit that the Constitution of the United States is not supreme and is not obeyed in the Southern tier of States. . . .

When by force of arms the Republican party saved the Union from dissolution; and Abraham Lincoln decreed Emancipation to an enslaved race, the dominant classes in the South sullenly and reluctantly submitted, because they no longer had the power to resist openly; and since then by one device, scheme, contrivance or another they have sought to indirectly accomplish within the Union what they failed to do on the battle-field. The forum was changed, but largely the same questions in essence and spirit remained, and now confront the American people for settlement on the basis of loyalty and supremacy of the Constitution. Under this pressure Southern orators come North and imitate the action of the scuttle-fish in seeking to escape condemnation by muddying and beclouding the real issue with an overflow of ornate rhetoric and dramatic professions of fidelity to the Union.

The presence of the Negro is not offensive if he will only appear in a cringing, menial attitude. He must forego all his rights as a citizen, and appear and supplicate "as a servant," and then, and only then, can he obtain an audience and protection. The Democratic design is to keep him as a useful servant in social matters and a mere tool in politics to increase the abnormal power of the Solid South in the Union . . .

It is said the Negro gets justice in the State courts, and yet to be "impolite," "indolent," or "impertinent" are capital offenses in the South, for which the Negro is mercilessly shot down, and in all the Court Records since the war not a single white man has been hung for wantonly killing a colored man . . . In the South, a colored man who protests respectfully against the barbarities and enormities heaped upon his race, and insists upon his rights under the law, is "insolent," or an "incendiary," and forthwith he is marked for destruction.

In many parts of the South a system of terrorism and guerrilla warfare exists, to which open war, with two contending armies in the field, gov-

* The reference is to Henry W. Grady and John B. Gordon.

erned by the usages of Christian nations, would be an improvement . . .

The purpose is to give the Negro just enough coarse food to keep him from starvation, and keep him "down," humble and submissive, so that he will be a docile laborer, with no views and no aspirations above the hoe and plow, and walking behind a mule in the furrow from one year's end to the other. . . . A society in Philadelphia was recently formed to mitigate the sufferings of the Russian prisoners in Siberia. These good people need not go very far away to employ their good offices for poor, down-trodden humanity. They have an excellent field for their missionary work much nearer home, right here in this supposed land of freedom and humanity, where innocent Negroes are hung, shot, and then riddled with bullets until they look like a sieve, and where colored women, innocent of all offense, except accused of being "impertinent," are stripped and then brutally thrashed. Think of it, Christian people! Helpless women divested of all clothing, stripped stark naked, and exposed to the rude stare of a gaping mob, and then the lash applied until the blood spurted from their quivering bodies!!! [Cries of "Shame!"] And yet all this and more was done by the white lynchers in the recent riot at Jesup, Georgia.

3. A Petition to Congress:

Whereas, The predominance of Afro-Americans in the States of Alabama, South Carolina, Louisiana, Mississippi, and other Southern States makes the situation painful and uncomfortable for the small minority of white fellow citizens residing therein; therefore, be it

Resolved, That we do petition the Honorable Congress of the United States to make and provide for an appropriation of $10,000,000,000, to furnish the unhappy white citizens of these States, who may desire to settle in other and more favored States, free from Afro-American majorities, with free transportation and lunch by the way to any of the States north of the Mason and Dixon line. Be it further

Resolved, That the Congress designate Senator Morgan, of Alabama; Senator Hampton, of South Carolina, and Senator Gibson, of Tennessee, to be the "Moses" to lead the unhappy people out of the States of their misfortune.

4. Constitution of the Afro-American League of the United States— Article II:

The objects of the League are to protest against taxation; to secure a more equitable distribution of school funds in those sections where separate schools exist; to insist upon a fair and impartial trial by a judge and jury of peers in all causes of law wherein we may be party; to resist by all legal and reasonable means mob and lynch law whereof we are made the action; and to insist upon the arrest and punishment of all such offenders against our legal rights; to resist tyrannical usages of all railroad, steamboat and other corporations, and the violent or unlawful conduct of their employees in all cases where we are concerned, by prosecution of all such corporations and their employers, in State and Federal Courts; to the labor of the reformation of all penal institutions where barbarous, cruel and unchristian treatment of convicts is practiced, and to assist healthy immigration from terror-ridden sections to others and more law-abiding sections. The objects of the League are to encourage all State and local Leagues in their efforts to break down the color bars, and in obtaining for the Afro-American equal chance with others in the avocations of life, and to unite with such branch Leagues for organized and effective work in securing the full privileges of citizenship.

The objects of the League shall be attained by the creation of healthy public opinion through the medium of the press and pulpit, public meetings and addresses, and by appealing to the court of law for redress of all denial of legal and constitutional rights; the purpose of this League is to secure the ends desired through legal and peaceable and lawful methods.

The Birth of the Afro-American National League . . . *Chicago, Illinois, January 15–17, 1890* (Chicago, 1890). Copy in Library of Congress.

[1]

Address of the Convention of Colored Americans, 1890

To The People of the United States:

The colored American citizens of the United States, in convention assembled, respectfully submit their grievances to the country and ask a favorable decision at the bar of public opinion. We regret that there exists in certain parts of our country a condition of affairs which renders it necessary for the colored American citizens to meet in a separate body for the consideration of grave and important questions that are national in their character. Being a part of the citizenship of this country, we can assure our countrymen that we do not meet in a separate convention from choice, but from necessity. It is because we have been made special and distinct objects of attack and oppression that are are compelled to meet in separate convention as colored American citizens, and suggest ways and means to remedy the evils of which we complain, and to prevent, if possible, a repetition of them.

We call attention to the fact, which no well-informed person who has any regard for the truth will deny, that popular elections, Federal as well as local, in many States of the South are, in a great measure, nothing more than farcical formalities. The votes of colored American citizens in such States are suppressed by violence or neutralized by fraud. The fact has also been made apparent within the last few years that differences of opinion among and separate party affiliations on the part of colored American citizens in those States afford no relief and bring no remedy for the wrongs of which we complain. It seems to be the settled policy of one of the two principal political parties in said States to regard "Negro suffrage" as an evil within itself, and that the leaders and members of said party are determined to violently suppress the votes of colored American citizens, it matters not with what party said voters may affiliate.

Contrary to the letter and spirit of the Constitution and laws of our country, our rights and privileges in the States referred to are not curtailed and abridged, but positively denied. We are made the special objects of unfriendly State legislation. Our wives and our daughters, our mothers and sisters, are forced, in consequence of such legislation, to occupy seats, when traveling, in filthy and inferior cars. Colored American citizens who may be convicted of petty offenses through unfriendly courts are subjected, while undergoing the sentence of said courts, to such cruel and inhuman treatment as to make their condition worse than abject slavery.

In addition to this, colored American citizens, when suspected of having committed certain offenses, and while in the custody of the so-called officers of the law, are in many instances, and, as we believe, with the knowledge and through the connivance of said officers, cowardly lynched and murdered without a hearing and without even a semblance of a trial. Our children in many of said States are not afforded the school facilities to which they are justly entitled, and which are essential to the future prosperity, not only of our race, but of both races and all sections of our country.

The labor system in most of the Southern States is unjust and unfair to the colored Americans. Being the principal laborers of that section, they are necessarily the sufferers to a greater extent than any other class from any unfavorable legislation on the subject of labor. The present system, at least in its results, is so injurious to the colored laborers in many parts of the South, that they seldom, if ever, enjoy a fair and reasonable portion of the fruits of their labor.

Under the Constitution and laws of the land we are entitled to the same rights and privileges enjoyed by any other class of citizens, and yet in defiance of law we find that we are subjected to taxation without representation.

We are compelled to obey laws that we have no voice in making. We are obliged in many localities to submit to the verdict of juries and decision of the courts in the creation and composition of which we are not allowed to participate. We, therefore, feel and believe that it is our duty, as it is certainly our privilege, to inform the country, through the medium of a national convention, of our grievances, having full faith in the fairness and justice of the American people. Public opinion, after all, especially in a democratic republic, is the supreme law of the land. To that tribunal we make our earnest appeal for justice and fair play. Political parties are the instruments through which the will of the people is executed. Our purpose is to impress upon the public mind the justice and fairness of our claims so that no political party can safely afford to ignore them.

If it is true that all our friends are in one party and our enemies in another, which we do not assert, that is a misfortune for which we are not responsible, and the existence of which we sincerely regret.

We feel that it is our duty to applaud the acts and indorse the utterances of our friends, it matters not where they are or to what party they may belong. We therefore urge upon the colored American voters of the United States, especially in localities the public sentiment of which secures to them the efficacy and potency of their votes, to support in the future only such candidates for public office as are known to be in favor of justice to the colored American citizen. To us this should be the paramount consideration. Questions relating to governmental policy and administration, as, for instance, the tariff, civil service reform and the financial policy of the Government, we should make secondary and subordinate. Without regard to the attitude of parties upon such questions, and without regard to our own views upon them, we feel that it is our duty to support only that party and only such candidates for office as are known to be friendly to our course, until all political parties will accord to us the rights and privileges to which we are entitled under the Constitution and laws of the land.

We earnestly petition the present Congress to so amend the Federal judiciary law as will make it possible for the Federal courts to organize juries that will be favorable to the enforcement of the laws.

We also petition the present Congress to enact into a law some such bill as the "Blair educational bill," believing, as we do, that it is the duty of the National Government to assist the several States in the education of the people, and that the money thus appropriated be apportioned on the basis of illiteracy.

We also petition the present Congress to so amend the national interstate commerce law as will nullify the effects of such State legislation as provides separate cars for white and colored passengers, believing, as we do, that such State legislation, so far as the same may be applicable to interstate roads, is clearly unconstitutional, to say nothing of its injustice.

We also petition the present Congress to pass such a law as will put Federal elections under Federal control.

We also petition Congress to pass a law re-imbursing the depositors of the late Freedman's Savings and Trust Company for the losses sustained by them through the failure of that institution.

The propositions now pending in Congress looking to the deportation or emigration of colored American citizens of this country to any other country, or even to any other part of our own country, through governmental aid, meets with our most emphatic condemnation and disapproval, for we cannot receive governmental aid to exile ourselves from this country as a neutralizing element against our own growing numbers or as an excuse for the nation not doing its duty toward us as American citizens. While we recognize the right of colored American citizens to go to any country they may desire, or to any part of our country, yet we do not believe that it is any part of the duty of the general Government to render any aid or assistance from the Federal Treasury for that purpose, and we do not ask it. All we ask is justice, equal rights, and fair play. If, under such circumstances, we cannot survive, we will have none to blame but ourselves.

We recommend the adoption of the following resolution by this convention:

Resolved, That the national organization created by this convention be authorized and instructed to call upon the President of the United States [Benjamin Harrison] and present him with a copy of this address, and also to thank him in the name of the convention for his friendly allusions to the Colored American in his message to Congress. Also to appear before the different committees of Congress having jurisdiction of the subject-matters referred to in this address, for the purpose of urging upon said committees the necessity for said proposed legislation, and to give reasons in detail for the same.

Senate Miscellaneous Document No. 82, 51st Cong., 1st Sess.

[m]

T. Thomas Fortune on Tuskegee

I have spent a week at Tuskegee, forty miles from Montgomery, investigating and studying the great work being done here, in the Tuskegee Normal and Industrial Institute, of which Mr. Booker T. Washington is the originator and projector. Mr. Washington is well known to New England people, and many of them have done much towards sustaining him and his work here. And a grand work it is, in the midst of a black population; the density of which is only exceeded by that of the black belt of South Carolina. Like a beacon light towering on high, among rocks and shoals, upon a dangerous coast, the Tuskegee Normal and Industrial Institute lifts its majestic head amid the blackness of this section of Alabama and the South. I heard of the work before I came here, but I had a very small idea of the necessity, the vastness and the thoroughness of it.

Here we have under control a thousand acres of land; here we have 400 colored sons, drinking in knowledge from the faithful ministrations of twenty-eight colored teachers, male and female. A more interesting spectacle can no where else be seen and studied. A great problem, mental, moral and industrial, is being solved and simplified even as we stand by and observe it. This vast gathering of souls eager to master the problems of life, is gathered into fourteen buildings of all degrees of size and architecture, every one of which was designed, the brick and lumber shaped, the work of construction done by these students, under the management and directions of colored superintendents. Splendid farm equipments, stock-raising, fruit culture, laundry work, practical housekeeping in all its branches, blacksmithing, wheelwrighting, carpentering, printing and building, shoe and harness making, masonry are all taught in their practical forms, while a splendid Normal school system is maintained to prepare school teachers for the great work before them. The saw and planing mill is a marvel in its way.

Only the English branches, the sciences and music are taught.

No time is wasted on dead languages or superfluous studies of any kind. What is practical, what will best fit these young people for the work of life, that is taught, and that is aimed at. Nor is moral and religious culture neglected. While being strictly non-sectarian, I never found a community more devout, more familiar with the Scriptures, more versed in the great truths of the Redeemer of mankind anywhere. This work is only eight years old. It began from nothing. It is worth to-day in dollars and cents more than $100,000. It is a monument to northern philanthropy and the execution and directing ability of our Washington. It costs $30,000 a year to run it. Twenty thousand dollars are given by philanthropists all over the country, $3,000 by the State of Alabama and the remainder is made up out of the school industries and the like. It is impossible to estimate the good the Tuskegee Normal and Industrial Institute has done and is doing. It is impossible to estimate the value of such a man as Booker T. Washington. It is to the eternal praise and glory of Northern and Western women and men that year after year they contribute liberally of their abundance to sustain the man and the work.

Christian Recorder, May 15, 1890.

III.

EXODUS

As the 1870's wore on and state after state in the South passed out of the hands of the Radical Reconstructionists, the Negro people thought more and more seriously of migration. Indeed during Reconstruction itself when the Radicals lost a particular state, movement of Negroes out of that area was characteristic. Normally this movement remained within the South, but some of it spilled out into the North or the West.

With the Hayes-Tilden agreement of 1877 sealing the murder of Reconstruction, certain Negro organizations—open and secret—and Negro leaders began to plan definitely for a mass exodus. The first major explosion occurred in January and February, 1879, and was centered in, though not confined to, southern Louisiana. A bad crop, a devastating yellow fever epidemic, an unsuccessful effort on the part of Negro tenants to force a reduction in rent, the end of Reconstruction, peonage, violence, absence of educational facilities, widespread disfranchisement, and abuse of Negro women produced—after years of careful planning and preparation—an exodus which saw something like 50,000 Negroes move North within a few months.

Most of these men, women and children headed for Kansas—the land whence came John Brown. In doing this, these Negroes were joining, for their own particular reasons, a swelling torrent of humanity for it must be remembered that the population of Kansas leaped from 364,000 in 1870 to 1,428,000 in 1890.

In the past this great Negro exodus has been treated as a spontaneous movement inspired by a Moses in the guise of the aged Benjamin Singleton. The fact is, as already indicated, that the exodus was the culmination of a steady process of migration and came in response to years of preparation, in the latter of which the somewhat eccentric Singleton played a secondary role.

After this first great outpouring subsided early in 1880, a trickling of movement continued and occasionally reached flood proportions. Notable among these were the migration of several thousand Negro families out of South Carolina in 1881 and out of Alabama in 1889. These phenomena gave rise to widespread consideration among Negro leaders of the wisdom, in terms of the struggle for liberation, of the tactic of migration.

To illustrate the facts concerning these organized mass flights and the expression of opinions among Negroes concerning them, five sets of documents are published below.

The first group [a] consists of the final report of the Business Committee of a Convention of Louisiana Negroes devoted to the question of migration held in New Orleans in April, 1879. The second group [b] consists of the testimony of Negro participants in the 1879 exodus given before a Senate Committee appointed December 18, 1879 to investigate the movement. The Negroes were Henry Adams, John H. Burch, John H. Johnson, Daniel Parker and Benjamin Singleton, of whom more will be said as they appear. In the third group [c] will be found extracts pertinent to migration from the proceedings of the National Conference of Colored Men held in Nashville in May, 1879, and attended by 140 delegates from 19 states and the District of Columbia, including such figures as John R. Lynch of Mississippi, John W. Cromwell of Washington,

William Still of Philadelphia, N. W. Cuney of Galveston and Richard R. Wright of Georgia.

The fourth group [d] consists of extracts from addresses on migration delivered in September, 1879 by Frederick Douglass and Professor Richard T. Greener, formerly of the University of South Carolina and then of Howard University. Greener favored the movement as an important and necessary element in the liberation struggle, while Douglass, though seeing some tactical value to the move, nevertheless held it to be ill-advised in strategic terms, as representing a tendency to abandon rather than heighten the liberation effort.

The last item in this section [e] consists of a letter dated February 1, 1889, dealing with the mass movements of that year. It was written by Booker T. Washington and sent to George W. Cable, the distinguished Louisiana author, whose *The Silent South* (1885) aroused great indignation from the very articulate masters of that South.

[a]

Louisiana Negro Convention, 1879

The committee * find that the primary cause of this [exodus] lies in the absence of a republican form of government to the people of Louisiana. Crime and lawlessness existing to an extent that laughs at all restraint and the misgovernment naturally induced from a State administration, itself the product of violence, have created an absorbing and constantly increasing distrust and alarm among our people throughout the State. All rights of freemen denied and all claims to a just recompense for labor rendered, or honorable dealings between planter and laborer disallowed, justice a mockery, and the law a cheat, the very officers of the courts being themselves the mobocrats and violators of law, the only remedy left the colored citizen in many parishes of our State today is to emigrate. The fiat to go forth is irresistible. The constantly recurring, nay, ever present, fear which haunts the minds of these our people in the turbulent parishes of the State is, that slavery in the horrid form of peonage is approaching; that the avowed disposition of the men now in power is to reduce the laborer and his interest to the minimum of advantages as freemen and to absolutely none as citizens, has produced so absolute a fear that in many cases it has become a panic. It is flight from present sufferings and from the wrongs to come. The committee finds that this exodus owes its effectiveness to society organizations among plantation laborers; that it began with the persecutions and political

* This report of the Committee of Business was dated April 21, 1879. The Committee's chairman was George T. Ruby, then editor of the New Orleans *Observer*. Mr. Ruby was born in New York City in 1841 and had written for the New York *Tribune* and *Times*. During the Civil War he went to New Orleans, serving as a teacher from 1864 to 1866. He then went to Texas, edited the Galveston *Standard*, 1866–68, and later served in the Texas Senate. He returned to New Orleans in 1874.

mobs of the years 1874 and 1875, and was organized as a colonization council in August, 1874, for emigration. This organization beginning in Caddo Parish, spread rapidly from parish to parish until it has permeated the State, and in sections particularly known as the cotton belt, where lawlessness and outrages upon black citizens are most frequent, the society has been most active.

Today this organization, as your committee has definitely learned, numbers on its rolls 92,800 names of men, women and children over twelve years of age, in Louisiana, Northwestern Texas, Arkansas, Mississippi, and Alabama; 69,000 of these are represented in the different parishes of this State. The cohesiveness of this organization in its secrecy and management being entirely committed to plantation laborers and their direct representatives, has secured its potency. The representative political leader was neither intrusted with nor informed of its existence. Year by year since 1874 the organization, as encroachment after encroachment was made on the rights of the colored people, grew and strengthened, and now when reduced to virtual peonage and the threatened deprivation of all rights as freemen and citizens is imminent, the exodus has ensued and its consequences are manifest.

Your committee, had it the power in its recommendations or councils to stem the tide of this mighty movement, would not prove so delinquent to all ties of brotherhood and to every attribute of manliness as to impede or offer a single check to so righteously just an emigration. On the contrary, we would wisely and practically aid it.

Senate Report 693, 46th Cong., 2d Sess., part 2, p. 39.

[b]

Negroes Discuss the Exodus

1. Henry Adams: *

Question: † Now tell us, Mr. Adams, what, if anything, you know about the exodus of the colored people from the Southern to the Northern and

---

* Henry Adams appears to have been the single most influential person behind the 1879 exodus. He was born a slave in Georgia in 1843 and came to Louisiana in 1850. He was "at hard work all my life" and the War freed him. In 1865 he was in Shreveport and the next year entered the Army. The rest of his story to 1879 appears in his testimony.

† The questions were put early in 1880 by various members of the Senatorial committee. The committee consisted of three Democrats—Daniel W. Voorhees (Indiana), Zebulon B. Vance (North Carolina), George H. Pendleton (Ohio); and two Republicans, William Windom (Minnesota), and Henry W. Blair (New Hampshire). After the first question and answer, the "question" and "answer" given in the source are dropped.

Western States; and be good enough to tell us in the first place what you know about the organization of any committee or society among the colored people themselves for the purpose of bettering their condition, and why it was organized. Just give us a history of that as you understand it. *Answer:* Well, in 1870, I believe it was, or about that year, after I had left the Army— I went into the Army in 1866 and came out the last of 1869—and went right back home again where I went from, Shreveport; I enlisted there, and went back there. I enlisted in the Regular Army, and then I went back after I came out of the Army. After we had come out a parcel of we men that was in the Army and other men thought that the way our people had been treated during the time we was in service—we heard so much talk of how they had been treated and opposed so much and there was no help for it—that caused me to go into the Army at first, the way our people was opposed. There was so much going on that I went off and left it; when I came back it was still going on, part of it, not quite so bad as at first. So a parcel of us got together and said that we would organize ourselves into a committee and look into affairs and see the true condition of our race, to see whether it was possible we could stay under a people who had held us under bondage or not. Then we did so and organized a committee.

What did you call your committee? We just called it a committee, that is all we called it, and it remained so; it increased to a large extent, and remained so. Some of the members of the committee was ordered by the committee to go into every State in the South where we had been slaves there, and post one another from time to time about the true condition of our race, and nothing but the truth.

You mean some members of your committee? That committee; yes, sir.

They traveled over the other States? Yes, sir; and we worked some of us, worked our way from place to place and went from State to State and worked—some of them did—amongst our people in the fields, everywhere, to see what sort of living our people lived; whether we could remain in the South amongst the people who had held us as slaves or not. We continued that on till 1874.

Now, before you come to 1874, let me ask you how extensive was the operation of your committee? Did they go into almost all the Southern States? Nearly all of the States we could get reports from as to how our race was living there.

Whom did you report to? To the committee; we reported to the Committee there.

To the committee at Shreveport? Yes. The reports were sent, and our committee met, so that they would be read at the meeting.

Were they addressed to the committee or to some individual? They were addressed to some individual of the committee—just addressed to the members or ones that we knowed belonged to the committee, and knowed would get the letters we would write to them.

Was the object of that committee at that time to remove your people from the South, or what was it? O, no, sir; not then; we just wanted to see whether there was any State in the South where we could get a living and enjoy our rights.

The object, then, was to find out the best places in the South where you could live? Yes, sir; where we could live and get along well there and to investigate our affairs—not to go nowhere till we saw whether we could stand it.

How were the expenses of these men paid? Every one paid his own expenses, except the one we sent to Louisiana and Mississippi. We took money out of our pockets and sent him, and said to him you must now go to work. You can't find out anything till you get amongst them. You can talk as much as you please, but you have got to go right into the field and work with them and sleep with them to know all about them.

Have you any idea how many of your people went out in that way?

At one time there was five hundred of us.

Do you mean five hundred belonging to your committee? Yes, sir.

I want to know how many traveled in that way to get at the condition of your people in the Southern States? I think about one hundred or one hundred and fifty went from one place or another.

And they went from one place to another, working their way and paying their expenses and reporting to the common center at Shreveport, do you mean? Yes, sir.

What was the character of the information that they gave you?

Well, the character of the information they brought to us was very bad, sir.

In what respect? They said that in other parts of the country where they traveled through, and what they saw they was comparing with what we saw and what we had seen in the part where we lived; we knowed what that was; and they cited several things that they saw in their travels; it was very bad.

Do you remember any of these reports that you get from members of your committee? Yes, sir; they said in several parts where they was that the land rent was still higher there in that part of the country than it was where we first organized it, and the people was still being whipped, some of them, by the old owners, the men that had owned them as slaves, and some of them was being cheated out of their crops just the same as they was there.

Was anything said about their personal and political rights in these reports, as to how they were treated about these? Yes, some of them stated that in some parts of the country where they voted they would be shot. Some of them stated that if they voted the Democratic ticket they would not be injured.

But that they would be shot, or might be shot, if they voted the Republican ticket? Yes, sir.

State what was the general character of these reports—I have not yet got down to your organization of 1874—whether what you have given was the general character; were there some safer places found that seemed a little better? Some of the places, of course, were a little better than others. Some men that owned some of the plantations would treat the people pretty well in some parts. We found that they would try to pay what they had promised from time to time; some they didn't pay near what they had promised; and in some places the families—some families—would make from five to a hundred bales of cotton to the family; then at the end of the year they would pay the owner of the land out of that amount at the end of the year, maybe one hundred dollars. Cotton was selling then at twenty-five cents a pound, and at the end of the year when they came to settle up with the owner of the land, they would not get a dollar sometimes, and sometimes they would get thirty dollars, and sometimes a hundred dollars out of a hundred bales of cotton.

What were the best localities that you heard from, if you remember, where they were treated the best? In Virginia was what they stated was the State that treated them best in the South; Virginia and Missouri, and Kentucky, and Tennessee.

There the treatment was better was it? Yes, sir; it was better there.

Had you any reports from North Carolina? Some few from North Carolina.

Do you remember anything about them; or is your knowledge of that State only general? Well, they reported that some parts of North Carolina was very bad and other parts was very good. . . .

I am speaking now of the period from 1870 to 1874, and you have given us the general character of the reports that you got from the South; what did you do in 1874? Well, along in August sometime in 1874, after the white league sprung up, they organized and said this is a white man's government, and the colored men should not hold any offices; they were no good but to work in the fields and take what they would give them and vote the Democratic ticket. That's what they would make public speeches and say to us, and we would hear them. We then organized an organization called the colonization council.

What was the difference between that organization and your committee, as to its objects? Well, the committee was to investigate the condition of our race.

And this organization was then to better your condition after you had found out what that condition was? Yes, sir.

The result of this investigation during these four years by your committee was the organization of this colonization council. Is that the way you wish me to understand it? It caused it to be organized.

It caused it to be organized. Now, what was the purpose of this colonization council? Well, it was to better our condition.

In what way did you propose to do it? We first organized and adopted a plan to appeal to the President of the United States and to Congress to help us out of our distress, or protect us in our rights and privileges.

Well, what other plan had you? And if that failed our idea was then to ask them to set apart a territory in the United States for us, somewhere where we could go and live with our families.

You preferred to go off somewhere by yourselves? Yes.

Well, what then? If that failed, our other object was to ask for an appropriation of money to ship us all to Liberia, in Africa; somewhere where we could live in peace and quiet.

Well, and what after that? When that failed then our idea was to appeal to other governments outside of the United States to help us to get away from the United States and go there and live under their flag.

Well, what did your council do now under these various modes of relief which they had marked out for themselves? Well, we appealed, as we promised.

Did you make any appeal to Congress and to the President? Yes, sir.

Who, in your association, authorized that appeal; how was it gotten up? It was gotten up by resolution.

By resolution? Yes, sir; and just passed by the organization.

Well, by "the organization," what do you mean? I mean the members of it.

Did they have meetings? Yes, sir.

How were these meetings held and where did you hold them? We held them in rooms and houses.

Were they secret meetings or public? We didn't allow nobody in there but our friends. If he was not a member he couldn't get in until we came out in public. When we called a public meeting we came out to the park or anywhere, and didn't care who heard. Then anybody could participate who believed in our movement.

Now, let us understand, before we go any further, the kind of people who composed that association. The committee, as I understand you, was composed entirely of laboring people? Yes, sir.

Did it include any politicians of either color, white or black?

No politicianers didn't belong to it, because we didn't allow them to know nothing about it . . . we didn't trust any of them . . .

Now, when you organized the council what kind of people were taken into it? Nobody but laboring men . . . When we met in committee there was not any of us allowed to tell our name . . . We first appealed to President Grant . . . That was in September, 1874 . . . at other times we sent to Congress . . . We told them our condition, and asked Congress to help us out of our distress and protect us in our lives and property, and pass some law or provide some way that we might get our rights in the South, and so forth . . . After the appeal in 1874, we appealed when the time got so hot down there they stopped our churches from having meetings after nine o'clock at night. They stopped them from sitting up and singing over the dead, and so forth, right in the little town where we lived, in Shreveport. I know that to be a fact; and after they did all this, and we saw it was getting so warm—killing our people all over the whole country—there was several of them killed right down in our parish—we appealed . . . We had much rather staid there [South] if we could have had our rights . . . In 1877 we lost all hopes . . . we found ourselves in such condition that we looked around and we seed that there was no way on earth, it seemed, that we could better our condition there, and we discussed that thoroughly in our organization along in May. We said that the whole South—every State in the South—had got into the hands of the very men that held us slaves—from one thing to another and we thought that the men that held us slaves was holding the reins of government over our heads in every respect almost, even the constable up to the governor. We felt we had almost as well be slaves under these men. In regard to the whole matter that was discussed, it came up in every council. Then we said there was no hope for us and we had better go . . . Then, in 1877 we appealed to President Hayes and to Congress, to both Houses. I am certain we sent papers there; if they didn't get them that is not our fault; we sent them. . . . Mighty few ministers would allow us to have their churches [for meetings]; some few would in some of the parishes . . . When we held our meetings we would not allow the politicians to speak. . . . it is not exactly five hundred men belonging to the council . . . they have now got at this time 98,000 names enrolled . . . men and women, and none under twelve years old . . . some in Louisiana—the majority of them in Louisiana, and some in Texas, and some in Arkansas . . . a few in Mississippi . . . a few in Alabama [and] in a great many of the others . . .

Now, Mr. Adams, you know, probably, more about the causes of the exodus from that country than any other man, from your connection with it; tell us in a few words what you believe to be the causes of these people going away? Well, the cause is, in my judgment, and from what information I have received, and what I have seen with my own eyes—it is because the largest majority of the people, of the white people, that held us as slaves treats our people so bad in many respects that it is impossible for them to stand it. Now, in a great many parts of that country there our people most as well be slaves as to be free; because, in the first place, I will state this: that in some times, in times of politics, if they have any idea that the Republicans will carry a parish or ward, or something of that kind, why, they would do anything on God's earth. There ain't nothing too mean for them to do to prevent it; nothing I can make mention of is too mean for them to do. . . .

Senate Report 693, 46th Cong., 2nd Sess., part 2, pp. 101–111.

2. John H. Burch: *

I want to ask you how the colored women, the wives of these colored men down there, look upon this exodus? Well, the women have had more to do with it than all the politics and men in the country. These women since reconstruction, have followed their husbands and brothers and all who had a vote, from morning to night, around the parishes demanding that they should vote the Republican ticket, especially if they heard that their husband, or brother, or father, was likely to vote the Democratic ticket. They have been very active since 1868 in all the political movements; they form a large number in all the political assemblages, and they have evidenced a deep interest in all that pertains to politics so far as their husbands and fathers and brothers were concerned; they have always placed their desire that they should vote the Republican ticket on the ground that it was only through the Republican party and the principles of that party that they could secure homes for themselves and educational advantages for their children, and protection in all the rights accorded to them by the Constitution of the nation. And so they have followed up their husbands and brothers and fathers until they have seen their Republican government swept away from under them; and now they have turned their attention to emigration. There is in New Orleans today a committee formed in 1878, that was called then the "committee of five hundred women," of which Mrs. Mary J. Garrett is president; her name is now Mary Jane Nelson—she married this year. Are they colored women? Yes, sir; they are all colored women. This

* John H. Burch was connected with the New Orleans *Louisianian* in 1870 and the Baton Rouge *Courier* in 1871. He served in the Louisiana House and Senate.

committee published an address in 1878, that I am very sorry I have not with me now, in which they demanded every right and privilege that the Constitution guarantees to their race, and that they should use every power in their hands to get it.

Senate Report 693, 46th Cong., 2nd Sess., part 2, pp. 232–33.

3. John H. Johnson: *

What did the Negroes give as their reasons for migrating? They stated that they had no security for life, limb, or property; that they worked year in and year out, and, notwithstanding they raised good crops, they were at the end of the year in debt; that they were charged exorbitant prices for provisions, and all these things kept them down and in debt. The high prices charged them for lands and the denial of their rights as citizens induced them to leave and seek a genial spot where they could have an opportunity to build up themselves and their families. Some of them stated that they had been on plantations alongside of theirs where men were shot down for political purposes, and the women stated all the impositions practiced on colored women in the South. . . . We tried to get some of them to return, and consulted with them on the subject, and they said they would rather go into the open prairie and starve there than go to the South to stand the impositions that were put on them down there. . . . If they were treated as human beings, to say nothing of their citizenship they would remain. The South is the home of the colored man . . . He has improved that part of the country, and done more to advance the material interests of the South than any other race or nation can do . . . If he had his rights under the Constitution he would remain. If he were allowed the opportunity of purchasing a homestead in the South he would remain. If he were encouraged in his efforts to get along he would remain.

Senate Report 693, 46th Cong., 2nd Sess., part 2, pp. 290–94.

4. Affidavit of Daniel Parker:

My name is Daniel Parker; my age is about twenty-nine years; I have been living for the last few years on Widow Crane's place, about 3 miles from Delta, Louisiana; made a very bad living; paying $10 an acre rent; the colored people in the South received no favors at all from the white people; the reason I left the South was we had organized a club to get a reduction in rent, and I had been made president of the club, on Widow Crane's place; I was accused of teaching the people to leave the South, and heard that threats had been made against my life; I was afraid they would make away with me at night; a young man had lived right next me moved in Tensas

---

* John H. Johnson was a 34 year old Negro attorney of St. Louis who was Secretary of the Colored Refugee Board of that city.

Parish, told me that the bulldozers along in August or September, 1878, came into that parish and killed and slaughtered men there just for fun; his name was Ed. Danby; I said, "Ed, do you go round there now and tell the people how to vote?" He said no, he had taken to preaching now—if he told the people how to vote there would be a man short there . . . I want to go to Topeka, Kans.; my wife and two children are down in Madison Parish; I had to leave without them . . . the landowners in the South did everything they could to prevent us from leaving. . . .

Senate Report 693, 46th Cong., 2nd Sess., part 3, p. 51.

5. Benjamin Singleton: *

What made you help in the migration? Well, my people, for the want of land—we needed land for our children—and their disadvantages that caused my heart to grieve and sorrow; pity for my race, sir, that was coming down, instead of going up—that caused me to go to work for them. . . . Right emphatically, I tell you today, I woke up the millions right through me! The great God of glory has worked in me. I have had open interviews with the living spirit of God for my people; and we are going to leave the South. We are going to leave it if there ain't an alteration and signs of a change.

What do you mean by a change? Well, I am not going to stand bulldozing and half pay and all those things. . . . I am the whole cause of the Kansas migration! . . . Allow me to say to you that confidence is perished and faded away; they have been lied to every year . . . My plan is for them to leave the country and learn the South a lesson . . . We don't want to leave the South, and just as soon as we have confidence in the South, I am going to be an instrument in the hands of God to persuade every man to go back, because that is the best country.

Senate Report 693, 46th Cong., 2nd Sess., part 3, pp. 380–83.

[c]

The National Conference of Colored Men, 1879

1. Resolution introduced by W. H. Councill of Alabama: †

Resolved, That whereas the principal business men and farmers have entered into contracts for the present year, we deem this an untimely season

---

* Benjamin Singleton was born in Tennessee in 1810. In 1869 he formed, in Nashville, the Tennessee Real Estate and Homestead Association and from that date to 1880 he assisted some 7,000 Negroes in leaving the deep South. In June, 1879 he and other Negroes incorporated The Singleton Colony of Morris and Lyon Counties, Kansas, which became one of the many centers to which the refugees moved. Singleton's own claims of being "the whole cause" of the exodus were grossly exaggerated, though later writers on the subject have treated the movement in that way.
† William H. Councill was President of the State Normal School at Huntsville. His ideas and conduct were at least as conservative as those of Booker T. Washington.

to agitate the question of migration; believing that it would prove detrimental to the interests of all concerned.

2. That we are opposed to a general and sudden exodus of our people for any part of the country, but recommend a careful consideration of the matter for all who desire to migrate, and after such mature consideration and calm reflection, if they are satisfied that their condition can be improved by emigration we advise gradual migration.

3. That the emigration question should be considered apart from politics, and should be based upon business calculation.

2. Letter from Charleston, S.C. Colored Western Emigration Society:

What is mere freedom to man without civil and political rights? . . . The boast is proudly made that this.is a white man's government. Let us appeal to the good people of the country to aid us in changing the place of our abode to the free States and Territories. We have willing hands as ever; we have strong arms still. We are sneeringly told that we are poor and have not the means of defraying our expenses in removing from here to the free States . . . We have no apology to make for our poverty. It comes illy from those who have enjoyed our unrequited labor for hundreds of years the taunt that we are poor . . .

3. Report of the Committee on Address: *

The disposition to leave the communities in which they feel insecure, is an evidence of a healthy growth in manly independence, and should receive the commendation and support of all philanthropists . . . In the light of these facts [the Negro's contributions to the nation] we demand, in the name of the citizenship conferred by the organic law of the land, in the name of humanity and Christian brotherhood, the same treatment accorded the other nationalities of our common country—nothing more, nothing less.

Proceedings of the National Conference of Colored Men of the United States, held in the State Capitol at Nashville, Tenn., May 6–9, 1879 (Washington, 1879), pp. 12, 16–17, 95.

[d]

Douglass and Greener on the Exodus, 1879

1. Frederick Douglass:

The Negro, long deemed to be too indolent and stupid to discover and

* The chairman of this committee was P. B. S. Pinchback, formerly Acting Governor of Louisiana.

adopt any rational measure to secure and defend his rights as a man, may now be congratulated upon the telling contradiction which he has recently and strikingly given to this withering disparagement and reproach. He has discovered and adopted a measure which may assist very materially in the solution of some of the vital problems involved in his sudden elevation from slavery to freedom, and from chattelhood to manhood, and citizenship . . . he has adopted a simple, lawful and peaceable measure. It is emigration—the quiet withdrawal of his valuable bones and muscles from a condition of things which he considers no longer tolerable. Innocent as this remedy is for the manifold ills, which he has thus far borne with marvellous patience, fortitude, and forbearance, it is none the less significant and effective. . . . This exodus has revealed to southern men the humiliating fact that the prosperity and civilization of the South are at the mercy of the despised and hated Negro. . . .

Political tricksters, land speculators, defeated office seekers, Northern malignants, speeches and resolutions in the Senate, unaided by other causes, could not, of themselves, have set such a multitudinous Exodus in motion . . . We have the story of the emigrants themselves, and if any can reveal the true cause of this Exodus they can . . . They tell us with great unanimity that they are very badly treated at the South . . .

[As a strategy, however] it is a surrender, a premature, disheartening surrender, since it would make freedom and free institutions depend upon migration rather than protection; by flight, rather than right . . . It leaves the whole question of equal rights on the soil of the South open and still to be settled . . . it is a confession of the utter unpracticability of equal rights and equal protection in any State, where those rights may be struck down by violence . . . The dissemination of this doctrine by the agents of emigration, cannot but do the cause of equal rights much harm. It lets the public mind down from the high ground of a great national duty, to a miserable compromise, in which wrong surrenders nothing and right everything . . . Does not one exodus invite another, and in advocating one do we not sustain the demand for another? . . .

As an assertion of power by a people hitherto held in bitter contempt; as an emphatic and stinging protest against high-handed, greedy and shameless injustice to the weak and defenceless; as a means of opening the blind eyes of oppressors to their folly and peril, the Exodus has done valuable service. Whether it has accomplished all of which it is capable in this particular direction for the present, is a question which may well be considered. With a moderate degree of intelligent leadership among the laboring class at the South, properly handling the justice of their cause, and wisely using the Exodus example, they can easily exact better terms for their labor than ever before. Exodus is medicine, not food. If it is attempted by force or fraud to compel the colored people to stay, then they should by all means go; go quickly, and die, if need be, in the attempt . . . In no case must the Negro be "bottled up" or "caged up" . . . Woe to the oppressed and destitute of all countries and races if the rich and powerful are to decide when and where they shall go or stay . . . The cry of "Land and Liberty," the watchword of the Nihilistic party in Russia, has a music in it sweet to the ear of all oppressed peoples, and well it shall be for the landholders of the South if they shall learn wisdom in time and adopt such a course of just treatment towards the landless laborers of the South in the future as shall make the popular watchword uncontagious and unknown among their laborers, and further stampede to the North wholly unknown. . . .

2. Richard T. Greener:

While time has modified his [Douglass'] extreme views, and more recent events have blunted the edge of his sarcasm, and while most of his objections are of the negative rather than the positive order, against the methods and men who seek to help the movement, rather than against the Exodus itself, still the *morale* of his influence is in opposition . . . it may be said, no favorer of migration claims it as the sole, proper or only permanent remedy for the aggravated relation of landlord and tenant at the South. It is approved as one remedy, thus far the most salutary, in stopping lawlessness and exactions. . . .

We must organize societies, contribute our dimes, and form a network of communication between the South and every principal point North and West. We should raise $200,000 to form a company; we should have a National Executive Committee, and have agents to buy land, procure cheap transportation, disseminate accurate information, and see to it that they are neither deluded nor defrauded. Such an organization, working through our churches and benevolent societies, would do more to develop our race than all the philanthropic measures designed to aid us since the war.

Addresses delivered before the American Social Science Association, September 12, 1879 and published in the *Journal of Social Science* (Boston, May, 1880), XI, pp. 1–35.

[e]

Washington to Cable, 1889

I have kept you waiting in order to get what information I could on the subject of your letter. Within the last year about 1 dozen families in good circumstances have left Montgomery [Alabama] & vicinity and settled in California. But those [who] are now leaving and have been doing so since Xmas in large numbers are the common plantation hands. I suppose 600 have gone from Montgomery and adjoining counties within the time mentioned. The majority are going to La. and Mississippi bottoms where flattering inducements are held out by labor agents who are paying the traveling expenses. As to the causes, I feel quite sure it is to be found in the fact that the colored people are tired [of] working hard all the year and getting nothing for it. It is simply impossible under the present mortgage system for them to get ahead—they can not pay 25 & 30 per cent interest on the dollar and many of them have reached the conclusion that no change can make their condition worse.

The Journal of Negro Education (Fall, 1948), XVII, p. 463.

IV.

NEGRO PARTICIPATION IN GENERAL MASS ORGANIZATIONS

Mass organizations favoring democratic reforms have always included Negro members. In the post-Reconstruction years, many thousands of Negroes actively participated in political and economic struggles carried on by such groups as the Greenbackers, Readjusters, Fusionists, Union Laborites and Knights of Labor. Within the Knights of Labor, a labor organization welcoming men and women, Negro and white, there were, in the 1880's, about 75,000 Negroes including such outstanding leaders as the New York machinist, Frank J. Ferrell; and within the protest parties enumerated above which prepared the soil for the flowering of the People's or Populist Party in 1892, Negroes were quite active, particularly, of course, in the South.

To illustrate this type of activity five documents are published below. The first [a] is a letter dated Lynchburg, Virginia, November 20, 1879 from George M. Arnold to his Philadelphia friend, Isaiah H. Wears. This deals with the formation of the Readjuster Party in Virginia—a coalition of anti-Democratic and Radical Republican whites and Negroes—which controlled the state apparatus from 1879 to the November election of 1883.

The second document [b] consists of the speech made by John R. Lynch of Mississippi to the Federal House of Representatives on April 27, 1882, as the culmination of his eighteen-month-long struggle contesting the seating of his opponent. Mr. Lynch's speech demonstrates the existence of strong post-Reconstruction political activity by the Negro people, even in Mississippi, and the presence of Negro-white unity. Lynch won this battle, the House voting to seat him, April 29, 1882, by a vote of 124–84.

The third document [c] is a campaign circular issued by Virginia Negroes just prior to the state election of November 6, 1883, appealing for support of the Readjuster party and enumerating its substantial accomplishments of the previous three years. The party was defeated by fraud and violence, as will be seen in a document appearing in the following section of this work.

The final documents relate to the Knights of Labor. The fourth [d] consists of a letter from an anonymous Negro calling, in 1886, for the support of the

Knights of Labor and referring to a high degree of unity achieved in his New York Assembly District. The last document [e] exemplifies the presence of white supremacist thinking and activity even within so progressive an organization as was the Knights of Labor. This failing accompanied, and in turn accelerated, the decline of that labor organization. In this document John Lucus Dennis, a Negro puddler at the Black Diamond Steel Works in Pittsburgh, writes, August 8, 1887, on a strike then in progress and expresses his concern with prevalent anti-Negro attitudes within the local organization of Knights.

[a]

Letter to Wears,* 1879

I take the liberty to drop you a word in reference to the late election in this State, for the purpose of endeavoring to explain to you and through you other representative men in the North, the real and absolute state of affairs, having special reference to the matter of Colored Republicans voting with the so-called Readjusters in this state Nov. 4th 1879.

I am a colored man, southern born, an ex-Union Soldier, and I venture to hope, a Republican of a devoted faith in the principals of the party. The vote that I will speak of *did* somewhat surprise me, and the causes that led to such a large vote, in the way 'twas given, is what I take this occasion to explain from an unprejudiced standpoint. To be brief, and at the same time plain, I beg leave to say that the large number of votes polled by Colored Citizens, for candidates of the Readjusters, was not done to approve of Repudiation [of the State debt], not at all. The leaders, and the leaders' followers, that were known during the campaign as Readjusters, disclaimed any intention whatever of such a thing as Repudiation.

Still to be frank I will state that some one or two candidates avowed themselves as frankly as language could convey the matter, as out and out repudiationists. I dont remember at this writing of but these two cases. To tell the real issue as it *was*. Square and frankly it is to say that it was *not* whether or not the debt should be settled by the McCollouch Bill of the last general assembly, or otherwise, but whether or not a new set of rulers for the Democratic conservative party of Virginia should supercede those that have had absolute control since the administration of Ex-Governor Gilbert C. Walker. Now, be it understood that under the rule of the Democratic party in this state every judge is elected by the legislature, which is and has been two-thirds Democratic, and all nominations that have been agreed to by the general assembly have been the caucus party choice, and

---

* Isaiah T. Wears was born free in Baltimore in 1822, and lived most of his life in Philadelphia where he died in 1900. He was prominent in the Abolitionist movement, and a leader in the post-Civil War Philadelphia Negro community.

the bitterest and violent partisans have been made judges, and these judges control the selection of juries absolutely without appeal!

Under this state of affairs there has not been, since Gov. Walker's day, three colored men in this State on petty juries. Add to this the fact that the street corner democratic bummer and striker, ballot box stuffer, gamblers, and men of the party faith who live open and above board in open adultery with Negro and white mistresses, have been put on the juries, and in the last circuit court here the foreman thereof is known as a man who has for years publicly lived in open and bold adultery with a Negro woman: also on recent juries I *have seen this with my own eyes*, men were on the jury to try cases wherein colored men were to be tried, who from one day the beginning of the year, to the last day the ending of it, have no visible means of support and are known as "men of the town." I need not tell you that the cities of Norfolk, Richmond, Petersburg and Lynchburg have a large intelligent business colored community, and for all other purposes, save to sit on juries, they are considered exceptionally good, and when these people voted last election who can and will blame them for casting their vote against the men and the measures that strive to deprive them of their civil and political liberties?

It is the way and manner that colored men and women have been treated in this state by the Democratic conservative party, that party that has cheated them out of two congressmen, and counted in one more who has never been elected; the party that takes the black man's school-tax dollar, but will not count his vote, that gives him teachers for his colored children that will not teach them as pupils but as brutes should be taught; this party that enacts a law, extra of the state constitution, that puts in the state prison men and women for the crime(?) of marrying according to the dictates of their inclinations, and consciences, but allows the fullest liberty to whites who live in open and public adultery with colored women, and even honor them by placing them in high civil, municipal and state places. . . .

One word more about the colored people. You know how true the colored Virginian was to the union in the dark and stormy days of the War both as a friend to the captive Union soldier, and then himself as a soldier. I say you know this because you were in a position to observe well and think well. You also have had ample opportunities to find out his devotion to the Union and the love of liberty since he was introduced as a voter. He is as true now as in the past—and when the great party of Nationality Union Freedom and Liberty wants his help, it will not be withheld. He is no Repudiationist, nor did he vote so in the last election. On the other hand he is by nature a National Republican, but in the contest just decided he voted to do away with a party and parties that have well-nigh made him wish he had never been made a citizen. Patience, time will vindicate the position of the colored voters, who sustained the Readjusters in the election in this state Nov. 4th 1879.

MS. in Papers of Isaiah T. Wears, in Leon Gardiner Collection on Negro History, library of the Pennsylvania Historical Society.

[b]

Speech by John R. Lynch, 1882

Mr. Speaker, in presenting this case to the House and to the country I will not discuss the legal questions that are involved; nor will I review the testimony that has been taken. These points have been and will be forcibly presented by members of the committee who have familiarized themselves with the case. I will content myself with calling public attention to the disreputable system of elections of which the pending case is a natural and necessary growth.

Out of 21,143 votes polled the contestee [James R. Chalmers] actually received about 5,000. In the counties of Adams, Claiborne, Jefferson, Washington, and Wilkinson something over 5,000 votes were counted and returned for him that were polled against him. Giving him the benefit of these frauds, he was still defeated by a majority of 663. His pretended claim to the seat is based upon the action of election commissioners or county returning boards in several counties in throwing out over 5,000 Republican tickets that had been received, counted, and returned by the precinct inspectors. . . .

The Southern Bourbons are simply determined not to tolerate honest differences of opinion upon political questions. They make no distinction between those who have the courage, the manhood, and the independence to array themselves in opposition to Bourbon methods and measures. It matters not what name the opposition may assume nor of what elements it may be composed. They may call themselves Republicans, or Greenbackers as in some localities, or Independents as in others, or Readjusters as in Virginia. The fact that they oppose the ascendency of Bourbon Democracy makes them, from a Bourbon standpoint enemies to the South, to its interests and to its people. All that is needed at the South today is the inculcation of a just and liberal public sentiment which will destroy political proscription and intolerance. That being done a full vote, a free ballot, and a fair count will necessarily follow, for it is an indisputable fact that fraud and violence have, as the basis of their existence, proscription and intolerance. [Applause.] . . .

I am aware of the fact that Southern Republicans are sometimes reproached because they do not make forcible resistance to the perpetration of these frauds; but it must be remembered that the frauds are always committed under some sort of color of law. . . . The frauds are always committed either by the sworn officers of the law or by others with their knowledge and approval. What lawful redress have Republicans, then, except to do just what I am now doing?

You certainly cannot expect them to resort to mob law or brute force, or to use what may be milder language, inaugurate a revolution. My opinion is that revolution is not the remedy to be applied in such cases. Our system of government is supposed to be one of law and order, resting upon the consent of the governed, as expressed through the peaceful medium of the ballot. . . .

The impartial historian will record the fact that the colored people of the South have contended for their rights with a bravery and a gallantry that is worthy of the highest commendation. Being, unfortunately, in dependent circumstances, with the preponderance of the wealth and intelligence against them in some localities, yet they have bravely refused to surrender their honest convictions, even upon the altar of their personal necessities. They have said to those upon whom they depended: You may deprive me for the time being of the opportunity of making an honest living; you may take the bread out of the mouths of my hungry and dependent family; you may close the school-house door in the face of my children; yea, more, you may take that which no man can give, my life, but my manhood, my principles you cannot have! [Applause.] . . .

Mr. Speaker, this disgraceful system of election frauds in several of the Southern States through and by which that section was made solid in its support of one of the great political parties of the day ought, must, and will be destroyed. [Applause.] . . .

Congressional Record, April 27, 1882, 47th Cong., 1st Sess., XIII, pp. 3384–87.

[c]

The Virginia Readjuster Party, 1883

An address to the colored voters of the State of Virginia

THE RECORD OF THE BOURBON-DEMOCRATIC AND LIBERAL READJUSTER PARTIES CONTRASTED—WHAT THE LEADING, MOST INFLUENTIAL, INTELLIGENT, AND REPRESENTATIVE COLORED MEN OF VIRGINIA HAVE TO SAY TO THEIR PEOPLE.

Read and circulate.

Citizens of Virginia:

We hope that our acquaintance with you, and our well-known interest in every measure, every aim, and every cause which has for its end the prosperity of Virginia and the bettering of the condition of all of her citizens, will be a sufficient apology for thus addressing you at this late day in the present canvass. But remembering that on the 6th of November you will be called upon to decide by your ballot—so far as that ballot can decide—which of the political parties in Virginia—Bourbon or Liberal-Readjuster—shall control the destinies of this State for the next two years, at least, we ask you to pass with us, for but a short while, over the records of these two parties. In this we do not include those nondescripts called Straight-out Republicans, for they have no party allegiance, either State or national, except that of being assistant Bourbon-Democrats, that is serving as tools for Democratic trash. They are neither the bosses nor the middlemen; they are neither the gun nor the charge of powder; but they serve as a kind of touch-stick to fire off Democratic charges. . . .

But still, the question arises as to which of the two parties the colored men of Virginia should give their support. Just here we beg to differ very materially from Messrs. J. B. Syphax and W. J. S. Bowe,* who said, in their recent address, that the "colored people owed allegiance to no party any more than any other people." We do, for we are not as intelligent, nor as strong, financially, as any other people. We are just out of slavery; we are struggling upward, we need friends. And our allegiance, future prosperity, financially, intellectually and otherwise, is due to the party and the people who are willing, and who have shown that willingness by their acts, to give us the SAME CHANCE IN THE RACE OF LIFE THAT OTHER MEN HAVE.

And if we think, for a moment, of what the Democratic party has done and is doing today, we may be well assured of the fact that we cannot look to them for succor and aid, for that party has lost no opportunity to oppress us; to disfranchise us by means of the whipping-post, the prepayment of capitation taxes, and other class legislation . . . They were making petit larceny an offense, for the commission of which even the smallest boy would be disfranchised forever. The whipping-post was an easy road to the disfranchisement of the black men who did not know their rights and had not friends to defend them when they were invaded. This hateful system went on, until today we have about eight thousand blacks disfranchised.† They were engaged in closing the schools against our children, in taking the money appropriated by the laws of the State to public education, and using it for other purposes, until $1,500,000 were taken from the children of the State and given to the bondholders, who neither knew nor cared for the condition of our people.

---

* Negro leaders of the rump "Straight-out Republicans."
† That is, the law provided that anyone sentenced to punishment by whipping was thereby disfranchised.

THE READJUSTER PARTY grew out of the mass of disorganization and mismanagement of the Democratic party; indeed, they are what may be called the law-respecting element of what was the former Democratic-Funder party; they were and are, of course, largely aided by the Republicans of the State. The Readjusters, in the work of restoring the State to her former prosperous and happy condition, have not been unmindful of the claims of their friends. They are not Democrats in the old sense—they are Virginians, and all men, white and black alike, are welcome to their ranks, and all are treated as men.

We know that some will ask, WHAT HAS THE READJUSTER PARTY DONE?

In answer to this, thank God, we can say that they have done much for Virginia, and in doing this they have not acted for one class of men more than another, but have worked for the benefit of all alike. They found Virginia poor, downtrodden, and oppressed. They have begun to make her strong, independent, and rich. They found her with a debt of over $31,000,000. They settled that debt, after deducting West Virginia's share— one-third—upon a fair and honorable basis, at $21,000,000. They found the whipping-post a relic of the barbarous ages, the savage state of society— a Funder institution in our State. They wiped it away as the morning sun melts the dew-drops from the grass. They found that a man was compelled to pay $1 before he could vote, and in many instances he could not find the Democratic tax collector when he wanted to pay this tax to vote, if the collector knew that he was not going to vote his way. And the Readjuster party said that this requirement before voting was wrong, and that a man should be allowed to vote and pay his taxes when he got able. So they wiped away that requirement which in former years, by Democratic manipulations, had disfranchised thousands of colored voters, and they made us free once again.

They found that our lunatics were kept in barracks which had been left as a relic of the war, and now little better than horse stables. So they said this was wrong, and they gave us $100,000 to build an asylum for the care and protection of our insane, and $56,000 annually for the support of this institution. They found that there were several colleges in the State for the higher education of white young men and women, supported in whole or in part by State funds, and none for the colored people: so they appropriated $100,000 for the building of a college * for the education of our sons and daughters, and put the management and control of this institution entirely in the hands of colored men, and today that institution is open, with a competent corps of colored teachers, and though it has only been open since the first of October, there are now more than one hundred young colored

* Virginia State, Petersburg, organized 1882.

men and women there drinking from the fountain of knowledge, preparing themselves for teachers, lawyers, and doctors, to work among and educate our children for the duties of life. They found that we had no representation in the various State offices at Richmond, and they gave us the messenger to the governor, in the person of a colored man. They gave us a colored man as clerk in the first auditor's office, and another bright-eyed, smart colored youngster as clerk in the second auditor's office.

They gave us fifteen colored men as guards at the State penitentiary. They gave us a colored man as assistant postmaster at Norfolk, and in the Federal offices we have more colored men than ever before. They have given us colored men as members of school trustee boards. They have given us colored men as jurors. Now, we pause to ask if this is not a good showing for that party, and if you do not consider it your duty to give it your earnest and hearty support? We think we hear the answer, "Yes," from every true man. . . .

W. N. STEVENS	J. R. JONES
D. N. NORTON	

State Senators

PETER J. CARTER	W. H. PLEASANTS
REV. WILLIAM TROY	R. L. MITCHELL

Visitors to the Virginia Normal and Collegiate Institute

A. W. HARRIS	ROSS HAMILTON
SHED. DUNGEE	DABNEY SMITH
LITTLETON OWENS	R. G. L. PAIGE
GUY POWELL	ARCHIE SCOTT
E. D. BIAND	ROBERT NORTON
ARMISTEAD GREEN	

Members of House of Delegates

W. H. FERGUSSON	R. T. TANCIL

Physicians at Central Lunatic Asylum

Jos. P. EVANS	P. G. MORGAN
R. W. SMITH	J. W. POINDEXTER
RUFUS JONES	P. K. JONES
GEORGE FAVERMAN	

Ex-Members of the Legislature

plus 280 names from throughout state.

Senate Report No. 579, 48th Cong., 1st Sess., pp. 787–91.

[d]

A Negro Worker on the Knights of Labor, 1886

I am a colored man. I had a letter sent me from Georgia by a colored man asking if colored men would be recognized in the Knights of Labor, and I have had similar questions from others of my race, both in New York and Brooklyn. My answer is Yes and I especially refer to the case of the colored delegate to Richmond from D.A. 49. I myself belong to a local that is wholly composed of white men, with two exceptions, and I hold a very high position of trust in it. I was elected junior delegate to the D.A., and there is no office in the organization that I could not be elected to.

I will say to my people, Help the cause of labor. I would furthermore say to colored men, Organize. I also appeal to you to support Henry George * and the K. of L. You will never gain anything from the Republican Party . . . You are a man. Let us break this race prejudice which capital likes. Let us put our shoulders to the wheel as men and victory is ours.

John Swinton's Paper (N.Y.), October 10, 1886.

[e]

A Negro Worker Calls for Unity, 1887

As a strike is now in progress at the Black Diamond Steel Works, where many of our race are employed, the colored people hereabouts feel a deep interest in its final outcome. As yet few colored men have taken any part in it, it having been thus far thought unwise to do so. It is true our white brothers, who joined the Knights of Labor and organized the strike without conferring with, or in any way consulting us, now invite us to join with them and help them to obtain the desired increase in wages and control by the Knights of Labor of the works. But as we were not taken into their scheme at its inception and as it was thought by them that no trouble would be experienced in obtaining what they wanted without our assistance, we question very much the sincerity and honesty of this invitation. Our experience as a race with these organizations has, on the whole, not been such as to give us either great satisfaction or confidence in white men's fidelity. For so often after we have joined them, and the desired object has been attained, we have discovered that sinister and selfish motives were the whole and the only cause that led them to seek us as members . . .

Now, Mr. Editor, I am not opposed to organized labor. God forbid that

* The author of *Progress and Poverty* was then running, on a Labor Party ticket, for Mayor of New York City.

I should be when its members are honest, just, and true! But when I join any society, I want to have pretty strong assurance that I will be treated fairly. I do not want to join any organization the members of which will refuse to work by my side because the color of my skin happens to be of a darker hue than their own. Now what the white men in these organizations should and must do, if they want colored men to join with and confide in them, is to give them a square deal—give them a genuine white man's chance—and my word for it they will flock into them like bees into a hive. If they will take . . . the colored man by the hand and convince him by actual fact that they will be true to him and not a traitor to their pledge, he will be found with them ever and always; for there are not under heaven men in whose breasts beat truer hearts than in the breast of the Negro.

The N.Y. *Freeman*, August 13, 1887.

V.

MORE BOURBON VIOLENCE

Typical of the methods by which the Bourbons beat back the efforts to unseat them were those employed in the 1883 elections in Virginia and Mississippi. In Virginia, as already seen, the Liberal Readjuster Party had won in 1879 and had instituted reforms very important to the Negro people. In Mississippi, Green-backers, Radical Republicans and Independent Democrats threatened the domination of the planters after 1877. In 1881 a fusion of anti-Bourbon elements in Mississippi resulted in local victories in several counties, notably in Copiah where over half of the 27,000 population were Negroes.

Thus it came about that in the 1883 elections wholesale violence directed particularly, but not solely, against the Negro people appeared and in this manner Bourbon rule was once again secured.

The first two documents that follow consist of the sworn testimony of Negro sufferers from this reactionary terror in Copiah County, Mississippi and Danville, Virginia. They were Mrs. Selina Wallis of Mississippi and Mrs. Violet Keeling of Virginia, who were responding to questioning, early in 1884, from members of Senatorial investigating committees.

Violence was also regularly used by the plantation owners throughout the period to suppress the numerous attempts at union organization by Negro workers. A notable example occurred in 1887 when Negro sugar plantation workers of Lafourche, Terrebonne, St. Mary, St. Martin and Iberia parishes, organized as District Assembly Number 149, Knights of Labor.

The workers averaged $13 a month and their wages were paid in scrip usable only at stores operated by the planters. In October they presented demands for wages of about $8 a week, to be paid every week and in cash. Most of the planters rejected the demands and in November about 9,000 Negroes and 1,000 whites went on strike. The workers were evicted, some strikebreakers were imported, the state militia and sheriff's posses were employed, scores of strikers were jailed, about thirty were murdered and two of the leading organizers, Negro brothers named George and Henry Cox, were taken from prison and lynched.

In this manner the strike was crushed, and armed terror was maintained for several weeks thereafter.

The third document in this group consists of an address to the American people relative to these events, drafted at a mass meeting held in New Orleans in August, 1888. The eight signers of this appeal were Negro ministers of the area, one of whom, the Rev. T. B. Stamps, was also proprietor of *The Louisiana Standard,* a local weekly newspaper.

[a]

Mrs. Selina Wallis, 1883

Question: You live in Copiah County, do you? *Answer:* Yes, sir.

You are the widow of Thomas Wallis? Yes, sir.

Thomas Wallis was killed, was he? Yes, sir.

When? Friday morning before the election.

Friday morning before the last election? Yes, sir.

Who killed him? I don't know.

Tell the committee what you saw in regard to the matter. The men came there to my gallery and hailed.

How many men? I don't know, sir, how many there was.

A dozen? I think there was more than a dozen.

Twenty? I reckon; I couldn't tell how many there was.

Did they come on horseback? Yes, sir.

Did they have guns? Yes, sir.

What time of the day was it? It wasn't in the day; it was in the night.

What time in the night? It must have been between one and two o'clock.

You and your husband were in the house. Yes, sir.

In bed? Yes, sir.

Who else was in the house? None but my baby and my other little son in that end of the house I was in.

What did you first hear? They hailed, and I heard them when they hailed.

What did they do? They called and told him to get up and open the door and kindle a light, and he was trying to kindle a light up and couldn't kindle it up as quick as they wanted, and they told him to make haste; he told them to give him a little time, and they said "damn little time," and they told him to open the door, and I told them the door wasn't fastened, and they shoved it once, and it didn't shove open because a chair was against it, and they shoved it again, and that time it flew wide open and knocked the chair from behind it, and two come in, and, as well as I could see, there was about five or six on the gallery; I couldn't tell how many there was— me in the house and them out-of-doors.

What did they do after they got in? They asked Tom who he was, and he told them he was Wallis; they asked him which one of the Wallises, and he told them old man Wallis; they asked him what was his given name, and he told them Tom Wallis; then they told him he was the man that they was after; that they had a writ for him. But when they hailed, my other son asked them who it was, my son that was in the little back room, and he said it was the sheriff from Brookhaven; he said, "which Sheriff?" and he told him "Mr. Cummings from Brookhaven." When Tommy told them he was Tom Wallis, they said he was the man they was after; he said, "All right, you are the very one I am after," and Tom says, "All right"; and when they said they had a writ, one of them pulled a line out of his pocket and started to put it over his neck.

A rope, you mean? Yes, sir. When he went to put it over, he throwed up his hand and said, "Hold on, gentlemen," and as soon as he said that, one of them shot him. Then they hollered to them that was outside to come in, and they came in from the gallery and pulled him out, and when they got him to the door, his axe was lying at the door, and he catched at the axe, and got hold of the handle.

Who did, Thomas? Yes, sir. And another one shot, and he shot sort of up inside of the house and it went through the ceiling of the house, and another one shot and it went up through the gallery and up in the top of the house, and another one shot right through the door and that went through his neck.

It went through your arm and through his neck? Yes, sir.

And then he was dead? Yes, sir; he fell right on my dress-tail behind.

How long did they stay there? They didn't stay a minute after they shot him.

Did they do anything more? They just went and jumped right on their horses and went right off.

Are there many colored people living around in that neighborhood? Yes, sir; right smart.

Did they threaten them? Yes, sir.

What did they do, take to the woods? Yes, sir.

How long did they stay away from their houses at night? Two or three weeks.

Do you know where they went to? To the woods, most of them did.

Where did you stay? Sometimes in the woods and sometimes over to my sister's house.

How long was your arm sore? It ain't quite well yet.

Which arm was it? The left arm. I can't do a thing with my arm now.

How many children have you? . . . I think I got nine.

How many at home with you there? I ain't got but two.

What did you do with them when you were sleeping out in the woods? Carried them with me.

What did you do with your wounded arm? I carried it with me.

Did you have anybody to take care of it? No, sir; nobody but my baby.

How many nights did you sleep out of the house? Four weeks.

Do you know whether they visited your house again? They came the night before the election again. They didn't go in the house that time; they came out in the road and shot all over the house, and all around, and went right on up the road.

Firing their guns? Yes, sir.

How many times should you say they fired? I don't know; I couldn't tell you that.

Were they firing around there occasionally? Yes, sir . . .

Was your husband a Republican? Yes, sir.

Did he take an interest in politics? Did he generally vote? Yes, sir.

Senate Report No. 512, 48th Cong., 1st Sess., pp. 69 ff.

[b]

Mrs. Violet Keeling, 1883

Q. Do you know whether your husband voted at that election? *A.* Yes, sir; I know whether he voted. He didn't vote.

Why didn't he vote, if you know? I will tell you the reason he didn't vote. I didn't want to trust him at the ballot-box, because life was better to him than the ballot-box, and I thought it was best for him to stay at home and save his life. My husband didn't even have a pocket-knife, I had a little pen-knife and I took that. He didn't even have a pocket-knife, and I thought it was best to take that even going to my work.

In other words, he was afraid to go to vote? Yes, sir; and I was afraid to go to work.*

Didn't I understand you to say that you staid away from your work on election day? Yes, sir; I staid at home that day.

Was there a general fear among the colored people that this trouble would break out again on the day of the election? I will tell you what way I looked at it, the way they talked when I would get in the presence of them, it seemed they were all afraid to go to the polls as bad as they wanted to vote, which I believe every colored one there was a Republican and wanted to vote.

* The witness worked in a tobacco factory.

Were they afraid to vote? They were afraid to vote.

Did that fear grow out of this firing on the 3d of November, you have described? * I don't believe they got really over that until today; up to this present time.

Did their staying away from the polls grow out of that fear? Did they stay away from the polls from the fear that grew out of the firing there on Saturday? Yes, sir; they staid away and I reckon it was better; and most of them staid home and didn't go about, and I saw less pass on the day of election amongst the colored people than I ever did.

Do you think your husband has got over his scare yet? He says if it continued like it is, which I like to see him vote all the time, when the time comes to vote, I like to see him go to the poll and vote, and I asked him if he would vote and he said that if it continued like it was he didn't think he would ever go and vote any more.

Didn't he think he would ever vote any more? No, sir.

Are any of the colored people in your country Democrats? I don't know. I don't have nothing to do with that sort.

I ask you if any of them are Democrats? I am telling you just what I know; I don't have nothing to do with that sort.

Well are any of them Democrats? Sir?

You heard the question.† No sir; I didn't heard.

Are any of the colored people Democrats? I don't know; I don't ask them, because I generally talks with them like myself I don't have much to do with people. But, as for my part, if I hear of a colored man voting the Democratic ticket, I stay as far from him as I can; I don't have nothing in the world to do with him.

You don't speak to him? No, sir; I don't 'tallow him to come in my house.

That is not the rule among all the colored people? I don't know for anybody but myself.

Why do you have such a dislike to a colored man that votes the Democratic ticket? I will tell you as near as I know. I think that if the race of colored people that has got no friends nohow, and if they don't hang together they won't have none while one party is going one way and another the other. I don't wish to see a colored man sell himself when he can do without. Of course we all have to live, and I always like to have a man live even if he works for 25 cents a day, but I don't want to see him sell himself away.

Cannot a colored man vote the Democratic ticket without selling him-

---

* Four Negroes were murdered in Danville on November 3, 1883.
† The questioner at this point was Sen. Z. B. Vance, Democrat, of North Carolina.

self? I think if a colored man votes the Democratic ticket he has always sold himself, because the white man is no friend to him anyway.

Now, when you find a white man voting with the colored people, don't you think he sold himself? I will tell you what I think of him. I think he is a man who has a judgment of his own head and knows what he is doing. . . .

It is a pretty general rule down there, that if a colored man sells himself you won't have anything to do with him? If I knew a colored man that voted the Democratic ticket to come to my house, I would tell him to go somewhere else and visit.

Suppose your husband should go and vote a Democratic ticket? I would just pick up my clothes and go to my father's, if I had a father, or would go to work for 25 cents a day. . . .

Are not the white people down there good friends to the colored people? Yes, friends to them; rather kill them.

But you said in your testimony, if I recollect aright, that you were astonished; that you did not believe the white folks had anything against the black folks. No, sir; I didn't say that, but I believe by hearing several of them talk, that I knew they must have had something in their heart against them, because they said they feared the colored people were going to carry the election, and I believe they had something against them on account of that. . . .

Senate Report No. 579, 48th Cong., 1st Sess.; testimony dated February 18, 1884.

[c]

New Orleans Mass Meeting, 1888

To the people of the United States:

We, citizens of New Orleans, as well as of neighboring parishes, from which we have been driven away without warrant or law, assembled in mass meeting at New Orleans, La., on Wednesday, August 22, [1888] at Geddes Hall, declare and assert: That a reign of terror exists in many parts of the state; that the laws are suspended and the officers of the government, from the governor down, afford no protection to the lives and property of the people against armed bodies of whites, who shed innocent blood and commit deeds of savagery unsurpassed in the dark ages of mankind.

For the past twelve years we have been most effectively disfranchised and robbed of our political rights. While denied the privilege in many places of voting for the party and candidates of our choice, acts of violence have been committed to compel us to vote against the dictates of our conscience for the Democratic party, and the Republican ballots cast by us have been counted for the Democratic candidates. The press, the pulpit, the commercial organizations, and executive authority of the State have given both open and silent approval of all these crimes. In addition to these methods, there seems to be a deep laid scheme to reduce the Negroes of the State to a condition of abject serfdom and peonage.

It is being executed by armed bodies of men, styling themselves regulators, all of whom are white, except when a Negro is occasionally forced to join them to give color to the pretense that they represent the virtue of their communities in the suppression impartially of vicious and immoral persons. With that pretense as a cloak these lawless bands make night hideous with their unblushing outrages and murders of inoffensive colored citizens. They go out on nightly raids, order peaceable citizens away never to return, whip some, fire into houses of others—endangering the defenseless lives of women and children—and no attempt is being made to indict them. No virtuous element in the State is found among the whites to rise up in their might and sternly repress these outrageous crimes.

These acts are done in deliberate defiance of the Constitution and laws of the United States, which are so thoroughly nullified that the Negroes who bore arms in defense of the Union have no protection or shelter from them within the borders of Louisiana. During the past twelve months our people have suffered from the lawless regulators as never before since the carnival of bloodshed conducted by the Democratic party in 1868. . . . Fully aware of their utter helplessness, unarmed and unable to offer resistance to an overpowering force which varies from a "band of whites" to a "sheriff's posse" or the "militia," but which in reality is simply the Democratic party assembled with military precision and armed with rifles of the latest improved patents, toilers forbidden to follow occupations of their choice, compelled to desist from the discussing of labor questions, and being whipped and butchered when in a defenseless condition.

In the instances where the Negroes have attempted to defend themselves, as at Pattersonville and Thibodeaux, they have been traduced in a spirit of savage malignity, the governor of the State, with scarce an observance of the forms of the law has hastened his mercenaries or militia to the scene with cannon and rifles ostensibly to preserve the peace, but actually to re-enforce the already too well fortified Negro murderers falsely assuming to be lawful posses.

A single volume would scarcely afford sufficient space to enumerate the outrages our people have suffered, and are daily suffering at the hand of their oppressors. They are flagrantly deprived of every right guaranteed them by the Constitution; in many parts of the State they are free only in name; they cannot assemble in place to indicate and discuss an equitable rate of wages for their labor; they do not feel safe as property holders and tax-payers, and are permitted to enjoy but very few public conveniences. . . .

We have exhausted all means in our power to have our wrongs redressed by those whose sworn duty it is to impartially execute the laws, but all in vain, until now, because of our murdered fellow-citizens, and apprehensive for our own safety, we appeal to the awakened conscience, the sense of justice and sympathy of the civilized world, and of the American people in particular, to assist us with such moral and material support, as to secure the removal of our people, penniless as many of them are under the feudal system under which they live, to the public lands and other places of the northwest where they can enjoy some security for their persons and property. To this end we have organized a bureau of immigration. . . .

To our people we advise calmness and a strict regard for law and order. If your homes are invaded expect no mercy, for none will be shown, and if doomed to die, then die defending your life and home to the best of your ability. If convinced that you will not be permitted to live where you are in peace and perfect security quietly go away. If you are without other means to travel take to the public roads or through the swamps and walk away.

Steamboats and railroads are inventions of recent years; your forefathers dared the bloodhounds, the patrollers, and innumerable obstacles, lived in the woods on roots and berries in making their way to Canadian borders.

Invoking the guiding favor of Almighty God and the sympathy of mankind, we are your brethren in affliction and the common bond of humanity.

Rev. Ernest Lyon, Rev. A. E. P. Albert, Rev. J. H. Coker, M.D., Rev. T. B. Stamps, Rev. M. C. B. Mason, Rev. W. Paul Green, Rev. J. D. Kennedy, Rev. C. B. Wilson, *Committee.*

The Louisiana (New Orleans) *Standard,* August 25, 1888, in *Congressional Record,* 50th Cong., 1st Sess., appendix, pp. 8993–94.

VI.
MISCELLANEOUS MATTERS

To illustrate the large area of miscellaneous matters relative to the Negro's particular history, six documents are published below. The first [a] is the earliest printed appeal—so far as the editor knows—for capitalizing the word "Negro." It appeared as an editorial in the Chicago *Conservator* in 1878, a paper founded that year by Ferdinand Lee Barnett, a lawyer and later the first Negro assistant state's attorney of Illinois. In 1895 he married Ida B. Wells, of whom more will be said later.

Notwithstanding great obstacles, the scientific and inventive contributions of the Negro people have been numerous and significant. Many industries, such as whaling, railroading, meat-packing, sugar-refining and shoe-manufacturing, have been stimulated in a basic sense by the work of Negro scientists and inventors.

To illustrate this, the second document [b] is a reproduction of the original patent drawings of the shoe-lasting machine invented in 1883 by Jan E. Matzeliger. Matzeliger, who died in 1889 at the age of thirty-seven, poor as he had lived, had been a cobbler in Philadelphia and Lynn. His lasting machine, the first appliance ever made capable of holding a shoe on its last, gripping and pulling the leather down around the heel, guiding and driving the nails into place and then discharging the completed shoe, was bought for a pittance by the president of the United Shoe Machinery Corporation. By immensely speeding up the process of shoemaking and by cutting production costs in half, Matzeliger's machine revolutionized this basic industry.

The third document [c] consists of a series of typical "Information Wanted" advertisements that appeared regularly in the Negro press until about 1895. These ads were appeals for information concerning relatives separated by slavery and are illustrative of the Negro people's efforts to overcome that institution's devastating effects upon the family.

The fourth document [d] comes from the Rev. R. W. Spearman, a minister and teacher in the little community of Belen, Mississippi. Here, in a brief letter written in April, 1888, will be found a dramatic presentation of the educational facilities open to most Negroes in the post-Reconstruction era.

The fifth document [e] consists of a letter written October 8, 1889, by Booker T. Washington to George W. Cable. This is a good firsthand account of the great difficulties faced by Southern tenant farmers, particularly Negroes, and forms excellent background material for understanding the origins of the militant rural protest movements of the nineties.

The sixth document [f] comes from the pen of the Rev. Robert Davis of the A.M.E. Church and is dated Rocky Mount, Virginia, August 29, 1890. It is descriptive of a quarterly meeting of the Church held at the same time and place as the hanging of Negroes found guilty of having burned a considerable portion of the town the previous November.

[a]

Barnett's Editorial, 1878

SPELL IT WITH A CAPITAL

We have noticed an error which all journalists seem to make. Whether from mistake or ill-intention, we are unable to say, but the profession universally begins Negro with a small letter. It is certainly improper, and as no one has ever given a good reason for this breach of orthography, we will offer one. White men began printing long before Colored men dared read their works; had power to establish any rule they saw fit. As a mark of disrespect, as a stigma, as a badge of inferiority, they tacitly agreed to spell his name without a capital. The French, German, Irish, Dutch, Japanese, and other

(*continued on p. 746*)

[b]

Matzeliger's Shoe-Lasting Machine, 1883

J. E. MATZELIGER
LASTING MACHINE

No. 274,207.   PATENTED MAR. 20, 1883.

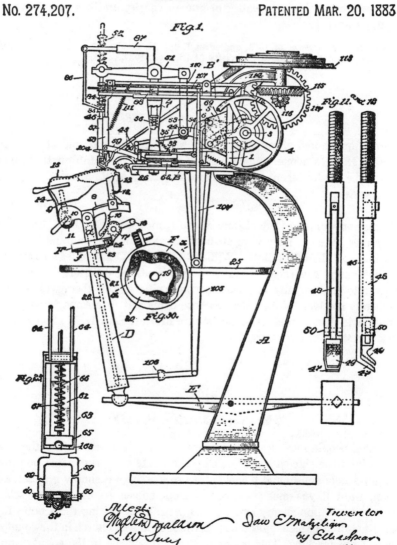

nationalities are honored with a capital letter, but the poor sons of Ham must bear the burden of a small *n*.

To our Colored journalistic brothers we present this as a matter of self-interest. Spell it with a capital. To the Democratic journals we present this as a matter of good grammar. To the Republicans we present it as a matter of right. Spell it with a capital. To all persons who would take from our wearied shoulders a hair's weight of the burden of prejudice and ill will we bear, we present this as a matter of human charity and beg you SPELL IT WITH A CAPITAL.

The Chicago Conservator of 1878, quoted in Ralph N. Davis, "The Negro Newspaper in Chicago," unpublished M.A., University of Chicago, 1939, p. 13.

[c]

"Information Wanted"; 1887

Information wanted of my sister Betty Mitchell. She was sold at New Orleans in 1860 to a man named Edward Summer. Any information about her will be gladly received by her brother, Rev. A. R. Mitchell, Mineral Springs, Ark.

Information wanted of my sisters, whose names were Elizabeth, Catherine and Agnes Massey. They were all from Clarks County, Va., and belonged to a man by the name of Dr. William McGuire. Our mother's name was Susan Massey. My three sisters were sold South at different times before the war to traders. Any information concerning any of them will be very thankfully received by their sister, whose name was Arie Anna Massey, but is now Arie Anna Green. Address in care of Rev. Seth D. W. Smith, P.O. Lock Box 40, Chambersburg, Pa.

Christian Recorder (Phila.), October 20, 1887.

[d]

Education in Mississippi, 1888

. . . Our people must learn many lessons of self-denial before they can successfully compete with the "pale brother." Here the law makes no provision for school houses and school furniture. A school is simply granted, and if you want it you must provide a school house; so we country school teachers teach in a shanty or an old church. I am writing these notes in a Baptist church (which, by the way, is the second best church in the county), where I am teaching. This is one of the best schools in the county and I receive $45.00 per month. The house is minus windows, doors, stove and, I might say, roof. It is a crazy old shanty made of cypress boards—cold and comfortless. I have to make my own fire, and, what is more, I have to get my own wood. Attendance is very irregular and nobody seems interested. This is one case, it is true, but it is a fair sample of a majority of our country schools.

Christian Recorder, May 3, 1888.

[e]

Tenant Farming in Alabama, 1889

I am very sorry to be so late answering your letter regarding the operation of the crop lien law in Alabama, but every minute of my time has seemingly been employed since receiving your letter. I am glad you are going to give the subject attention and trust that my information is not too late for use.

Of course when the war ended the colored people had nothing on which to live while the first crop was being made. Thus, in addition to renting the land on which to make the first crop they had to get the local merchant or someone else to supply the food for the family to eat while the first crop was being made. For every dollar's worth of provisions so advanced the local merchant charged from 12 to 30 per cent interest. In order to be sure that he secured his principal and interest a mortgage or lien was taken on the crop, in most cases not then planted. Of course the farmers could pay no such interest and the end of the first year found them in debt—the 2nd year they tried again, but there was the old debt and the new interest to pay, and in this way the "mortgage system" has gotten a hold on everything that it seems impossible to shake off. Its evils have grown instead of decreasing, until it is safe to say that ⅚ of the colored farmers mortgage their crops every year. Not only their crops before, in many cases, they are actually planted, but their wives sign a release from the homestead law and in most every case mules, cows, wagons, plows and often all household furniture is covered by the lien.

At a glance one is not likely to get the full force of the figures representing the amount of interest charged. Example, if a man makes a mortgage with a merchant for $200 on which to "run" during the year the farmer is likely to get about $50 of this amount in February or March, $50 May, $50 in June or July and the remainder in Aug. or Sept. By the middle of Sept. the farmer begins returning the money in cotton and by the last of Oct. whatever he can pay the farmer has paid, but the merchant charges as much for the money gotten in July or Aug. as for that gotten in Feb. The farmer is charged interest on all for the one year of 12 months. And as the "advance" is made in most cases in provisions rather than cash, the farmer, in addition to paying the interest mentioned, is charged more for the same goods than one buying for cash. If a farmer has 6 in a family say wife and 4 children, the merchant has it in his power to feed only those who work and sometimes he says to the farmer if he sends his children to school no rations can be drawn for them while they are attending school.

After a merchant has "run" a farmer for 5 or 6 years and he does not "pay out" or decides to try mortgaging with another merchant the first merchant in such cases usually "cleans up" the farmer, that is takes everything, mules, cows, plows, chicken's fodder—everything except wife and children.

It is not very often that the merchant furnishing the supplies owns the land, this in most cases is rented from a different party. So you see that the 2 parties, farmer and merchant, who have the most contact with the land, have no interest in it except to get all they can out of it.

The result of all this is seen in the "general run down" condition of $\frac{4}{5}$ of the farms in Alabama—houses unpainted—fences tumbling down, animals poorly cared for, and the land growing poorer every year. Many of the colored farmers have almost given up hope and do just enough work to secure their "advances." One of the strongest things that can be said in favor of the colored people is, that in almost every community there are one or two who have shaken off this yoke of slavery and have bought farms of their own and are making money—and there are a *few* who rent land and "mortgage" and still do something.

The practices that I have referred to are in most cases sanctioned by the laws of the legislature and are not prohibited by law. . . .

For the good of the work to which I am devoting my life I prefer that my name should not be used in any printed matter. If I can help at anytime in the good cause I shall be only too glad to do so.

The Journal of Negro Education, (1948), XVII, pp. 46–65.

[f]

Rocky Mount Executions, 1890

We held quarterly meeting at Rocky Mount, Va., August 23–28th . . .

Last November this town was set on fire and twenty-six stores and dwellings were burned. George Early, William Brown, Bird Woods and Nannie Woods, all colored, were charged with the burning. They were tried at the December term of the county court and sentenced to be hanged August 24th '90. Our quarterly conference occurred on the same day. George Early and Bird Woods were hanged. William Brown and Nannie Woods will be hanged September 19th. The authorities seem to like the fun so well that instead of making one do all, they got the governor to respite the other two till September 19th.

Our people were at a loss what to do. Some said the quarterly meeting would not go on and then came to me to know about it. I told them yes, the meeting would go on just the same. I told them that the white people had been hanging our people for nearly three hundred years and it was not worth while for me to stop my meeting. So we went on and had more people present than ever before. We prayed, sang and preached as though no one had been hanged, notwithstanding the occasion was one of great solemnity— an awful time. These men faced death boldly and in a firm voice protested their innocence, and said, "It was hard to die for an infamous offense of which they were not guilty." How long, oh Lord, with greatest depths will colored men have to stand on the scaffolds of the South and plead for their innocence in vain? O, Lord, that thy judgments may sit on our oppressors. Our people generally believe that these parties were innocent, hence it has inspired deep unrest and dissatisfaction among the colored people here.

Christian Recorder, September 11, 1890.

VII

The Appearance of Imperialism

192

AMERICAN IMPERIALISM APPEARS, 1890–1900

The Sherman Anti-Trust Act—passed in 1890, "less to curb trusts than to curb discontent," as Orville H. Pratt, Republican Senator from Connecticut, put it—signalizes the onset of the stage of monopoly capitalism in the United States. More trusts were organized in the ten years following the passage of the "anti-trust" law than had been organized in the preceding thirty. The process was capped, in 1901, with the setting up of the first billion dollar trust in history, the United States Steel Corporation.

This monopoly capitalism in these ten years also captured American agriculture in the West and in the South, launched an imperialist war against Spain, appropriated Hawaii, Puerto Rico, Cuba, Guam, and the Philippine Islands, and attempted to resubjugate the Negro people.

Documents to illustrate the many-sided participation of the Negro people in the history of this fateful decade are grouped within seven main divisions. This includes, firstly, a section devoted to presenting general analyses and programs put forth by individual Negroes. This is followed by a group of documents descriptive of the viewpoints and proposals of various Negro organizations, while the third section presents some petitions on specific issues offered to various government bodies or officials. Section four consists of various documents pertinent to the beginning and development of a national struggle against lynching. The fifth section presents documents illustrative of the demands and role of the Negro people in the Populist movement, later independent political battles and various labor struggles of the period, while the next section offers a few documents revealing the opinions of Negroes concerning the Republican and Democratic parties of the decade. The last group presents some material on the Spanish-American War and the Negroes' attitude toward the conquest of colonies and the campaign of subjugation waged in the Philippines.

I.

WHAT IS TO BE DONE?

Eight documents appear in this section. The first of these [a], entitled "A Negro's View of the Negro Question in the United States," originally appeared in the Manchester *Guardian* of England in 1891. Its author was W. S. Scarborough, a Greek scholar and professor at Wilberforce University and a regular contributor to the leading periodicals of his time.

Document two [b] consists of personal notes made by a young student named William Edward Burghardt Du Bois in 1893 at Berlin, in which the twenty-five year old man states his aim and purpose. The third document [c] is the speech delivered at the Atlanta Cotton Exposition, September 18, 1895, which gained national, though not unanimous, acclaim for Booker T. Washington. The fourth document [d] is a typical address by the "Back-To-Africa" protagonist, Bishop Henry M. Turner, delivered in December, 1895.

The fifth document [e] expresses the viewpoint of John Hope, President of Atlanta University. Mr. Hope's remarks were made in Nashville, February 22, 1896, before that city's Negro Debating Society, as a protest against the policy of Booker T. Washington. The next document [f], from the poet, Paul Laurence Dunbar, appeared in 1898 and likewise took issue with Washington. In this case the latter's absorption with industrial education was attacked.

The seventh document [g] consists of the remarks of an early representative of the Negro bourgeoisie, John Merrick of Durham, North Carolina, who had been put in business by two Southern millionaires, Julian S. Carr and Washington Duke. The speech, made in 1898, is fittingly "reasonable." Document eight [h] consists of abstracts from a remarkable paper on "The Disfranchisement of the Negro" published in 1899. Its author was John L. Love, a member of the Executive Committee of The American Negro Academy, headed at that time by Dr. Du Bois. More will be said of this Academy at another point.

[a]

W. S. Scarborough, 1891

The trouble is the Negro is advancing too rapidly for many of the white-liners of the South, and there is a determination to call a halt. Consequently all sorts of schemes are devised to impede the progress of the blacks. They are shot down if they testify against white men; they meet the same fate if they refuse to do so. If they attempt to assert their civil and political rights in any manly way they are mobbed, butchered, and killed. If they nominate or assist in nominating one of their own number for office, it matters not how well qualified he may be, a cry is raised that "Negroes are drawing the race issue." The Negro has been patient—yes, more than this; he has prostrated himself at the feet of the government, and has remonstrated with it to give him protection in the enjoyment of his rights. The

Government has utterly failed to do its duty, in that it has disregarded his request. . . .

The end is not yet. In fact the struggle has just begun. The blacks themselves intend to have something to say as to what shall be done with them. They intend to have a hand in the settlement of this question, and until they do the question will never be settled. . . .

He has seen so many broken pledges, violations of oaths, and disregard for platforms and public declarations on the part of political parties, that it is found no longer advisable for the colored people to have great faith in them. This is the conclusion many have come to.

Recent outrages in the South and the tendency in the North to unite with Southern leaders against the blacks, the efforts of religious bodies to rid themselves of their colored membership, the desire of political parties to manage and carry elections without the Negro vote, prejudice and ostracism, are all having their effect, and are making new creatures of the more thoughtful American Negroes. They impel the Negroes to adopt plans and measures that will in some way aid them in changing their present condition for something more desirable. . . .

It is not a wise policy to continue alienating the affections of the Negro, especially when there is no possibility of removing him from the country. As the whites have all to lose and the Negro but little, wisdom should dictate a conciliatory policy at least. Whatever be the methods adopted by the blacks to ensure safety and protection, I am justified in saying that no radical measures will be taken until all other efforts fail. It is believed by us all that education, wealth and a radical change in the Negro's present status will bring about the results desired. To acquire these will take time. Therefore the blacks must content themselves with their present condition till they are able to change it, defending themselves as best they can against all assaults while they contend and fight for their rights. Their cause is a just one, and they are bound to win. They are full of hope and courage, and though desperate, they are not as yet dangerous. The so-called "Negro Problem," (or the "white man question") can be settled in time peaceably, and will be thus settled if the whites permit it. Our American white citizens may defer a solution by all sorts of schemes and devices, but the time will come when they—North and South—will have to confront the inevitable, and grant the Negro the rights that belong to him or suffer the consequences.

Christian Recorder, June 18, 1891.

[b]

W. E. B. Du Bois, 1893

Program for the celebration of my twenty-fifth birthday. . . . I awoke at eight and took coffee and oranges, read letters, thought of my parents, sang, cried &c (O yes—the night before I heard Shubert's beautiful unfinished symphony. . . ,). Then I wandered up to the reading room, then to the art gallery, then to a fine dinner. . . . Then went to Potsdam for coffee & saw a pretty girl. Then came back to the seminar, took a wander, supped on cocoa, wine, oranges and cake, wrote my year book & letters—and now I go to bed after one of the happiest days of my happy life.

Night—grand and wonderful. I am glad I am living. I rejoice as a strong man to run a race. And I am strong—is it egotism or is it assurance? . . . I know that I am either a genius or a fool. O I wonder what I am—I wonder what the world is—I wonder if life is worth the striving. I do not know— perhaps I never shall know; but this I do know: be the Truth what it may I shall seek it on the pure assumption that it is worth seeking—and Heaven nor Hell, God nor Devil shall turn me from my purpose till I die. . . .

I am striving to make my life all that life may be—and I am limiting that strife only in so far as that strife is incompatible with others of my brothers and sisters making their lives similar. The crucial question now is where that limit comes . . . God knows I am sorely puzzled. I am firmly convinced that my own best development is not one and the same with the best development of the world and here I am willing to sacrifice. . . . The general proposition of working for the world's good becomes too soon sickly sentimentality. I therefore take the world that the Unknown lay in my hands & work for the rise of the Negro people, taking for granted that their best development means the best development of the world. . . .

These are my plans: to make a name in science, to make a name in literature and thus to raise my race. . . .

I wonder what will be the outcome? Who knows?

I will go unto the King—which is not according to the law & if I perish— *I Perish.*

MS. in Du Bois' papers.

[c]

Booker T. Washington, 1895

Mr. President, Gentlemen of the Board of Directors, and Citizens:
One-third of the population of the South is of Negro race. No enter-

prise seeking the material, civil, or moral welfare of this section can disregard this element of our population and reach the highest success. I but convey to you, Mr. President and Directors, the sentiment of the masses of my race, when I say that in no way have the value and manhood of the American Negro been more fittingly and generously recognized, than by the managers of this magnificent Exposition at every stage of its progress. It is a recognition which will do more to cement the friendship of the two races than any occurrence since the dawn of our freedom.

Not only this, but the opportunity here afforded will awaken among us a new era of industrial progress. Ignorant and inexperienced, it is not strange that in the first years of our new life we began at the top instead of the bottom; that a seat in Congress or the State Legislature was more sought than real estate or industrial skill; that the political convention or stump speaking had more attractions than starting a dairy farm or truck garden.

A ship lost at sea for many days suddenly sighted a friendly vessel. From the mast of the unfortunate vessel was seen the signal: "Water, water, we die of thirst." The answer from the friendly vessel at once came back, "Cast down your bucket where you are." A second time the signal, "Water, water, send us water," ran up from the distressed vessel and was answered, "Cast down your bucket where you are," and a third and fourth signal for water was answered "Cast down your bucket where you are." The captain of the distressed vessel, at last heeding the injunction cast down his bucket and it came up full of fresh, sparkling water from the mouth of the Amazon River. To those of my race who depend on bettering their condition in a foreign land, or who underestimate the importance of cultivating friendly relations with the Southern white man who is their next door neighbor, I would say, cast down your bucket where you are, cast it down in making friends, in every manly way, of the people of all races by whom you are surrounded. Cast it down in agriculture, in mechanics, in commerce, in domestic service, and in the professions. And in this connection it is well to bear in mind that, whatever other sins the South may be called upon to bear, when it comes to business pure and simple it is in the South that the Negro is given a man's chance in the commercial world; and in nothing is this Exposition more eloquent than in emphasising this chance. Our greatest danger is, that, in the great leap from slavery to freedom, we may overlook the fact that the masses of us are to live by the productions of our hands, and fail to keep in mind that we shall prosper in the proportion as we learn to dignify and glorify common labor and put brains and skill into the common occupations of life; shall prosper in proportion as we learn to draw the line between the superficial and the substantial, the ornamental gewgaws of life and the useful. No race can prosper till it learns that there is as much dignity in tilling a field as in writing a poem. It is at the bottom of life we must begin and not the top. Nor should we permit our grievances to overshadow our opportunities.

To those of the white race who look to the incoming of those of foreign birth and strange tongue and habits for the prosperity of the South, were I permitted, I would repeat what I say to my own race, "Cast down your bucket where you are." Cast it down among the 8,000,000 Negroes whose habits you know, whose loyalty and love you have tested in days when to have proved treacherous meant the ruin of your firesides. Cast it down among those people who have, without strikes and labor wars, tilled your fields, cleared your forests, builded your railroads and cities, and brought forth treasures from the bowels of the· earth and helped make possible this magnificent representation of the progress of the South. Casting down your bucket among my people, helping and encouraging as you are doing on these grounds, and with education of head, hand and heart, you will find that they will buy your surplus land, make blossom the waste places in your fields, and run your factories. While doing this you can be sure in the future, as you have been in the past, that you and your families will be surrounded by the most patient, faithful, law-abiding, and unresentful people that the world has seen. As we have proved our loyalty to you in the past, in nursing your children, watching by the sick beds of your mothers and fathers, and often following them with tear-dimmed eyes to their graves, so in the future, in our humble way, we shall stand by you with a devotion that no foreigner can approach, ready to lay down our lives, if need be, in defense of yours; interlacing our industrial, commercial, civil, and religious life with yours in a way that shall make the interests of both races one. In all things that are purely social we can be as separate as the fingers, yet one as the hand in all things essential to mutual progress.

There is no defense or security for any of us except in the highest intelligence and development of all. If anywhere there are efforts tending to curtail the fullest growth of the Negro, let these efforts be turned into stimulating, encouraging and making him the most useful and intelligent citizen. Effort or means so invested will pay a thousand per cent interest. These efforts will be twice blessed—"blessing him that gives and him that takes."

There is no escape, through law of man or God, from the inevitable:

> "The laws of changeless justice bind
> Oppressor with oppressed,
> And close as sin and suffering joined
> We march to fate abreast."

Nearly sixteen millions of hands will aid you pulling the load upwards, or they will pull against you the load downwards. We shall constitute one-third and much more of the ignorance and crime of the South, or one-third its intelligence and progress; we shall contribute one-third to the business and industrial prosperity of the South, or we shall prove a veritable body of death, stagnating, depressing, retarding every effort to advance the body politic.

Gentlemen of the Exposition: As we present to you our humble effort at an exhibition of our progress, you must not expect over much; starting thirty years ago with ownership here and there in a few quilts and pumpkins and chickens (gathered from miscellaneous sources) * remember, the path that has led us from these to the invention and production of agricultural imple-ments, buggies, steam engines, newspapers, books, statuary, carvings, paint-ings, the management of drug stores and banks, has not been trodden with-out contact with thorns and thistles. While we take pride in what we exhibit as a result of our independent efforts, we do not for a moment forget that our part in this exhibit would fall far short of your expectations but for the constant help that has come to our educational life, not only from the Southern States, but especially from Northern philanthropists who have made their gifts a constant stream of blessing and encouragement.

The wisest among my race understand that the agitation of questions of social equality is the extremest folly, and that progress in the enjoyment of all the privileges that will come to us must be the result of severe and con-stant struggle, rather than of artificial forcing. No race that has anything to contribute to the markets of the world is long in any degree ostracized. It is important and right that all privileges of the law be ours, but it is vastly more important that we be prepared for the exercise of these privi-leges. The opportunity to earn a dollar in a factory just now is worth in-finitely more than the opportunity to spend a dollar in an opera house.

In conclusion, may I repeat, that nothing in thirty years has given us more hope and encouragement and drawn us so near to you of the white race as the opportunity offered by this Exposition; here bending, as it were, over the altar that represents the results of the struggles of your race and mine, both starting practically empty-handed three decades ago, I pledge that, in your effort to work out the great and intricate problem which God has laid at the doors of the South, you shall have at all times the patient, sympathetic help of my race. Only let this be constantly in mind, that while, from representations in these buildings of the products of field, of forest, of mine, of factory, letters and art, much good will come—yet, far above

---

* This "humorous" aside was typical of Washington's speeches before white audiences and was bitterly resented by many Negroes.

and beyond material benefit, will be that higher good, that let us pray God will come, in a blotting out of sectional differences and racial animosities and suspicions, and in a determination, even in the remotest corner, to administer absolute justice; in a willing obedience among all classes to the mandates of law, and a spirit that will tolerate nothing but the highest equity in the enforcement of law. This, this, coupled with material prosperity, will bring into our beloved South new heaven and new earth.

Alice M. Bacon, *The Negro and the Atlanta Exposition* (Baltimore, 1896), pp. 12–16.

[d]

Bishop Turner, 1896

I believe that the Negroid race has been free long enough now to begin to think for himself and plan for better conditions than he can lay claim to in this country or ever will. *There is no manhood future in the United States for the Negro.* He may eke out an existence for generations to come, but he can never be a *man*—full, symmetrical and undwarfed. Upon this point I know thousands who make pretensions to scholarship, white and colored, will differ and may charge me with folly, while I in turn pity their ignorance of history and political and civil sociology. . . . The colored man who will stand up and in one breath say that the Negroid race does not want social equality and in the next predict a great future in the face of all the proscription of which the colored man is the victim, is either an ignoramus, or is an advocate of the perpetual servility and degradation of his race variety. I know as Senator Morgan [of Alabama] says, and as every white man in the land will say, that the whites will not grant social equality to the Negroid race, nor am I certain that God wants them to do it.

And as such, I believe that two or three millions of us should return to the land of our ancestors, and establish our own nation, civilization, laws, customs, style of manufacture, and not only give the world, like other race varieties, the benefit of our individuality, but build up social conditions peculiarly our own, and cease to be grumblers, chronic complainers and a menace to the white man's country, or the country he claims and is bound to dominate. . . .

It is idle talk to speak of a colored man not being a success in skilled labor or fine arts. What the black man needs is a country and surroundings in harmony with his color and with respect for his manhood. Upon this point I would delight to dwell longer if I had time. Thousands of white people in this country are ever and anon advising the colored people to keep out of politics, but they do not advise themselves. If the Negro is a man in keeping with other men, why should he be less concerned about politics than any one else? Strange, too, that a number of would-be colored leaders are ignorant and debased enough to proclaim the same foolish jargon. For the Negro to stay out of politics is to level himself with a horse or a cow, which is no politician, and the Negro who does it proclaims his inability to take part in political affairs. If the Negro is to be a man, full and complete, he must take part in everything that belongs to manhood. If he omits a single duty, responsibility or privilege, to that extent he is limited and incomplete.

J. W. E. Bowen, ed., *Africa and the American Negro* . . . (Atlanta, 1896), pp. 195–98. Copy in the Library of Congress.

[e]

John Hope, 1896

If we are not striving for equality, in heaven's name for what are we living? I regard it as cowardly and dishonest for any of our colored men to tell white people or colored people that we are not struggling for equality. If money, education, and honesty will not bring to me as much privilege, as much equality as they bring to any American citizen, then they are to me a curse, and not a blessing. God forbid that we should get the implements with which to fashion our freedom, and then be too lazy or pusillanimous to fashion it. Let us not fool ourselves nor be fooled by others. If we cannot do what other freemen do, then we are not free. Yes, my friends, I want equality. Nothing less. I want all that my God-given powers will enable me to get, then why not equality? Now, catch your breath, for I am going to use an adjective: I am going to say we demand social equality. In this Republic we shall be less than freemen, if we have a whit less than that which thrift, education, and honor afford other freemen. If equality, political, economic, and social, is the boon of other men in this great country of ours, then equality, political, economic, and social, is what we demand. Why build a wall to keep me out? I am no wild beast, nor am I an unclean thing.

Rise, Brothers! Come let us possess this land. Never say: "Let well enough alone." Cease to console yourselves with adages that numb the moral sense. Be discontented. Be dissatisfied. "Sweat and grunt" under present conditions. Be as restless as the tempestuous billows on the boundless sea. Let your discontent break mountain-high against the wall of prejudice, and swamp it to the very foundation. Then we shall not have to plead for justice nor on bended knee crave mercy; for we shall be men. Then and not until then will liberty in its highest sense be the boast of our Republic.

Ridgely Torrence, *The Story of John Hope* (N.Y., 1948, Macmillan), pp. 114–15.

[f]

Paul Laurence Dunbar, 1898

. . . The statement has been so strongly and so frequently urged that the Negro should work with his hands, that the opposite of the proposition has been implied. People are taking it for granted that he ought not to work with his head. And it is so easy for these people among whom we are living to believe this; it flatters and satisfies their self-complacency.

At this late date the Negro has no need to prove his manual efficiency. That was settled fifty years ago, when he was the plantation blacksmith and carpenter and shoemaker. But his intellectual capacity is still in doubt. Any attempt at engaging in pursuits when his mind is employed is met by an attitude that stigmatizes his effort as presumption. Then if the daring one succeeds, he is looked upon as a monster. . . .

I would not counsel a return to the madness of that first enthusiasm for classic and professional learning; but I would urge that the Negro tempt. this newer one with a right idea of the just proportion in life of industry, commerce, art, science and letters, of materialism and idealism, of utilitarianism and beauty!

The Independent (N.Y.), August 18, 1898, I, pp. 469–71.

[g]

John Merrick, 1898

There has been lots and lots said about the Negro and his condition in North Carolina. So much so that I think that the least of us have a perfect right to give vent to our feelings if we wish; and on these grounds, I take the privilege to say a few words about me and my people the way I see it.

We are here and we are going to stay. And why not stay? We have the same privileges that other people have. Every avenue is open to us to do business as it is to any other people. We are allowed to own homes and farms, run farms, do banking business, insurance, real estate business and all other minor businesses that are done in this Commonwealth. . . . Now to show you why we have not been benefitted by politics and why we ought to let them alone: In the first place, our good men and lots of our best men have turned their attention to party and office. A man goes into politics a good man and he goes to pulling the wires and soon is classed a politician. This naturally makes him lose interest along business and industrial lines; then he has to stick to it for protection, and that settles him as a businessman. This happens with very few exceptions. . . . What difference does it make to us who is elected? We got to serve in the same different capacities of life for a living. . . . We got to haul wood, and don't care who is elected.

Now let us think more of our employment and what it takes to keep peace and to build us a little house and stop thinking we are the whole Republican Party and without us the whole thing would stop.

Now don't the writers of the race jump on the writer and try to solve my problem. Mine is solved. I solved mine by learning to be courteous to those that courtesy was due, working and trying to save and properly appropriate what I made.

I do think we have done well and I think we could have done better. Now let us make better use of the years we have left than we have the years that have past, as we have the past to look back over and see the many mistakes.

W. K. Boyd, *The Story of Durham* . . . (Duke University Press, Durham, 1927), pp. 282–83.

[h]

John L. Love, 1899

The assault, under the forms of law, which is being made upon the political rights of the Negro is the symptom of an animus which has its roots imbedded in the past. It does not mark a revival, but rather the supreme desperate effort of the spirit of tyranny to compass the political subjection and consequent social degradation of the black man. Its provocation does not consist in any abnormal or perilous condition in southern communities arising from a numerical preponderance of Negroes. It is not made to meet a merely temporary emergency with the intent to return to the principles of republican government upon the advent of intelligence and wealth to the Negro. Indeed, the very intent and purpose of the assault is to prevent such an advent, in so far as human ingenuity and tyrannical violence can do so.

It cannot find its justification in a necessity of averting by radical measures any imagined perils to social order which might arise from the political domination of ignorance; for the spirit which prompts the assault has ever fostered ignorance and endeavored to perpetuate it. In fact, the assault is so iniquitous in its conception and is being executed with such wicked and violent disregard of political morals and human rights, as by comparison to render almost beneficent the realization of the perils which the imagination of the assailants pretends to fancy.

There may be those who see in this assault nothing more than a supreme effort of a benign civilization to save itself from utter ruin. It is, however, to be borne in mind that the apostles of this civilization which is of a peculiarly local type, have ever asserted that its maintenance and future glory are inseparably connected with the subjection of the Negro. Always they have spoken the language of tyranny, which, in spite of its embellishments and jugglings, amounts to this: the social well-being and political privileges of the Negro are inconsistent with the economic interests and political ambitions of a few southern white men. Into this language all of the feigned social perils and political nightmares of southern planters and politicians easily resolve themselves. [There follows a twelve page summary of the political history of Reconstruction.]

With the disgraceful dicker of 1877, this era closed, and with it passed away for a time, whose limit has not yet been fixed, whatever there has been of republican government in the South. How the overthrow of Reconstruction government was accomplished is well-known. The significance of its overthrow is that it marked the arrogant reassertion of the malignant and desperate purpose of the southern oligarchy, trained in the absolutism of slave mastery, to despoil the Negro of the rights of citizenship, and to reduce him to a state of serfdom.

In the preparation for the execution of this infamous purpose, they attempted and succeed in accomplishing what does great credit to the sheer audacity of southern political leadership. By sublime dissimulation they hoodwinked the other sections of the country in regard to the South's attitude to the Negro. Their first maneuver was to give the Negro a bad reputation and denounce as mischievous meddlers those who insisted that he be dealt with justly. The Southern oligarchy put forward its youngest and best men. Its first point of attack was Massachusetts; and thither went Grady and Gordon and Watterson who with persuasive accent plead the cause of the "New South." With charming recklessness of statement, they proclaimed the era of sectional fraternity and with consummate cunning set forth in the next breath to eastern capitalists the industrial possibilities of the South. Gradually they reached the climax of their mission, to wit: Leave the Negro to us: we are his friends, his natural guardians: we know him better than you do, and can more wisely fix his status in our social scheme. Then the old, old story was repeated with endless refrain, of the Negro's ignorance, criminal tendencies (fully attested by timely news dispatches from the South), of his inferiority, and of the menace he is to Anglo-Saxon domination.

Thus while the sons of slave masters were poisoning the minds of the north and west, the slave drivers were at home perfecting the conspiracy against Negro citizenship.

The year 1890 witnessed the beginning of the execution of this conspiracy which promises to continue until the Negro is divested of every right which is worth the having. In 1890 a minority of the people of the state of Mississippi arrogated to themselves the right to despoil the majority of the citizens of that state of the rights of free men by nullifying the Fifteenth Amendment. . . .

The Constitution of Mississippi has served as the pattern for the disfranchising enactments of South Carolina and Louisiana.

When the present Constitution of South Carolina was in process of construction, the Supreme Court of the United States had not passed upon the legality of the so-called educational provision of the Mississippi Constitution, and the possibility that it might in the near future declare all such enactments repugnant to the Constitution of the United States deterred the members of the South Carolina constitutional convention from going the full length of the Mississippi plan. Although they had assembled for no other purpose than to disfranchise the Negro, yet out of fear of the Fifteenth Amendment to the Federal Constitution, they failed to do all they purposed.

George L. Tillman, the brother of the present United States Senator from that state, spoke in the convention the following significant and pathetic words:

"Mr. President, we can all hope a great deal from the constitution we have adopted. It is not such an instrument as we would have made had we been a free people. We are not a free people; we have not been since the war. I fear it will be some time before we can call ourselves free. I have had that fact very painfully impressed upon me for several years. *If we were free, instead of having Negro suffrage we would have Negro slavery; instead of having the United States Government we would have the Confederate States Government; instead of paying $300,000 pension tribute we would be receiving it. . . .*"

These enactments have never received the approval of the people of the states. Of a total of 235,604 male citizens of voting age in South Carolina in 1890, more than 102,000 of whom were white men, only 60,925 participated in the election of November 6, 1894, at which the members of the constitutional convention were elected. Of the number thus voting only 31,402 were counted in favor of holding the convention. Thus one-seventh of the citizens called a convention and enacted a constitution which disfranchised more than one hundred thousand electors. The constitutions of Mississippi and Louisiana were adopted in the same way.

These so-called constitutions, besides being repugnant to the spirit and purpose of the Fifteenth Amendment are also violative of the acts of Congress restoring the rebellious states to the Union, which acts the Federal Supreme Court has on several occasions declared constitutional. . . .

What effect have these disfranchising enactments had upon the status of the Negro? Has he lost nothing more than the bare right to vote? Has he been deprived of nothing but an abstract right to a voice in the affairs of government and of no other privilege than the possibility of a share of political power?

Surely the loss of any one of the foregoing is not unimportant in a democratic form of government. But he has lost much more, and the probabilities are that, if these obvious discriminations are allowed to continue, he will be brought to his deepest humiliation. The law which deprives him of the badge of citizenship, changes at once his legal status and cuts him off from respect. His disqualification as an elector shuts him out of the jury box in courts where what few rights he has left are adjudicated and his grievances redressed. His disqualification as an elector and as a juror discredits him as a witness. In the states which have adopted these disfranchising constitutions, more than three hundred thousand citizens have been thereby disqualified as jurors. This is all the more outrageous, because in the same states advantage has been taken in criminal legislation of what the Supreme Court of Mississippi has termed "certain peculiarities of habit and character of the Negro" whereby "furtive offenses," which in other communities are treated as mere misdemeanors, are made felonies and are usually visited with greater punishment than are the "robust crimes" of the whites. In South Carolina, for instance, the breach of a labor contract has been made a crime, the object being to reduce the Negro to a state of serfdom.

Not only has the legal status of the Negro been gravely affected by these disfranchising enactments; his economic status has also been lowered. A Mississippian states the following as the reason for disfranchising the Negro in his state:

"It is a question of political economy which the people of the North cannot realize nor understand *and which they have no right to discuss as they have no power to determine.* If the Negro is permitted to engage in politics his usefulness as a laborer is at an end. *He can no longer be controlled or utilized.* The South has to deal with him as an industrial and economic factor *and is forced to assert its control over him in sheer self-defense.*" *

Thus Negro labor must be managed, and control must be asserted over him. His possession of the ballot would make him a free laborer and would enable him to demand the wages of free labor. It is truly an "economic prob-

* Chicago *Inter-Ocean*, No. 4, 1890. (Footnote in original.)

lem," in which not only the Negro of the South is concerned, but also the interests of free labor in every section of this country.

These disfranchising enactments in that they lower the legal and economic status of the black man, also tend to lower his educational and social status. The political and economic supremacy of the southern oligarchy is dependent upon the ignorance and the social degradation of the Negro. It is, therefore, not surprising that the politicians now dominant in the South assert that education disqualifies him as a field hand—as a manageable factor— and that consequently there must be a decrease in the amount of money expended for his education or that his education must be directed along lines which will make him more adaptable to management as an economic factor for their sole benefit. . . .

The nation cannot put up with many more of these instruments of disfranchisement. It cannot endure the present ones very much longer. The question is ceasing to be one of interest merely to the Negro; it is rapidly becoming one of national moment. It is becoming a contest between democracy and oligarchy in which the stability and integrity of republican institutions are involved. Already a few thousand minions of oligarchy are exerting a larger influence in the national government than do millions of freemen who are obeying the Federal Constitution by maintaining a republican form of government. . . .

The total vote cast in the twenty congressional districts of South Carolina, Louisiana, and Mississippi in the election of 1898 was 91,184; while that polled in the ten congressional districts of Wisconsin was 332,204. Thus, although these states cast nearly two hundred and fifty thousand votes less than the state of Wisconsin, they control twice as much power as that state in the national legislature.

The southern people themselves cannot permit these violent infringements of the principles of republican government to continue without irrevocable detriment to their best and highest interests. In the degree that they stand by in silence and see the Negro stripped of his civil and political rights by a band of unscrupulous men who seek no higher end than their personal aggrandizement, they compromise their own civil and political freedom, and put in jeopardy the industrial progress of the South. The bane of the South today is her selfish and misguided political leadership, the men who will not scruple to sacrifice upon the altars of their insatiable ambition for power every interest linked with her economic prosperity and all consideration for civic virtue by which alone the greatness of a people is measured.

John L. Love, *The Disfranchisement of the Negro* (Washington, 1899).

II.

NEGRO ORGANIZATIONS—VIEWS AND PROPOSALS

Many organizations appeared among the Negro people during the last decade of the nineteenth century in response to the pressures and changes produced by developing imperialism. Five documents are published below to illustrate the various facets of this activity.

The first [a] is the founding statement, in the form of a memorial to Congress, of the short-lived National Association of Colored Men. Its organizing convention was held in Detroit in January, 1896, with its leaders, like Richard T. Greener, D. Augustus Straker and Joseph Dickinson, being largely confined to Negro professionals from New York, Illinois and Michigan. The whole tenor of this group was opposed to the Washington policy and its statement is in many ways a precursor of the Du Bois-founded Niagara Movement to appear a decade later.

Beginning in 1892, under the leadership of Booker T. Washington there were held annual Tuskegee Negro Conferences which were notable for their "down-to-earth" nature and avoidance of "theorizing," especially in terms of political activity. As an example of these is offered [b] the description of the Fifth Tuskegee Negro Conference (1896) by John Q. Johnson, formerly a mathematics instructor at Tuskegee.

Anticipatory of Du Bois' concept of Negro liberation as the work of a "talented tenth," of an intellectual elite, fully propounded by him in the 1900's, was the founding in March, 1897, of The American Negro Academy. The leader and first president of this organization was the Rev. Alexander Crummell, and prominent in it were three other ministers—F. J. Grimke, L. B. Moore and J. Albert Johnson—and four professors, W. E. B. Du Bois, W. H. Crogman, W. S. Scarborough and Kelly Miller, while its secretary was the newspaper editor and historian, John W. Cromwell. Its essential objects were, in its own words, "the promotion of literature, science and art . . . the fostering of higher education, the publication of scholarly work and the defense of the Negro against vicious assault." As expressive of this point of view, the third document [c] consists of the inaugural address of Mr. Crummell delivered before the Academy on March 5, 1897.

As this decade is marked by the significant development of a Negro professional group, so it witnesses the same phenomenon for a Negro bourgeoisie. This results in 1900 in the founding of the Negro Business Men's League, to be dealt with hereafter, but that, too, had forerunners. Indicative of these was The Invincible Sons and Daughters of Commerce founded in February, 1896. Among its leaders were Augustus M. Hodges of Brooklyn, N.Y., Miss Lucy L. Owens of Kempsville, Va., Amos W. Watkins of Oakland, Cal., L. L. Jackson of Bradley, Miss., George P. Isaacs of Brenham, Tex., and Mrs. Mary J. Smith of Vineland, N.J. To demonstrate the program of this organization, one of its advertisements, published in 1899, is reprinted as the fourth document [d] in this group.

The fifth document [e] consists of an article by Dr. Du Bois, published in 1899, descriptive of the conventions held that year by the National Afro-American Council and the National Association of Colored Women. The article is quite self-explanatory, so it need be said here merely that the organization of

Negro women described by Dr. Du Bois exists today as the National Council of Negro Women.

[a]

National Association of Colored Men, 1896

ADDRESS To The Congress of the United States:

This national conference of colored men, assembled upon call in Detroit, Mich., asserts, in support of this address to the American people, that the status of the colored race in the United States bears a closer analogy to that of denizens than to the honorable and indefeasible rights of native-born citizenship; that a national citizenship weakly subordinate to and timid in the face of state citizenship is a pitiful and humiliating spectacle under our amended constitution; that in at least three States of this Union today United States citizenship is a farce. . . . This conference neither assumes to dictate a conclusive and final form of "a more perfect union" than now obtains among our people, nor does it assume to have any other purpose in view in meeting than to assert its opposition to every species of injustices perpetrated upon our race by law or otherwise.

It aims to render more effective the great moral, educational, and social forces which eight millions of freemen ought to exercise in a free Republic. We aim to form a compact national organization, free and untrammeled in its local sectional interests but absolutely harmonious and resolute on all questions affecting the primary duties of our race as men and as citizens.

We aim at the present time to take on a new form and assume a new attitude among the citizens of this nation—not unduly arrogant nor assuming, but one which shall resent alike the assumption of any inferiority of our person or any subordination of our claims for rights—and to oppose even the presumption of a denial of any of our privileges.

Our further aim is the assertion of every claim due us as native-born citizens of the United States, a class next to the persecuted and disfranchised Indian, one of the oldest representatives in the United States, identified with the nation by ties of blood, by years of unrequited and still unpaid-for toil, by services in both arms of the United States during each war of the nation's history.

In seeking to unite and consolidate our interests, we do so not because we prefer to consider them apart from or incompatible with the interest of all other Americans, native and adopted, but for the more overwhelming and patent fact, demonstrated after a generation of freedom, that a selfish indifference to our rights, an un-American, a non-Christian contempt, and a universal assumption of our contentment with ostracism is equivalent to an inexorable *lex non scripta* which makes it at once our duty to step into line, form into solid columns, advance upon, and resolutely meet either those who negatively deny our assumption by pen, by voice, [or those who] by legislative action seek to degrade us as citizens or as human beings.

And while seeking to band ourselves together we disclaim all intention of setting up the interest of our race against those of other Americans by birth or naturalization, conscious that the welfare of the humblest citizen is as important to the state as that of the most powerful and the most intelligent.

We look for no superiority over others and we emphatically deny the assumption of superior rights by others over us. . . .

We recognize the efforts made hitherto in conventions and conferences toward the ends we are now aiming at as neither abortive nor useless. On the contrary, we regard them as of value as precedents for us in the efforts now being made to accomplish some lasting good for our race.

We desire to recall the fact also, by no means well-known, that the American Negro has at no time in the past been either unmindful or indifferent to or failed to assert and contend for his own rights. . . .

Our advance along the lines of industry, with the exception of church and educational philanthropy, is due mainly to our great capacity for work, the eagerness to embrace every opportunity for advancement, and our adaptability for every avenue and vocation in life.

While we are grateful for the millions which have been contributed North and South for the benefit of our race we assert that it is not one-tenth of what was due us for the fields reaped down, and the value of soil tilled and watered with tears or our blood.

Much of the opposition to the Negro today, South and North, in factory, bench, and shop, is not based as formerly on the ground of the Negro's fundamental incapacity, but is publicly stated and stoutly defended on the theory that the superior race must be protected from the Negro's physical prowess, his enthusiasm and acknowledged capacity. The truth of this proposition is shown from the frequency with which it is admitted openly at the court, discussed privately in the shop, or debated in synods and councils, or made the basis of ethnological or physical inquiry—a plain confession that the prevailing secret opinion of the Negro of 1895–96 is that he is not an inferior but a formidable competitor, whose efforts and presence are of so much account and so imminent that he must be repressed.

This conference desires to place itself on record as relying in its demand for rights and assertion of principles on fundamental grounds of human and civil rights, as expounded by the leading publicists, the leaders of liberty and thought in all ages. . . .

We aim at nothing unattainable, nothing Utopian, not what "the society of the future" is seeking, but merely what other citizens of this civilization are now enjoying. . . .

We begin, moreover, the second generation since the rebellion. We mark the opening of the militant period of our race in this country. . . . We hail and accept the burdens of the new time without fear and without favor. We understand that aggrieved persons must intelligently know first the ground upon which their rights rest, the limitations and coincidence with the rights of others, and the occasion and the measure of their assertion.

That time we conceive to be now. Our calm, deliberate advice is for every member of the race henceforth to employ every weapon of every kind of warfare legitimately and courageously in the demand for every right.

We are not frightened at the Mumbo-Jumbo of so-called social equality. We are not at pains to disclaim our aspiration after this myth; nor do we hasten to acknowledge our unfitness for it. We know that under the existing conditions of American society the same laws which apply to our other fellow-citizens apply equally to us. We recognize the universal law that no man or race gets more social or political preferment than he fights for and can maintain.

We do not acquiesce in the dictum that we must trust to time and to the pleasure or disposition of our enemies to grant rights. We hold it to be our duty to contend ourselves, and to teach our brothers to contend also; to confirm the wavering, rebuke the coward, inform the ignorant, strengthen the weak and despairing, knowing it is the part of the tyrants everywhere to continue to oppose and curtail the natural privileges of others, those they have oppressed. We trust we are not without some gifts of reason, and we trust we are not destitute of those elements of intelligence which will enable us to methodize our strength in the race now before us, to contend for all our rights thoughtfully and manfully.

We do not acknowledge that we now lack or have ever failed to feel at any stage of our career in this country, that warmth of patriotic imagination, that glow of race enthusiasm, which is so necessary for high endeavor.

We trust, too, the chastening hand of slavery and caste have only served to temper and deepen confidence in the ultimate right settlement of all our demands as men and citizens. . . .

Senate Document No. 61, 54th Cong., 1st Sess.

[b]

Tuskegee Negro Conference, 1896

Call to the Conference:

The Negro Conferences held at Tuskegee, Alabama, the last four years, under the auspices of the Tuskegee Normal Industrial Institute, Tuskegee, Alabama, have proved so helpful and instructive in showing the masses of colored people how to lift themselves up in their industrial, educational, moral and religious life, and have created so much general interest throughout the country, that it has been decided to hold another session of this Conference, Thursday, March 5, 1896.

The aim will be, as in the four previous years, to bring together for a quiet Conference, not the politicians, but the representatives of the common, hard-working farmers and mechanics—the bone and sinew of the Negro race—ministers and teachers.

Two objects will be kept in view—first, to find out from the people themselves the facts as to their condition and get their ideas as to the remedies for the present evils—second, to get information as to how the young men and women now being educated can best use their education in helping the masses.

At the last Conference there were nearly 800 representatives present and a large number gave encouraging evidence of how, as a result of previous meetings, homes had been secured, school-houses built, school terms extended, and the moral life of the people bettered.

In view of the economy which the people have been forced to practice during the last two years, owing to poor crops and low prices of cotton, this Conference will present an excellent medium through which to teach permanent economy and thrift.

It is planned to devote a portion of this Conference to a Woman's Conference.

On Friday, March 6th, the day following the Conference, there will be a meeting of the officers and teachers of the colored schools in the South, who may be at the Conference, for the purpose of comparing views and taking advantage of the lessons that may have been gotten from the Conference of the previous day.

It is believed that such a meeting for the elevation of the Negro, held in the Black Belt, with the lessons and impressions of the direct contact with the masses of the colored people the previous day fresh before them, can only result in much practical good to the cause of Negro education.

Aside from the work to be done in the South in an educational and moral sense, there can be no permanent prosperity till the whole industrial system, (especially the "Mortgage System") is revolutionized and put on a right basis, and there can be no better way to bring about the desired result than through such organizations as this Negro Conference.

Remarks by J. Q. Johnson:

When Mr. Booker T. Washington issued the call for the first Negro Conference, Feb. 23, 1892, he thought there would not be more than seventy-five who would respond, but to his surprise nearly 500 came. In February, 1893, about 800 attended the Conference, representing, it is safe to say, a Negro population of 200,000. In 1894 and '95 and especially 1896, the conference idea had become so prevalent in the South, that there were representatives from sister conferences which had been formed in almost every Southern State from Virginia to Texas.

Many conventions have been held, and many resolutions against wrongs, real and imaginary, have been passed by the Negro of the South since the war. But the Tuskegee movement seems to be the first serious effort whose wisdom, as voiced in the Conference declarations, is approved by the general suffrage of the Nation, North and South, white and black. It certainly tends to make the Negro a free man in deed and truth.

Welcoming remarks of Mr. Washington:

I want to thank you for your presence today. I know how busy you are at this season of the year, and how anxious you are to get back to your mules and oxen, but I think that you all will be helped by a day like this, and go back with your hearts lightened by hearing of each other's encouragements and discouragements.

I want to emphasize the object of these conferences. When they were first instituted, it was to confine ourselves mainly to conditions within our own power to remedy. We might discuss many wrongs which should be righted; but it seems to me that it is best to lay hold of the things we can put right rather than those we can do nothing but find fault with. Be perfectly frank with each other; state things as they are; do not say anything for mere sound, or because you think it will please one or displease another; let us hear the truth on all matters. We have many things to discourage and disappoint us, and we sometimes feel that we are slipping backward; but, I believe, if we do our duty in getting property, Christian education, and character, in some way or other the sky will clear up, and we shall make our way onward.

Declarations by the Conference:

1. We are more and more convinced, as we gather in these Annual Conferences, that we shall secure our rightful place as citizens in proportion as we possess Christian character, education, and property. To this end we urge parents to exercise rigid care in the control of their children, the doing away with the one-room cabin and the mortgage habit; we urge the purchase of land, improved methods of farming, diversified crops, attention to stock-raising, dairying, fruit-growing, and more interest in learning the trades, now too much neglected.

2. We urge that a larger proportion of our college educated men and women give the race the benefit of their education, along industrial lines, and that more educated ministers and teachers settle in the country districts.

3. As in most places the public schools are in session only three or four months during the year, we urge the people by every means possible, to supplement this time by at least three or four additional months each year, that no sacrifice be considered too great to keep the children in school, and that only the best teachers be employed.

4. We note with pleasure, the organization of other Conferences, and we advise that the number be still more largely increased.

John Q. Johnson, *Report of the Fifth Tuskegee Negro Conference* (Baltimore, 1896).

[c]

The American Negro Academy, 1897

. . . Nothing has surprised and gratified me so much as the anxiousness of many minds for the movement which we are on the eve of beginning. In the letters which our Secretary, Mr. Cromwell, has received, and which will be read to us, we are struck by the fact that one cultured man here and another there—several minds in different localities—tell him that this is just the thing they have desired, and have been looking for.

I congratulate you, therefore, gentlemen, on the opportuneness of your assemblage here. I felicitate you on the superior and lofty aims which have drawn you together. And, in behalf of your compeers, resident here in the city of Washington, I welcome you to the city and to the important deliberations to which our organization invites you.

Just here, let me call your attention to the uniqueness and specialty of this conference. It is unlike any other which has ever taken place in the history of the Negro, on the American Continent. There have been . . . numerous conventions of men of our race. There have been religious assemblies, political conferences, suffrage meetings, educational conventions. But *our* meeting is for a purpose which, while inclusive in some respects of these various concerns, is for an object more distinct and positive than any of them.

What then, it may be asked, is the special undertaking we have before us, in this Academy? My answer is the civilization of the Negro race in the United States, by the scientific processes of literature, art, and philosophy, through the agency of the cultured men of this same Negro race. And here, let me say, that the special race problem of the Negro in the United States is his civilization.

I doubt if there is a man in this presence who has a higher conception of Negro capacity than your speaker; and this of itself, precludes the idea, on my part, of race disparagement. But, it seems manifest to me that, as a race in this land, we have no art; we have no science; we have no philosophy; we have no scholarship. Individuals we have in each of these lines; but mere individuality cannot be recognized as the aggregation of a family, a nation, or a race; or as the interpretation of any of them. And until we attain the role of civilization, we cannot stand up and hold our place in the world of culture and enlightenment. And the forfeiture of such a place means, despite, inferiority, repulsion, drudgery, poverty, and ultimate death! Now gentlemen, for the creation of a complete and rounded man, you need the impress and the moulding of the highest arts. But how much more so for the realizing of a true and lofty *race* of men. What is true of a man is deeply true of a people. The special need in such a case is the force and application of the highest arts; not mere mechanism; not mere machinery; not mere handicraft; not the mere grasp on material things; not mere temporal ambitions. These are but incidents; important indeed, but pertaining mainly to man's material needs, and to the feeding of the body. . . .

What is the great difficulty with the black race, in this era, in this land? It is that both within their ranks, and external to themselves, by large schools of thought interested in them, material ideas in divers forms are made prominent, as the master-need of the race, and as the surest way to success. Men are constantly dogmatizing theories of sense and matter as the salvable hope of the race. Some of our leaders and teachers boldly declare, now, that *property* is the source of power; and then, that *money* is the thing which commands respect. At one time it is *official position* which is the masterful influence in the elevation of the race; at another, men are disposed to fall back upon *blood* and *lineage,* as the root (source) of power and progress.

Blind men! For they fail to see that neither property, nor money, nor station, nor office, nor lineage, are fixed factors, in so large a thing as the destiny of man; that they are not vitalizing qualities in the changeless hopes of humanity. The greatness of peoples springs from their ability to grasp the grand conceptions of being. It is the absorption of a people, of a nation, of a race, in large majestic and abiding things which lifts them up to the skies. These once apprehended, all the minor details of life follow in their proper places, and spread abroad in the details and the comfort of practicality. But until these gifts of a lofty civilization are secured, men are sure to remain low, debased and grovelling. . . .

Who are to be the agents to lift up this people of ours to the grand plane of civilization? Who are to bring them up to the height of noble thought, grand civility, a chaste and elevating culture, refinement, and the impulses or irrepressible progress? It is to be done by the scholars and thinkers, who have secured the vision which penetrates the center of nature, and sweeps the circles of historic enlightenment; and who have got insight into the life of things, and learned the art by which men touch the springs of action.

For to transform and stimulate the souls of a race or a people is a work of intelligence. It is a work which demands the clear induction of world-wide facts, and the perception of their application to new circumstances. It is a work which will require the most skillful resources, and the use of the scientific spirit.

But every man in a race cannot be a philosopher: nay, but few men in any land, in any age, can grasp ideal truth. Scientific ideas however must be apprehended, else there can be no progress, no elevation.

Just here arises the need for the trained and scholarly men of a race to employ their knowledge and culture and teaching and to guide both the opinions and habits of the crude masses. The masses, nowhere are, or can be, learned or scientific. The scholar is exceptional, just the same as a great admiral like Nelson is, or a grand soldier like Caesar or Napoleon. But the leader, the creative and organizing mind, is the master-need in all the societies of man. But, if they are not inspired with the notion of leadership and duty, then with all their Latin and Greek and science they are but pedants, trimmers, opportunists. For all true and lofty scholarship is weighty with the burdens and responsibilities of life and humanity.

But these reformers must not be mere scholars. They must needs be both scholars and philanthropists. For thus, indeed, has it been in all the history of men. In all the great revolutions, and in all great reforms which have transpired, scholars have been conspicuous; in the reconstruction of society, in formulating laws, in producing great emancipations, in the revival of letters, in the advancement of science, in the renaissance of art, in the destruction of gross superstitions and in the restoration of true and enlightened religion.

And what is the spirit with which they are to come to this work? My answer is, that *disinterestedness* must animate their motives and their acts. Whatever rivalries and dissensions may divide man in the social or political world, let generosity govern *us*. Let us emulate one another in the prompt recognition of rare genius, or uncommon talent. Let there be no tardy acknowledgment of worth in *our* world of intellect. If we are fortunate enough, to see, of a sudden, a clever mathematician of our class, a brilliant poet, a youthful, but promising scientist or philosopher, let us rush forward, and hail his coming with no hesitant admiration, with no reluctant praise.

It is only thus, gentlemen, that we can bring forth, stimulate, and uplift all the latent genius, garnered up, in the by-places and sequestered corners of this neglected Race.

It is only thus we can nullify and break down the conspiracy which would fain limit and narrow the range of Negro talent in this caste-tainted country. It is only thus, we can secure that recognition of genius and scholarship in the republic of letters, which is the rightful prerogative of every race of men. It is only thus we can spread abroad and widely disseminate that culture and enlightenment which shall permeate and leaven the entire social and domestic life of our people and so give that civilization which is the nearest ally of religion.

Alexander Crummell, *Civilization the Primal Need of the Race* (Washington, 1898).

[d]

The Invincible Sons and Daughters of Commerce, 1899

"BUSINESS, WEALTH AND RACE UNITY"
To have been first, denotes antiquity; to become first denotes progression.

THE INVINCIBLE SONS AND DAUGHTERS OF COMMERCE
(A national incorporated secret society of Colored merchants and buyers, organized February 12, 1896—Lincoln's birthday—is NOT the first Colored secret society organized for the betterment of the Colored American. It is however pushing its way to the front for the following reasons:)

The members of the I.S.D.C. are pledged and duly sworn to purchase all their goods from COLORED MERCHANTS AND SHOPKEEPERS, when said merchants and shopkeepers are members of the order, also to start stores in locations where there are none kept or owned by colored people.

The Supreme Board of Stockholders loans lodges MONEY TO START STORES. You cannot become nonfinancial as in the old societies. For every cent you put in your lodge you get a part of it back. THE I.S.D.C. IS NOT A DEATH

BENEFIT SOCIETY, BUT ONE TO BENEFIT YOU WHILE YOU LIVE, not after death, although we bury our dead. We differ from the old societies. Their motto is: "We care for the sick and bury the dead."

We believe that the key to wealth is BUSINESS. We believe that the key to business is RACE UNITY. We believe that the key to the so-called Negro problem is BUSINESS, WEALTH and RACE UNITY. We believe that race unity along the avenues of Business and Commerce will open to us all the gateways to true and full-fledged American citizenship, and have, therefore, organized the I.S.D.C., with the hope and belief that its membership will soon include every progressive colored man, woman and child in the United States. 509 subordinate lodges, "Family Leagues," "Housewives and Daughters Circles," "State Boards of Directors," one Junior Merchants' Club (boys), two "Little Mother's Lodges," and one "Merchants' Commandery," uniformed rank, have been set apart in the following States, to wit: Texas, Alabama, Virginia, Delaware, South Carolina, New York, New Jersey, Tennessee, Mississippi, Illinois, Massachusetts, Indiana and California, with all the rights, signs, grips, degrees, passwords, etc., of the order of I.S.D.C. OUR MOTTO: "We care for the well and raise the living. . . ."

The Indianapolis Freeman, February 18, 1899.

[e]

Du Bois on Two Negro Conventions, 1899

There can be no doubt as to the wave of intense feeling which has recently stirred American Negroes. Events of grave significance to them have followed fast and faster in the last ten years; the Wilmington riot, the murder of Postmaster Baker, the crucifixion of Hose,* continued lynchings and disturbances, progressive disfranchisement, the treatment of Negro soldiers, and the hostile attitude of trades-unions—all these things have profoundly moved these people, and to the student of race problems their action under such circumstances is of great interest. Moreover, in any consideration of the Negro problems we cannot longer ignore the progressive formation of a strong public opinion among these nine millions of men. This process has been slow and tedious but steady, as was natural among a group with common blood and similar history.

In local centers organizations became (after the Civil War) strong and successful, and today it would be difficult to find a Negro who does not belong to several distinctively Negro organizations in religious, business, or social lines. From such local groups to a national organization is a long step, but a natural one. Such organizations might grow from the local bodies by

* Later documents will elucidate these references.

accretion, as was the case with the African Methodist Church with its 500,000 members; or local bodies might federate into a national body, or finally a national body might be established and then plant local branches. Manifestly the last method would be most difficult to carry out among an inexperienced people, and yet the largeness of the plan is attractive. One of the earlier organizations of this sort was the Colored National League. It was organized in the early eighties, and established branches throughout the United States. It was modeled in some respects after the Irish Land League. It was never a strong organization, and internal dissensions and personal jealousies caused it to sink into inactivity after one or two meetings. It was one of those failures on which success is built.

Meantime an attempt at federation made by colored women was more successful. The Colored Woman's League of Washington, under the presidency of Mrs. John F. Cook, began some six years ago an excellent work in local reformatory enterprises. At the same time Colored Women's Clubs were formed in various parts of the country, and through the agency of Mrs. J. St. P. Ruffen, of Boston, and her bright little paper, the *Woman's Era,* these clubs were federated under the title of "The National Association of Colored Women."

Renewed signs of race conflicts in the South brought such a demand for the revival of the Colored National League that its last president, Mr. T. T. Fortune, of the *New York Age,* called a meeting in Rochester on the occasion of the dedication of the Frederick Douglass monument. At that meeting * the old League was merged into a new organization, to be known as the National Afro-American Council, under the presidency of Bishop Alexander Walters, of the [A.M.E.] Zion Church.

This summer it has happened that the third biennial session of the National Association of Colored Women, and the first annual conference of the National Afro-American Council met in Chicago during the same week, and the sessions were not only significant in themselves, but of singular importance as marking the development of this race. . . . Undoubtedly the women assembled at Chicago (on August 15) were rather above the average of their race, and represented the aristocracy among the Negroes. Consequently their evident intelligence and air of good-breeding served also to impress the onlookers. Some striking personalities were noticeable. Mrs. Mary Church Terrell, a tall, handsome woman, the wife of a Harvard man,† now principal of the Washington Colored High School, was the president, and presided with dignity and tact. Perhaps the finest specimen of Negro womanhood present was Mrs. Josephine S. Yates, of Kansas City, a dark-

* Held September 15, 1898.
† Robert H. Terrell, appointed by Pres. Wilson as judge of Washington's municipal court.

brown matron, with a quiet air of dignity and earnestness. The widow of ex-Senator B. K. Bruce and the wife of Booker T. Washington were also noticeable figures.

The best papers of the meeting were those by Mrs. Yates on "An Equal Moral Standard for Men and Women," by Miss J. E. Holmes, of Atlanta, on "The Convict Lease System," and by Mrs. Elizabeth C. Carter, of New Bedford, on "Practical Club Work." In these papers, as in many others, the keynote struck was the necessity of work among children—a line of thought which especially characterized the meeting.

On the day that the women adjourned, August 17th, the National Afro-American Council met. . . . The Council was a far different body from the Association; its members were mostly male, its scope and aims far wider, and in its attendance, it was more faithfully representative of the rank and file of the American Negroes. While then its culture and taste were in painful contrast to the women's session, yet its candid earnestness and faithful striving made it a far more reliable reflex of the mental attitude of the millions it represented. The opposing forces present were easily distinguished; those who desired radical action in regard to lynch law, those who desired to defend the Republican administration from attack, those who favor some schemes of migration, some who saw a chance to use the assembly for their own interests, and those who desired above all to strengthen this national organization. The set papers were of varying merit, and not as interesting as the spontaneous debates on the floor. Uppermost in the minds of all were the subjects of Southern lynchings and the attitude of President McKinley.

On the whole, the effect of the debating and conference was good, and behind all froth and intemperate or irrelevant talk there was distinct evidence of sensible restraint and careful well-reasoned leadership. This was especially shown in the resolutions adopted, which were short, concise and clear. The resolution with regard to lynching was as follows:

"*Resolved,* That it is the duty of the United States Government to see to it that its citizens are not deprived of life and liberty without due process of law, and we solemnly demand such national and constitutional legislation as shall at least guarantee to American citizens as great protection from mob violence as is given citizens of foreign birth resident here.

"The widespread crime of lynching persons accused of lawbreaking is an offense against civilization which demands punishment; and we believe it lies in the power of Congress to provide such repressive legislation as shall prevent justice in America from becoming a byword and a mockery."

The second and third resolutions condemned "the despoiler of homes and the degrader of womanhood, be he white or black," and urged Negroes to become artisans and businessmen. Over the fourth resolution there was long and sharp debate, and attempts were made by some to make it less pointed, and by others to make it more scathing. It reads:

"*Resolved,* That we are heartily grieved that the President of the United States and those in authority have not from time to time used their high station to voice the best conscience of the nation in regard to mob violence and fair treatment of justly deserving men . . ."

And finally, the Council affirmed: ". . . we declare it to be our unalterable purpose to strive by all proper and manly means to vindicate the rights and perform our duties right here in the land of our birth."

The convention was composed largely of professional men and school teachers, with a few clerks in public service, merchants, farmers and workingmen. They were men of average ability, rather talkative and excitable. There were some conspicuous figures: The erratic Bishop Turner, the tall and genial President Walters; Henderson, who lost home and property at the Wilmington riot—a sad-faced, earnest man; the secretary, Mrs. [Ida B.] Wells Barnett, who began the anti-lynching crusade, and the dark-faced [Isaiah T.] Montgomery, who alone represented his race in the Mississippi Constitutional Convention.

There can be little doubt that these two conventions have had a good effect. They are an earnest of what we may look for when careful, thoughtful organization among Negroes shall enable them to act for themselves; rescuing and protecting their weak ones and guiding the strong.

The Independent (N.Y.), September 7, 1899, LI, pp. 2425–27.

III.

NEGROES STRUGGLE AGAINST DISABILITIES

Petitions against existing grievances, and memorials and addresses appeared from Negroes throughout this decade of heightened oppression. One of the subjects to which particular attention was given was that of lynching, with which a later section will deal. In addition, protests were levied against the Bourbons' disfranchisement efforts, their attacks upon already meager educational provisions and their general policy of terror.

Five documents are reprinted below to illustrate this. The first document [a] is in two parts and deals with the South Carolina constitutional convention of 1895. Here the masters of this state were following the example set by their class brothers in Mississippi five years before and were engaged in disfranchising Negroes through the use of poll taxes, literacy and property qualifications for voting. The document is indicative of the efforts of the six Negro delegates at this convention to block this antidemocratic move. Its first part consists of the ordinance proposed by Thomas E. Miller, a former Congressman and a lawyer from Beaufort, which would have required submitting to the vote of the people the constitution coming out of the 1895 convention; the second part represents the attempt by William J. Whipper, likewise a Negro lawyer from Beaufort, to provide for the enfranchisement of all in South Carolina, regardless of sex or color. The four other Negroes taking part in these unsuccessful moves were the former Congressman, Robert Smalls, a teacher from Georgetown, R. B. Anderson, a merchant, James Wigg and a lawyer, Isaiah R. Reed, both of Beaufort.

In a category quite by itself is the petition of Harriet Tubman which forms the second document [b] of this group. References have recurred in this work to this remarkable woman. Harriet Tubman, escaped slave, underground railroad agent and conductor, Abolitionist organizer, friend of John Brown, fighter for women's rights, nurse, scout, spy during the Civil War, and battler for Negro liberation until her death in 1913, was one of the truly towering figures of American history.

She was poverty-stricken all her life and after the Civil War attempted to persuade the government to pay her for services rendered the Union. Assisting her was a prominent up-state New Yorker named Charles P. Wood. In 1868, he submitted documentary proof (including letters from the Secretary of War and various Army officers) of her wartime services, but no action was forthcoming from Congress for thirty years. Finally, in 1897, a Senate Committee recommended that Harriet Tubman be given $25 a month for the rest of her life, but $5 was whittled from this miserable pittance by Southern Congressmen before, in 1898, the Government of the United States enacted a law in her favor.

The document printed below was an affidavit sworn to by Harriet Tubman on January 1, 1898 in connection with the final effort to obtain a government pension.

The third document [c] is an open letter sent by Booker T. Washington to the Louisiana Constitutional Convention of 1898 in a vain attempt to keep that body from disfranchising Negroes.

The fourth document [d] is a petition signed by twenty-four leading Negroes of Georgia, including John Hope, W. A. Pledger and W. E. B. Du Bois, the latter of whom was its author. This was submitted to the Georgia legislature in November, 1899 and protested the Hardwick Bill which, by literacy and property devices, sought to deprive the Negro of the vote. The Bill was defeated, but a constitutional amendment later accomplished the purpose.

The last document [e] is a stirring anti-imperialist clarion call for resistance from the Massachusetts branch of the Colored National League, meeting in Boston in October, 1899. It took the form of an open letter to President McKinley and was signed by I. D. Barnett, Edward E. Brown, Archibald H. Grimke, Edwin G. Walker and many others.

[a]

The South Carolina Constitutional Convention, 1895

1. Thomas E. Miller's Proposed Ordinance:

Mr. Miller introduced the following ordinance, which was read the first time and referred to the Committee on Judicial Department: *

---

* Mr. Miller's proposed ordinance was buried in committee. The 1895 Constitution of South Carolina was not submitted to a vote of the people.

An Ordinance to Provide that the Constitution Shall Be Submitted to the People To Be Ratified.

Be it Resolved: 1. That after the Constitution shall have been passed in convention and duly attested the said Constitution shall be submitted to the qualified electors of the State to be voted for, and if a majority of all votes cast be in favor of said Constitution, it shall then be, and become, the Constitution of the State of South Carolina.

2. The said vote shall be taken on the second Tuesday in January, A.D. 1896, at the various voting precincts in each and every County of the State.

3. The Governor shall, on the first Tuesday in December, 1895, issue an order for said vote to be taken under the election laws of the State. The ballot shall be plain white paper two and one-half inches wide by five inches long. The favorable ballot shall contain the words, "I am in favor of the new Constitution"; the ballot against shall contain the words, "I am not in favor of the new Constitution." Any and all other ballots, save as above provided, found in any box shall not be counted or included in the count of the votes for or against the ratification of the said Constitution.

2. William J. Whipper's proposed suffrage law:

Mr. Whipper offered the following . . .

Section 1. All elections by the people shall be by ballot.

Section 2. Every qualified elector shall be eligible to any office to be voted for.

Section 3. Every citizen * of the United States of the age of twenty-one years and upwards not laboring under the disabilities named in this Constitution and otherwise qualified shall be a legal elector.

Section 4. The qualifications for suffrage shall be residence in the State one year and in the County sixty days before any general election. The General Assembly shall provide for the election or appointment of one registrar for each County, who shall register all persons over the age of twenty-one years not disqualified by this Section. . . .

Section 5. Any person denied registration shall have the right to appeal to any Court or Judge thereof to determine any question that may arise in consequence of such denial.

Section 6. For the purpose of voting no person shall be deemed to have gained or lost a residence by reason of his presence or absence while employed in the service of the United States, nor while engaged in the navigation of the waters of this State or of the United States or on the high seas.

Section 7. Each political party shall be represented on the Board of

---

* Observe that this includes women.

County Canvassers for each County; also on the Board of Managers at each precinct. . . .*

Journal of the Constitutional Convention of the State of South Carolina . . . Sept. 10–Dec. 4, 1895 (Columbia, 1895), pp. 89, 412–13.

[b]

Harriet Tubman's Petition, 1898

I am about 75 years of age. I was born and reared in Dorchester County, Md. My maiden name was Araminta Ross. Sometime prior to the late War of the Rebellion I married John Tubman who died in the State of Maryland on the 30th day of September, 1867. I married Nelson Davis, a soldier of the late war, on the 18th day of March, 1869, at Auburn, N.Y.

I furnished the original papers in my claim to one Charles P. Wood, then of Auburn, N.Y., who died several years ago. Said Wood made copies of said original papers which are herewith annexed. I was informed by said Wood that he sent said original papers to one James Barrett, an attorney . . . Washington, D.C., and I was told by the wife of said Barrett that she handed the original papers to the Hon. C. D. MacDougall, then a member of the House of Representatives.

My claim against the U.S. is for three years' service as nurse and cook in hospitals, and as commander of several men (eight or nine) as scouts during the late War of Rebellion, under directions and orders of Edwin M. Stanton, Secretary of War, and of several generals.

I claim for my services above named the sum of eighteen hundred dollars. The annexed copies have recently been read over to me and are true to the best of my knowledge, information and belief.

Earl Conrad, "The Charles P. Wood Manuscripts of Harriet Tubman," in *The Negro History Bulletin*, Jan. 1950, pp. 94–95.

[c]

Washington to Louisiana Constitutional Convention, 1898

In addressing you this letter, I know that I am running the risk of appearing to meddle with something that does not concern me. But since I know that nothing but sincere love for our beautiful Southland, which I hold as near to my heart as any of you can, and a sincere love for every black and white man within her borders, is the only thing actuating me to write, I am willing to be misjudged, if need be, if I can accomplish a little good.

* The Convention rejected Mr. Whipper's proposal by a vote of 130 to 6. The six positive votes came from the Negro delegates.

But I do not believe that you, gentlemen of the Convention, will misinterpret my motives. What I say will, I believe, be considered in the same earnest spirit in which I write.

I am no politician; on the other hand, I have always advised my race to give attention to acquiring property, intelligence and character, as the necessary bases of good citizenship, rather than to mere political agitation. But the question upon which I write is out of the region of ordinary politics; it affects the civilization of two races, not for a day alone, but for a very long time to come: it is up in the region of duty of man to man, of Christian to Christianity.

Since the war, no State has had such an opportunity to settle for all time the race question, so far as it concerns politics, as is now given in Louisiana. Will your Convention set an example to the world in this respect? Will Louisiana take such high and just grounds in respect to the Negro that no one can doubt that the South is as good a friend to the Negro as he possesses elsewhere? In all this, gentlemen of the Convention, I am not pleading for the Negro alone, but for the morals, the higher life of the white man as well. For the more I study this question, the more I am convinced that it is not so much a question as to what the white man will do with the Negro, as to what the Negro will do with the white man's civilization.

The Negro agrees with you that it is necessary to the salvation of the South that restriction be put upon the ballot. I know that you have two serious problems before you; ignorant and corrupt government on the one hand, and on the other, a way to restrict the ballot so that control will be in the hands of the intelligent, without regard to race. With the sincerest sympathy with you in your efforts to find a way out of the difficulty, I want to suggest that no State in the South can make a law that will provide an opportunity or temptation for an ignorant white man to vote and withhold the same opportunity from an ignorant colored man, without injuring both men. No State can make a law that can thus be executed without dwarfing for all time the morals of the white man in the South. Any law controlling the ballot, that is not absolutely just and fair to both races, will work more permanent injury to the whites than to the blacks.

The Negro does not object to an educational or property test, but let the law be so clear that no one clothed with State authority will be tempted to perjure and degrade himself, by putting one interpretation upon it for the white man and another for the black man. Study the history of the South, and you will find that when there has been the most dishonesty in the matter of voting, there you will find today the lowest moral condition of both races. First, there was the temptation to act wrongly with the Negro's ballot. From this it was an easy step to dishonesty with the white man's ballot, to the carrying of concealed weapons, to the murder of a Negro, and then to the murder of a white man, and then to lynching. I entreat you not to pass such a law as will prove an eternal millstone about the neck of your children. . . .

I beg of you, further, that in the degree you close the ballot-box against the ignorant, that you open the school house. More than one-half of the people of your State are Negroes.* No State can long prosper when a large percentage of its citizenship is in ignorance and poverty, and has no interest in government. I beg of you that you do not treat us as alien people. We are not aliens. You know us; you know that we have cleared your forests, tilled your fields, nursed your children and protected your families. There is an attachment between us that few understand. While I do not presume to be able to advise you, yet it is in my heart to say that if your Convention would do something that would prevent, for all time, strained relations between the two races, and would permanently settle the matter of political relations in our Southern States, at least, let the very best educational opportunities be provided for both races; and add to this the enactment of an election law that shall be incapable of unjust discrimination; at the same time providing that in proportion as the ignorant secure education, property and character, they will be given the right of citizenship. Any other course will take from one-half your citizens interest in the State, and hope and ambition to become intelligent producers and taxpayers—to become useful and virtuous citizens. Any other course will tie the white citizens of Louisiana to a body of death.

The Negroes are not unmindful of the fact that the white people of your State pay the greater proportion of the school taxes, and that the poverty of the State prevents it from doing all that it desires for public education, yet I believe you will agree with me, that ignorance is more costly to the State than education; that it will cost Louisiana more not to educate her Negroes than it will cost to educate them. In connection with a generous provision for public schools, I believe that nothing will so help my own people in your State as provision at some institution for the highest academic and normal training, in connection with thorough training in agriculture, mechanics and domestic economy. . . . An institution that will give this training of the hand, along with the highest mental culture, will soon convince our people that their own salvation is in the ownership of property, industrial and business development, rather than in mere political agitation.

The highest test of the civilization of any race is in its willingness to extend a helping hand to the less fortunate. A race, like an individual, lifts

* According to the 1900 census there were 650,804 Negroes and 729,612 whites in Louisiana.

itself up by lifting others up. Surely no people ever had a greater chance to exhibit the highest Christian fortitude and magnanimity than is now presented to the people of Louisiana. It requires little wisdom or statesmanship to repress, to crush out, to retard the hopes and aspirations of a people, but the highest and most profound statesmanship is shown in guiding and stimulating a people so that every fibre in the body, mind and soul shall be made to contribute in the highest degree to the usefulness and nobility of the State. It is along this line that I pray God the thoughts and activities of your Convention be guided.

An Open Letter by Booker T. Washington to the Louisiana Constitutional Convention, February 19th, 1898 (n.p., n.d.).

[d]

Georgia Negroes on the Hardwick Bill, 1899

We, your petitioners, understanding that there lies before your honorable body a bill known as the Hardwick Bill, designed to change radically the basis of suffrage in this Commonwealth, desire respectfully to lay the following considerations before you.

It is a solemn moment when a free community proposes to change the fundamental form of its Government, and especially to determine what voice its citizens shall have in the conduct of its affairs. Such changes and decisions, affecting the very root of Democratic institutions in this country, ought not to be undertaken and carried through without careful deliberation, wise forethought and a broad and statesmanlike spirit of Justice.

Especially is this true in Georgia today. The future prosperity of our State depends upon the preservation within her borders of peace and security, good government and the impartial administration of law. Whatever tends to excite strife and restlessness, or opens the door to unfair dealing, or spreads the sense of injustice among the masses of the people is unwise and impolitic.

It has come to be the concensus of opinion in civilized Nations that in the long run government must be based on the consent of the governed. This is the verdict of more than three centuries of strife and bloodshed, and it is a verdict not lightly to be set aside. Nevertheless, the Nineteenth century with its broader outlook and deeper experience has added one modifying clause to this, to which the world now assents, namely: That in order to take part in government, the governed must be intelligent enough to recognize and choose their own best good; that consequently in free governments based on universal manhood suffrage, it is fair and right to impose on voters an educational qualification, so long as the State furnishes free school facilities to all children.

To these principles, we, as representatives of the Negroes of Georgia, give full assent. We join heartily with the best conscience of the State, of the Nation, and of the civilized world in demanding a pure intelligent ballot, free from bribery, ignorance, fraud and intimidation. And to secure this, we concur in the movement towards imposing fair and impartial qualifications upon voters, whether based on education, or property, or both.

Nor is this, gentlemen of the Legislature, a light sacrifice on our part. We Negroes are today, in large degree, poor and ignorant through the crime of the Nation. Through no fault of our own, are we here brought into contact with a civilization higher than that of the average of our race. We have not been sparing in our efforts to improve.

Notwithstanding all this, so far as the Hardwick Bill proposes to restrict the right of suffrage to all who, irrespective of race or color, are intelligent enough to vote properly, we heartily endorse it. But there are two features of the proposed law against which we desire hereby to enter solemn and emphatic protest. These are:

First. The so-called "Grandfather" clause, which provides "That no male person who was on January 1st, 1867 or any time prior thereto, entitled to vote under the laws of the State wherein he then resided, and no lineal descendant of such person shall be denied the right to register or vote at any election in this State by reason of his failure to possess the educational qualification provided for in this paragraph." And

Secondly. We protest against the clause which restricts the right to vote to those who can read and UNDERSTAND a clause in the Constitution; and which allows the local election officers to be the final judges of this "understanding." We firmly believe that the exceptions in the first mentioned clause are wrong in principle, unfair in application, and in flat contradiction to those very principles of reform upon which the whole proposal is based; while the second clause is a direct invitation to injustice and fraud. . . .

If ignorance is dangerous to Democratic institutions, then proscribe IGNORANCE and not COLOR.

If bribery and vote selling have too often made popular elections in Georgia a farce, then proscribe BRIBERY and VOTE SELLING, and not COLOR.

It is ignorance and crime that menace decent government in Georgia, and not the color of its citizens. Away then with ignorance and crime, but let the rule that regulates the restrictions apply to white and black alike. . . .

The "understanding clause" of the proposed bill is an open door to manipulation and dishonesty. In a free and just government no local election officer ought to be clothed with discretionary or judicial function. Wherever this has been done, fraud and chicanery have been the inevitable result. If this clause should become a law the registrars and election managers would virtually have the power of deciding who should vote. The Party in power today which places such a weapon in the hands of its appointees, may, in the future, find the very machinery turned against itself by the Party in power tomorrow. In such ways are the foundations of popular government sapped.

Against these two propositions, therefore, we desire to enter our earnest plea, being convinced that any law which proposes discrimination against 850,000 souls, and which openly clears the way for dishonesty in popular elections, is contrary to the genius of our Christian civilization, and a menace to free Democratic institutions.

We call attention to the fact that even under present conditions, Negro voters in Georgia have from time to time shown that sound judgment which seeks to put respectability and intelligence in control over the affairs of the State. Even in times of grave political excitement, when in more than fifty counties of the State the blacks had a clear majority of the registered vote, they never aspired to political supremacy, but preferred to use their votes to put in office some of the best white officials that have ever ruled the State. Seldom in the history of this Commonwealth have disturbances arisen by reason of the Negroes exercising the right of suffrage, and whatever good government Georgia has enjoyed in the last decade is due in no small degree to men who owe their election to Negro suffrage.

For these reasons, gentlemen of the Legislature, we plead for the defeat of the above mentioned features of the Hardwick Bill, which would tend to increase that race antagonism between citizens of our State which all good men deeply deplore. We know that there are among our white fellow citizens broad-minded men who realize that the prosperity of Georgia is bound up with the prosperity of the Georgia Negro; that no Nation or State can advance faster than its laboring classes, and that whatever hinders, degrades or discourages the Negroes weakens and injures the State. To such Georgians we appeal in this crisis: Race antagonism and hatred have gone too far in this State; let us stop here; let us insist that we go no further; let us countenance no measure or movement calculated to increase that deep and terrible sense of wrong under which so many today labor.

May the Twentieth century of the Prince of Peace dawn upon an era of generous sympathy and forbearance between these two great races in Georgia, and not upon a season of added injustice and antipathy.

A Memorial to the Legislature of Georgia on the Hardwick Bill—a printed folder in the papers of Dr. W. E. B. Du Bois.

[e]

Massachusetts Negroes to President McKinley, 1899

We, colored people of Massachusetts in mass meeting assembled to consider our oppressions and the state of the country relative to the same, have resolved to address ourselves to you in an open letter, notwithstanding your extraordinary, your incomprehensible silence on the subject of our wrongs in your annual and other messages to Congress, as in your public utterances to the people at large. We address ourselves to you, sir, not as suppliants, but as of right, as American citizens, whose servant you are, and to whom you are bound to listen, and for whom you are equally bound to speak, and upon occasion to act, as for any other body of your fellow-countrymen in like circumstances. We ask nothing for ourselves at your hands, as chief magistrate of the republic, to which all American citizens are not entitled. We ask for the enjoyment of life, liberty and the pursuit of happiness equally with other men. We ask for the free and full exercise of all the rights of American freemen, guaranteed to us by the Constitution and laws of the Union, which you were solemnly sworn to obey and execute. We ask you for what belongs to us, the high sanction of Constitution and law, and the Democratic genius of our institutions and civilization. These rights are everywhere throughout the South denied to us, violently wrested from us by mobs, by lawless legislatures, and nullifying conventions, combinations, and conspiracies, openly, defiantly, under your eyes, in your constructive and actual presence. And we demand, which is a part of our rights, protection, security in our life, our liberty, and in the pursuit of our individual and social happiness under a government, which we are bound to defend in war, and which is equally bound to furnish us in peace protection, at home and abroad.

We have suffered, sir—God knows how much we have suffered!—since your accession to office, at the hands of a country professing to be Christian, but which is not Christian; from the hate and violence of a people claiming to be civilized, but who are not civilized, and you have seen our sufferings, witnessed from your high place our awful wrongs and miseries, and yet you have at no time and on no occasion opened your lips in our behalf. Why? we ask. Is it because we are black and weak and despised? Are you silent because without any fault of our own we were enslaved and held for more than two centuries in cruel bondage by your forefathers? Is it because we bear the marks of those sad generations of Anglo-Saxon brutality and wickedness, that you do not speak? . . .

The struggle of the Negro to rise out of his ignorance, his poverty and his social degradation . . . to the full stature of his American citizenship, has been met everywhere in the South by the active ill will and determined race hatred and opposition of the white people of that section. Turn where he will, he encounters this cruel and implacable spirit. He dare not speak openly the thoughts which rise in his breast. He has wrongs such as have never in modern times been inflicted on a people, and yet he must be dumb in the midst of a nation which prates loudly of democracy and humanity, boasts itself the champion of oppressed people abroad, while it looks on indifferent, apathetic, at appalling enormities and iniquities at home, where the victims are black and the criminals white. The suppression, the terror wrought at the South is so complete, so ever-present, so awful, that no Negro's life or property is safe for a day who ventures to raise his voice to heaven in indignant protest and appeal against the deep damnation and despotism of such a social state. Even teachers and leaders of this poor, oppressed and patient people may not speak, lest their institutions of learning and industry, and their own lives pay for their temerity at the swift hands of savage mobs. But if the peace of Warsaw, the silence of death reign over our people and their leaders at the South, we of Massachusetts are free, and must and shall raise our voice to you and through you to the country, in solemn protest and warning against the fearful sin and peril of such explosive social conditions. We, sir, at this crisis and extremity in the life of our race in the South, and in this crisis and extremity of the republic as well, in the presence of the civilized world, cry to you to pause, if but for for an hour, in pursuit of your national policy of "criminal aggression" abroad to consider the "criminal aggression" at home against humanity and American citizenship, which is in the full tide of successful conquest at the South, and the tremendous consequences to our civilization; and the durability of the Union itself, of this universal subversion of the supreme law of the land, of democratic institutions, and of the precious principle of the religion of Jesus in the social and civil life of the Southern people.

With one accord, with an anxiety that wrenched our hearts with cruel hopes and fears, the Colored people of the United States turned to you when Wilmington, N.C. was held for two dreadful days and nights in the clutch of a bloody revolution; when Negroes, guilty of no crime except the color of their skin and a desire to exercise the rights of their American citizenship, were butchered like dogs in the streets of that ill-fated town; and when government of the people by the people and for the people perished in your very presence by the hands of violent men during those bitter November [1898] days for want of federal aid, which you would not and did not furnish, on the plea that you could not give what was not asked for by a coward and recreant governor. And we well understood at that time, sir, not withstanding your plea of constitutional inability to cope with the rebellion in Wilmington, that where there is a will with constitutional law-yers and rulers there is always a way, and where there is no will there is no way. We well knew that you lacked the will and, therefore, the way to meet that emergency.

It was the same thing with that terrible ebullition of mob spirit at Phoenix, S.C., when black men were hunted and murdered, and white men shot and driven out of that place by a set of white savages,* who cared not for the Constitution and the laws of the United States any more than they do for the Constitution and the laws of an empire dead and buried a thou-sand years. We looked in vain for some word or some act from you. . . .

And, when you made your Southern tour a little later, and we saw how cunningly you catered to Southern race prejudice and proscription; how you, the one single public man and magistrate of the country, who, by virtue of your exalted office, ought under no circumstances to recognize caste distinctions and discriminations among your fellow citizens, received white men at the Capitol in Montgomery, Ala., and black men afterward in a Negro church; how you preached patience, industry, moderation to your long-suffering black fellow citizens, and patriotism, jingoism and imperialism to your white ones; when we saw all those things, scales of illusion in respect to your object fell from our eyes. We felt that the President of the United States, in order to win the support of the South to his policy of "criminal aggression" in the far East, was ready and willing to shut his eyes, ears and lips to the "criminal aggression" of that section against the Con-stitution and the laws of the land, wherein they guarantee civil rights and citizenship to the Negro, whose ultimate reduction to a condition of fixed and abject serfdom is the plain purpose of the Southern people and their laws.

When, several months subsequently, you returned to Georgia, the mob spirit, as if to evince its supreme contempt for your presence and the federal executive authority which you represent, boldly broke into a prison shed [in Palmetto], where were confined helpless Negro prisoners on a charge of incendiarism and brutally murdered five of them. These men were Ameri-can citizens, entitled to the rights of American citizens, protection and trial by due process of law. . . . They ought to have been sacred charges in the hands of any civilized or semicivilized State and people. But almost in your hearing, before your eyes (and you the chief magistrate of a country loudly boastful of its freedom, Christianity and civilization), they were atrociously

---

* Beginning in November, 1898, and lasting several weeks, a reign of terror was directed against Negroes and white radicals in and around Phoenix, S.C. Six Negroes were murdered, and many others were wounded or lashed.

murdered. Did you speak? Did you open your lips to express horror of the awful crime and stern condemnation of the incredible villainy and complicity of the constituted authorities of Georgia in the commission of this monstrous outrage, which out-barbarized barbarism and stained through and through with indelible infamy before the world your country's justice, honor and humanity?

Still later, considering the age, the circumstances and the nation in which the deed was done, Georgia committed a crime unmatched for moral depravity and sheer atrocity during the century. A Negro [Sam Hose], charged with murder and criminal assault, the first charge he is reported by the newspapers to have admitted, and the second to have denied, was taken one quiet Sunday morning from his captors, and burned to death with indescribable and hellish cruelty in the presence of cheering thousands of the so-called best people of [Newnan,] Georgia—men, women and children, who had gone forth on a Christian Sabbath to the burning of a human being as to a country festival and holiday of innocent enjoyment and amusement. . . . The death of Hose was quickly followed by that of the Negro preacher, Strickland, guiltless of crime, under circumstances and with a brutality of wickedness almost matching in horror and enormity the torture and murder of the first; and this last was succeeded by a third victim; who was literally lashed to death by the wild, beastlike spirit of a Georgia mob, for daring merely to utter his abhorrence of the Palmetto iniquity and slaughter of helpless prisoners.

Did you speak? Did you utter one word of reprobation, of righteous indignation, either as magistrate or as man? Did you break the shameful silence of shameful months with so much as a whisper of a whisper against the deep damnation of such defiance of all law, human and divine; such revulsion of men into beasts, and relapses of communities into barbarism in the very center of the republic, and amid the sanctuary of the temple of American liberty itself? You did not, sir, but your Attorney-General did, and he only to throw out to the public, to your meek and long-suffering colored fellow citizens, the cold and cautious legal opinion that the case of Hose has no federal aspect. Mr. President, has it any moral or human aspect, seeing that Hose was a member of the Negro race, whom your Supreme Court once declared has no rights in America which white men are bound to respect? Is this infamous dictum of that tribunal still the supreme law of the land? We ask you, sir, since recent events in Arkansas, Mississippi, Alabama, Virginia and Louisiana, as well as in Georgia and the Carolinas, indeed throughout the South, and your own persistent silence, and the persistent silence of every member of your Cabinet on the subject of the wrongs of that race in those States, would appear together to imply as much.

Had, eighteen months ago, the Cuban revolution to throw off the yoke of Spain, or the attempt of Spain to subdue the Cuban rebellion, any federal aspect? We believe that you and the Congress of the United States thought that they had, and therefore used, finally, the armed force of the nation to expel Spain from that island. Why? Was it because "the people of the Island of Cuba are, and of right ought to be free and independent?" You and the Congress said as much, and may we fervently pray, sir, in passing that the freedom and independence of that brave people shall not much longer be denied them by our government? But to resume, there was another consideration which, in your judgment, gave to the Cuban question a federal aspect, which provoked at last the armed interposition of our government in the affairs of that island, and this was "the chronic condition of disturbance in Cuba so injurious and menacing to our interests and tranquillity, as well as shocking to our sentiments of humanity"— Wherefore you presently fulfilled "a duty to humanity by ending a situation, the indefinite prolongation of which had become insufferable."

Mr. President, had that "chronic condition of disturbance in Cuba so injurious and menacing to our interests and tranquillity, as well as shocking to our sentiments of humanity," which you wished to terminate and did terminate, a federal aspect, while that not less "chronic condition of disturbance" in the South, which is a thousand times more "injurious and menacing to our interests and tranquillity," as well as far more "shocking to our sentiments of humanity," or ought to be, none whatever? Is it better to be Cuban revolutionists fighting for Cuban independence than American citizens striving to do their simple duty at home? Or is it better only in case those American citizens doing their simple duty at home happen to be Negroes residing in the Southern States?

Are crying national transgressions and injustices more "injurious and menacing" to the Republic, as well as "shocking to its sentiments of humanity," when committed by a foreign state, in foreign territory, against a foreign people, than when they are committed by a portion of our own people against a portion of our own people at home? There were those of our citizens who did not think that the Cuban question possessed any federal aspect, while there were others who thought otherwise; and these, having the will and the power, eventually found a way to suppress a menacing danger to the country and a wrong against humanity at the same time. . . . If, sir, you have the disposition, as we know that you have the power, we are confident that you will be able to find a constitutional way to reach us in our extremity, and our enemies also, who are likewise enemies to great public interests and national tranquillity.

Open Letter to President McKinley from the Colored People of Massachusetts (n.p., n.d.).

IV.

LYNCHING

According to the conservative figures of the Tuskegee Institute, 3,426 Negroes have been lynched in the United States from 1882 through 1947. Of this total, thirty-six percent, or 1,217, were lynched from 1890 through 1900. This, in terms of seared flesh and broken necks, was part of the mortal casualty list suffered by the Negro people as monopoly capitalism fastened its grip upon them and crushed the protest movements of its victims—Negro and white.

Against this depravity the Negro people fought bravely. They organized the anti-lynching movement in the United States and their letters, petitions and delegations forced this question upon the attention of the nation.

To illustrate this nine documents follow. The first [a] is a letter from a Negro minister, the Rev. E. Malcolm Argyle, dated Baxter, Arkansas, March 14, 1892, descriptive of the frightful conditions of violence in his state and indicating some organized forms of counteraction taken by Negroes.

The second document [b] consists of abstracts from an article on "Lynch Law in the South" by the aged Frederick Douglass which was published in August, 1892. Here Douglass is at pains to show that the blame for lynching's existence and continuance did not rest upon the South alone but, on the contrary, upon the nation as a whole.

Documents three through five [c, d, e] consist of typical reports or comments on lynchings appearing in the Negro press during this decade. The press approved when resistance was offered to the lynchers—which was frequent. The sixth document [f] is made up of the remarks of Mrs. Ida B. Wells-Barnett to President McKinley on March 21, 1898. Mrs. Barnett was acting as the spokesman of a Negro mass meeting held shortly before in Chicago. This Negro woman, whose career has been sorely neglected, had more to do with originating and carrying forward the anti-lynching crusade than any other single person. Beginning her career as a fearless opponent of Jim Crow and as editor of a Memphis newspaper, the *Free Press,* she was forcibly driven from that city in 1892, joined the Chicago *Conservator* and then lectured throughout the northern part of the United States and in Europe on lynching. She was among the first to point out the falsity of the charge of rape as "explaining" lynching and to expose it as a prime device for the maintenance of the plantation system.

The seventh document [g] consists of the appeal to the Negro people from the National Afro-American Council, in May, 1899, which resulted in a day of fasting on Friday, June 2 and special exercises in all Negro churches the following Sunday as a protest against oppression and, especially, lynching.

The record of lynchings for the single year 1900 as reported by the Negro journalist, John Edward Bruce, basing himself upon the listings in the Chicago *Tribune* and *Conservator,* forms the eighth document [h], while the last document [i] is an abstract from an article by Mrs. Wells-Barnett, then chairman of the Anti-Lynching Bureau of the National Afro-American Council, on "Lynching and the Excuse for It," published in 1901.

[a]

Report from Arkansas, 1892

There is much uneasiness and unrest all over this State among our people, owing to the fact that the people (our race variety) all over the State are being lynched upon the slightest provocation; some being strung up to telegraph poles, others burnt at the stake and still others being shot like dogs. In the last 30 days there have been not less than eight colored persons lynched in this State. At Texarkana a few days ago, a man was burnt at the stake. In Pine Bluff a few days later two men were strung up and shot, and this too by the brilliant glare of the electric lights. At Varner, George Harris was taken from jail and shot for killing a white man, for poisoning his domestic happiness. At Wilmar, a boy was induced to confess to the commission of an outrage, upon promise of his liberty, and when he had confessed, he was strung up and shot. Over in Toneoke County, a whole family consisting of husband, wife and child were shot down like dogs. Verily the situation is alarming in the extreme.

At this writing 500 people are hovering upon wharves in Pine Bluff, awaiting the steamers to take them up the Arkansas River to Oklahoma. The *Arkansas Gazette* a white Democratic journal of this date says 1,200 more are passing through the upper country, enroute to Oklahoma and what is most pitiable, these poor people are comparatively destitute; yet are being imposed upon by unprincipled sharks of their own race. What is the outcome of all this? It is evident that the white people of the South have no further use for the Negro. He is being worse treated now, than at any other time, since the surrender. The white press of the South seems to be subsidized by this lawless element, the white pulpits seem to condone lynching. The colored press in the South are dared to take an aggressive stand against lynch law. The Northern press seems to care little about the condition of the Negroes South. The pulpits of the North are passive. Will not some who are not in danger of their lives, speak out against the tyrannical South, will not the [Philadelphia] *Christian Recorder,* the [New York] *Age,* the [Indianapolis] *Freeman* and all other journals devoted to the especial interest of the Afro-Americans, speak out against these lynchings and mob violence? For God's sake, say or do something, for our condition is precarious in the extreme.

A few days ago a convention of colored clergymen met in the city of Little Rock to take under advisement the drafting of an address to be presented to the Governor of this State. There were a few representative men from all different branches of the christian church in this State, but it was surprising to note the conspicuous absence of some of our leading pastors. These were severely condemned, and set down on as unworthy of recognition and the support of the race, in that they lacked that paramount perquisite that makes up race pride—interest. The convention was composed of the best brains of the A.M.E., Baptist, M.E., Campbellite, A.M.E. Zion, C.M.E., and Presbyterian Churches of this State, also representatives of the Congregational Church, the Negro bar and the press. Much interest was manifested in the formulating of an address to the Governor. Some desired that the address be in strong language, while others desired that it take the appearance of a mild appeal for redress. The effect of this convention is watched with the deepest interest; the preachers all over the State promising to lecture upon and counsel quietness. Will not the *Christian Recorder* ask the prayers of the connection in behalf of their brethren in Arkansas? Pray for us.

Christian Recorder (Phila.), March 24, 1892.

[b]

Frederick Douglass on Lynching, 1892

. . . . The crime which these usurpers of courts of law and juries profess to punish is the most revolting and shocking of any this side of murder. This they know is the best excuse, and it appeals at once and promptly to a prejudice which prevails at the North as well as the South. Hence we have for any act of lawless violence the same excuse—an outrage by a Negro upon some white woman. It is a notable fact, also, that it is not with them the immorality or the enormity of the crime itself that arouses popular wrath, but the emphasis is put upon the race and color of the parties to it. Here, and not there, is the ground of indignation and abhorrence. The appeal is not to the moral sense but to the well-known hatred of one class to another. . . .

For 200 years or more white men have in the South committed this offense against black women, and the fact has excited little attention, even at the North, except among Abolitionists; which circumstance demonstrates that the horror now excited is not for the crime itself, but that it is based on the reversal of color in the participants. . . .

Now where rests the responsibility for the lynch law prevalent in the South? It is evident that it is not entirely with the ignorant mob. The men who break open jails and with bloody hands destroy human life are not alone responsible. These are not the men who make public sentiment. They are simply the hangmen, not the court, judge, or jury. They simply obey the public sentiment of the South—the sentiment created by wealth and respectability, by the press and pulpit. A change in public sentiment can be easily effected by these forces whenever they shall elect to make the effort. Let the press and the pulpit of the South unite their power against the cruelty, disgrace and shame that is settling like a mantle of fire upon these lynch-law States, and lynch law itself will soon cease to exist.

Nor is the South alone responsible for this burning shame and menace to our free institutions. Wherever contempt of race prevails, whether against African, Indian or Mongolian, countenance and support are given to the present peculiar treatment of the Negro in the South. The finger of scorn at the North is correlated to the dagger of the assassin at the South. The sin against the Negro is both sectional and national; and until the voice of the North shall be heard in emphatic condemnation and withering reproach against these continued ruthless mob law murders, it will remain equally involved with the South in this common crime.

Christian Recorder, August 11, 1892.

[c]

Jack Trice Resists Lynchers, 1896

Jacksonville, Fla.—Jack Trice fought fifteen white men at 3 A.M., on the 12th, killing James Hughes and Edward Sanchez, fatally wounding Henry Daniels and dangerously wounding Albert Bruffum. The battle occurred at Trice's humble home near Palmetto, a town six miles south of here, to prevent his 14-year-old son being "regulated" (brutally whipped and perhaps killed) by the whites. On the afternoon of May 11, Trice's son and the son of Town Marshal Hughes, of Palmetto, fought, the white boy being badly beaten. Marshal Hughes was greatly enraged and he and 14 other white men went to Trice's house to "regulate" his little boy. The whites demanded that the boy be sent out. Trice refused and they began firing. Trice returned the fire, his first bullet killing Marshal Hughes. Edward Sanchez tried to burn the house, but was shot through the brain by Trice. Then the whites tried to batter in the door with a log, which resulted in Henry Daniels getting a bullet in the stomach that will kill him. The "regulators" then ran. A final bullet from Trice's deadly rifle struck Albert Bruffum in the back. The whites secured re-enforcements and returned to Trice's home at sunrise, vowing to burn father and son at the stake; but the intended victims had fled. Only Trice's aged mother was in the house. The old lady was driven out like a dog and the house burned. Posses with bloodhounds are chasing Trice and his boy, and they will be lynched if caught. It is sincerely hoped that both will escape.

Cleveland *Gazette,* May 30, 1896.

[d]

"Can't Lynching Be Stopped?"—1897

Among the first editorial utterances we published through the columns of this paper with respect to the practice of lynching, as carried on by the Southern whites upon the blacks, was the assertion that the only way those barbarians can be made to desist from engaging in such brutal butcheries is to assure them that they will run a great risk of being compelled to bite the dust on every occasion of their entering upon such devilish pastime . . .

The action of the Negroes at Key West, Fla., last week, points to the true solution of the lynching problem . . . The Negroes of Key West had prepared themselves for just such an emergency, as the crazy Col. Pendleton sprung upon them when he called for "white men" to lynch a Negro prisoner. So far from succeeding in lynching the Negro, the valiant ex-rebel managed to save his own neck by the thickness of a hair . . . Had the colored men failed to rise up in defense of the law the helpless prisoner would of course have been murdered . . . It speaks volumes to the credit of the Afro-American residents of Key West to note the fact that they did not attempt to rescue the prisoner from the custody of the officers, nor did they defend him against the regular process of the law. They merely defended the community against being outraged by having all order overthrown by a lot of villains whose existence is a constant menace to the peace of society, and for doing so they merit the commendation of all good citizens.

It was a wise precaution on the part of our Florida brethren to have provided themselves with guns and ammunition. It was a glorious thing that they possessed sufficient courage to use them so well. Let colored men everywhere imitate the brave example of those at Key West, and lynching will soon become rare. . . .

The Afro-American Sentinel (Omaha), July 3, 1897.

[e]

The Lynching of Postmaster Baker, 1898

Lake City, S.C.—George Washington's birthday was ushered in in this section on Tuesday morning at 1 o'clock with the most revolting crime ever perpetrated . . . Postmaster Baker, an Afro-American of this little town, and his family at the time stated above were burned out of their home, the postmaster and a babe in arms killed, his wife and three daughters shot and maimed for life, and his son wounded.

Mr. Baker was appointed postmaster three months ago. Lake City is a town of 500 inhabitants, and the Afro-American population in the vicinity is large. There was the usual prejudiced protest at his appointment. Three months ago as the postmaster was leaving the office at night in company with several men of our class, he was fired on from ambush. Since then he moved his family into a house in which he also established the post office.

Last week Tuesday night a body of scoundrels (white) who were concealed behind buildings and fences in the neighborhood, riddled the building with shot and rifle bullets. They shot high and no one was hurt. It was simply an effort to intimidate him. A short time before Senators Tillman and McLauren and Congressman Horton had asked the postmaster general to remove Mr. Baker because of his color and the request had been refused. The refusal was wired here. Mr. Baker did not remove his family and gave no evidence of being frightened. Being a government official he felt confident of protection from Washington.

At 1 o'clock Tuesday morning a torch was applied to the post office and house. Back, just within the line of light, were over a hundred white brutes—murderers—armed with pistols and shotguns. By the time the fire aroused the sleeping family, consisting of the postmaster, his wife, four daughters, a son and an infant at the breast, the crowd began firing into the building. A hundred bullet holes were made through the thin boarding and many found lodgment in members of the family within.

The postmaster was the first to reach the door and he fell dead just within the threshold, being shot in several places. The mother had the baby in her arms and reached the door over her husband's body, when a bullet crashed through its skull, and it fell to the floor. She was shot in several places. Two of the girls had their arms broken close to the shoulders and will probably lose them. Another of the girls is fatally wounded. The boy was also shot.

Only two of the seven occupants of the house escaped with slight injuries. The bodies of Mr. Baker and the infant were cremated in the building. All mail matter was destroyed. A coroner's jury was impanelled Tuesday evening. It visited the charred remains and adjourned until today. Nothing will be done to apprehend the infernal brutes and murderers. The whelps that shot almost to death some time ago Isaac H. Loftin, the Afro-American postmaster of Hogansville, Ga., are still at liberty—walking the streets of that town, with more freedom than the man they all but murdered. No effort to arrest and punish them has ever been or ever will be made by local, state or federal authorities. The same will be true in this case. This is a great country, a great government! Not even Spain respects it.

Cleveland *Gazette*, February 26, 1898.

[f]

Mrs. Ida Wells-Barnett Calls on President McKinley, 1898

Washington, D.C.—The Chicago delegation of Illinois congressmen, headed by Senator Mason, called on the president at the White House the 21st ult., with Mrs. Ida B. Wells-Barnett, concerning the lynching of Postmaster Baker, of Lake City, S.C. Mrs. Barnett, who is better known as Ida Wells, has agitated the subject of lynching both in this country and Great Britain, and came to present the resolutions recently adopted at a mass meeting in Chicago. Senator Mason introduced Mrs. Barnett, telling of her work. She said:

"Mr. President, the colored citizens of this country in general, and Chicago in particular, desire to respectfully urge that some action be taken by you as chief magistrate of this great nation, first, for the apprehension and punishment of the lynchers of Postmaster Baker, of Lake City, S.C.; second, we ask indemnity for the widow and children, both for the murder of the husband and father, and for injuries sustained by themselves; third, we most earnestly desire that national legislation be enacted for the suppression of the national crime of lynching.

"For nearly twenty years lynching crimes, which stand side by side with Armenian and Cuban outrages, have been committed and permitted by this Christian nation. Nowhere in the civilized world save the United States of America do men, possessing all civil and political power, go out in bands of 50 to 5,000 to hunt down, shoot, hang or burn to death a single individual, unarmed and absolutely powerless. Statistics show that nearly 10,000 American citizens have been lynched in the past 20 years. To our appeals for justice the stereotyped reply has been that the government could not interfere in a state matter. Postmaster Baker's case was a federal matter, pure and simple. He died at his post of duty in defense of his country's honor, as truly as did ever a soldier on the field of battle. We refuse to believe this country, so powerful to defend its citizens abroad, is unable to protect its citizens at home. Italy and China have been indemnified by this government for the lynching of their citizens. We ask that the government do as much for its own."

The president assured the delegation that he was in hearty accord with the plea, and that both the department of justice and post office department would do all that could be done in that matter. The attorney general, he said, had been instructed to see what could be done by the government.*

Cleveland *Gazette*, April 9, 1898.
* Nothing was done.

[g]

The Fast of Protest, 1899

The National Afro-American Council of the United States has issued a proclamation calling upon the colored people of this country to set apart Friday, June 2, as a day of fasting and prayer, and has called upon all colored ministers to devote the sunrise hour of the following Sunday, June 4, to special exercises in order that "God, the Father of Mercies, may take our deplorable case in His own hands, and that if vengeance is to be meted out let God himself repay." It sets forth the "indescribable barbarous treatment" of the Negro—refers to role in wars, denounces lynchings "in the most strenuous language." It says, in part:

"We pay out millions of dollars yearly to ride in 'jim-crow' cars, some of them scarcely fit for cattle, yet we are compelled to pay as much as those who have every accommodation and convenience. Indians, Chinamen and every other race can travel as they please. Such unjust laws make the railroad highway robbers. In some sections of the country we may ride for thousands of miles and are denied a cup of tea or coffee because no provision is made, or allowed to be made, to accommodate us with something to eat, while we are ready to pay for it. Waiving hundreds of inconveniences, we are practically outlawed by many States, and also by the general Government in its endorsement of silence and indifference.

"We are dragged before the courts by thousands and sentenced to every form of punishment, and even executed, without the privilege of having a jury composed in whole or in part of members of our own race, while simple justice should guarantee us judges and juries who could adjudicate our cases free from the bias, caste and prejudice incident to the same in this country.

"In many sections we are arrested and lodged in jails on the most frivolous suspicion of being the perpetrators of most hideous and revolting crimes, and, regardless of established guilt, mobs are formed of ignorant, vicious, whiskey-besotted men, at whose approach the keys of these jails and prisons are surrendered and the suspicioned party is ruthlessly forced from the custody of the law and tortured, hanged, shot, butchered, dismembered and burned in the most fiendish manner. Nor is this fate limited to a few unfortunate and monstrous wretches, which we, like other people, doubtless have among our race, but instances have multiplied into hundreds, thousands and tens of thousands. And, horrible to conceive, these mobs no longer conceal themselves in the shadows of the night, but in open day plunder the prisons for the victims of their lawless vengeance and defiantly walk into courts and rob the sheriffs and judges of their prisoners and butcher them without even time to commune in prayer with God, a privilege that no barbaric age has ever denied a soul about to be ushered into the presence of his Maker.

"Owing to these and many other calamitous conditions which time forbids a recital of, unhistoric, unprecedented and dreadfully abnormal, we are impelled by a sense of duty and the instincts of our moral nature to appeal to the Afro-Americans in the United States to put forth some endeavors by ceasing to be longer silent, and to appeal to some judiciary for help and relief. If earth affords none for our helpless and defenceless race, we must appeal to the bar of Infinite Power and Justice, whose Judge holds the destinies of nations in His hands."

N.Y. *Tribune,* May 4, 1899.

[h]

One Year's Lynching Record, 1900

CHARGE OF MURDER *

January 9, Henry Giveney, Ripley, Tenn.
January 9, Roger Giveney, Ripley, Tenn.
March 11, Unknown Negro, Jennings, Neb.
March 24, Walter Cotton, Emporia, Va.
March 27, William Edward, Deer Creek Bridge, Miss.
April 16, Moses York, near Tunica, Miss.
April 28, Mindee Chowgee, Marshall, Mo.
May 4, Marshall Jones, Douglas, Ga.
May 13, Alexander Whitney, Harlem, Ga.
May 14, William Willis, Grovetown, Ga.
May 14, Unknown Negro, Brooksville, Fla.
May 14, Unknown Negro, Brooksville, Fla.
May 22, Calvin Hilburn, Pueblo, Col.
June 10, Unknown Negro, Snead, Fla.
June 17, Nat Mullins, Earl, Ark.
June 21, Robert Davis, Mulberry, Fla.
July 12, John Jennings, Creswell, Ga.
July 26, Robert Charles, New Orleans, La.
Sept. 11, Unknown Negro, Forest City, N.C.
Sept. 11, Thomas J. Amos, Cheneyville, La.
Sept. 7, Frank Brown, Tunica, Miss.

* The group titles are in the original document and record the accusations reported by the press.

Sept. 14, David Moore, Tunica, Miss.
Sept. 14, William Brown, Tunica, Miss.
Oct. 9, Wiley Johnson, Baton Rouge, La.
Oct. 23, Gloster Barnes, near Vicksburg, Miss.
Nov. 16, Preston Porter, Lymon, Col.
Dec. 16, Bud Rowland, Rockford, Ind.
Dec. 16, Thomas Henderson, Rockford, Ind.
Dec. 19, Unknown Negro, Arcadia, Miss.
Dec. 20, ——— Lewis, Gulf Port, Miss.

PLOT TO KILL WHITES

April 22, John Hughley, Allentown, Fla.

SUSPECTED ROBBERY

June 17, S. A. Jenkins, Searcy, Ark.

RAPE

June 5, W. W. Watts, Newport News, Va.
March 4, George Ratliffe, Clyde, N.C.
March 10, Thomas Clayton, Hernando, Miss.
March 26, Lewis Harris, Belair, Md.
April 3, Allen Brooks, Berryville, Ga.
April 20, John Peters, Tazewell, W. Va.
May 4, Henry Darley, Liberty, Md.
May 7, Unknown Negro, Geneva, Ala.
June 3, Dago Pete, Tutwiler, Miss.
June 23, Frank Gilmore, Livingstone Parish, La.
July 23, Elijah Clark, Huntsville, Ala.
July 24, Jack Hillsman, Knoxville, Ga.
Aug. 13, Jack Betts, Corinth, Miss.
Aug. 19, Unknown Negro, Arrington, Va.
Aug. 26, Unknown Negro, S. Pittsburg, Tenn.
Oct. 19, Frank Hardeneman, Wellaston, Ga.
Dec. 8, Daniel Long, Wythe County, Va.
Dec. 21, Unknown Negro, Arkadelphia, Ark.

ATTEMPTED ASSAULT

March 18, John Bailey, Manetta, Ga.
March 18, Charles Humphries, Lee County, Ala.
April 19, Henry McAfee, Brownsville, Miss.
May 11, William Lee, Hinton, W. Va.
May 15, Henry Harris, Lena, La.

June 9, Simon Adams, near Columbia, Ga.
June 11, Senny Jefferson, Metcalf, Ga.
June 27, Jack Thomas, Live Oak, Fla.
July 6, John Roe, Columbia, Ala.
Sept. 10, Logan Reoms, Duplex, Tenn.
Sept. 12, Fred Floyd, Wetumpka, Kan.
Oct. 2, Winfield Thomas, Eclectic, Ala.
Oct. 18, Fratur Warfield, Elkton, Ky.

RACE PREJUDICE

July 25, Unknown Negro, New Orleans, La.
July 25, August Thomas, New Orleans, La.
July 25, Baptiste Filean, New Orleans, La.
July 25, Louis Taylor, New Orleans, La.
July 25, Anna Marbry, New Orleans, La.
July 25, Unknown Negro, New Orleans, La.
July 25, Silas Jackson, New Orleans, La.
Oct. 24, James Suer, Liberty Hill, Ga.
Oct. 24, James Calaway, Liberty Hill, Ga.

GIVING TESTIMONY

Mar. 23, Luis Rice, Ripley, Tenn.

ATTACKING A WHITE MAN

May 1, Henry Ratcliff, Gloucester, Miss.
May 1, George Gordon, Albin, Miss.
Sept. 8, Grant Weley, Thomasville, Ga.

SUSPICION OF MURDER

June 10, Askew, Mississippi City, Miss.
June 10, Reese, Mississippi City, Miss.

COMPLICITY OF MURDER

June 10, John Sanders, Snead, Fla.
Dec. 17, John Rolla, Booneville, Ind.

UNKNOWN OFFENSES

June 27, Jordan Hines, Molina, Ga.
June 20, James Barco, Panasoffkee, Fla.

NO OFFENSE

May 7, Unknown Negro, Amite. Miss.

ARSON

April 5, Unknown Negro, Southampton County, Va.
Dec. 28, George Faller, Marion, Ga.

SUSPICION OF ARSON

Jan. 11, Rufus Salter, West Spring, S.C.

AIDING ESCAPE OF MURDERERS

Jan. 16, Anderson Gause, Henning, Tenn.

UNPOPULARITY

July 9, Jefferson Henry, Greene's Bayou, La.

MAKING THREATS

Mar. 4, James Crosby, Selo Hatchel, Ala.
June 12, Seth Cobb, Devall's Bluffs, La.

INFORMER

Mar. 22, George Ritter, Canhaft, N.C.

ROBBING

May 26, Unknown Negro, West Point, Ark.
Oct. 8, ——— Williams, Tiptonville, Tenn.

BURGLARY

Sept. 21, George Beckham, Ponchatoula, La.
Sept. 21, Charles Elliott, Ponchatoula, La.
Sept. 21, Nathaniel Bowman, Ponchatoula, La.
Sept. 21, Isaiah Rollins, Ponchatoula, La.

ATTEMPT TO MURDER

June 12, John Brodie, Lee County, Ark.
Nov. 15, Unknown Negro, Jefferson, Tex.
Nov. 15, Unknown Negro, Jefferson, Tex.
Nov. 15, Unknown Negro, Jefferson, Tex.

THREATS TO KILL

Feb. 17, William Burts, Basket Mills, S.C.

ASSAULT

May 16, Samuel Hinson, Cushtusha, Miss.
Oct. 30, ——— Abernathy, Duke, Ala.

John E. Bruce, *The Blood Red Record* . . . (Albany, 1901). Copy in Wisconsin State Library, Madison.

[i]

Ida B. Wells-Barnett on Lynching, 1901

. . . . If the Southern citizens lynch Negroes because "that is the only successful method of dealing with a certain class of crimes," then that class of crimes should be shown unmistakably by this record. Now consider the record.

It would be supposed that the record would show that all, or nearly all, lynchings were caused by outrageous assaults upon women; certainly that this particular offense would outnumber all other causes for putting human beings to death without a trial by jury and the other safeguards of our Constitution and laws.

But the record makes no such disclosure. Instead, it shows that five women have been lynched, put to death with unspeakable savagery during the past five years. They certainly were not under the ban of the outlawing crime. It shows that men, not a few, but hundreds, have been lynched for misdemeanors, while others have suffered death for no offense known to the law, the causes assigned being "mistaken identity," "insult," "bad reputation," "unpopularity," "violating contract," "running quarantine," "giving evidence," "frightening children by shooting at rabbits," etc. Then, strangest of all, the record shows that the sum total of lynchings for these offenses—not crimes—and for the alleged offenses which are only misdemeanors, greatly exceeds the lynchings for the very crime universally declared to be the cause of lynching . . . Instead of being the sole cause of lynching, the crime upon which lynchers build their defense furnishes the least victims for the mob. In 1896 less than thirty-nine per cent of the Negroes lynched were charged with this crime; in 1897, less than eighteen per cent; in 1898, less than sixteen per cent; in 1899, less than fourteen per cent; and in 1900, less than fifteen per cent, were so charged.

The Independent (N.Y.), May 16, 1901, LIII, pp. 1133–36.

V.

POPULISM AND STRIKES

The broadest anti-monopoly coalition formed by the people of the United States was the Populist movement of the 1890's. It had three main organizational bases— the Farmers' Mutual Benefit Association, located largely in the west, the Southern Alliance, and the Colored Farmers' Alliance. The last two achieved a high degree of unity and this unity resulted in the Alliance and Populists capturing several state governments. These governments then dealt blows to Jim Crow, enhanced appropriations for education, appointed many Negro officeholders on a local and state level, democratized county administration, curbed interest charges, regulated railroads and equalized the taxation system.

The efforts of the Negro people in these respects were fought by the classical methods of fraud, violence and the deliberate playing upon racist and chauvinist notions. To illustrate these aspects of the Populist era, eleven documents have been selected and are published below. The first [a] is a brief extract from a speech by H. J. Spencer at a meeting of the Texas State Colored Alliance, held in Palestine in October, 1890. This Alliance had been formed in 1886 and Spencer was its first secretary. The report was published originally in the organ of this Alliance, the *National Alliance*, founded in Houston in 1889, of which, unfortunately, no known copy is in existence. Mr. Spencer, in prophesying a bright future for the Colored Farmers' Alliance, spoke truly for by 1891 it had organizations in twenty states and nearly one and a quarter million members, of whom 750,000 were adult males, 300,000 females and 150,000 males under twenty-one years of age.

The second document [b] comes from the Rev. J. L. Moore of Crescent City, Florida, superintendent of the Putnam County Colored Farmers' Alliance. It is descriptive of the proceedings at Ocala, Florida, in December, 1890, when the three Farmers' organizations formed a united force anticipating the launching two summers later of the People's or Populist Party. Moore here is especially concerned with the Negroes' own particular demands. The third document [c] consists of a letter written in 1891 by Joseph H. Powell, state agent of the Mississippi Colored Alliance, placing his organization on record as opposing endorsement of the Democratic candidate for U.S. Senator, the incumbent, J. Z. George, because of his anti-Negro record—a position subsequently adopted by the Mississippi Alliance as a whole.

Document four [d] is the fullest account the editor has seen of the demands made by the cotton-picker strikers in 1891. The strike appears to have centered in Texas, though it had repercussions elsewhere. The National Farmers' Alliance as a whole disapproved of the move as did certain of the Negro Farmers groups and it was not successful. The fifth document [e] is a typical editorial in the Negro press hailing the constructive work of Populist officials. This appeared in the Republican N.Y. *Age* and complimented Ben Tillman, then an Alliance-elected Governor of South Carolina (and later a rabid anti-Negro Bourbon Senator) for his vigorous activities in preventing a lynching.

Documents six and seven [f, g] are concerned with strikes by Negro workmen. The earlier of these, won by the men, involved two thousand Negro longshoremen in St. Louis in 1892 and the reprinted item is an editorial from a Negro newspaper of the time. The second consists of a speech made August 30, 1898 by George Patrick, Negro screwman and leader of some 2,300 Negro longshore members of the A.F. of L. in their strike against the Malloy lines in Galveston. After the killing and arrest of some of the Negroes and the use of the state militia, the strike, which had lasted four weeks, was broken.

The last four documents in this section concern events in North Carolina from 1898–99. The state is selected as representative of the methods used to overthrow a progressive government provided by the fusion of Populist and Negro Republican groups in an anti-Bourbon coalition. This coalition gained control of North Carolina in 1894 and held it until overthrown in the 1898 elections. During this time strides were made in assisting education, eliminating restrictions upon the suffrage, giving Negroes something approaching their due in terms of public office, reducing interest charges, and equalizing the taxation system. Perhaps the single act most significant of the new values of the Fusion-controlled legislature was its adjourning, on February 21, 1895, to mark the death of Frederick Douglass.

In 1898 the Democrats, assisted by defections from Fusionists of those interested in reducing taxes on expanding railroad and manufacturing properties, regained control. They did this by using, in the words of Professor James S. Bassett of Trinity College, who witnessed the campaign, "a great deal of intimidation and a great deal of fraud." The high point in the intimidation came in Wilmington where organized counter-revolutionary terror, personally participated in by "the best people," deposed, by murder, the city administration on November 11, 1898, the day following the election. This city with 17,000 Negroes and 8,000 whites had four Negroes among the ten members of the Board of Aldermen, Negro as well as white firemen and policemen, one Negro jailer, some Negro magistrates, one of the county's representatives to the state legislature was a Negro (John T. Howe), and the county treasurer, recorder of deeds and coroner were also Negroes.

After months of planning, buying guns, organizing, whipping up race hatred, the assault came, the administration was deposed and a new city government headed by A. M. Waddell, who had led in the march on City Hall, was installed.

Document eight [h] consists of the editorial which appeared early in 1898 in Alex Manly's *Wilmington Record* and which was revived and widely reprinted in the Bourbon's chauvinistic campaign just before the day of voting. Document nine [i] consists of an eye-witness account of the Wilmington outbreak by a Negro refugee, the Rev. Charles S. Morris. The tenth document [j] is an abstract from an address by Thomas O. Fuller, a Negro elected to the State Senate in this election of 1898 from Warren and Vance counties which remained Republican despite the state-wide terror. The very compromising remarks made by Senator Fuller show clearly, however, that the terror was not without its effects upon him. In 1899 he voted against the act disfranchising Negroes and soon thereafter left to take up a teaching career in Tennessee.

The last document [k] in this series is an article entitled "The Injustice to the Colored Voter" by George H. White, which appeared in January, 1900. This piece is representative of the efforts made by Negro leaders to enact legislation, in accordance with the provisions of the 14th Amendment, cutting down on the number of Congressmen allowed to states which disfranchised Negro citizens. George H. White was a Negro Fusion Congressman from North Carolina having been elected in 1896. He was the last Southern Negro to hold a seat in Congress. A graduate of Howard University, he had previously been a member of both houses of the North Carolina legislature and prosecuting attorney for the Second Judicial District of his state. As a Congressman he introduced and fought for Federal anti-lynching legislation.

[a]

The Secretary of the Texas Colored Farmers' Alliance, 1890

He spoke of other organizations among the colored people. How, from time to time, efforts had been made to draw them together and unite them in one solid body, but those efforts all had failed and all former organizations had utterly broken down. On the contrary, the National Alliance Movement had now been in existence for about three years. It had gathered strength every hour of that time. It was peculiarly a movement of the people, by the people and for the people. The colored race had been educated and elevated; they had saved millions in money, and had been trained to look forward to homes of their own and independence and happiness around their own firesides; and these were some of the causes why the National Alliance had prospered and would continue to prosper, and would finally bring the entire colored race together as a unit.

The National Alliance, n.d., quoted in The National Economist (official organ of The National Farmers' Alliance, Washington) November 1, 1890.

[b]

The Florida Colored Farmers' Alliance, 1891

Upon perusing said article * I found it to be an attack upon the National Colored Farmers' Alliance and Co-operative Union on their action while in session at Ocala, Fla., in passing resolutions asking Congress to pass the federal election bill, now pending before the Senate of the United States. Now, as I was a member of that body, and you have taken us to task because of our action, I hereby reply and only ask that you will do me the kindness of publishing my reply, as it may be the means of you and others seeing us just as we are. I notice you, as others, call it the force bill, and you remarked, "How the force bill could benefit the Negro even in the slightest degree passes comprehension. . . ." But our object was to have protection of the ballot boxes, because none sees the need of reform more than we do. How is that reform to be brought about while the present parties have control of the ballot boxes (unless it comes through the now existing parties, which is not likely if their past history argues anything)? The Hon. Alonzo Wardell, of Huron, South Dakota, informed us while at Ocala, that in his State the Republicans were 22,000 majority, but when the independent party sprang up and votes were counted at the last election there were 10,000 more votes than registered voters, which, of course, called for a contest, and when a contest comes up under those circumstances those who are in sympathy with their kind win and the other fellows must stay out. That was in a State largely Republican; and should the reformist begin to operate in our own sunny land of flowers, or in any State that can boast of her Democratic fidelity, they would meet with the eight-ballot box system and tickets spread on top at their proper places for the Democratic voters, and the other fellows would have to do the best they could; and if they voted

* An editorial in an unnamed Jacksonville, Florida, newspaper.

right they would not be allowed a chance as inspectors at the ballot box, and the result would be increased Democratic majorities. And while the federal election bill is not satisfactory to us throughout as it reads, yet we want something guaranteeing every man a free vote and an honest count. The federal election bill being the only thing that ever emanated from our halls of legislation that pointed in that direction, we, in body assembled as representatives of our race, asked Congress to pass it.

In all the discussions of the whites in all the various meetings they attend and the different resolutions, remarks, and speeches they make against the Negro, I never hear you, Mr. Editor, nor any of the other leading journals, once criticize their action or say they are antagonizing the races, neither do you ever call a halt. But let the Negro speak once, and what do you hear? Antagonizing races, Negro uprising, Negro domination, etc. Anything to keep the reading public hostile toward the Negro, not allowing him the privilege to speak his opinion, and if that opinion be wrong show him by argument, and not at once make it a race issue . . . as members of the Colored Farmers' Alliance we avowed that we were going to vote with and for the man or party that will secure for the farmer or laboring man his just rights and privileges, and in order that he may enjoy them without experiencing a burden.

We want protection at the ballot box, so that the laboring man may have an equal showing, and the various labor organizations to secure their just rights, we will join hand with them irrespective of party, "and those fellows will have to walk." We are aware of the fact that the laboring colored man's interests and the laboring white man's interests are one and the same. Especially is this true at the South. Anything that can be brought about to benefit the workingman, will also benefit the Negro more than any other legislation that can be enacted. . . . So I for one have fully decided to vote with and work for that party, or those who favor the workingman, let them belong to the Democratic, or Republican, or the People's Party. I know I speak the sentiment of that convention, representing as we do one-fifth of the laborers of this country, seven-eighths of our race in this country being engaged in agricultural pursuits.

Can you wonder why we have turned our attention from the few pitiful offices a few of our members could secure, and turned our attention toward benefiting the mass of our race, and why we are willing to legislate that this mass be benefited? And we ask Congress to protect the ballot box, so they may be justly dealt with in their effort to gain that power. We know and you know that neither of the now existing parties is going to legislate in the interest of the farmers or laboring men except so far as it does not conflict with their interest to do so. . . .

But, Mr. Editor, can we do anything while the present parties have control of the ballot box, and we (the Alliance) have no protection? The greatest mistake, I see, is this: The wily politicians see and know that they have to do something, therefore they are slipping into the Alliance, and the farmers, in many instances, are accepting them as leaders; and if we are to have the same leaders, we need not expect anything else but the same results. The action of the Alliance in this reminds me of the man who first put his hand in the lion's mouth and the lion finally bit it off; and then he changed to make the matter better and put his head in the lion's mouth, and therefore lost his head. Now the farmers and laboring men know in the manner they were standing before they organized; they lost their hands, so to speak; now organized in one body or head, if they give themselves over to the same power that took their hand, it will likewise take their head.

Now, Mr. Editor, I wish to say, if the laboring men of the United States will lay down party issues and combine to enact laws for the benefit of the laboring man, I, as county superintendent of Putnam County Colored Farmers' Alliance, and member of the National Colored Farmers, know that I voice the sentiment of that body, representing as we did 750,000 votes, when I say we are willing and ready to lay down the past, take hold with them irrespective of party, race, or creed, until the cry shall be heard from the Heights of Abraham of the North, to the Everglades of Florida, and from the rock-bound coast of the East, to the Golden Eldorado of the West, that we can heartily endorse the motto, "Equal rights to all and special privileges to none."

The National Economist (Washington), March 7, 1891.

[c]

Mississippi Colored Farmers' Alliance, 1891

I notice in the State papers a departure of Mr. McAllister, assistant lecturer of the Alliance, from the leading principles of the Alliance platform; also that gentleman is not in favor of a third party. In the latter we are with him, but in the former not. The Colored Alliance in the State of Mississippi was organized for the common good and benefit of the farmer and national reform. This we expect to obtain by legislation brought about through our choice of candidates. So long as we hold to those who have misrepresented the farmer in the past it shows our inability to act for ourselves. Let the old party plow his own field over. It has cost too much for our education in politics of old political economy to old politicians. We will support a new Alliance man and not Mr. George or any other candidate from the present list. Mr. McAllister wants Mr. George returned to the Senate, the man who was foremost in the origination of the constitution that has disfranchised so much of the Alliance vote of the State of Mississippi, which was the severest blow ever struck at a party. Mr. McAllister is not in favor of the sub-treasury plan. But he is in favor of returning a candidate to Congress who is opposed to every interest of our plans. We heartily indorse Mr. Burkitt in his defence of the Alliance.

The National Economist (Washington), April 11, 1891. The editor is indebted to Mr. Jack Abramowitz of New York City for calling this item to his attention.

[d]

The Cotton Pickers' Strike, 1891

The colored cotton pickers in Texas have agreed not to pick cotton after September 20 for less than $1 per hundred pounds and board. This organ-ization of cotton pickers has been perfected through the Colored Alliance, and now numbers more than half a million, with thousands being added every day throughout the Southern states. Col. R. A. Humphrey, general superintendent of the Colored Alliance, with headquarters at Galveston, admitted the existence of the organization, saying it had been induced by organizations some time ago, of planters and merchants in certain sections, notably Memphis and Charleston—to reduce the price for picking to a very low standard, and that the colored pickers had combined to protect themselves from this dictation, and he thought they would be able to do so. It is learned that a circular has been mailed at Houston, Tex., to every colored sub-alliance throughout the country, fixing the date when the strike of the pickers will be simultaneously inaugurated, and how it shall be con-ducted.

Cleveland Gazette, September 26, 1891.

[e]

An Alliance Governor and Lynching, 1891

Governor Tillman of South Carolina has set his face against lynch and mob law. He recently called out the Morgan Rifles, to protect the black man who shot the Mayor of Spartanburg, and laid down the following mandatory law for the guidance of Sheriffs: "It may as well be understood once and for all in South Carolina that the law must be enforced, and that the Sheriffs, instead of dodging real or imaginary mobs, must defend their prisoners with their lives, if necessary. If an officer of the law cannot protect a prisoner then he has no business to arrest him, and the prisoner once arrested must be safe from molestation of any authority except that of the court."

It looks as if the Farmers' Alliance Governor of South Carolina understands his business and possesses the manhood and the courage to attend to it. If all the Governors of the South would follow his example, crime would decrease and respect for the law would increase.

N.Y. *Age,* quoted in the *Christian Recorder,* October 29, 1891.

[f]

Strike of St. Louis Negro Longshoremen, 1892

The threatened river strike is on, and over 2,000 Afro-American laborers are idle on the levee. Four steamers arrived last Wednesday night and were unable to land their cargoes. A number of boats are lying at their docks waiting to be loaded, but are unable to get a pound of freight carried on board. The cause of the strike is a demand by the marine firemen that the union scale of wages be paid and none but union men be employed on the boats. This was refused by the owners, and a tie-up of the river traffic is the consequence. The marine firemen struck work Thursday morning of last week and were followed by the members of the longshoremen and roustabouts unions. The men are quiet and orderly, and no serious trouble is anticipated. They are firm in their demands, however. and say the company must accede to their terms. As the men on strike are all Afro-Americans, thoroughly organized, and members of the Federation of Labor, it is believed they will force the company to accept their requests. The general opinion among river men is that the strike will last but a few days.

Cleveland *Gazette,* April 9, 1892.

[g]

Strike of Galveston Negro Longshoremen, 1898

It requires something to subsist upon. We are not farmers; we cannot get out and raise that on which we have to subsist. It requires spot cash. You know what the trouble is. It is not necessary for me to tell you here. The Mallory Line steamer is here offering reduced wages upon which we cannot live. Many of you have read my letter giving the scale of wages we ask. Now the Mallory Line is charging the merchants of this town 85¢ a hundred for freight. They refuse to pay us 50¢ an hour for unloading that freight. They charge merchants 45¢ a hundred on sugar, and we have to pay a dollar for eighteen pounds of sugar, yet they will not pay us living wages.

We have not come here to prevent the Mallory Line from working, but we ask them to pay us what we pay them through our merchants. We don't want any trouble and don't mean to have any riotous conduct. We don't mean to stop the Mallory Line and say they shall not come into this port. We simply ask them for liberal wages upon which a laborer can subsist.

We mean to say that scab labor from the country, which comes here for three or four months every year after making a cotton crop to gobble our work and make a stake for Christmas, should not be employed at reduced wages. We stay here all the year around. We simply ask the cooperation of our white brethren. We have not committed any violence, and we don't intend to do so. We ask this labor from the country to disband and go back to the country. If we get more wages we will be able to pay them better prices for their produce and wages will be raised in the country; everybody will be happy and we will have two children born to one. . . .

I ask you all to do no acts of violence; do nothing that is against the law or against decency. The white labor unions are ready to give us their sympathy as long as we remain within the bounds of the law. Be cautious in this matter. Stay away from the Mallory docks for less than 40¢ an hour. When they are ready to consent to our terms, union men will do the work. We don't want scabs to do the work at union wages, but we want union men at union wages. Don't violate the law. Ask these laborers from the country not to go to work down there, and when you ask them see that they don't do it.

Galveston *Daily News,* August 31, 1898; I am indebted to Mr. Stanley Todd Lowry of Austin for bringing this item to my attention.

[h]

The Wilmington, N.C., Record's Editorial, 1898

We suggest that the whites guard their women more closely . . . thus giving no opportunity for the human fiend, be he white or black. You leave your goods out of doors and then complain because they are taken away. Poor white men are careless in the matter of protecting their women, especially on the farms. They are careless of their conduct toward them and our experience among poor white people in the country teaches us that the women of that race are not any more particular in the matter of clandestine meetings with colored men than the white men with colored women. Meetings of this kind go on for some time until the woman's infatuation or the man's boldness brings attention to them and the man is lynched for rape. Every Negro lynched is called "a Big Burly Black Brute" when in fact many of these who have been thus dealt with had white men for their fathers and were not only "not black and burly" but were sufficiently attractive for white girls of culture and refinement to fall in love with them as is well known to all.

Raleigh *News and Observer*, August 18, 1898, quoting the Wilmington *Record*, n.d. No copies of the *Record* appear to exist. The editor wishes to acknowledge his indebtedness to the doctoral dissertation by Helen G. Edmonds, "The Negro and Fusion Politics in North Carolina, 1894–1901," Ohio State University, 1946.

[i]

The Wilmington Massacre, 1898

Nine Negroes massacred outright; a score wounded and hunted like partridges on the mountain; one man, brave enough to fight against such odds would be hailed as a hero anywhere else, was given the privilege of running the gauntlet up a broad street, where he sank ankle deep in the sand, while crowds of men lined the sidewalks and riddled him with a pint of bullets as he ran bleeding past their doors; another Negro shot twenty times in the back as he scrambled empty handed over a fence; thousands of women and children fleeing in terror from their humble homes in the darkness of the night, out under a gray and angry sky, from which falls a cold and bone-chilling rain, out to the dark and tangled ooze of the swamp amid the crawling things of night, fearing to light a fire, startled at every footstep, cowering, shivering, shuddering, trembling, praying in gloom and terror: half-clad and barefooted mothers, with their babies wrapped only in a shawl, whimpering with cold and hunger at their icy breasts, crouched in terror from the vengeance of those who, in the name of civilization, and with the benediction of the ministers of the Prince of Peace, inaugurated the reformation of the city of Wilmington the day after the election by driving out one set of white office holders and filling their places with another set of white office holders—the one being Republican and the other Democrat. . . . All this happened, not in Turkey, nor in Russia, nor in Spain, not in the gardens of Nero, nor in the dungeons of Torquemada, but within three hundred miles of the White House, in the best State in the South, within a year of the twentieth century, while the nation was on its knees thanking God for having enabled it to break the Spanish yoke from the neck of Cuba. This is our civilization. This is Cuba's kindergarten of ethics and good government. This is Protestant religion in the United States, that is planning a wholesale missionary crusade against Catholic Cuba. This is the golden rule as interpreted by the white pulpit of Wilmington.

Over this drunken and blood-thirsty mob they stretch their hands and invoke the blessings of a just God. We have waited two hundred and fifty years for liberty, and this is what it is when it comes. O Liberty, what crimes are committed in thy name! A rent and bloody mantle of citizenship that has covered as with a garment of fire, wrapped in which as in a shroud, forty thousand of my people have fallen around Southern ballot boxes. . . . A score of intelligent colored men, able to pass even a South Carolina election officer, shot down at Phoenix, South Carolina, for no reason whatever, except as the Charleston *News and Courier* said, because the baser elements of the community loved to kill and destroy. The pitiful privilege of dying like cattle in the red gutters of Wilmington, or crouching waist deep in the icy waters of neighboring swamps, where terrified women gave birth to a dozen infants, most of whom died of exposure and cold. This is Negro citizenship! This is what the nation fought for from Bull Run to Appomattox!

What caused all this bitterness, strife, arson, murder, revolution and anarchy at Wilmington? We hear the answer on all sides—"Negro domination." I deny the charge. It is utterly false, and no one knows it better than the men who use it to justify crimes that threaten the very foundation of republican government; crimes that make the South red with blood, white with bones and gray with ashes; crimes no other civilized government would tolerate for a single day. The colored people comprise one-third of the population of the State of North Carolina; in the Legislature there are one hundred and twenty representatives, seven of whom are colored. There are fifty senators, two of whom are colored—nine in all out of one hundred and seventy. Can nine Negroes dominate one hundred and sixty white men? That would be a fair sample of the tail wagging the dog. Not a colored man holds a state office in North Carolina; the whole race has less than five per cent of all the offices in the state. In the city of Wilmington the Mayor was white, six out of ten members of the board of aldermen, and sixteen out of twenty-six members of the police force were white; the city attorney was white, the city clerk was white, the city treasurer was white, the superintendent of streets was white, the superintendent of garbage was white, the superintendent of health was white, and all the nurses in the white wards were white; the superintendent of the public schools was white, the chief and assistant chief of the fire department, and three out of five fire companies were white; the school committee has always been composed of two white men and one colored; the board of audit and finance is composed of five members, four of whom were white, and the one Negro was reported to be worth more than any of his white associates. The tax rate under this miscalled Negro regime was less than under its predecessors; this is Negro domination in Wilmington. This is a fair sample of that Southern scarecrow—conjured by these masters of the black art everywhere. . . .

The Good Samaritan did not leave his own eldest son robbed and bleeding at his own threshold, while he went way off down the road between

Jerusalem and Jericho to hunt for a man that had fallen among thieves. Nor can America afford to go eight thousand miles from home to set up a republican government in the Philippines while the blood of citizens whose ancestors came here before the Mayflower, is crying out to God against her from the gutters of Wilmington.

This speech, delivered by the Rev. Morris in January, 1899, at Boston before the Interdenominational Association of Colored Clergymen, was found in printed form in a folder, entitled "Writings of Charles H. Williams" in the library of the Wisconsin State Historical Society in Madison. Mr. Williams, a white man of Baraboo, Wis., showed great interest in the Negro question and wrote profusely on the subject in local newspapers.

[j]

Senator Fuller's Post-Election Speech, 1898

Without doubt, the field of expedients will be swept by the next legislature in order to counteract the influence, or obstruct the exercise of franchise by the ignorant colored element of the population, which franchise is held to be dangerous to our free institutions. Whether it will be an educational or property qualification, no one knows at present. The Constitution of Mississippi provides that an elector must be able to read and write and must have paid all taxes legally required of him. An exception is made for those who cannot read, that they must be able to understand the Constitution when explained to them or "give a reasonable interpretation thereof." By this provision it was easy to eliminate the ignorant vote and the United States Supreme Court, in a recent decision, held it to be constitutional, since it "discriminated against no particular race." In rendering its decision, the Court said, concerning our race, *"A patient, docile people; but careless, landless,* migratory within narrow limits; without forethought—the Convention (of Mississippi) discriminates against its *characteristics* and the *offenses* to which its criminal elements are prone. They reach weak and vicious *white* men as weak and vicious *black* men; and whatever is sinister in their intention if anything, can be prevented by both races by the exertion of that duty which voluntarily pays taxes and refrains from crime."

Hence, we see that the highest court of our land holds that we are careless, landless and unnecessarily migratory. We must be made to feel the force of this significant declaration. Since it is claimed that legislation is aimed at our moral, industrial and intellectual unfitness, the remedy is not far to seek. It is not with the office-seeker, the professional politician, nor with those who claim the inherent right to govern. It is with you and me . . . BE INDUSTRIOUS, HONEST, PATIENT and RESPECTFUL and you have nothing to fear . . . I shall go to the Senate, not as a politician, but as a Christian citizen. I shall DEFEND nothing, but shall gently and earnestly PLEAD for a continuance of the sympathetic and friendly relations which have been the proud boast of us all and which have given North Carolina an exalted place in the great sisterhood of states . . . In the meantime, let UNNECESSARY AGITATION CEASE. . . . I believe with Prof. Booker T. Washington. Shun ANARCHY, INTIMIDATION, and RIOT. . . .

Thomas O. Fuller, *Twenty Years in Public Life* . . . (Nashville, 1910), pp. 42–44. Copy in the Library of Congress.

[k]

Congressman White on Negro Disfranchisement, 1900

In Mississippi the vote cast at the last election for Congressmen, numbering seven in number, was 27,114. I do not mean the vote cast for the successful candidates. That was the total vote cast for all candidates. In Louisiana they did a little better. With six members of Congress the whole vote was 32,731. In South Carolina the vote for seven members of Congress elected was 28, 832. In my own district in North Carolina, on the other hand, notwithstanding fraud and rascality, 35,279 votes were recorded, though as a matter of fact some forty thousand votes were cast. Thus in a single district of my own State eight thousand more votes were declared than in seven Congressional districts in Mississippi, and almost seven thousand more than in seven districts in South Carolina. The population of the First District is 143,315, and the votes cast for a member of Congress 2,469. In the Sixth District of South Carolina but 1,916 votes were cast for a member of Congress out of a population of 158,851.

These figures on their very face show fraud or suppression. Under the new election law passed by North Carolina in 1899 should the Constitutional amendment be adopted and should it be decided that it is in harmony with the national Constitution, my own State would be reduced to the level of the other States mentioned in the matter of the franchise. . . .

The proposed constitutional amendment requires that every person presenting himself for registration shall be able to read and write any section of the Constitution in the English language. He is required likewise to pay his poll tax as prescribed by law. Then there is a provision, which we call "the grandfather clause," which provides that the requirement as to reading and writing shall not apply to any male person who was entitled to vote on January 1st, 1867, or at any time prior thereto. Nor shall it apply to the lineal descendant of any such person, who shall have registered prior to December, 1908. This provision, of course, excludes the illiterate Negroes while admitting to the suffrage the illiterate whites. By a law of 1835 North

Carolina forbade any Negro or person of Negro descent to vote, and the law remained in force till the adoption of the constitutional amendment. There may be five thousand colored people who can vote under that clause, largely made up of those who moved from other States, where they had the right to vote. In 1896 the Negro vote was 120,000, while the white Republican vote was 37,000. The whole white vote of the State was somewhere near two hundred thousand. We constitute not quite one-third of the population of the State. The white Republicans will be virtually united against the amendment and I think the Populists will fuse with the Republicans, and in a fair vote I believe the amendment would be defeated; but under the new election law, with absolute Democratic control, a fair vote is impossible.

For these reasons I favor the Crumpacker Bill, which proposes to determine by the Twelfth Census the number of persons who are denied the right to vote under these restrictions, so as to form a basis of apportionment to Congress next fall in accordance with the provision of Section 2 of the Fourteenth Amendment to the Constitution. I do not believe that anybody should be permitted to thrive by his own dishonesty and rascality. These frauds in the South while terribly unjust to the colored man will certainly react upon the white people.

The Independent (N.Y.), January 18, 1900, LII, pp. 176–77.

VI.

THE NEGRO AND THE TWO MAJOR PARTIES

The period of the development of monopoly capitalism, and the years immediately following the demise of the Populist movement, witnessed a sharpening disillusionment among many Negroes as concerns the Republican Party. While this in some cases eventuated in a drift to the Democratic Party—a man like Du Bois, for example, supporting Bryan—the general feeling was that the hostility of that party, especially its southern wing, towards the Negro made his affiliation with it impossible. Present with this, however, was quite distinctly a growing distrust of the Republican Party. This is significant background material for an understanding of the historic roots of the Negro people's dramatic break with Republicanism in the following generation.

To indicate this development four typical documents are published below. The first is a letter dated June 24, 1896, from John H. Kelley, a prominent Negro attorney of St. Joseph, Missouri, to Cyrus D. Bell, editor of a pro-Democratic newspaper, *The Afro-American Sentinel,* published in Omaha, Nebraska. The letter comments particularly upon the Jim Crow arrangement which characterized the Republican National Convention held in St. Louis. The second document is an editorial in this newspaper, later in 1896, referring caustically to the questioning concerning his position on the Negro put to William Jennings Bryan by Philip H. Brown, an official of the Afro-American Associated Press.

The third document is a letter dated July 30, 1900, from George E. Taylor, of Oskaloosa, Iowa to George L. Knox, editor of the pro-Republican newspaper, the Indianapolis *Freeman*. Mr. Taylor, president of the Negro National Democratic League, here explains why he prefers Bryan over McKinley. The last document is an editorial from the Indianapolis *Freeman* in which Mr. Knox, while commenting favorably on the anti-imperialist movement and the idea of political independence for the Negro, still states his preference for the Republican Party.

[a]

Kelley to Bell, 1896

I thank you for the copy of the *Sentinel* which I heartily enjoyed, and fully agree with your editorial upon the treatment accorded to the black contingent of the Republican party in the recent convention at St. Louis in respect to civil accommodations. We are greatly in need of more such men as yourself, possessed with a spirit to do justice to every one, and independence and manliness sufficient to complain when justice is not done. There was not one Negro, as you observed, at that convention, who had that courage. We have a cheap lot of spewed-out political scullions who exist in political cesspools, doing the bidding of designing white bosses, and who dare not show their heads outside the dark places in which they dwell, nor come into the light of independence and freedom of political action; and they were at the convention.

Frederick Douglass was the only Negro who spoke in season and out for his race and came nearer being a leader than all of the would-be leaders in the entire race. Every black delegate should have taken the first train for his home at the instant of the unpardonable insult on the part of the hotel keepers, and backed up by that stronger factor—public sentiment. . . . Some of the Negroes have received an immediate answer to their prayers, viz the visitation of another cyclone upon St. Louis, but it did not destroy any of the hotels or restaurants as they prayed for. If God does not interfere and help the Negro, his cause is surely a hopeless and helpless one. Again I congratulate you upon the manly stand you have taken for your race, and it is just this kind of men and papers that are actually doing good and making history for the Negro in America.

The Afro-American Sentinel (Omaha), June 27, 1896.

[b]

A Pro-Bryan Editorial, 1896

Some New York Negro, heretofore unheard of, whose leading trait is brass and whose principal lack is brains, has lately written a communication to

Mr. Bryan asking him (1) whether he thinks Negroes in the South should have the same rights as whites? (2) whether he condemns lynching in the South? and (3) whether he thinks "the separate car outrage as practiced in Louisiana is just?" The fool concludes his communication with what he doubtless intended as a terrifying remark: "Ten million of colored people will be interested in your reply. . . ."

What fact is there in the life of Wm. J. Bryan, whether inquiry be directed to his public or private career, that would justify the slightest suspicion that he would be in the least degree inclined to condone the outrages and injustices under which the colored people of the South—aye, and of some parts of the North, including New York—suffer?

During Mr. Bryan's first term in Congress, some five or six years ago, the Hon. H. P. Cheatham, an Afro-American Congressman from North Carolina, introduced a certain measure in the House designed particularly to promote the interest of the colored people of the South.* Although a large part—we think a majority—of the Republican members of that House opposed, and eventually defeated Mr. Cheatham's measure, the nobleman, Wm. J. Bryan, with that generosity of heart and earnest eloquence that are his brightest and most conspicuous characteristics, did his best from first to last for its success. The editor of this paper had the good fortune of getting possession of Mr. Cheatham's letter to Mr. Bryan acknowledging the latter's splendid and disinterested services in behalf of this race at that time. As our readers doubtless remember, we printed Mr. Cheatham's letter through several editions of this paper during the memorable campaign which ended in Mr. Bryan's second election to Congress from a district which was believed and conceded to be hopelessly Republican.

Let the mercenary mud slingers do their worst in their attempts to bedaub the character of the "boy orator of the Platte." The buzzards, whether blacks or whites, will find no carrion here upon which to feast their foul appetites.

The Afro-American Sentinel (Omaha), August 29, 1896.

[c]

A Pro-Democratic Letter, 1900

That a large percentage of the . . . Negro voters of the country are today arrayed with the Democratic party, no well informed person can deny. And, in order that our Republican brothers may know why we cherish the faith

* In 1892, Mr. Cheatham introduced a bill "to aid in the establishment and temporary support of common schools."

that is within us, I desire to say through the *Freeman,* that we believe that imperialism leads to despotism, and we consider that the present administration has strong imperialistic tendencies; we also believe in the rights of all men to govern themselves, hence we oppose the policy of the administration towards the Philippines; we are firm believers in the Monroe Doctrine, and since the present administration has practically annulled this doctrine we oppose the action; we are opposed to the propagation of private trusts and combines, and consider that the administration is in full sympathy with such; we in no wise feel benefited by the Dingley tariff, hence we oppose it; we are unalterably opposed to the present "gold standard" policy, believing that it tends to contract the currency of the country, thus hampering our chances for sustenance; hence, it is apparent that we stand for the principles of the Democratic Party and for Bryan, as against the principles of the present Republican Party and McKinley.

Indianapolis *Freeman,* August 11, 1900.

[d]

An Anti-Democratic Editorial, 1900

The Anti-Imperialist Convention,* which met in Indianapolis, decided to endorse Mr. Bryan, owing to his new and intense opposition to the government's policy of expansion. Its action in that matter was anticipated. However, that convention dared to declare, in a mild form, for the Constitution as it may be considered as applying to Negroes. It saw fit to deprecate the disfranchising tendencies that are being noted in some sections of the country.

It will be borne in mind that the great Democratic party at Kansas City did not have the courage to utter a single word in that direction. Mr. George Taylor, of Oskaloosa, Iowa, one of the Negro converts to that party, thinks that it ought to be excused because it was not informed as to its duty. Ignorance of the law excuseth no man. The Anti-Imperialist Convention needed no instructions, the great Republican party needed no such instructions. It is very strange that the party that "worships man rather than the dollar" should neglect such a large portion of mankind that need special attention.

What the Anti-Imperialists have done will not save the Negroes to the Democratic party. What they have done simply emphasizes what the Demo-

---

* The Anti-Imperialist League, consisting of men like Moorfield Storey, W. E. B. Du Bois and William Dean Howells, was formed after the Spanish-American War.

rrats did not do. Negroes who insist that they are right for dividing on issues as sensible white men do, are right, but the issue, as the case now stands, is the race itself. The Negroes' civil existence is threatened, their political status has been curtailed, and by whom?

What fine spun theories have the spellbinders to present to the Negroes now? Can North Carolina be omitted and South Carolina and Mississippi and Louisiana? Well, hardly. The charge of for revenue only will sound plausible this year when applied to those who are trying to convert Negroes to Democracy.

Indianapolis *Freeman*, August 25, 1900.

VII.

THE SPANISH-AMERICAN WAR AND THE PHILIPPINE ISLANDS

Typical of the published response of the Negro people to the Spanish-American conflict was that of restrained support. A sense of patriotism, a feeling that participation in battle might result in improved conditions at home and a keen interest in the welfare of the Negro people in Cuba as well as the Filipino people combined to produce this support. But ever present was resentment over Jim-Crowism in the armed forces and this was expressed vigorously.

Other documents appearing earlier have shown the anti-imperialist current running through Negro society. This developed especially during the brutal suppression by the American government of the insurrection in the Philippines.

Four documents are printed below relative to these phases of Negro history. The first is an editorial entitled "Let Afro-Americans Prove Their Loyalty" which appeared in a Negro newspaper shortly before war was declared. The second document is illustrative of the Negro troops' response to Jim-Crow and is from an article by the Rev. Theophilus G. Steward, Chaplain of the Negro Twenty-Fifth Infantry Regiment.

The third item consists of three parts, the first being an attack made in 1898, upon the War itself as being an imperialist one. It was written by a Providence, R.I., attorney, Charles G. Baylor, and was displayed very prominently in the Negro press. The second is a statement made in the summer of 1899 by Clifford H. Plummer, a Negro lawyer of Boston and Secretary of the National Colored Protective League. How authentic the details of this document may be is not known, but it is certainly indicative of a strong anti-imperialist feeling among Negroes. The third part consists of a letter dated Washington, October 19, 1899, and written by Lewis H. Douglass, son of Frederick Douglass, severely condemning United States expansionist policies. The fourth document is representative of letters from Negro soldiers engaged in the Filipino "pacification" campaign and indicates how troubling to the American Negro was this effort at subduing other colored peoples.

[a]

Anticipating the Outbreak of War, 1898

We hold to the conviction that in the event of a war with Spain, Afro-Americans will find resting upon themselves a responsibility equal with that on every other citizen of this republic. The interests involved in the issues of war are important with the Afro-American as with anyone else, because however much proscribed and circumscribed in the exercise of his personal and political immunities, his rights per se are as sacred and dear to himself as to any other citizen. As much as we abominate the terrible injustice done the Afro-American under his own government, yet we have never lost sight of the fact that this country and government are his rightful and inalienable heritage, and despite our murmurings we have deemed it our duty that every citizen should respond to the demands of the national defense. Our present administration is called to confront the grave threatenings of war, and it will be expected to deal with the present troubles wisely and effectively. Very assuredly every intelligent and loyal black man who feels the least personal concern for his surroundings will not only desire a peaceful settlement of the difficulties, but will in case of an actual break between Spain and our government feel himself in duty bound to lend all aid, encourage and support his government and if need be offer himself in vindication of the national defense. This is our opportunity. Let us not stand upon the asking, but show ourselves ready to maintain intact the government from which we derive our hopes for life, liberty and happiness.

Editorial in the Cleveland *Gazette*, March 26, 1898.

[b]

A Negro Chaplain on Jim Crow, 1898

After many changes and much telegraphing, the Twenty-fifth Infantry was finally ordered to leave the stations which it had so long occupied in Montana . . . the demonstrations were very hearty until we had passed Terre Haute, Ind.; but soon after passing this place, at 10 P.M., we were in Kentucky, and as daylight came upon us we realized that we had crossed the line that divides the world. The Twenty-fifth is a black regiment, and black soldiers are not cheered in Kentucky and Tennessee. On arriving at Nashville, the black chaplain and his family were given plainly and forcefully to understand, as they entered the railroad dining-saloon, that they could not eat with the other officers of the regiment under a Southern sky.

United States commission could not make clean what the South pronounces unclean; and these men whose brawny arms are expected to uphold the flag of the great nation had a "realizing sense" of the weakness of their flag as they saw the Government blue spit upon by a custom as mean as it is silly and degrading. A glorious dilemma that will be for the Cuban Negro, to usher him into the condition of the American Negro. . . . One over-curious man asked a soldier if he thought "you darkies would fight." He rose up from the earth inside of ten seconds perhaps, but within that time had finished his course in the school of experience, and was ready for his diploma. His question was answered to his full satisfaction; and, like the good old plantation song, he carries the witness in his breast.

The Independent (N.Y.), April 28, 1898, L, pp. 535–36.

[c]

The Negro's Anti-Imperialism, 1898–99

1. *Charles G. Baylor:*

. . . The central and important fact in this whole matter is that the revolution in Cuba was from the beginning, an Afro-Cuban Socialist up-rising against Spanish tyranny, capitalistic greed and rapacity, the church being the mainstay and prop of the entire infernation.

It was a struggle, which from the first aroused a universal revolutionary sympathy, nowhere more powerfully than in Spain itself. The Afro-Cuban revolt in Cuba drew to its side lovers of liberty all over the world. In the United States it penetrated all grades of society, arousing the masses, and alarming the plutocracy. It divided parties and shook the fabric of Jesuitism to its foundation.

The present war which has taken the place of that holy crusade, has from one cause or another degenerated finally in a bloody farce, the chief object of which is to put down that revolution in its socialistic aspect. . . .

Maceo, the great Afro-Cuban military leader was a full blooded Negro. General Gomez is an Afro-Cuban—a quadroon. Nearly all the leaders and fighters in the Cuban army of liberation are men who, if in South Carolina, Mississippi or Louisiana, would be made to ride in the "Jim Crow Cars," and would be refused the right to occupy a private residence on Beacon St., in Boston. You see the proposed Afro-Cuban Republic was too close to our own Cuba and Armenia to suit either the northern or southern pluto-crats. . . .

The question which must be answered in the face of such facts as these at such a time as this is, Shall the Liberty Cause in Cuba be thus betrayed and sacrificed without a determined resistance by liberty men and women everywhere? . . . I ask the question because the American Negro cannot become the ally of Imperialism without enslaving his own race. . . .

The Richmond Planet, July 30, 1898. I am indebted to Mrs. Cecille H. Harris of Los Angeles, for calling this document to my attention.

2. *Clifford H. Plummer:*

An uprising of the colored race against the Administration at Washington is being organized in Boston. This is the seat of the movement that it is proposed to carry wherever the colored people are populous. The instigators assert that it will mean the downfall of McKinley, imperialism and the Republican Party. They claim that it will divert the colored vote that has been the upholder of the Republican Party since the colored man received the right of franchise.

The object of this organization is a revolt at the ballot box; but there are those among its supporters who would willingly take part in an armed uprising, and who, were it possible, would offer their strength to aid the Filipinos in their struggle for independence. During the war with Spain a proportion of the more enthusiastic of the colored people of New England and of some of the Middle and Southwestern States were ready to make an armed revolt against the United States and to espouse the cause of Spain. That feeling still exists to a large degree, and, as has been already said, were it possible to render the fighting Filipinos armed assistance, it would be done. It was, in fact, only the cooler minds and trained intelligence of certain of the race that successfully prevented the more open expression of feeling and the actual offer of services. It was the purpose of some of the people to raise troops as quietly as possible, to get out of the country in detachments, and to join the forces of Spain.

N.Y. *Tribune,* July 17, 1899.

3. *Lewis H. Douglass:*

President McKinley, in the course of his speech at Minneapolis, said of the Filipinos under American sovereignty: "They will not be governed as vassals, or serfs, or slaves. They will be given a government of liberty, regulated by law, honestly administered, without oppressing exaction, taxation without tyranny, justice without bribe, education without distinction of social conditions, freedom of religious worship, and protection of life, liberty, and pursuit of happiness."

I do not believe that President McKinley has any confidence in the statement above. It cannot be successfully asserted that the great tariff statesman is blind to the fact of the race and color prejudice that dominates the greater percentage of the soldiers who are killing Filipinos in the name of freedom and civilization.

President McKinley knows that brave, loyal, black American soldiers, who fight and die for their country, are hated, despised, and cruelly treated in that section of the country from which this administration accepts dicta- tion and to the tastes of which the President, undoubtedly, caters. The President of the United States knows that he dare not station a regiment of black heroes in the State of Arkansas. He knows that at the race hating command of a people who sought destruction of the nation his administra- tion rescinded an order to send black soldiers to Little Rock. The admin- istration lacks the courage to deal with American citizens without regard to race or color, as is clearly demonstrated in the weak and contemptibly mean act of yielding to the demands of those who hold that this is a white man's government and that dark races have no rights which white men are bound to respect.

It is a sorry, though true, fact that whatever this government controls, injustice to dark races prevails. The people of Cuba, Porto Rico, Hawaii and Manila know it well as do the wronged Indian and outraged black man in the United States. . . .

The question will be asked: How is it that such promises are made to Filipinos thousands of miles away while the action of the administration in protecting dark citizens at home does not even extend to a promise of any attempt to rebuke the outlawry which kills American citizens of African descent for the purpose of gratifying blood-thirstiness and race hatred? . . .

It is hypocrisy of the most sickening kind to try to make us believe that the killing of Filipinos is for the purpose of good government and to give protection to life and liberty and the pursuit of happiness. . . .

When the United States learns that justice should be blind as to race and color, then may it undertake to, with some show of propriety, expand. Now its expansion means extension of race hate and cruelty, barbarous lynchings and gross injustice to dark people.

American Citizen (Kansas City, Kansas), Nov. 17, 1899.

[d]

Negro Soldiers on the Filipino Insurrection, 1901

1:

William Simms, a soldier in Bong-a-bong, Philippine Isles, whose home is in Muncie, Ind., writing to *The Freeman* says: "I was struck by a ques- tion a little boy asked me, which ran about this way—'Why does the American Negro come from America to fight us when we are much friend to him and have not done anything to him? He is all the same as me, and me all the same as you. Why don't you fight those people in America that burn the Negroes, that made a beast of you, that took the child from its mother's side and sold it?' " Simms admits that he was staggered.

Indianapolis *Freeman,* May 11, 1901.

2:

This struggle on the islands has been naught but a gigantic scheme of robbery and oppression. Many soldiers who came here in poverty to battle for the "stars and stripes" have gone home with gold, diamonds, and other valuables while the natives here who were once good livers, are hardly able to keep the wolf from the door. Graves have been entered and searches have been made for riches; churches and cathedrals have been entered and robbed of their precious ornaments; homes have been pillaged and moneys and jewelry stolen. The commissary scandal is being thoroughly investigated. . . . The way some of our officers have conducted themselves is enough to cause the worst insurrecto to shudder with fear when he knows the American flag is to wave over his people and that they are to look to the American government for protection. The natives say we have good men for soldiers but drunkards for officers—my lips are closed. The natives unequivocally denounce the attitude of our government and claim that its administration is unjust and humiliating. . . . If we are to unfurl our flag on these islands let us make these natives joint heirs in our citizenship. . . . The eyes of the civilized world are upon us and now is the time for action.

Letter from Pvt. William R. Fulbright of the 25th Inf. Regt., dated Manila, June 10, 1901, in the Indianapolis *Freeman,* August 3, 1901.

VIII
The Twentieth Century

THE DEVELOPING NEGRO LIBERATION
MOVEMENT, 1901–1910

Though monopoly capitalism emerges in 1900 as dominant in American life and transforms the United States into an imperialistic nation, its position was challenged constantly. Among no sector of the population was this more true than the Negro people, chief sufferers as they were from enveloping imperialism.

The documents which follow aim at demonstrating the impact of this imperialism upon the American Negro both in its oppressing aspects and in terms of the organization of resistance to and struggle against it. In doing this the material has been assembled within six groupings.

The first group contains material illustrative of the feelings of and conditions facing the largest segments among Negroes in the United States: the Negro woman, the plantation worker, the industrial worker and the bourgeoisie.

The second group presents material concerning the steadily growing Negro press and the types of influence to which it was subjected. The third group illustrates currents in Negro politics and especially the growing expressions of dissatisfaction with the Republican Party. Material is presented here, also, of the increasing interest in socialism characterizing the decade.

The fourth group is one containing documents of a miscellaneous character tied together by the fact that they are indicative of facets within the special experiences of the Negro population. These concern such things as the national sensation caused when a Negro dined with the President, the diary entries of a Negro noting how his white neighbors reacted to his presence, comments on the Atlanta Massacre of 1906 and reactions to the dishonorable discharge of three whole companies of a Negro infantry regiment.

The fifth section comprises documents relating to the principles and personalities involved in the Washington-Du Bois conflict, while the sixth group deals with the

organizational forms and ideas of the numerous collective expressions of struggle
and discontent during the ten year period. Particular attention is given to the
program of the Niagara Movement founded in 1905 and to the first formulations
of the aims of the National Association for the Advancement of Colored People
begun half a decade later.

I.

THE NEGRO'S LIFE, 1901–1910

In 1900 there were 8,800,000 Negroes in the United States, of whom all but
900,000 were in the South. Ten years later the total number had grown by one
million while those outside the South reached 1,000,000.

During this decade about half the Negro population consisted, of course, of
women and in the first document [a] an Alabama housewife describes in 1902 the
conditions facing them. At this same period, almost sixty percent of all employed
Negroes labored in agriculture under conditions equivalent, in most cases, to
peonage. One such Negro, from Georgia, tells in the second document [b] his
story as of 1905. Documents three and four [c, d] relate to conditions among and
strike experiences of Negroes in New York and Chicago, with some passing reference to Philadelphia as well. In those three cities there lived in 1910 almost a
quarter of a million Negroes, or over twenty percent of all Negroes residing in the
North.

The last two documents in the section deal with the National Negro Business
League which was founded in 1900 in Boston. Two years before, Dr. Du Bois had
prepared for the Atlanta University Conference a listing and study of Negroes
in business. In 1899, at the request of the Afro-American Council, he headed a
business bureau of the Council and gave Booker T. Washington a roster of businessmen. The next year the Boston meeting occurred, the League was organized,
but Dr. Du Bois was not among those present. The fifth document [e] is a report
on the 1901 convention of the National Negro Business League, while the sixth
[f] represents an estimation of its work written by Mr. Washington late in 1902.

[a]

A Negro Woman Speaks, 1902

I am a colored woman, wife and mother.* I have lived all my life in the South,
and have often thought what a peculiar fact it is that the more ignorant
the Southern whites are of us the more vehement they are in their denunciation of us. They boast that they have little intercourse with us, never see
us in our homes, churches or places of amusement, but still they know us
thoroughly.

They also admit that they know us in no capacity except as servants,
yet they say we are at our best in that single capacity. What philosophers

---

* This was published anonymously for it was feared that the author's life might be
endangered if her identity were known.

they are! The Southerners say we Negroes are a happy, laughing set of people, with no thought of tomorrow. How mistaken they are! The educated, thinking Negro is just the opposite. There is a feeling of unrest, insecurity, almost panic among the best class of Negroes in the South. In our homes, in our churches, wherever two or three are gathered together, there is a discussion of what is best to do. Must we remain in the South or go elsewhere? Where can we go to feel that security which other people feel? Is it best to go in great numbers or only in several families? These and many other things are discussed over and over.

People who have security in their homes, whose children can go on the street unmolested, whose wives and daughters are treated as women, cannot, perhaps, sympathize with the Southern Negro's anxieties and complaints. I ask forbearance of such people. . . .

I know of houses occupied by poor Negroes in which a respectable farmer would not keep his cattle. It is impossible for them to rent elsewhere. All Southern real estate agents have "white property" and "colored property." In one of the largest Southern cities there is a colored minister, a graduate of Harvard, whose wife is an educated, Christian woman, who lived for weeks in a tumble-down rookery because he could neither rent nor buy in a respectable locality.

Many colored women who wash, iron, scrub, cook or sew all the week to help pay the rent for these miserable hovels and help fill the many small mouths, would deny themselves some of the necessaries of life if they could take their little children and teething babies on the cars to the parks of a Sunday afternoon and sit under the trees, enjoy the cool breezes and breathe God's pure air for only two or three hours; but this is denied them. Some of the parks have signs, "No Negroes allowed on these grounds except as servants." Pitiful, pitiful customs and laws that make war on women and babes! There is no wonder that we die; the wonder is that we persist in living.

Fourteen years ago I had just married. My husband had saved sufficient money to buy a small home. On account of our limited means we went to the suburbs, on unpaved streets, to look for a home, only asking for a high, healthy locality. Some real estate agents were "sorry, but had nothing to suit," some had "just the thing," but we discovered on investigation that they had "just the thing" for an unhealthy pigsty. Others had no "colored property." One agent said that he had what we wanted, but we should have to go to see the lot after dark, or walk by and give the place a casual look; for, he said, "all the white people in the neighborhood would be down on me." Finally we bought this lot. When the house was being built we went to see it. Consternation reigned. We had ruined this neighborhood of poor people; poor as we, poorer in manners at least. The people who lived next door received the sympathy of their friends. When we walked on the street (there were no sidewalks) we were embarrassed by the stare of many unfriendly eyes.

Two years passed before a single woman spoke to me, and only then because I helped one of them when a little sudden trouble came to her. Such was the reception, I a happy young woman, just married, received from people among whom I wanted to make a home. Fourteen years have now passed, four children have been born to us, and one has died in this same home, among these same neighbors. Although the neighbors speak to us, and occasionally one will send a child to borrow the morning's paper or ask the loan of a pattern, not one woman has ever been inside of my house, not even at the times when a woman would doubly appreciate the slightest attention of a neighbor.

The Southerner boasts that he is our friend; he educates our children, he pays us for work and is most noble and generous to us. Did not the Negro by his labor for over three hundred years help to educate the white man's children? Is thirty equal to three hundred? Does a white man deserve praise for paying a black man for his work?

The Southerner also claims that the Negro gets justice. Not long ago a Negro man was cursed and struck in the face by an electric car conductor. The Negro knocked the conductor down and although it was clearly proven in a court of "justice" that the conductor was in the wrong the Negro had to pay a fine of $10. The judge told him "I fine you that much to teach you that you must respect white folks." The conductor was acquitted. "Most noble judge! A second Daniel!" This is the South's idea of justice.

A noble man, who has established rescue homes for fallen women all over the country, visited a Southern city. The women of the city were invited to meet him in one of the churches. The fallen women were especially invited and both good and bad went. They sat wherever they could find a seat, so long as their faces were white; but I, a respectable married woman, was asked to sit apart. A colored woman, however respectable, is lower than the white prostitute. The Southern white woman will declare that no Negro women are virtuous, yet she places her innocent children in their care. . . .

The Southerner says the Negro must "keep in his place." That means the particular place the white man says is his. . . . A self respecting colored man who does not cringe, but walks erect, supports his family, educates his children, and by example and precept teaches them that God made all men equal, is called a "dangerous Negro"; "he is too smart"; "he wants to be white and act like white people." Now, we are told that the Negro has the worst traits of the whole human family and the Southern white man the best; but we must not profit by his example or we are regarded as "dangerous Negroes."

White agents and other chance visitors who come into our homes ask questions that we must not dare ask their wives. They express surprise that our children have clean faces and that their hair is combed. You cannot insult a colored woman, you know. . . .

There are aristocrats in crime, in poverty, and in misfortune in the South. The white criminal cannot think of eating or sleeping in the same part of the penitentiary with the Negro criminal. The white pauper is just as exclusive; and although the blind cannot see color, nor the insane care about it, they must be kept separate, at great extra expense. Lastly, the dead white man's bones must not be contaminated with the dead black man's. . . .

Whenever a crime is committed, in the South the policemen look for the Negro in the case. A white man with face and hands blackened can commit any crime in the calendar. The first friendly stream soon washes away his guilt and he is ready to join in the hunt to lynch the "big, black burly brute." When a white man in the South does commit a crime, that is simply one white man gone wrong. If his crime is especially brutal he is a freak or temporarily insane. If one low, ignorant black wretch commits a crime, that is different. All of us must bear his guilt. A young white boy's badness is simply the overflowing of young animal spirits; the black boy's badness is badness, pure and simple. . . .

When we were shouting for Dewey, Sampson, Schley and Hobson, and were on tiptoe to touch the hem of their garments, we were delighted to know that some of our Spanish-American heroes were coming where we could get a glimpse of them. Had not black men helped in a small way to give them their honors? In the cities of the South, where these heroes went, the white school children were assembled, flags were waved, flowers strewn, speeches made, and "My Country, 'tis of Thee, Sweet Land of Liberty," was sung. Our children who need to be taught so much, were not assembled, their hands waved no flags, they threw no flowers, heard no thrilling speech, sang no song of their country. And this is the South's idea of justice. Is it surprising that feeling grows more bitter, when the white mother teaches her boy to hate my boy, not because he is mean, but because his skin is dark? I have seen very small white children hang their black dolls. It is not the child's fault, he is simply an apt pupil.

Someone will at last arise who will champion our cause and compel the world to see that we deserve justice; as other heroes compelled it to see that we deserved freedom.

The Independent (N.Y.), Sept. 18, 1902, LIV, pp. 2221–24.

[b]

A Negro Peon Speaks, 1905

I am a Negro and was born sometime during the war in Elbert County, Ga., and I reckon by this time I must be a little over forty years old. My mother was not married when I was born, and I never knew who my father was or anything about him. Shortly after the war my mother died, and I was left to the care of my uncle. All this happened before I was eight years old, and so I can't remember very much about it. When I was about ten years old my uncle hired me out to Captain ——. I had already learned how to plow, and was also a good hand at picking cotton. I was told that the Captain wanted me for his houseboy, and that later on he was going to train me to be his coachman. To be a coachman in those days was considered a post of honor, and young as I was, I was glad of the chance. But I had not been at the Captain's a month before I was put to work on the farm, with some twenty or thirty other Negroes—men, women and children. From the beginning the boys had the same tasks as the men and women. There was no difference. We all worked hard during the week, and would frolic on Saturday nights and often on Sundays. And everybody was happy. The men got $3 a week and the women $2. I don't know what the children got. Every week my uncle collected my money for me, but it was very little of it that I ever saw. My uncle fed and clothed me, gave me a place to sleep, and allowed me ten or fifteen cents a week for "spending change," as he called it. I must have been seventeen or eighteen years old before I got tired of that arrangement, and felt that I was man enough to be working for myself and handling my own wages. The other boys about my age and size were "drawing" their own pay, and they used to laugh at me and call me "Baby," because my old uncle was always on hand to "draw" my pay. Worked up by these things, I made a break for liberty. Unknown to my uncle or the Captain I went off to a neighboring plantation and hired myself out to another man. The new landlord agreed to give me forty cents a day and furnish me one meal. I thought that was doing fine. Bright and early one Monday morning I started for work, still not letting the others know anything about it. But they found it out before sundown. The Captain came over to the new place and brought some kind of officer of the law. The officer pulled out a long piece of paper from his pocket and read it to my employer. When this was done I heard my new boss say:

"I beg your pardon, Captain. I didn't know this Negro was bound out to you, or I wouldn't have hired him."

"He certainly is bound out to me," said the Captain. "He belongs to me until he is twenty-one, and I'm going to make him know his place."

So I was carried back to the Captain's. That night he made me strip off my clothing down to my waist, ordered his foreman to give me thirty lashes with a buggy whip across my bare back, and stood by until it was done. After that experience the Captain made me stay on his place night and day—but my uncle still continued to "draw" my money.

I was a man nearly grown before I knew how to count from one to one hundred. I was a man nearly grown before I ever saw a colored teacher. I never went to school a day in my life. Today I can't write my own name, though I can read a little. I was a man nearly grown before I ever rode on a railroad train, and then I went on an excursion from Elberton to Athens. What was true of me was true of hundreds of other Negroes around me— 'way off there in the country, fifteen or twenty miles from the nearest town.

When I reached twenty-one the Captain told me I was a free man, but he urged me to stay with him. He said he would treat me right, and pay me as much as anybody else would. The Captain's son and I were about the same age, and the Captain said that, as he had owned my mother and uncle during slavery, and as his son didn't want me to leave them (since I had been with them so long), he wanted me to stay with the old family. And I stayed. I signed a contract—that is, I made my mark—for one year. The Captain was to give me $3.50 a week, and furnish me a little house on the plantation—a one-room log cabin similar to those used by his other laborers.

During that year I married Mandy. For several years Mandy had been the house-servant for the Captain, his wife, his son and his three daughters, and they all seemed to think a good deal of her. As an evidence of their regard they gave us a suit of furniture, which cost about $25, and we set up housekeeping in one of the Captain's two-room shanties. I thought I was the biggest man in Georgia. Mandy still kept her place in the "Big House" after our marriage. We did so well for the first year that I renewed my contract for the second year, and for the third, fourth and fifth year I did the same thing. Before the end of the fifth year the Captain had died, and his son, who had married some two or three years before, took charge of the plantation. Also, for two or three years, this son had been serving at Atlanta in some big office to which he had been elected. I think it was in the Legislature or something of that sort—anyhow, all the people called him Senator. At the end of the fifth year the Senator suggested that I sign up a contract for ten years; then, he said, we wouldn't have to fix up papers every year. I asked my wife about it; she consented; and so I made a ten-year contract.

Not long afterward the Senator had a long, low shanty built on his place. A great big chimney, with a wide, open fireplace, was built at one end of it, and on each side of the house, running lengthwise, there was a row of frames or stalls just large enough to hold a single mattress. The places for these mattresses were fixed one above the other; so that there was a double row of these stalls or pens on each side. They looked for all the world like stalls for horses. Since then I have seen cabooses similarly arranged as sleeping quarters for railroad laborers.

Nobody seemed to know what the Senator was fixing for. All doubts were put aside one bright day in April when about forty able-bodies Negroes, bound in iron chains, and some of them handcuffed, were brought out to the Senator's farm in three big wagons. They were quartered in the long, low shanty, and it was afterward called the stockade. This was the beginning of the Senator's convict camp. These men were prisoners who had been leased by the Senator from the State of Georgia at about $200 each per year, the State agreeing to pay for guards and physicians, for necessary inspection, for inquests, all rewards for escaped convicts, the cost of litigation and all other incidental expenses.

When I saw these men in shackles, and the guards with their guns, I was scared nearly to death. I felt like running away, but I didn't know where to go. And if there had been any place to go to, I would have had to leave my wife and child behind. We free laborers held a meeting. We all wanted to quit. We sent a man to tell the Senator about it. Word came back that we were all under contract for ten years and that the Senator would hold us to the letter of the contract, or put us in chains and lock us up—the same as the other prisoners. It was made plain to us by some white people we talked to that in the contracts we had signed we had all agreed to be locked up in a stockade at night or at any other time that our employer saw fit; further, we learned that we could not lawfully break our contract for any reason and go and hire ourselves to somebody else without the consent of our employer; and, more than that, if we got mad and ran away, we could be run down by bloodhounds, arrested without process of law, and be returned to our employer, who, according to the contract, might beat us brutally or administer any kind of punishment that he thought proper. In other words, we had sold ourselves into slavery—and what could we do about it? The white folks had all the courts, all the guns, all the hounds, all the railroads, all the telegraph wires, all the newspapers, all the money, and nearly all the land—and we had only our ignorance, our poverty and our empty hands. We decided that the best thing to do was to shut our mouths, say nothing, and go back to work. And most of us worked side by side with those convicts during the remainder of the ten years.

But this first batch of convicts was only the beginning. Within six months another stockade was built, and twenty or thirty other convicts were brought to the plantation, among them six or eight women! The Senator had bought an additional thousand acres of land, and to his already large cotton plantation he added two great big sawmills and went into the lumber business. Within two years the Senator had in all 200 Negroes working on his plantation—about half of them free laborers, so called, and about half of them convicts. The only difference between the free laborers and the others was that the free laborers could come and go as they pleased, at night— that is, they were not locked up at night, and were not, as a general thing, whipped for slight offenses. The troubles of the free laborers began at the close of the ten-year period. To a man they all refused to sign new contracts— even for one year, not to say anything of ten years. And just when we thought that our bondage was at an end we found that it had really just begun. Two or three years before, or about a year and a half after the Senator had started his camp, he had established a large store, which was called the commissary. All of us free laborers were compelled to buy our supplies—food, clothing, etc.—from that store. We never used any money in our dealings with the commissary, only tickets or orders, and we had a general settlement once each year, in October. In this store we were charged all sorts of high prices for goods, because every year we would come out in debt to our employer. If not that, we seldom had more than $5 or $10 coming to us—and that for a whole year's work. Well, at the close of the tenth year, when we kicked and meant to leave the Senator, he said to some of us with a smile (and I never will forget that smile—I can see it now):

"Boys, I'm sorry you're going to leave me. I hope you will do well in your new places—so well that you will be able to pay me the little balances which most of you owe me."

Word was sent out for all of us to meet him at the commissary at 2 o'clock. There he told us that, after we had signed what he called a written acknowl- edgement of our debts, we might go and look for new places. The store- keeper took us one by one and read to us statements of our accounts. According to the books there was no man of us who owed the Senator less than $100; some of us were put down for as much as $200. I owed $165, according to the bookkeeper. These debts were not accumulated during one year, but ran back for three and four years, so we were told—in spite of the fact that we understood that we had had a full settlement at the end of each year. But no one of us would have dared to dispute a white man's word—oh, no; not in those days. Besides, we fellows didn't care anything about the amounts—we were after getting away; and we had been told that we might go, if we signed the acknowledgements. We would have signed anything, just to get away. So we stepped up, we did, and made our marks. That same night we were rounded up by a constable and ten or twelve white men, who aided him, and we were locked up, every one of us, in one of the Senator's stockades. The next morning it was explained to us by the two guards appointed to watch us that, in the papers we had signed the day before, we had not only made acknowledgement of our indebtedness, but that we had also agreed to work for the Senator until the debts were paid by hard labor. And from that day forward we were treated just like convicts. Really we had made ourselves lifetime slaves, or peons, as the laws called us. But call it slavery, peonage, or what not, the truth is we lived in a hell on earth what time we spent in the Senator's peon camp.

I lived in that camp, as a peon, for nearly three years. My wife fared better than I did, as did the wives of some of the other Negroes, because the white men about the camp used these unfortunate creatures as their mistresses. When I was first put in the stockade my wife was still kept for a while in the "Big House," but my little boy, who was only nine years old, was given away to a Negro family across the river in South Carolina, and I never saw or heard of him after that. When I left the camp my wife had had two children by some one of the white bosses, and she was living in a fairly good shape in a little house off to herself. But the poor Negro women who were not in the class with my wife fared about as bad as the helpless Negro men. Most of the time the women who were peons or convicts were compelled to wear men's clothes. Sometimes, when I have seen them dressed like men, and plowing or hoeing or hauling logs or working at the blacksmith's trade, just the same as men, my heart would bleed and my blood would boil, but I was powerless to raise a hand. It would have meant death on the spot to have said a word. Of the first six women brought to the camp, two of them gave birth to children after they had been there more than twelve months—and the babies had white men for their fathers!

The stockades in which we slept, were, I believe, the filthiest places in the world. They were cesspools of nastiness. During the thirteen years that I was there I am willing to swear that a mattress was never moved after it had been brought there, except to turn it over once or twice a month. No sheets were used, only dark-colored blankets. Most of the men slept every night in the clothing that they had worked in all day. Some of the worst characters were made to sleep in chairs. The doors were locked and barred, each night, and tallow-candles were the only lights allowed. Really the stockades were but little more than cow sheds, horse stables or hog pens. Strange to say, not a great number of these people died while I was there, though a great many came away maimed and bruised and, in some cases, disabled for life. As far as I can remember only about ten died during the last ten years that I was there, two of these being killed outright by the guards for trivial offenses.

It was a hard school that peon camp was, but I learned more there in a few short months by contact with those poor fellows from the outside world than ever I had known before. Most of what I learned was evil, and I now know that I should have been better off without the knowledge, but much of what I learned was helpful to me. Barring two or three severe and brutal whippings which I received, I got along very well, all things considered; but the system is damnable. A favorite way of whipping a man was to strap him down to a log, flat on his back, and spank him fifty or sixty times on his bare feet with a shingle or a huge piece of plank. When the men would get up with sore and blistered feet and an aching body, if he could not then keep up with the other men at work he would be strapped to the log again, this time face downward, and would be lashed with a buggy trace on his bare back. When a woman had to be whipped it was usually done in private, though they would be compelled to fall down across a barrel or something of the kind and receive the licks on their backsides.

The working day on a peon farm begins with sunrise and ends when the sun goes down; or, in other words, the average peon works from ten to twelve hours each day, with one hour (from 12 o'clock to 1 o'clock) for dinner. Hot or cold, sun or rain, this is the rule. As to their meals, the laborers are divided up into squads or companies, just the same as soldiers in a great military camp would be. . . . Each peon is provided with a great big tin cup, a flat tin pan and two big tin spoons. No knives or forks are ever seen, except those used by the cooks. At meal time the peons pass in single file before the cooks, and hold out their pans and cups to receive their allowances. Cow peas (red or white, which when boiled turn black), fat bacon and old-fashioned Georgia cornbread, baked in pones from one to two and three inches thick, made up the chief articles of food. Black coffee, black molasses and brown sugar are also used abundantly. . . .

Today, I am told, there are six or seven of these private camps in Georgia —that is to say, camps where most of the convicts are leased from the State of Georgia. But there are hundreds and hundreds of farmers all over the State where Negroes, and in some cases poor white folks, are held in bondage on the ground that they are working out debts, or where the contract which they have made hold them in a kind of perpetual bondage, because, under those contracts, they may not quit one employer and hire out to another except by and with the knowledge and consent of the former employer.

One of the usual ways to secure laborers for a large peonage camp is for the proprietor to send out an agent to the little courts in the towns and villages, and where a man charged with some petty offense has no friends or money the agent will urge him to plead guilty, with the understanding that the agent will pay his fine, and in that way save him from the disgrace of being sent to jail or the chain-gang! For this high favor the man must sign beforehand a paper signifying his willingness to go to the farm and work out the amount of the fine imposed. When he reaches the farm he has to be fed and clothed, to be sure, and these things are charged up to his account. By the time he has worked out his first debt another is hanging over his head, and so on and so on, by a sort of endless chain, for an indefinite period, as in every case the indebtedness is arbitrarily arranged by the employer. In many cases it is very evident that the court officials are in collusion with the proprietors or agents, and that they divide the "graft" among themselves. . . .

But I didn't tell you how I got out. I didn't get out—they put me out. When I had served as a peon for nearly three years—and you remember that they claimed I owed them only $165—when I had served for nearly three years one of the bosses came to me and said that my time was up. He happened to be the one who was said to be living with my wife. He gave me a new suit of overalls, which cost about seventy-five cents, took me in a buggy and carried me across the Broad River into South Carolina, set me down and told me to "git." I didn't have a cent of money, and I wasn't feeling well, but somehow I managed to get a move on me. I begged my way to Columbia. In two or three days I ran across a man looking for laborers to carry to Birmingham, and I joined his gang. I have been here in the Birmingham district since they released me, and I reckon I'll die either in a coal mine or an iron furnace. It don't make much difference which. Either is better than a Georgia peon camp. And a Georgia peon camp is hell itself!

Hamilton Holt, *The Life Stories of Undistinguished Americans As Told By Themselves* (N.Y., 1906), pp. 183–99.

[c]

The Negro in the Chicago Labor Movement, 1900–1905

The question of earning a living—how to get a job and how to hold a job— is the most serious and most difficult question now confronting the Chicago Negro. He must work where he can rather than where he will. Times of industrial unrest, of which there are many in this city, have often offered to him opportunities for work which were before closed. The three most significant instances of such unrest in which Negroes had conspicuous part were the building trades strike of 1900, the stockyards' strike of 1904, and the teamsters' strike of 1905. Prior to 1900, Negroes played but little part in the industrial situation on account of the smallness of the Negro population. . . . The [1900] strike lasted all the summer and the number of Negroes increased until they were an important issue. There was, however, no wholesale importation from the South. On one of the largest buildings in the city, the Mandel Department Store, a large number of Negroes were employed, and their presence caused much violence, despite police protection. Violence, however, did not frighten the Negroes, and more peaceful means were used. The Chicago Federation of Labor, representing all the organized labor bodies of the city, issued an appeal to the Negroes, which because of its significance is given here:

"The frequency with which unscrupulous employers of labor are of late supplanting white men by their colored brethren in times of industrial troubles is a question of most serious moment to the wage earners of this country. In calling attention to this question it is not our intention to arouse sentiment which might lead to race prejudice, or a race war, which would be deplorable in its results, but rather in a friendly spirit to lay before our colored brethren a statement of facts which we hope may convince them of their error. . . . We do not even condemn them, believing they are most justly entitled to our sympathy and support. In the slavery days, now happily gone by, when the traffic in human flesh and blood remained a blot on our civilization, the Negro was unable to free himself from the bondage. His white brother rose in arms and declared that the slave should be free. Today the Negro is being used to keep the white man in industrial slavery. The colored man, more simple in his ways, with fewer wants and these more easily satisfied, is contented to work under conditions which are irksome to the white workman, and he is today, perhaps unconsciously, being used to try to drag the white man down to a level lower than was the Negro before he was freed from slavery. . . .

"It is to remedy this that we appeal to him, to welcome him into our fold, to elevate him to our standard and to better his condition as well as our own. The trades-union movement knows no race or color. Its aims are the bettering of the condition of the wage earner, whatever his color or creed. In this spirit we appeal to the colored workman to join us in our work. Come into our trades unions, give us your assistance and in return, receive our support, so that race hatred may be forever buried, and the workers of the country united in a solid phalanx to demand what we are justly entitled to— a fair share of the fruits of our industry."

This appeal was taken seriously by many Negroes, who left the ranks of strikebreakers to join the unions. Some of these indeed became so zealous for the cause of unionism, that they even tried the persuasion of violence upon other members of their race, when words were not found strong enough to stop them from work.

The strike ended in the fall, the Building Trades' Council was disrupted, and the unions left in a weak condition. But in the recuperation many more Negroes were among the members of the unions than before. Of these the Negro membership of the hod carriers was especially strong, for in this kind of work the Negroes had been the strongest competitors.

The next great struggle in which Negroes were engaged was the stockyards' strike. On Tuesday, July 12 [1904], nearly fifty thousand men, many of whom were Negroes, stopped work at the command of Michael Donnelly, president of the Amalgamated Meat Cutters and Butcher Workmen, who had organized the stockyards' unions and who conducted the strike. The grounds for the strike were the refusal of the packers to grant to the unskilled men a minimum wage of eighteen and one-half cents per hour, and an equalization of the wages of skilled men. The strike was general in the West and involved all the large houses. Ten days later, however, the packers and labor men came to a tentative agreement. On July 23, the men applied for their former positions. But in a few hours they were called out again, as it was charged that the packers discriminated in hiring the old men. Thus begun a second strike, which was to continue nearly two months. The packers determined to break the strike after the efforts at peace failed. To do this they turned to the Negroes. For more than twenty years there had been Negroes employed in the stockyards. Both Mr. Armour and Mr. Swift were friendly to them. There had been but little premeditated effort to break the strike, and in recruiting strikebreakers there was very little system. Employment agencies, private individuals, "runners," and others, scoured the city. Thousands of Negroes were imported and in a few days more than ten thousand Negroes were in the various plants. Lodginghouses, commissaries, and pleasure rooms were hastily provided; Negroes were eager to seize the situation. . . .

Most of the Negroes employed were unskilled and were so indiscriminately gotten that it cannot be said that they were effective workers, or even the better type of strikebreakers. They served a purpose, however, by the greatness of their numbers, of weakening the strikers. Within one month an industry which had used ninety-five per cent white labor now threatened to use eighty-five per cent Negro labor. It was more than unionism could bear. The more thoughtless strikers and their friends used violence, and made it positively dangerous for a black face to appear in "Packingtown." But the thoughtful few saw another side of the subject, and used persuasion and proffers of future friendliness to Negroes. . . .

On September 9 [1904], the strike ended, the unions surrendered unconditionally, and the men went back to work. The majority of the Negroes had not gained in proficiency, and quit or were discharged. A fair proportion remained. Today no industry in Chicago employs more Negroes than the packing industries, where in nearly every branch they find employment.

The teamsters' strike began April 6 [1905] in sympathy for the garment workers of the mail-order house of Montgomery Ward & Co., who had been upon a strike since November. On Friday, April 7, seventy-one teamsters employed by that firm quit work. The next day strikebreakers, among them many Negroes, took their places, and delivered goods under police protection. There was a brief but futile effort at settlement; then a grim determination on the part of both employers and teamsters to win. The strike spread to the railway express drivers, department store drivers, coal drivers, parcel and baggage delivery drivers, furniture, lumber and truck drivers, and other teamsters who refused to deliver goods to strike-bound houses, in all about 5,000 men.

Among the first strikebreakers were a large number of Negroes. Negroes drove for such firms as Marshall Field, Carson, Pirie, Scott & Co., J. V. Farwell, Johnson Chair Co., and others who had not before employed Negro teamsters. The coal companies were freshly manned almost entirely with Negroes. This was, as usual, the signal for violence. For one hundred and five days there was a fierce struggle; and for at least forty days it seemed that there was war. Over five hundred cases of violence were known to the police, and at least a score of deaths resulted. During the second month the teamsters weakened considerably, and the end came July 20 when the Teamster's Joint Council declared the strike off without condition. The coal teamsters, however, did not go back to work, but kept up the strike against the coal companies who were employing Negroes. August 23, however, the coal teamsters decided to call it off; but at this writing, August 30 [1905], policemen are still guarding Negro drivers of coal wagons.

After the first three weeks of the strike Negroes constituted an ever-decreasing number of strikebreakers. Of the total number of men employed by the Employers' Association, there were 700 white men from Chicago to 200 Negroes; 4,300 white men were imported from St. Louis, Toledo, Buffalo, Cleveland, Minneapolis, Indianapolis, Omaha, Peoria, Rock Island, Moline, Davenport, and other cities, while about 450 Negroes were brought from St. Louis and 150 from Kansas City. At the end of the strike there were only about two per cent Negro strikebreakers. The cause of this decrease was chiefly the violence which the strike incited. Officers of the Employers' Association assure me that the Negroes were quite as competent as the whites, but that white strikebreakers objected to working with them; and that Negroes were often especially singled out for violent attacks by strikers and strike sympathizers. The race issue was raised by strikers, encouraged by exaggerated reports of some of the daily papers. The populace was in a fever, condemning Negro strikebreakers more than white strikebreakers, and deriding and committing violence upon them, even when they did not approve of the grounds of the strike. Many of the Negroes left their work voluntarily; but the majority remained until they were discharged. Now about eighty Negroes hold places gotten during the strike.

After this review, comes the question: Why do Negroes become strike-breakers? A prominent labor editor of this city writes me in answer to this question; that the cause is "a certain prejudice which exists against them (Negroes) in the minds of white men, no matter how we might try to disguise the feeling, which operates against them in securing employment under normal conditions." Of course it must be borne in mind that Negroes seldom constitute the majority of strikebreakers. The public is in danger of being misled on this point. In the teamsters' strike the impression was abroad that Negroes were the majority of strikebreakers. No less a personage than a Negro secretary of the teamsters' union wrote me that Negroes constituted ninety per cent of the strikebreakers during the first weeks of the strike, and forty per cent at the time of his writing (July 1). The fact is Negroes never made up as high as ninety per cent of the strikebreakers, and July 1 were only about five per cent. The bulk of Negro workmen never consisted of strikebreakers. Nor are Negroes opposed to unions. Many struck with the unions and remained loyal to them at the stockyards. In the teamsters' strike, while there were 800 Negro strikebreakers, the unions held a membership of nearly two thousand Negro teamsters, and one of their number represented the coal drivers at the Philadelphia convention of the Brotherhood of Teamsters in August. There are a half dozen Negro delegates to the Chicago Federation of Labor, and several Negro local union officers. Yet it still remains that in times of industrial peace the more desirable places are closed against Negroes, either because the employers will not hire them or the men will not work with them.

Negroes become strikebreakers, also, because of the high wages paid during strikes. The union scale, and even higher, is paid. Teamsters receive $4 and $5 per day, which is paid every evening. Lodging was often furnished and sometimes board. This has great force with the unemployed and discontented classes . . . the part of Negroes in strikes is bringing the unions to deal with less of insincerity than heretofore with the Negroes. They are beginning to realize in fact, what they have asserted in theory, that the cause of labor cannot be limited by color, creed or any other extraneous condition. . . .

R. R. Wright, in *Charities* (N.Y.), October 7, 1905, XV, pp. 69–73. Mr. Wright was the Negro pastor of Chicago's Trinity Mission and son of the President of the Georgia State College for Negroes.

[d]

The Negro in the New York Labor Movement, 1906–10

1. White and Negro Unity:

On last Thursday [July 5, 1906] New York was treated to the extraordinary spectacle of white union men striking to compel a company of contractors to recognize the Afro-American members of the union.

The Cecelia Asphalt Paving company, which has the contract for paving the square around Cooper Union, began by filling the places of the Afro-American pavers and rammersmen with Irish and Germans. Immediately Mr. James S. Wallace, the Afro-American agent of the International Union of Pavers and Rammersmen, reported to the officers of the union that his men were not getting a square deal.

"Then we'll call out all of our union members," replied the officers; and in a short while nearly all the white workmen laid down their tools.

The superintendent of the company hustled to the spot posthaste and tried to persuade the white men to go back to work.

"Beat it," replied they, "unless you give us a written guarantee to recognize all the members of our union, black as well as white."

"I'll give you the letter tomorrow at 10 o'clock," conceded the contractor.

"Then we'll go back to work tomorrow at 10 o'clock," said the union men.

The next day the letter was forthcoming, and all the men triumphantly went back to their tools.

N.Y. *Age*, July 12, 1906.

2. A Negro Official Discusses Trade Unions:

Since I * have been brought in touch with so many prominent men of both races who seem to be engaged in uplifting the Negro race, and as each seems to have a different idea to express, it seems that I am called upon to say something on a question which most of our well-wishers seem to overlook or ignore. Years of experience have impressed upon my mind that a mutual understanding between the white and Negro men whom you may call the laborers and mechanics, or the common people, would have a good and wholesome effect upon both races. . . .

There are in New York many unions, viz., plasterers, carpenters, printers, teamsters, pavers, engineers, drillers, longshoremen, cigarmakers, etc., and I find in no instance that a Negro has committed any breach of etiquette. These unions have a large Negro membership, and they are treated as men.

* The writer was James S. Wallace, referred to in the preceding document.

Labor and capital will never be reconciled, and he who advances the capitalist ideas cannot be looked upon as a friend of labor. . . . When the millions of poor working people recognize that the interest of one poor man is the concern of all, and that a blow struck at the Negro's progress affects the entire working class; when they agree to stand for one object, and let that object be better conditions, racial troubles will be reduced to the minimum. . . . In the paving industry Negroes, Italians and other nationalities are in an International union with a Negro Third Vice-President, myself, in New York, and a Negro Fifth Vice-President in Chicago, Mr. Theodore Payne. Wages are now unprecedented for the Negro—$4.96 per day of 8 hours. Engineers, plasterers and all men who have joined mutually in unions are getting good wages, but still nonunion advocates menace the interest of all.

N.Y. *Age,* August 30, 1906.

3. *Negroes and the Ladies Waist Makers Union:*

Regardless of our * opinions as to the merits of the particular case of the recent strike of the Waist Makers in New York and Philadelphia, it cannot be gainsaid that the matter of the attitude of "Union Labor" toward our people, and of our people toward it, is of great and growing importance.

The following letter from one of the officers [Elizabeth Dutcher] of the Women's Trade Union League speaks for itself and should be carefully pondered, especially by those persons and editors who, some unwittingly, are assisting in the present insidious effort to make our people Ishmaelites in the world of labor; or, as someone has put it, to make us the "Cossacks" of America.

February 23rd, 1910

To the Editor of the *Horizon,*

Dear Sir:—I note in an issue of the New York *Age,* of Thursday, Jan. 20th, 1910, an editorial on the Waist Makers Strike. In this editorial it is stated that the editor of the paper had refused to induce colored girls to join the union and had also refused to dissuade other colored girls from taking the place of those on strike because they had no assurance that the union would in the future admit without discrimination colored girls to membership. The editorial goes on to say that "Trade Unionism is hostile to the colored race and that the Negro will continue to be the pivot upon which future strikes will turn so long as labor will ignore his right to work and thwart his ambition to advance in the mechanical world." I cannot help feeling that the editor of the *Age* was misinformed. In both Philadelphia

* The writer was F. H. M. Murray, a militant Negro leader of Washington.

and New York, some of the most devoted members of the Ladies Waist Makers Union are colored girls. In Philadelphia several of the girls going on strike were colored girls and two of these were the best pickets the union had in that city. They were not only able to persuade the girls of their own race and color from acting as strikebreakers, but they were able to keep wavering white girls from going back to work.

In New York, colored girls are not only members of the union but they have been prominent in the union. One colored girl has been secretary of her shop organization all through the strike and has been very frequently at the union headquarters doing responsible work. The editor should also know that meetings were held during the strike at the Fleet Street Methodist Memorial Church (colored) in Brooklyn and St. Marks Methodist Church in Manhattan and that in both, members of the Ladies Waist Makers Union said definitely and publicly that colored girls were not only eligible but welcome to membership. . . .

It is not our purpose now to discuss, with those who may be inclined to doubt, the advisability of our people joining the ranks of "Union Labor" but to throw a little light on the question brought forward by the [N.Y.] *Age;* whether or not, as is persistently claimed, "Trade Unionism is hostile to the colored race," and the further claim that the Unions will not take us in. . . .

The Horizon (Washington), March, 1910, V, no. 5, p. 9. Copy in the library of Dr. W. E. B. Du Bois.

[e]

Negro Businessmen, 1901

The second convention of the National Negro Business League has just closed, and its proceedings add an inspiring chapter to the history of the American Negro. At this convention Massachusetts shook hands with California and Illinois and Wisconsin promenaded with Louisiana and Florida.

Nearly two hundred delegates were present, representing nearly every walk of life from the small storekeeper to the wholesale merchant; from the artisan to the inventor and manufacturer; from the truck gardener to the planter; and from the teacher, doctor and lawyer to the ripe scholar, skilled surgeon and diplomat.

The convention extended through three days, August 21, 22, and 23, and no time was lost in vain babbling, parliamentary wrangles and petty squabbles. "I am here for business" was the expression on the face of every delegate. . . .

The convention was called to order at 10 o'clock on the morning of

August 21 by President Booker T. Washington, who called on Rev. J. W. E. Bowen, of Atlanta, Ga., to make the opening prayer. Addresses of welcome were then delivered by Mr. Fieldhouse on behalf of Governor Yates, who could not be present, and City Attorney Taylor, the representative of Mayor Carter Harrison, who was out of the city [Chicago]. . . .

Following this, President Booker T. Washington stepped forward to deliver his annual address amidst the greatest demonstration. He spoke briefly, but his sound advice, downright earnestness and rugged eloquence set the convention on fire. "Let no legislation or attempted legislation," said he, "dishearten or discourage us. Every step must be forward. The opinion of the world is not influenced permanently by what we say ourselves, nor by what others say of us, but by what we do. . . ." Giles B. Jackson, of Richmond, Va., was introduced, who addressed the convention on "The Business League of Virginia." . . . According to his statement the Negroes pay taxes on $17,000,000 worth of real estate in Virginia.

The next speaker was from Richmond also, Rev. W. L. Taylor, president, True Reformers. He spoke on "Business Features of the Order of True Reformers." No speaker during the three days' session of the convention was more heartily received. He told how the order was started twenty years ago with one hundred members and the methods employed to increase the membership to 42,872, the present enrollment. . . .

Mr. J. A. Wilson, of Kansas City, Mo., was next called on, and he told how the businessmen of Kansas City, Mo., and Kansas City, Kan., are drawing trade by serving ice water and refreshments occasionally free. . . .

The morning session was closed with an address by T. W. Jones, of Chicago, Ill., on "Can the Negro Succeed As a Business Man?" There is no better answer to this question than Mr. Jones himself. Mr. Jones is a furniture mover and in a few years he has accumulated a snug fortune by reason of his business acumen. His business is the largest of its kind in this great city. It is needless to state that his paper was warmly received.

The first speaker at the evening session of the first day was Mrs. Alberta Moore Smith, of Chicago, Ill., on "Negro Women's Business Clubs a Factor in the Vexed Problem." The first and oldest women's business club in this country is the Chicago club and Mrs. Smith is its president. She said "that there are five avenues of employment open to white women to every two for colored women, and one of the missions of the Chicago club is to secure work for colored women in keeping with their training. Last year this club put seventeen colored women in good positions and secured situations for fifty. . . ."

From Dr. Sterr's* paper we learned that there are two hundred and thirty

* Dr. W. S. Sterr was from Decatur, Alabama.

Negro drug stores operated in this country, fifteen of which are in Alabama. The amount invested in the drug business is $500,000. . . .

Indianapolis *Freeman,* September 7, 1901.

[f]

Booker T. Washington on the Business League, 1902

The National Negro Business League has justified its existence as a stimulus to the race in commercial activity. The third annual meeting, held in Richmond, Virginia, late in August, was attended by Negro businessmen from almost every State east of the Mississippi River, and some from States which lie still farther west. Every one of the common business occupations was represented, and many that are less common. Women as well as men are members of the League and come to its meetings. . . . The success of the organization from the first has been most gratifying. Indeed, the fact that the Negroes of the United States, barely thirty-five years out of slavery, should have become engaged in business to an extent that suggested the formation of a national business organization is, in itself, a cause for gratification.

The machinery of the League is very simple. Any Negro man or woman who is engaged in any business is eligible for membership upon the payment of an annual fee of two dollars. It is desirable, however, and it is recommended, that local leagues be formed to cooperate with the central body to extend its influence in their own fields; and in many cases this has been done—in places as far distant from each other as Boston, Pensacola, Chicago, Richmond, and Little Rock, Arkansas. Over three thousand persons are now in touch with the central organization through these local leagues. . . .

The National Negro Business League has set going an earnest and active inquiry among our people as to each other's success in business, and has brought to view from far and wide many business enterprises which were not known beyond the immediate town or vicinity in which they are located. This knowledge has given a feeling of fellowship among our people which serves to strengthen and encourage them. We are led to feel and know that we are playing an important part in a field which for many years has been almost wholly occupied and operated by other races. It has strengthened us in the eyes of the world in that it is being shown that we are beginning to get that in hand which makes us brave men and women, and that we are contributing materially to the financial, commercial and manufacturing interests of our great country.

World's Work (N.Y.), October, 1902, IV, pp. 2671–76.

II.

THE NEGRO PRESS

The freedom and integrity of the Negro press became an object of increasing attack from the Bourbon and from Big Business during the early years of the twentieth century.

Five documents follow to illustrate this and to indicate something of the response to it. The first [a] is a portion of a letter from the distinguished Negro novelist, Charles W. Chesnutt, to Dr. Du Bois, dated Cleveland, June 27, 1903. The second document [b] is a letter written by Booker T. Washington in the summer of 1903 to J. E. Dickerson, editor of the Norfolk, Va. *News*. It is representative of the type of influence exerted by Mr. Washington to win over or to hold newspapers to his own view of the wisest course for Negroes to pursue.

The third document [c] is part of an editorial, "The South and Free Speech," appearing in 1904 in *The Voice of the Negro*, the leading Negro magazine of the period, then published in Atlanta. This piece gives one some idea of the pressures to which Negro editors, especially in the South, were subjected.

Early in 1905, Dr. Du Bois publicly accused several Negro newspapers of being corrupt. Some prominent white men including William H. Ward, editor of *The Independent*, and Oswald Garrison Villard, of the New York *Evening Post*, wrote him seeking further details. The reply Dr. Du Bois sent to Mr. Ward, from Atlanta, March 10, 1905, is the fourth document [d].

The attempt of Big Business and its politicians to influence the press reached a high point prior to important elections. Typical of this as concerns the Negro press is the presidential election of 1908, when the Republican Party, through Booker T. Washington, expended much effort in this direction.

The Tuskegee machine's direct representative for this work in Washington was one Ralph W. Tyler, of Ohio, made an assistant auditor in the Treasury Department in 1907 at Mr. Washington's recommendation. He contacted, successfully, the editors of the Washington *Bee*, Chicago *Conservator*, Indianapolis *Freeman* and New York *Age*, and set up a Colored Press Bureau at the capital whose expenses were met by the Republican Party. In charge of this Bureau was placed Mr. Richard W. Thompson who was also employed as a watchman in a Federal building. The last document [e] illuminates this whole arrangement. It is a letter written by Tyler to Emmett J. Scott, Mr. Washington's private secretary, dated October 15, 1908.

[a]

Chesnutt to Du Bois, 1903

. . . . I have not forgotten what you say about a national Negro journal. It is a matter concerning which one would like to think and consult before committing himself. There are already many "colored" papers; how they support themselves may be guessed at from the contents—most of them are mediums for hair straightening advertisements and the personal laudation of "self-made men," most of whom are not so well made that they really ought to brag much about it. The question of support would be the vital one for such a journal. What the Negro needs more than anything else is a medium through which he can present his case to thinking white people, who after all are the arbiters of our destiny. How helpless the Negro is in the South your own writings give ample proof; while in the North he is so vastly in the minority in numbers, to say nothing of his average humble conditions, that his influence alone would be inconsiderable. I fear few white people, except the occasional exchange editors, read the present newspapers published by colored people. Whether you could reach that class of readers and at the same time get a sufficient subscription list from all sources to support the paper is the thing which I would advise you to consider carefully before you risk much money.* The editing of a newspaper is the next vital consideration. To do it properly would require all the time of a good man—he ought to be as good a man as yourself. . . .

Du Bois MSS.

[b]

Washington to Dickerson, 1903

I am in receipt of your kind letter of July 9 [1903] and greatly regret my delay in answering it. I have been away from my mail a great deal of late and could not reach your letter sooner.

I am very grateful to you for the policy your paper has pursued and is pursuing. I have asked my publishers [Doubleday, Doran & Co.] to send you an advertisement for my book *Up from Slavery* and I think they will do so. In addition, I shall place in the *News* an advertisement for my Agricultural Department at Tuskegee Institute. I shall be glad to hear from you from time to time and to see copies of your paper.

I hope you will see your way clear to attend the meeting of the National Negro Business League at Nashville, Tenn., during August 19, 20 and 21. It is an excellent organization and you would meet many fine men. We could thus become better acquainted.

The Norfolk News, n.d., clipping in Du Bois MSS. Pencilled beneath this, in the handwriting of Dr. Du Bois, appears: "The above letter was printed in the *News* and kept standing for several issues. The *News* has severely attacked all newspapers criticising Mr. W."

* In 1906 Du Bois launched a weekly, *The Moon*. It lasted one year. In 1907 there appeared his *Horizon*, a monthly, which lasted to 1910.

[c]

Voice of the Negro *Editorial, 1904*

Certainly there can be but few persons in the United States who do not know that neither freedom of speech nor freedom of the press has ever been tolerated in the South. . . . One of our agents writes us from a certain village in Louisiana that he could not venture to sell the September number of the *Voice* in that section for the reason that it was a political number and colored people were not allowed to discuss politics in those parts. . . . Here in Atlanta within the last month, because a colored editor has some self-assertion and independence in speaking of the policy of a white newspaper [the Atlanta *Constitution*], the answer from the white editor has been that the Negro is constantly and emphatically assuming "an equality that can never exist" and that "Negroes of this temper ought not to be allowed in these troublous times to hold positions in which they can threaten or disturb the peace of society. The law ought to find a way to suppress a pestilent nuisance like this. And if the law confesses itself ineffective, then the usual result is likely to follow, and some fine morning this insolent coon is likely to wake up and find his type—if he has any—on the ground, and himself sitting or leaning on top of it, as the state of his anatomy may prescribe."

We have heard many prominent white men say that they were opposed to such an editorial and yet not one dare to say so over his signature in public print. . . .

Will the mind of the South be forever hag-ridden with fratricidal hatred? . . . It is our duty to counsel moderation, to seek by right living to secure the confidence of the better element of the white people. . . .

The Voice of the Negro (Atlanta), November, 1904.

[d]

Du Bois to Ward, 1905

My dear Dr. Ward: The only Negro papers that are taking vigorous exception to my plain statement are the ones who have sold out to the "Syndicate," viz: the N.Y. *Age,* the Chicago *Conservator,* the Boston *Citizen,* the Washington *Colored American,* the *Colored American Magazine,* & the Indianapolis *Freeman.* Two of these papers have recently died and one is sick seriously. Of course I do not propose to wash our dirty linen in public & consequently I shall say nothing further in print on the subject until I think a further warning necessary. What I have already said is absolutely true and is well-known to leading colored men & provable by documentary evidence: * viz that in order to forestall criticism of certain persons & measures money has been freely furnished a set of Negro newspapers in the principal cities; part of this has come as a direct bonus, part in advertising & all of it has been given on condition that these papers print certain matter & refrain from other matter. This movement has been going on now for 3 or 4 years until it is notorious among well-informed Negroes & a subject of frequent comment. You must not be at all worried at my losing the confidence of Negroes—I never had the confidence of those who are aroused over my declaration and never expect it.

Du Bois MSS.; marked "Personal and Confidential."

[e]

Tyler to Scott, 1908

A rather amusing thing came up this week that bears on [Richard W.] Thompson, though he regards it in anything but an amusing light.

It seems that the storehouse over which Thompson serves as night watchman is to be abandoned in about 30 days, and the two watchmen—Dick being the colored one—were ordered dropped, as there was no need for their services. Of course this is a sad blow to Thompson. To think that a fellow with ambition to become the next Asst. Register of the Treasury must hustle around to save himself from losing a $720 watchmanship. Oh horrors! Oh how ungrateful are republics!

The amusing part is that Dick is now engaged in writing yards of dope telling why Ham should vote the Republican ticket and citing yards of statistics showing how many Negroes are on the government payroll, himself in the lot. . . . [Tyler explains that a new Federal job has been secured for Thompson.] So this, I think, disposes of Thompson's fears, and he can continue to write hope-freighted dope at $30 per week. . . .

Booker T. Washington MSS., Library of Congress.

III.
THE NEGRO AND POLITICS

The dominent trend in the politics of the Negro people in the first decade of the twentieth century was one towards an independent position. Thus, the New York *Age,* a leading Republican newspaper, entitled an editorial in its issue of April 11, 1907: "New Political Party Needed To Supplant Existing Ones."

* Such evidence is in the personal papers of Dr. Du Bois.

The movement showed itself in efforts to establish an all-Negro national party, to win away the northern wing of the Democratic Party from the southern and to revitalize the monopoly-bound Republican Party. There appeared, too, a growing interest in the Socialist Party despite that Party's official refusal to recognize the fact of the superexploitation of the Negro working and farming masses and the special oppression of the entire Negro people.

Five documents are published below as typical of these developments. The first of these [a] is a description of the aims of an all-Negro national political organization, the National Liberty Party. The description comes from George Edwin Taylor of Ottumwa, Iowa, the new party's presidential candidate in 1904. Negro political parties had been formed before—notably the Negro Protective Party of Ohio whose gubernatorial candidate, S. J. Lewis, polled about 5,000 votes in 1897 —but this is the first instance of such a party being formed on a national scale. Its life ended with the 1904 campaign.

George Edwin Taylor, whom we have already met as president, in 1900 of the Negro National Democratic League, had been born free in 1857 in Little Rock, Arkansas. As a youngster, and orphan, he lived in Alton, Illinois and later in La Crosse, Wisconsin. In the latter city he was active in journalism and politics, editing for a time in the eighties a local Knights of Labor paper and assisting a Labor candidate win the mayoralty. In 1887 he served as a Wisconsin delegate to the Cincinnati convention of the Union Labor Party. Shortly thereafter he moved to Iowa and attempted to work within the Republican Party, but in 1892 he publicly renounced it. From 1893 to 1900 he edited a weekly paper, *The Negro Solicitor,* in Oskaloosa, Iowa.

The National Liberty Party was formed in March, 1904 and Taylor was nominated at its convention, attended by delegates from thirty-six states, held that July in St. Louis. Taylor's speech is notable for its insistence upon the particular needs of the Negro people at the same time as it makes clear the essential identity of interests of all working people.

The second document [b], in three parts, is illustrative of the developing interest among Negroes in the program of the Socialist Party. In the first part, Jesse Max Barber, editor of *The Voice of the Negro* (published in Atlanta) comments very favorably, in 1904, on "The Spread of Socialism," while in parts two and three appear statements endorsing the Socialist Party from the Washington *Bee* and *The Georgia Baptist* in 1906.

The third document [c] consists of a statement, prepared by W. E. B. Du Bois for the 1908 campaign. It is part of the anti-Republican, and especially anti-Roosevelt and anti-Taft, agitation conducted under the auspices of The National Negro American Political League. Behind this League were men like Bishop H. M. Turner, Archibald H. Grimké, and William Monroe Trotter.

Taft's general anti-Negro bias, and the attempts made during his administration to build a "Lily-White" Republican machine in the South, exacerbated the drift away from him. To show this, editorial statements from two Negro newspapers, in 1910, one Southern and pro-Taft in 1908, the other midwestern and anti-Taft in 1908, are reprinted as the fourth document [d] in this group.

The fifth and last document [e] is the call of the National Independent Political League to its convention, meeting in Atlantic City, N.J., in August, 1910. It constitutes an excellent summary of the points in the indictment of Republicanism as of that year among growing sectors of the Negro people.

[a]

A Negro Presidential Candidate's Address, 1904

The National Liberty Party now confronts the people of the United States claiming their consideration for the first time, but though the organization is in its infancy, the principles for which it stands are fundamental to our republican form of government. In fact, we are struggling to revive the well-nigh deserted principles of the grand old Whig party (the mother of the Republican party), which declared for "popular rights," government of all the people, for all the people, and by all the people.

When the founders of this republic were called upon to frame the Declaration of Independence and a Constitution for the future guidance, protection and foundation rock of the government, through their inspired wisdom they drafted ordinances declaring their independence, and guaranteeing protection, equal privileges, equal opportunity and equal rights to all citizens of the government. It was at that time clear to them that upon no other premises could the American people hope to secure their freedom and independence, and maintain a popular government. And the history of the past 127 years, proves the correctness of their judgment, that to depart from these fundamental principles is to endanger the very perpetuity of our government.

The National Liberty Party calls the attention of the people of the United States to the bold fact that these fundamental principles are fast being covered up, ignored, disregarded, and practically nullified by the administrative power, the national governing forces of both the Republican and Democratic parties, and the controlling political forces of at least six states of the Union which have recently by state constitutional amendment, actually disfranchised over 2,000,000 American born citizens.

Practically all of these disfranchised people are Negroes, and it is also a fact that, under the Federal Constitution and Laws, we are as emphatically recognized as citizens as are the most aristocratic Caucasians. Why not?

The history of the National Liberty Party is very brief. It is the direct outgrowth of the Civil and Personal Liberty Leagues, which for years have thrived among the Negroes of the South, and portions of the East. Through the efforts of Stanley P. Mitchell (the head of the Liberty Leagues) of Memphis, Tenn., and his associates, the first National Convention of the National Liberty Party was held in the auditorium of the Douglas Hotel in the city of St. Louis, on the 5th and 6th days of July last, when a permanent and complete organization of the party was effected. Thirty-six states were represented in the convention.

We religiously adhere to the sacredness of our form of government, and subscribe to its every tenet, law and claim. We believe that the tendency of the dominant parties is to dissipate these tenets, laws, and demands, and that it is our duty and the duty of every sober-minded citizen to join us in the arrest of this wholesale dissipation, in the interests of good government, the maintenance of federal power and the perpetuity of our system of government, which the popular statement of the world pronounces the most beneficent the world has ever known.

It must be clear to all unprejudiced students of history that whenever a government fails to secure for all its subjects or citizens at home, as well as abroad, that which it guarantees, that such government is nearing dangerous ground—it matters not whether said neglected citizens belong to or represent a popular or unpopular class. For, in such neglect, a fundamental principle of government is abused, distorted, abandoned, and like a cancer it will continue to grow and spread until finally it gnaws in twain the very vital cords. The Negro who now suffers most directly, by reason of this neglect (disfranchisement) is not in fact the only sufferer, for his immediate calamity is the beginning of the end of the downfall of the producing element of the races who comprise the vast common working classes of this great republic. The Negro of the United States is distinctively a factor in the great and grand army of American working men, and whatever enhances, strengthens, retards or impedes his progress, happiness, manhood, or citizenship rights, proportionately affects all the citizens of his class and standing. Hence, the interest that all common people of every race or nationality in the United States should have in this government. Does the question "Am I my black brother's keeper?" arise in the minds of the common (white) people? If so, I refer to the history of the world from the days of Cain and Abel for your answer. Judas betrayed the Christ only to earn for himself eternal reproach and an ignominious death. Napoleon, through intrigue, captured and starved to the death in a dungeon, that gallant statesman and warrior, Toussaint l'Ouverture, and as a reward, died the death of an exile; the Spaniards, through deception and cunning, assassinated General Maceo, the greatest Negro soldier and general of modern times, and soon afterwards were subjected to banishment and disgraceful defeat as their reward. In short, the history of the world proves the ultimate defeat of wrong and the establishment of right.

It is the purpose of the National Liberty Party to point out some of the dangerous errors in our present system of government and work their correction, and we shall not cease until this end shall have been accomplished, for it appears to us to be patriotically obligatory.

As to the independence of the National Liberty Party, I do not hesitate to state that, in every sense of the word, we are, and propose to remain, purely independent, for the principles for which we stand are not now germane to the platform of principles of any other political party. If they were, there would be no room or occasion for the existence of this party. The National Liberty Party is purely a creature of necessity.

Never before in the history of American Negro citizenship has the time been so opportune for an independent political movement on the part of the race. And never before has there been a time when such a movement could draw materially from the race. But now in the light of the history of the past four years, with a Republican president in the executive chair, and both branches of Congress and a majority of the Supreme Court of the same political faith, we are confronted with the amazing fact that more than one-fifth of the race are actually disfranchised, robbed of all the rights, powers and benefits of true citizenship, we are forced to lay aside our prejudices, indeed, our personal wishes, and consult with the higher demands of our manhood, the true interests of the country and our posterity, and act while we yet live, ere the time when it shall be too late. No other race of our strength would have quietly submitted to what we have during the past four years without a rebellion, a revolution, or an uprising.

We, too, propose a rebellion, a revolution, an uprising, not by physical force, but by the ballot, through the promulgation of the National Liberty Party. Our education, our civilization and our natural disposition, all incline us to this course as the only rational, consistent, effective method of attaining the desired end, viz: representation *as well as* taxation; the full exercise of our Constitutional rights as citizens. The only truly effective way for the common people to correct a national evil lies in their power at the ballot box, if they will but exercise it judiciously.

Whenever the race and their co-laborers shall array themselves in one grand independent political phalanx, the very foundations of the two dominant political parties will be shaken and the leaders of both will be brought to a realization of the danger which threatens their organization, and *"the rights of the people"* will again be considered by them instead of that of special classes, as is the present rule.

It is the intention of the committee of the National Liberty Party to perfect all necessary arrangements to have placed upon the ballots of the several states, presidential electors, and in many instances to nominate by petition and otherwise, congressional candidates. Should we fail to complete the organization in all the states this year, we shall continue the work after the election. Our greatest strength, of course, lies in the Southern states, which have not as yet adopted disfranchisement amendments. We expect to make a good showing in Kansas, Indiana, Illinois, Ohio, Pennsylvania, W. Virginia, Tennessee, Iowa, Texas and many other states. It is conservative to estimate that at least sixty per cent of the Negroes of the states in which we secure a place upon the ballot for our candidates will vote for us. It is also fair to presume that a goodly number of the white independents in these states will support the movement. Why not? We stand for the text and the spirit of the Declaration of Independence and the Federal Constitution; for universal suffrage; for the pensioning of all veterans of the war of the rebellion; for the establishment of a National Arbitration Board with power to adjust all differences that may arise between employer and employee; for the abolition of polygamy; for the nullification and repeal of all class legislation; for unsubsidized competition in all lines of commerce, and industry, which means the abolishment of all trusts and combines; for the pensioning of ex-slaves . . . and for a reduction of the tariff. We do not consider the money standard an issue of any merit in this campaign.

Every Negro who is loyal to his race and the powers that made him a free man, must join with us in heart, if not in action, in this effort to emphasize the fact that the Constitution of the United States is no respecter of persons, but that all American citizens are entitled to exercise all the rights of citizenship regardless of race or color.

The Voice of the Negro (Atlanta), July, 1904.

[b]

The Socialist Party and the Negro, 1904–06

1:

The doctrine of Socialism is the doctrine of an industrial State, directed by modern science, with government ownership and control of all public utilities, and based upon the equality of mankind. . . . Mr. Debs has said repeatedly that the Socialist party is the black man's hope and friend. There are objections to Socialism in some of its aspects, but it is a splendid field for negotiations for the Negro in these days when the Republican party has forsook him to the persecutions of the Democrats. An examination of the field certainly could do no harm. We must affiliate with a party that will reward our endeavors with friendly co-operation.

The Voice of the Negro (Atlanta), June, 1904.

2:

Existing conditions in the American body politic demand an independent attitude on the part of the colored citizens, regardless of circumstances.

The Southern Republicans have about eliminated the colored American from politics. Democratic Legislatures have disfranchised him, and white Republican organizations have ignored him. Now, will colored Americans continue to force themselves in places on the councils of the party to which they have been identified, where they are not wanted? It is claimed by some that the Democratic party doesn't need the colored vote. Perhaps not, and if that party was the only one in existence, the colored voter might despair. But there is a party that is coming to the front, known as the Socialist Labor party, which recognizes equality of citizenship.

The Washington *Bee*, quoted in N.Y. *Age*, September 6, 1906.

3:

The Mirror, edited by Mr. John A. Mette of this city [Augusta], is the State organ of the Socialist party. Its words are, consequently, to be taken with reference to the position of the Socialist party in Georgia. We reproduce an article which appeared in that paper editorially August 11th, nearly two weeks previous to the white primary. We are of the opinion that the colored voters of Georgia will find it to their interest to vote the Socialist State ticket in October. Nine-tenths of the white people who belong to the Socialist party are laboring people; they must live daily upon the sweat of their brow. Nine-tenths of the colored people are laboring people, who must eat bread daily in the sweat of their brow. The consolidation of wealth during the past score of years must admonish all laboring classes that their hopes for the future devolves largely upon their coming together, and in one common cause, fighting the battle of labor against combinations of wealth.

The Georgia Baptist (Augusta), quoted in N.Y. *Age*, Sept. 6, 1906.

[c]

Negro Anti-Republicanism, 1908

Republicans and Democrats.

It would be well for thoughtful colored citizens to sit down a while before election and do some hard thinking.

We have been voting for forty years on the theory that Republicans freed the race from slavery and Democrats are responsible for southern prejudice.

Is this true? The Republican party never intended to free the slaves. It never began the war with any such idea. It was willing to end the war and not touch slavery.

The Democratic party consists of two parts: the "Solid South" and the Northern Democracy. The Northern Democracy stand for every progressive idea which is of interest to colored men—a lower tariff to reduce the cost of living, the curbing of great corporations, real popular government. The "Solid South" hates Negroes. The Northern Democracy has not been able hitherto to get into power except by help of the "Solid South." Why? Because of the Negro vote of New York, Ohio, Illinois, Indiana and other states. *You*, colored voters, have yourselves chained the Democratic party to the "Solid South."

The Democratic party has appealed to you to unchain them. They have appointed more Negroes to state and city offices in the North than Republicans ever have and never have Negroes fared better than under the Democrat, Grover Cleveland.

Not only that but today it is the Republican party that is courting the "Solid South." It is a Republican president, William Taft, who has gone further in depriving Negroes of office than any Democrat ever dared propose. He has dismissed colored men from office by the wholesale; no matter how competent and deserving they were he announced the extraordinary dictum that hereafter it is not a question of fitness but a question of race prejudice as to whether the black man shall be appointed to office.

Not only he, but his predecessor and would be successor, Theodore Roosevelt, have raised heaven and earth to placate the South. The crime of Brownsville * and Mr. Taft's Inaugural Address were nothing more than efforts to get Southern votes.

Not only have these two presidents, but the leaders of the Republican party acquiesced and even defended the disfranchisement of colored voters in the South. Mr. Taft has repeatedly said it was a good thing; Mr. Roosevelt has told us to stop whining; the "lily white" organizations have been recognized; a Republican Congress and a Republican Supreme Court have refused to act, and in every way the Republican party for ten years have told the Negro that if he did not like what they were doing he can get out.

Isn't it time then for the colored voters to get out and try and see if they can in the great pivotal states of the North put a Northern Democrat in power and give them so much power and influence in their party that they will be in the future less and less dependent upon the "Solid South?" It is the greatest chance that the black voters have had in a generation. . . .

Du Bois MSS.

---
* Later documents will describe this.

[d]

The Negro and President Taft, 1910

1:

As we see it our amiable president who it is stated wishes to hear from the "people" themselves what they wish the government to do for them has adopted the Southern Democratic politician's application of the term "people." It means only white people. President Taft has not yet in any way indicated or intimated that he desires to learn the wishes of the Negro in respect to matters affecting the Negro. On the contrary, he has shown in the plainest and most direct manner possible that he does not wish to know from the Negro what he desires but prefers to be guided and advised by those whose every move since the war has been hostile to the advancement or uplift of the Negro.

2:

When Afro-American Republican "spellbinders" were touring Ohio, during the presidential campaign of 1908, the burden of their argument was to defeat Bryan to save the United States Supreme Court from being dominated by prejudiced southerners. They said, if he was elected, the many vacancies to occur during the next four years would be filled by Negro-hating southern Democrats, ex-rebels, and to avoid this danger, Mr. Taft, the Republican candidate, should be elected. This was done, and with the assistance of thousands of Afro-American votes. A vacancy on the Supreme Court bench occurred recently and President Taft promptly announced his intention to and did do the very thing the aforementioned Afro-American "spellbinders" were so fearful, Mr. Bryan, as President, would do. He has placed Judge Lurton of Tennessee, a Negro-hating Democrat and ex-rebel, on the United States Supreme Court bench, and "rubs it in" good by following this with the announcement that he intends to appoint Gen. Luke E. Wright of the same state and "stripe," to the United States Circuit Court as Judge Lurton's successor.

1), Sumter, S.C. *Defender;* 2), Cleveland *Gazette;* both undated, in *The Horizon* (Washington), February, 1910. Copy in library of Dr. Du Bois.

[e]

The National Independent Political League, 1910

This national convention of Colored citizens is called under grave conditions touching the object of this organization, the supreme aim of which is to maintain and secure for all Colored Americans the same rights and privileges of citizenship as are enjoyed by other citizens of these United States of America.

In the Southern States 95 per cent of the nine million Colored citizens of the United States are deprived of the exercise of the ballot, the fundamental right under our system of government, without which there is for citizens neither protection nor freedom. This rape of the ballot is consummated in plain violation of the national constitution which forbids denial of the right to vote because of race or color. The executive head of the federal government within sixteen months officially admitted this disfranchisement in inaugural address and palliated the violation of the federal constitution instead of declaring his purpose to enforce the law in obedience to the oath he had just solemnly taken. President Wm. H. Taft even intimated the legality of these devices for nullifying the 15th Amendment by State laws which are as much worse than fraudulent practices as law is stronger than custom. The Legislative branch of the federal government, specifically clothed with power to enforce the suffrage articles of the constitution, has viewed with apathy and inaction their flagrant violation save when actively condoning it by seating congressmen elected under the violation as against contestants entitled to seats if the federal law had been obeyed in their districts in the South. The judicial branch has dodged the issue in all cases brought involving Southern disfranchisement laws, thus by persistent refusal of relief strengthening the nullification and emboldening the nullifiers of the supreme law of the land.

But what train of evils were let loose upon Colored Americans with disfranchisement! In the Southern States unequal and oppressive laws have destroyed all their civil rights, excluding them from public places of business, of accommodation, or resort, even public parks and public libraries, barring from State quasi-public and public schools, forcing them into separate and inferior schools, fastening upon them the public ignominy and caste stigma of segregation in public travel, casting them even into peonage. They are under the tyranny of taxation without representation. Left in that hopeless and helpless condition of citizens without voice as to lawmaker, law enforcer, or law interpreter they are not only the victims of injustice in the courts, but denied all trial by court or jury, are the prey of the fiendish white mob, until now the almost daily lynching of human beings has disgraced our country before the civilized world.

Inevitably this race persecution infects the North. Color prejudice is on the increase. Discrimination based on color in civil rights and in economic opportunities is gaining ground. Jim Crow cars have reached the borders of the national capital, twice color disfranchisement has raised its horrid head above Mason and Dixon's line, while bloody race riots and barbarous lynchings have reached up to Illinois, even to the home of the martyred Lincoln.

Most harmful and portentous of all in this crusade of race hate and color prejudice is the action, under the present administration, of the federal government itself. For the first time in the United States a President has officially proclaimed color a political disability. By his declaration that he would not appoint colored citizens to office where white citizens objected, he completed Southern disfranchisement. It is Colored soldiers who are the victims when for the first time a battalion is discharged wholesale and without trial because of an alleged affray with civilians, and the new departure, aggravated by the failure to establish individual guilt after trial, is boldly continued. That unique degradation of free citizens, segregation by color in public carriers, has been sanctioned and nationalized by a federal commission, while the federal court in support declares the right of even an interstate railroad to segregate Colored passengers.

Unless one-eighth of the citizens of the United States are to be reduced to political serfdom, unless our Republic is to abandon democracy for the caste of color, this present trend must be resolutely opposed. Graver crisis in a Republic could hardly be.

The Horizon (Washington), July, 1910.

IV.

MISCELLANEOUS MATTERS, 1901–1910

As preceding portions of this work have shown, the American Negro's past has been marked by certain kinds of events quite unique to him. The most significant and representative of these for this decade are grouped together in this section of miscellany consisting of eleven documents.

On October 16, 1901 a dinner occurred which rocked a nation. On that day President Theodore Roosevelt and a few guests, including Mr. Booker T. Washington, dined together informally at the White House. The white press, particularly in the South, greeted this event with the type of vituperation credible only to those who have some knowledge of the bestiality white chauvinism can evoke. Booker T. Washington's brief and characteristic comment on this, as reported in the Negro press, forms the first document [a].

The second document [b] is a letter which Dr. Du Bois wrote from Atlanta University, January 7, 1905, to a Negro girl named Vernealia Fareira. The young lady was a student in a Berwyn, Pennsylvania high school, and her teacher, a white woman, informed Dr. Du Bois that while she was "very bright," still her school work was suffering. This was due to the fact that she refused to study, asserting that since she was a Negro she would "never have a chance to use her knowledge."

The third document [c] consists of brief notes entered from June to October, 1905, in the diary of John E. Bruce, a leading Negro Republican and publisher of the New York *Chronicle*. Mr. Bruce and his wife had just rented a home in a white neighborhood in Yonkers and the entries are indicative of the reaction this provoked.

Philanthropy—especially the heavy endowment, and strict control, of educational institutions—was a favorite device in the rulers' attempt to curb grass-roots Negro protest movements. Objection to this from Negroes grew in this decade and indicative is an article on the subject written in 1905 by Dr. Du Bois. Extracts from it form the fourth document [d].

The fifth document [e], in three parts, deals with the Atlanta Massacre of September, 1906, the most outrageous instance of organized violence against the Negro people to occur during the decade. A local political campaign, with Negro disfranchisement as an issue, was used as the occasion for whipping up through speeches and, especially, the press, hatred against Negroes. On the evening of September 22 the fury broke loose and when on the 24th, Negroes, with women particularly prominent, turned to self-defense, the police joined in the mob attacks. Even the aged president of the Gammon Theological Seminary, Dr. Bowen, was beaten about the head with a rifle butt by a uniformed brute. Total casualties, according to the hastily formed Atlantic Civic League, came to two whites and ten Negroes (including two women) killed, and ten whites and sixty Negroes seriously injured. The press of *The Voice of the Negro* was closed and its editor, Jesse Max Barber, forced to flee for his life to Chicago.

The first part of this fifth document is the letter sent to the New York *World* by Mr. Barber on September 26, in reply to the justification of the outbreak from John Temple Graves, of the Atlanta *Georgian*, which the New York paper had already published. It is this letter which directly led to Mr. Barber's flight, for after its appearance he was told by Captain James English—the Governor's Chief of Staff, a member of the city's Board of Police Commissioners, and president of the Fourth National Bank of Atlanta—to get out while he could still walk. The second part consists of the headlines of the event in the New York *Age* and its report of the reaction to the event by Booker T. Washington, while the third part brings the bitter comments of Lewis H. Douglass, son of Frederick Douglass.

There were occasional reports during these years of conspiratorial or incendiary activities by southern Negroes, but the truth concerning these was found to be elusive by contemporaries and remains difficult to discover with certainty now. A typical example of such a report, involving a widespread fire in Seneca, South Carolina, in 1906, forms the sixth document [f].

The seventh document [g], in two parts, deals with the dishonorable discharge from the United States Army of three companies of the Twenty-Fifth Infantry Regiment whose enlisted men were all Negroes. This was done by President Roosevelt in November, 1906, following an investigation by the Army's Inspector-General of a shooting affray in Brownsville, Texas, the evening of August 13. The baiting of Negro troops in this city had been notorious for weeks but the details of the actual event are unclear. Certainly the basic aggressions and provocations came from the whites and how many or what Negroes were in fact involved was never established. The Negro people fought against the peremptory and vindictive act of the government, won some white allies, notably Senator Joseph B. Foraker of Ohio, and in 1909 the dishonorable discharges were revoked. The first part of this document is made up of the original news report of President Roosevelt's act as displayed in the Negro press; the second part consists of the affidavit of the First Sergeant of one the companies involved—Mingo S. Sanders.

In the 1890's, as we have seen, there was considerable discussion concerning the advisability or practicality of forging an all-Negro State somewhere in the South, and notably in what is now Oklahoma. The migratory action accompanying and stimulating this discussion resulted in the founding of several all-Negro communities in Alabama, Mississippi and particularly Oklahoma. A description of one of these—Boley, Oklahoma—by Booker T. Washington appeared in 1908 and this forms the eighth document [h].

With the legalization of Jim Crow in the towns and states of the South, in the 1890's and thereafter, Negroes in many communities established their own transportation companies. One of the last of these was a railway located in Jacksonville, Florida and the notice of its foreclosure and sale appearing in the Negro press in 1908 makes up the ninth document [i].

A striking instance of the developing Negro liberation movement in this decade was the Negro people's growing interest in the resurrection of their own history. This culminated, in 1915, in the founding, under the leadership of Dr. Carter G. Woodson, of the Association for the Study of Negro Life and History and the appearance of its publication, *The Journal of Negro History*. In this, as in so much else, Dr. Du Bois was a pioneer, his *History of the Suppression of African Slave Trade* appearing in 1896 as Harvard Historical Studies Number 1. Indicative of this development is a letter written July 12, 1909, to Du Bois, about the need for a reinvestigation of the Reconstruction Period. This letter, written by James R. L. Diggs, who was President of The Virginia Theological Seminary and College of Lynchburg, together with Du Bois' favorable reply, dated July 24, form the tenth document [j].

Early in 1910, Howard University students rebelled against the singing of Negro spirituals—or "plantation melodies" as they were then often called—before white audiences, insisting that this was demeaning. Provocative remarks on this action, and on the music involved, came from F. H. M. Murray's pen and these form the last document [k] in this section.

[a]

Mr. Washington Dines With President Roosevelt, 1901

Booker T. Washington, the Negro orator and president of Tuskegee Institute, when asked as to the meaning of the violent denunciation of President Roosevelt by a number of Southern newspapers for entertaining him at dinner in the White House, said:

"I think the newspapers of the South do not voice the opinion of the Southern people. However, they are hurting the entire South more than they are President Roosevelt. They represent a transient emotional sentiment on the part of a class of the white people of the South, but such feelings do not indicate the general feeling and opinion of Southern people.

"I have known President Roosevelt for a number of years. We have consulted together many times over matters pertaining to my race in the South. As far as I can learn of him he makes no distinction as to the color of a man's cuticle when he wants to get at facts, and is as ready to consult with the Negro, Indian or Chinaman as he is with the Anglo-Saxon.

"There were two or three other guests with us at the dinner given by the President. It was a private affair."

"Have you not been received at the homes of some of the best white people of the South?" he was asked.

"I have," said Mr. Washington.

The Indianapolis *Freeman*, October 26, 1901.

[b]

Dr. Du Bois Writes a Negro Schoolgirl, 1905

I wonder if you will let a stranger say a word to you about yourself? I have heard that you are a young woman of some ability but that you are neglecting your school work because you have become hopeless of trying to do anything in the world. I am very sorry for this. How any human being whose wonderful fortune it is to live in the 20th century should under ordinarily fair advantages despair of life is almost unbelievable. And if in addition to this that person is, as I am, of Negro lineage with all the hopes and yearnings of hundreds of millions of human souls dependent in some degree on her striving, then her bitterness amounts to crime.

There are in the U.S. today tens of thousands of colored girls who would be happy beyond measure to have the chance of educating themselves that you are neglecting. If you train yourself as you easily can, there are wonderful chances of usefulness before you: you can join the ranks of 15,000 Negro women teachers, of hundreds of nurses and physicians, of the growing number of clerks and stenographers, and above all of the host of homemakers. Ignorance is a cure for nothing. Get the very best training possible & the doors of opportunity will fly open before you as they are flying before thousands of your fellows. On the other hand every time a colored person neglects an opportunity, it makes it more difficult for others of the race to get such an opportunity. Do you want to cut off the chances of the boys and girls of tomorrow?

Du Bois MSS.

[c]

The Diary of John E. Bruce, 1905

June—Am once more established in a home, after existing for over a year in two stuffy rooms . . . my dear little wife, a typical homebody, is inexpressibly happy and of course I am. I live for her and am happiest when she is happy.

July—The microbe of prejudice has followed us to this place and I now hear that my "happy home" is for sale. The neighborhood is white and the colors do not blend harmoniously.

August—Am once more disestablished domestically. The happy home established in June, and which I dreamed would be a long continued source of pleasure and comfort to us all must be broken up in September. . . .

October—This threatened calamity did not eventuate. The old house it was found was not worth the cost of improvements necessary to make it habitable for white folks and so it was patched up and the rent raised and we were permitted to repossess ourselves of our happy home idea.

MS. in Schomburg Collection, New York Public Library.

[d]

Du Bois on Philanthropy, 1905

There is a feeling today among Negroes that certain classes of men are more desirous of making the Negro problem one of almsgiving and charity rather than of manhood and manhood rights. To this they are righteously opposed, and when in good faith some earnest workers in this great field point to the columns of figures showing the money spent for Negro churches and schools, there prevails among colored people, along with all their thankfulness, a spirit which a widely read Negro paper has recently voiced:

"For all time, charity, which neither pauperizes nor patronizes heaven's unfortunates, but gives itself with its gifts, all praises and thanks are due. But chilling, unfeeling, vaunting pretension, masquerading in the mantle of charity, deserves neither respect nor consideration. The neediest prefer to bear the ills of want and wretchedness rather than be the miserable objects of prying pity or condescending curiosity which proffers alms today, that it may defer justice and fair play tomorrow; which comes, if ever, only to keep the word of promise to the ear and break it to the hope."

Such words and such a feeling must be respected. It contains the germs of manhood, self-respect and self-hope. The period of universal Negro charity is passing—slowly, to be sure, all too slowly—but passing.

The Independent (N.Y.), December 7, 1905, LIX, p. 1316.

[e]

The Atlanta Massacre, 1906

1. Mr. Barber's letter to the N.Y. World:

John Temple Graves assumes a grand air of fairness in his letter of two days ago to *The New York World*. But in all that pageantry of high-sounding phrases he seeks an excuse for a mob which was as lawless and as godless as any savages that ever shocked civilization.

There has been no "carnival of rapes" * in and around Atlanta. There has been a frightful carnival of newspaper lies. First Hoke Smith, governor-elect of Georgia, formerly supposed to be a Christian and liberal man, transformed himself into a human moccasin, and for eighteen long months he abused the Negro to the snarling riffraff of this state. The day before his election the newspapers were thick with rumors of attempts at assaults. A prominent banker of Atlanta stated to the writer that it was all a trick to further fire race hatred, so that Smith would be elected on his Negro-hating platform. Some of his emissaries blacked their faces, knocked down a few white women and fled. Smith was elected overwhelmingly.

The proof of this hellish conspiracy is found in the fact that every time bloodhounds were placed on the tracks where one of the women was assaulted they trailed a scent to a white man's house and stopped. However, the white man was not arrested. A suspicious looking Negro was arrested remote from the scene, and without question he will pay for the deed with his life.

One of the women who at first claimed that she was assaulted and had her throat partly cut by a "burly black brute" later confessed that she herself had tried to commit suicide because of family troubles. The newspapers made very obscure mention of this fact. For days armed posses had scoured the woods looking for a Negro. . . .

Remember that Charles Daniel, editor of the Atlanta *News*, had for more than a month sought by every hellish device to precipitate a race war. He had called for the reorganization of the Ku Klux Klan, had offered a reward to lynchers, and had written daily fire-eating and reckless editorials against the Negro.† Remember that Mr. Graves himself had written repeatedly in limpid and classic style about "The Shadow of the Black Terror." Remember that the Atlanta *Journal* had exhausted its vocabulary abusing the Negro, while the *Constitution* was mum. Then, finally, there came these

---

* Barber is quoting Graves' letter.
† Here is a brief sample: "Vicious blacks are sounding the doom of their race. The wonder is that the white men do not begin in earnest a real warfare on the blacks."— Atlanta *News*, Sept. 23, 1906.

extras with alarming rapidity on Saturday night with headlines a foot deep.

There had to be some blood letting. There was some blood letting, but the innocent were the only ones to suffer.

The cause of this riot: Sensational newspapers and unscrupulous politicians. The remedy: An impartial enforcement of the laws of the land. The authorities must protect the people. Although the newspapers have not said so, almost as many white people were killed and as many were wounded as colored in this riot.

The Voice of the Negro (Chicago), November, 1906, pp. 470–72.

2. N.Y. Age *and Booker T. Washington:*

ATLANTA SLAYS BLACK CITIZENS SCORES KILLED

INFERNAL RESULT OF AGITATIONS BY WHITES

HOKE SMITH IS GUILTY

ABOMINABLE CAMPAIGN OF "THE NEWS" ALSO

RESPONSIBLE

BLACK MEN RETALIATE

BUT ARE DISARMED BY MILITIA—

CLARK UNIVERSITY INVESTED—

DR. BOWEN ARRESTED

TO RETALIATE FATAL—WASHINGTON

As a rule I never discuss the matter of mob violence except when I am in the South,* but in this case I make an exception.

In answer to your request, I will state that in my address in Atlanta to the National Negro Business League, a few days ago, I spoke plainly against the crime of assaulting women and of resorting to lynching and mob law as a remedy for any evil. I feel the present situation too deeply to give any extended utterance at this time, except to say that I would strongly urge that the best white people and the best colored people come together in council and use their united efforts to stop the present disorder.

I would especially urge the colored people in Atlanta and elsewhere to exercise self-control and not make the fatal mistake of attempting to retaliate, but to rely upon the efforts of the proper authorities to bring order and security out of confusion. If they do this they will have the sympathy of good people the world over.

Let me repeat that wherever I have met them, without exception, I have found the leading colored people as much opposed to crime as the leading white people; but what is needed now is to get the best element of both races together and try to change the present deplorable condition of affairs. We of

* Mr. Washington was then in New York City.

both races must learn that the inflexible enforcement of the laws against all criminals is indispensable, and in this I will do my utmost to have my race cooperate.

The Atlanta outbreak should not discourage our people, but should teach a lesson from which all can profit. And we should bear in mind also that while there is disorder in one community there is peace and harmony in thousands of others. As a colored man I cannot refrain from expressing a feeling of very deep grief on account of the death of so many innocent men of both races because of the deeds of a few despicable criminals.

N.Y. *Age*, September 27, 1906.

3. *Lewis H. Douglass:*

. . . . Too much has been said in the way of warning our people to refrain from criminality. What should be said to our innocent and law-abiding people who overwhelmingly outnumber the criminals among us and who can do nothing and can effect nothing in the way of checking the criminal classes white or black? You say the right word and I will say amen. Our people must die to be saved and in dying must take as many along with them as it is possible to do with the aid of firearms and all other weapons. . . .

In no instance was there a colored man injured who was guilty of any offense against the law of nature, morals or the laws of his country at Atlanta.

N.Y. *Age*, October 4, 1906.

[f]

The Burning of Seneca, S.C., 1906

The evil conscience of the whites, which persuaded them that they richly deserved such reprisals, probably initiated the report sent out last week that the Afro-Americans of Seneca, S.C., had set the town on fire in revenge for the recent dynamiting by the whites of Harrell College, an Afro-American institution.

This suspicion seems to have been quieted by the activity of the Afro-Americans in helping extinguish the flames. But the origin of the fire is still a mystery, and it is quite possible that some Afro-Americans started it without the knowledge of the others.

The buildings burned were two hotels, two stores adjoining the hotels, a clothing store, a drug store, grocery store and one hardware store, embracing the business part of the town. . . . No casualties are reported, as the occupants of the hotels had ample time to get out. The loss amounted to over $75,000.

N.Y. *Age,* October 25, 1906.

[g]

The Brownsville, Texas Case, 1906

1. The News Report:

Washington, November 6—By order of President Roosevelt, acting upon a report made to him by Brig-Gen. E. A. Garlington, Inspector-General of the Army, every man of companies B, C, and D of the Twenty-Fifth Infantry, the Afro-American regiment, will be discharged without honor from the army and forever debarred from reenlisting in the army or the navy, as well as from employment by the Government in any civil capacity.

The action is one of the most drastic ever taken by the President and is sure to cause a sensation throughout the service. The refusal of members of the battalion to give Gen. Garlington or to their immediate superiors the names of the men implicated in the shooting of citizens at Brownsville, Texas, near Fort Brown, on August 13, led the Inspector-General to recommend the discharge of all the men and the President concurred. . . .

This action of President Roosevelt is sure to arouse the bitterest surprise and anger everywhere among Afro-Americans. They believe that the Afro-American soldiers were heroic in refusing to betray their comrades to an unfair trial and certain death, and that they are merely another sacrifice offered by the President upon the altar of Southern race prejudice. It is said the soldiers have entered into a compact never to divulge the evidence.

N.Y. *Age,* November 8, 1906.

2. The Affidavit of First Sergeant Mingo Sanders:

TERRITORY OF OKLAHOMA, *County of Canadian, ss:*

Personally appeared before me, the undersigned, duly authorized to administer oaths in and for the county and Territory aforesaid, one Sergt. M. S. Sanders, a member of Company B, Twenty-Fifth United States Infantry, and he deposes and says that he is 50 years old; that he has served for a period of twenty-five years, six months and seven days, being a noncommissioned officer for a period of thirteen years and a sergeant for a period of six years; that he has served in Cuba and the Philippines, two months in Cuba, and was continually on the firing line. . . .

Affiant doeth further say that he was garrisoned at Fort Brown, Tex., on the 13th day of August, 1906, and a member of Company B, Twenty-Fifth United States Infantry. That on August 13, 1906, near 4 o'clock, Lieut. George C. Lawson, and company commander, said to him, "Sergeant, are there any men in town on pass?" to which he replied "No, sir; no men on pass." Lieutenant Lawson said, "Send me two responsible men." Affiant obeyed said order, and sent Sergt. Walker McCurcy and Corporal Waddington. Said Officer Lawson told the men to go all over town and if they saw any of Company B's men to tell them to report at quarters at once.

Said officer asked affiant to publish on retreat that no man of the company would be allowed in town after 8 o'clock.

Affiant further says that on the evening of the 13th of August, 1906, he retired to his quarters, about 500 yards east of Company B's quarters; that he was aroused about 12:30 by his wife, and that he heard firing, which, from his long army experience, he knew that there were mixed arms being fired. He at once rushed to his company's quarters, gave the order to fall in, and proceeded to call the roll. The time when he was first aroused and the calling of the roll consumed about ten minutes. That on roll call only 4 men were absent out of 57, and that the men absent were Elmer Brown, detailed at Major Penrose's stables as help; John Brown, assistant baker at post bake house; William Smith, who was upstairs in quarters asleep; Alfred N. Williams, on duty quartermaster corral; that as he called the roll the firing was still going on downtown. After roll call he reported the result to Company Commander Lawson, and company was ordered around rear of quarters, where orders were issued to take position of defense to support C on walls. Company remained in that position about one hour; orders were then issued to form company and call roll again, which he did, and men answered to roll call except two men, Elmer P. Brown and John Brown. Affiant then received orders from Major Penrose to send an officer after them. He sent Corporal Harris, who returned with the two men, which made the roll complete and all men accounted for. Company was dismissed and ordered to remain on until further orders. Company then to put away rifles and go to bed. Next morning at 7 o'clock a.m., at drill, rifles were inspected and company then relieved Company C, Twenty-Fifth Infantry.

Affiant further says, according to his best knowledge and belief, that every gun was intact and locked the previous evening. Affiant further says that the men of Company B who were called before Inspector-General Garlington were only 7 men out of the 57 in the company. . . .

Affiant further says that majority of company are now on their second and third enlistment, and has about 15 men on long enlistment and service in the United States Army, and that this affiant has only one year and five months before retiring.

MINGO SANDERS

Subscribed and sworn to before me this 24th day of November, 1906.

E. T. BARBOUR, *Notary Public.*

Summary Discharge or Mustering out of Regiments or Companies. Message from the President of the United States transmitting a report from the Secretary of War together with several documents . . . (Washington, 1907), Part I, pp. 227, 228.

[*h*]

Booker T. Washington on an All-Negro Town, 1908

Boley, Indian Territory, is the youngest, the most enterprising, and in many ways the most interesting of the Negro towns in the United States. A rude, bustling, Western town, it is a characteristic product of the Negro immigration from the South and Middle West into the new lands of what is now the State of Oklahoma.

The large proportions of the northward and westward movement of the Negro population recall the Kansas Exodus of thirty years ago, when within a few months more than forty thousand helpless and destitute Negroes from the country districts of Arkansas and Mississippi poured into eastern Kansas in search of "better homes, larger opportunities, and kindlier treatment."

It is a striking evidence of the progress made in thirty years that the present northward and westward movement of the Negro people has brought into these new lands, not a helpless and ignorant horde of black people, but land-seekers and home-builders, men who have come prepared to build up the country. In the thirty years since the Kansas Exodus the Southern Negroes have learned to build schools, to establish banks and conduct newspapers. They have recovered something of the knack for trade that their forefathers in Africa were famous for. They have learned through their churches and their secret orders the art of corporate and united action. This experience has enabled them to set up and maintain in a raw Western community, numbering 2,500, an orderly and self-respecting government.

In the fall of 1905 I spent a week in the Territories of Oklahoma and Indian Territory. During the course of my visit I had an opportunity for the first time to see the three races—the Negro, the Indian and the white man—living side by side, each in sufficient numbers to make their influence felt in the communities of which they were a part, and in the Territory as a whole. . . .

One sees them [Negroes] everywhere, working side by side with white men. They have their banks, business enterprises, schools, and churches. There are still, I am told, among the "natives" some Negroes who cannot speak the English language, and who have been so thoroughly bred in the customs of the Indians that they have remained among the hills with the tribes by whom they were adopted. But, as a rule, the Negro natives do not shun the white man and his civilization, but, on the contrary, rather seek it, and enter, with the Negro immigrants, into competition with the white man for its benefits. . . .

In 1905, when I visited Indian Territory, Boley was little more than a name. It was started in 1903. At the present time it is a thriving town of two thousand five hundred inhabitants, with two banks, two cotton gins, a newspaper, a hotel, and a "college," the Creek-Seminole College and Agricultural Institute.

There is a story told in regard to the way in which the town of Boley was started, which, even if it is not wholly true as to the details, is at least characteristic, and illustrates the temper of the people in that region.

One spring day, four years ago, a number of gentlemen were discussing, at Wilitka, the race question. The point at issue was the capability of the Negro for self-government. One of the gentlemen, who happened to be connected with the Fort Smith Railway, maintained that if the Negroes were given a fair chance they would prove themselves as capable of self-government as any other people of the same degree of culture and education. He asserted that they had never had a fair chance. The other gentleman naturally asserted the contrary. The result of the argument was Boley. . . .

It is said that during the past two years not a single arrest has been made among the citizens. The reason is that the majority of these Negro settlers have come there with the definite intention of getting a home and building up a community where they can, as they say, be "free." What this expression means is pretty well shown by the case of C. W. Perry, who came from Marshall, Texas. Perry had learned the trade of a machinist and had worked in the railway machine shops until the white machinists struck and made it so uncomfortable that the Negro machinists went out. Then he went on the railway as a brakeman, where he worked for fifteen years. He owned his own home and was well respected, so much so that when it became known that he intended to leave, several of the County Commissioners called on him. "Why are you going away?" they asked; "you have your home here among us. We are behind you and will protect you."

"Well," he replied, "I have always had an ambition to do something for myself. I don't want always to be led. I want to do a little leading."

Other immigrants, like Mr. T. R. Ringe, the Mayor, who was born a slave in Kentucky, and Mr. E. L. Lugrande, one of the principal stockholders in the new bank, came out in the new country, like so many of the white settlers, merely to get land. Mr. Lugrande came from Denton County, Texas, where he had 418 acres of land. He had purchased this land some years ago for four and five dollars an acre. He sold it for fifty dollars an acre, and, coming to Boley, he purchased a tract of land just outside the town and began selling town lots. Now a large part of his acreage is in the center of the town. . . .

A large proportion of the settlers of Boley are farmers from Texas, Arkansas, and Mississippi. But the desire for Western lands has drawn into the community not only farmers, but doctors, lawyers, and craftsmen of all kinds. The fame of the town has also brought, no doubt, a certain proportion of the drifting population. But behind all other attractions of the new colony is the belief that here Negroes would find greater opportunities and more freedom of action that they have been able to find in the older communities North or South.

Boley, like the other Negro towns that have sprung up in other parts of the country, represents a dawning race consciousness, a wholesome desire to do something to make the race respected; something which will demonstrate the right of the Negro, not merely as an individual, but as a race, to have a worthy and permanent place in the civilization that the American people are creating.

In short, Boley is another chapter in the long struggle of the Negro for moral, industrial, and political freedom.

The Outlook (N.Y.), January 4, 1908.

[i]

A Negro-Owned Railway, 1908

The Negroes in Jacksonville, Fla., owned a street railway in North Jacksonville. This was the only street railway owned by Negroes in the United States. They had colored motormen, conductors, president and directors. The road was financed with Negro capital. Henry M. Endicott, Jr., of Boston, Mass., bought the road for $70,000. The sale was made to satisfy the judgment in a foreclosure of a mortgage in which W. D. Parnet was trustee. The property now will be operated by whites. Many years ago, the Negro owned a street railway in Pine Bluff, Ark., which was a valuable piece of property. It was operated by mules. This was sold. It is to be regretted that the Jacksonville Negroes failed to meet their obligations. The enterprise was certainly a credit to the race.

Christian Index (Jackson, Tenn.), January 16, 1908, p. 3.

[j]

The Need for Rewriting Negro History, 1909

1. Mr. Diggs to Dr. Du Bois:

For some time I have been thinking of a work that ought to be done by the men who are of our way of thinking. The Educated Negro owes the world a history of reconstruction. No subject has been treated in a way more harmful to our race than this one subject.

We have the men. We ought to have a series of ten volumes or more covering the reconstruction periods in Virginia, North Carolina, South Carolina, Georgia, Florida, Alabama, Mississippi, Louisiana, Texas and Arkansas. I have mentioned the matter to Mr. J. W. Cromwell of Washington, D.C., and he thinks it is the supreme need of the day. We must get our views of that period before the public. The series of works by southern writers present our white brothers' side of the question but I do not find the proper credit given our people for what of good they really did in those trying days.

Now it has occurred to me that Hon. John R. Lynch, who is now retired on a good salary, Dr. Theophilus G. Steward, Gen. Robert Smalls and others might give the facts from which a good case might be made out for our cause. Mr. Cromwell was active in the Virginia Constitutional Convention, was an editor and knows the men. Now would this work, if done say within the next three years, not form a splendid array of facts for the larger work you are planning? Should we not have both sides of reconstruction?

I am willing to write up either State if no one who lived during those days and who for such reasons can do it better than I, can be found. Perhaps if Cromwell will take North Carolina, I will work at Virginia. If you will take the lead, we will follow. If not, perhaps Cromwell might be Editor-in-Chief. Any plan you suggest will suit me. I simply want the work done.

2. Du Bois' Reply:

Your scheme for the set of histories of reconstruction from the Negro point of view, is excellent, and will fit into my encyclopedia project * perfectly.

I shall take it up in the fall.

Du Bois MSS.

---

* Dr. Du Bois had conceived of a multi-volumed Encyclopedia of the Negro People. Forty years later he edited a *Preparatory Volume* offering a projected index for such a work.

[k]

The Singing of Spirituals, 1910

Considerable was said in the race press and elsewhere a few weeks back regarding the "revolt" of the students at Howard University against the singing of "Plantation Melodies."

The season for the making up of commencement and school-closing programs being at hand prompts us to say a few words about one phase of the matter but little touched upon; entering the case not as an attorney for either side but as a proctor for the melodies.

Primarily it should be said that few or none of these Plantation Melodies are "songs" or "Folk Songs," neither in the ordinary sense nor according to the dictionary definitions. Though crude, they were composed and sung as hymns in religious worship or for private and personal consolation. Yet it was claimed that the students were regularly called upon to render these melodies for the "entertainment" of visitors; and, it may be assumed from their acts and associations, many of these visitors—though prominent and powerful personages—regard these soul-yearnings of our fathers and mothers much as the general public does the "living skeleton" and the "fat woman" in the sideshow; as things curious and "funny." . . .

Again, however unique or expressive and beautiful may be the music (tunes) of some of these melodies—and like all "popular" songs many are scarcely melodious—let them be recast so as to express correct and elevating conceptions and let them be couched in grammatical language, and their "popularity" with the class referred to would quickly vanish. How much, for example, would these folks be entertained or enraptured by the music, the really beautiful melody, of "Steal Away" were it not for the wording; as in the refrain: "I ain't got long to stay hyar"? And wherein lies the great popularity of "Roll, Jordan, Roll," unless in its muddled theological geography—"I want to go to Heaven when I die, to hear sweet Jordan roll"?

True these hymns or some of them express and attest the cruel character of the oppression under which our fathers and mothers groaned and the hope and faith which sustained them. By us they are rightly held in appreciation, even reverence. But to render them in season and out, to excite and tickle the jaded and satiated "entertainment" appetites of those whose clamor for them is most insistent—and who are edified and touched by them much as we would be by an Indian Ghost Dance or a Chinese funeral service—is to pervert their spirit and intent and is close to sacrilege. If there were no other objection to their use for "entertainment" purposes, this would be an all-sufficient one. . . .

The Horizon (Washington), May, 1910.

V.

BOOKER T. WASHINGTON: PRO AND CON

Mr. Washington's policy amounted objectively to an acceptance by the Negro people of second-class citizenship. His appearance upon the historical stage and the growth of his influence coincided with and reflected the propertied interests' resistance to the farmers' and workers' great protest movements in the generation spanning the close of the nineteenth and the opening of the twentieth centuries. American imperialism conquers the South during these years and Mr. Washington's program of industrial education, ultra-gradualism and opposition to independent political activity and trade-unionism assisted in this conquest.

At the same time it is clear that no love was lost between Washington and the Carnegies with whom he dealt; rather, it appears to have been the educator's conviction that since they had the money and the power, it was incumbent upon him —who needed that money and influence for his educational work—to come to terms with them. This would require, of course, that the education suited the donors—an essential part of the agreement—but any other program, to the Washingtonians, was visionary at best and demagogic and dangerous at worst.

The six documents that follow are offered in an effort to picture this complex situation and the types of reactions it produced. The first document [a], dated Chicago, July 20, 1903, is a letter to Dr. Du Bois from the Rev. Kittredge Wheeler, of the Fourth Baptist Church, expressive of the misgivings felt by many Negroes concerning Washington's program. The second document [b] is a typical pro-Washington editorial from the influential Indianapolis *Freeman* of the same year.

To understand the third document [c] it is necessary to know that in January, 1904, a closed meeting of about fifty outstanding Negro leaders—both pro- and anti-Washington—was held in Carnegie Hall, New York City. This meeting had been a year in the making and the initiative for it came from the Tuskegee forces with the money—for transportation and other expenses—coming from Andrew Carnegie. Notwithstanding these auspices and the fact that Mr. Carnegie favored the private meeting with an address lauding Mr. Washington, frank expressions of opinions were made by the assembled leaders. From this meeting developed the Committee of Twelve for the Advancement of the Interests of the Negro Race, but when its control was captured by Washington, Du Bois resigned and the Committee soon disintegrated.

It is to this that Dr. Du Bois is referring in his letter, dated Atlanta, April 2, 1907, sent to Miss A. P. Moore of the Women's Home Baptist Mission Society in Chicago. The lady had written urging unity between Du Bois and Washington and in this letter the former tells of his experiences growing out of the 1904 conference.

A letter from Du Bois, dated Atlanta, December 28, 1905, forms the fourth document [d]. This was addressed to the New York financier, George Foster Peabody, founder in 1867, of the Peabody Education Fund for southern Negro and white schools. Dr. Du Bois' independence was becoming embarrassing to Atlanta University in terms of its chronic need for funds. Here he is explaining his position on Washington and his estimate of the radical William Monroe Trotter of the Boston *Guardian*. So bitter had been Mr. Trotter's objections to Mr. Washington when the latter appeared in Boston's Zion Church that a disturbance ensued and the editor was jailed. It is to this event that Dr. Du Bois makes reference in his letter.

Document five [e] is a brief letter, dated March 10, 1910, from Dr. Du Bois to a lady named Edith R. Force of Oak Park, Illinois. Miss Force had inquired for Du Bois' views on industrial education and his response is remarkable for its succinctness and clarity. The last document [f] in this group is dated New York City, October 26, 1910 and was issued by twenty-three Negro leaders acting as a National Negro Committee. It was a reply to the glowing reports concerning the Negro's situation which had been brought to Europe earlier that year by Booker T. Washington. The author was Dr. Du Bois and the signers with their identifications are given as they appeared in the original document.

[a]

Wheeler to Du Bois, 1903

I am very greatly interested in everything of a public character which concerns the Negro race. My father belonged to the Underground Railway in an early day, when to be a black Abolitionist took nerve and courage and conscience. Some five or six years ago, at my own charges and as a private individual, I visited our schools in the South, including schools at Jackson, Miss., Selma, Montgomery, New Orleans, Nashville, Tuskegee, Atlanta and others. Now to commit myself, and not to commit you, without your knowledge, while I believe in Mr. Washington and Tuskegee, as far as it goes, yet I believe most emphatically that the battle cry "Manual training for the Negro" is fundamentally false, and harmful, and pernicious.

The South and the North both like it. Why? Because they are willing to meet the Negro on the fairest, broadest and unrestricted ground before God and man, or because on its very face, it assumes, asserts a limitation in connection with the Negro, and is a discrimination against him? I deplore this fact more than I can tell you; and I know, perhaps better than you, if you have been living some time in the South, how this catchword is eagerly, gladly, selfishly, accepted here. It relieves us in the North of any great responsibility! The education of the hands is easy, simple, a short cut, and if neglected, well, what of it? The body perishes—dust to dust. The education of the heart and mind, and soul, the lifting up of a man—this is difficult and long and painstaking. This means—in a word—the giving of one's self to that man who is to be lifted, or to be helped! This is the way of Calvary! Not an easy road.

This catchword has filled the minds of the people—North and South! It is misleading! It has done incalculable harm, it will take a generation and more to dislodge it. Now, the only reason, why I mention Mr. Washington's name here is this: He, more than any other one man is responsible for this idea; and because he is the confessed representative of it. "Booker Washington says so; he knows." "He is the foremost man of his race." And this is an answer to every objection. This is the only reply the people of the North deem it necessary to make. Indeed this is such a finality in the consideration of this race problem (I do not like this expression) that few men here in the North stop to give it a careful consideration. Now if Mr. Washington would say "I believe in Education for all men alike, but manual training, or industrial education for the Negro of the South seems for the present, to be most needed, or expedient," I would not have anything to say.

Or, if Mr. Washington would say: "There are many schools of higher education in the South for the Negro, and in my work in Tuskegee I am best adapted to give manual training." Very good! But you know that is not his attitude; not his position before the public. Mr. Washington of course says in public that Tuskegee gives academic training, and is engaged in fitting many of the students there, to become *school teachers;* but that is kept in the background, that is not his message to the people.

His name, his work, his school, all are used here in the North, even as an argument against the education of the Negro. Why is it that the ignorant, illiterate, low, profane white man of the North catches at the words—"Industrial education; Manual training for the Negro." He is not interested in any moral or educational question under heaven. How is it that such a man is so sure and clear on the best and only thing, for the Negro? I wish Mr. Washington might be persuaded to define his position more sharply; and if he believes in the *education* of the Negro, without limitations or discriminations, or differentiations, that he would speedily say so. The sentiment "Industrial Education for the Negro" is the shackle—not removed from his hands but in addition, put upon head and heart—upon the whole man—the whole race. Let us fear him, who casts body and soul into hell! Jesus said.

This sentiment inculcated, re-enslaves the Negro race. When the iron manacle was on the slave's limbs, that iron visibly marked the degree or extent of his abject condition. Physical slavery had not yet dared to invade the realm of the soul. And the implication of his subjection or inferiority did not go beyond the iron band, or the physical body.

But now this sentiment is a manacle upon the intellectual, moral, spiritual, upon the higher, nature; upon the whole man.

I think someone should endeavor to make Mr. Washington see his position; or if it be not his position, then for the sake of the Negro, and the Caucasian, the North and the South, that he should come out publicly and clear the air, of this damaging and damnable misrepresentation on his part, and misapprehension on the part of the country. The position is untenable. If he does not hold it, he should say; if he does hold it, he should be driven from it. . . .

Du Bois MSS.

[b]

A Pro-Washington Editorial, 1903

With pleasure we present in this issue several features of Tuskegee, the great institution conducted by the world-famed Booker T. Washington. Very little can be said of the man or the institution that will increase the general admiration for either, yet they are incentives and of the best kind, and as such, too much publicity cannot be given them. This world is fairly informed concerning the struggles of Mr. Washington in his work, which began in the humblest manner, and to which beginning he seems to take pride in referring. In fact, his spirit of humility is his virtue; he is not too proud to reckon back to the whence from which he came. He is not, however, unconscious of the vast strides he has made, but it has not destroyed his balance; he is the same Mr. Washington of the years ago when he was fighting apparently insurmountable financial difficulties.

Tuskegee is truly a magical institution as concerns growth. None in the world, perhaps, has reached its proportions within the given time; the growth is not to be attributed to opportunity merely, for it is so often said that the industrial education idea was not new, and that other institutions of a similar character by many years antedated his; it was the genius of the individual. Tuskegee is as it is because of Prof. Booker T. Washington, and shame to anyone who would attempt to detract from him one jot or tittle.

From one insignificant building at the beginning, in 1881, on the 4th of July, Tuskegee has to its credit many buildings, among which are seven magnificent halls named in honor of the donors. They are Rockefeller, Huntington, Alabama, Sassedy, Phelps, Porter, Olivia Davidson Hall, and a science hall. The office building, the girls' dormitory and the Collis P. Huntington memorial building are noteworthy structures that are both useful and ornamental.

The Carnegie Library is a splendid structure, built on the colonial style of architecture, and cost $20,000. . . . Eleven new buildings are under the process of erection at this time. Mr. Washington places an estimate of $525,-000 on the properties of the institution and does not think it too high. The endowment fund is something like $1,000,000.

Students of Tuskegee are required to attend Sunday School and Church services regularly every Sunday. There are among the students five religious organizations and societies: The Young Men's Christian Association, Young People's Society of Christian Endeavor, The Young Women's Christian Temperance Union, the Young Women's Christian Association, and the Edna D. Cheney Missionary Society. Although Tuskegee is primarily a Normal and Industrial Institute, the religious side of the work is not neglected or slighted.

It is apparent that the religious training is one of the strong features of Tuskegee, which is at variance with a notion that sought circulation recently.

The Tuskegee Student is an excellent little publication, edited by Mr. Emmett J. Scott, Mr. Washington's private secretary. Mr. Scott is an able, scholarly writer and well-fitted for his responsible task. *The Southern Letter* is a monthly journal, containing a record of the achievements of the graduates of the institution and goes more particularly to philanthropic persons throughout the country.

A military system has long since been in vogue at Tuskegee, of which Mr. Washington says: "The military system has been introduced for the reason that it cultivates habits of order, neatness and unquestioned obedience. Besides, the drill is good physical training, promoting, as it does, a manly bearing. 'Setting-up' exercises according to the very latest methods used in the United States Army have been introduced. No guns are used."

As to Mr. Washington's educational views, he has tried to have all understand that he stands for one phase of education, and that is manual training. He does not feel that his effort along that line should interrupt the progress of the other phases of education, but he means, as it is clearly shown by his almost superhuman effort, to leave no stone unturned in the promotion of the side he has chosen. His views on the educational phases amount to a principle, which is as follows:

A liberal education for those who are able to be liberal, which is the jewel—consistency—the thing so often lost to view.

Booker T. Washington is the man of the age—the age of achievements—the age in which things are being done. The dreamers, wiseacres or dunces may dream on, theorize on, but the world will "pay them no mind" until they carry out some of their plans now on paper.

The Freeman (Indianapolis), December 26, 1903.

[c]

Du Bois to Miss Moore, 1907

Replying to your letter of March 31st perhaps if I tell you the history of my last attempt to cooperate with Mr. Washington, you will appreciate my present condition. It was about four years ago; Mr. Washington asked me and some other men to come to New York for a conference. I helped him arrange for the conference and went there. When we got there I told him frankly behind closed doors with the other men present, the things we objected to in his program.

We did not object to industrial education, we did not object to his enthusiasm for its advancement, we did object to his attacks upon higher training and upon his general attitude of belittling the race and of not putting enough stress upon voting and things of that sort. The result of the conference was that a committee was appointed to arrange for a Committee of Twelve, colored people throughout the United States, men of influence and prominence. Three men were to appoint that committee, Mr. Washington, Mr. Hugh Browne and myself. When I went to New York to appoint the committee, I found that Mr. Washington and Mr. Hugh Browne had been in conference for twenty-four hours or more and the people they appointed were elected voting always two to one against me.

Nevertheless I kept on, tried to do what I could. It was arranged that the whole committee should meet in St. Louis during the summer. That summer I had done so much work that the physician refused to let me go to the meeting and I had to write to Mr. Washington and ask him to postpone it. While I was away trying to recuperate, the meeting was held, Mr. Washington was made chairman, the whole work of the committee was put into the hands of an executive sub-committee, the appointment of that sub-committee had been put in Mr. Washington's hands. I found therefore, when to my astonishment I learned of these proceedings, that the whole power of this whole organization was at Mr. Washington's beck and call and that I was virtually bound hand and foot by anything the committee would do. There was simply one thing for me to do and that was for me to resign from the committee and that was what I did immediately and three or four others also resigned. As a result of that Mr. Washington told people in New York that I didn't keep my word and I could not be depended upon. I said after that that there was no use trying to cooperate with a man who would act like that and I am still of that opinion. Whatever I can do to promote harmony I will do so but I will not put myself under the control and command of Mr. Washington.

Du Bois MSS. For an account of this episode see the editor's article in *Science & Society* (1949), XIII, pp. 345–51.

[d]

Du Bois to Peabody, 1905

Some time ago Mr. Ware, our Chaplain, spoke to me of a letter received from you in which you spoke of certain rumors as to my connection with the disturbances over Mr. Washington in Boston last summer. Later Dr. Bumstead wrote me of a similar letter not mentioning from whom he had received it, but I took it that it was probably from you.*

I want therefore to write you frankly of my position in this matter that there may be no misapprehension, and I want you to feel at liberty to use the letter as you may wish.

Mrs. Trotter, the wife of the editor of the *Guardian,* is an old friend of mine of school days. Mr. Trotter I have not known so long or so well but met him in college. I had then and afterward disagreed with him rather sharply over many questions of policy and particularly over Mr. Washington. But nevertheless both then and now I saw in him a clean-hearted utterly unselfish man whom I admired despite his dogged and unreasoning prejudices. Last summer while Mrs. Du Bois and I were looking for a boarding place, Mrs. Trotter offered to share her home with us and we gladly accepted. I went first to Tuskegee and then made a trip on a coast steamer. I did not arrive in Boston until after the Zion Church disturbance. Before seeing the account in the morning papers I had had no inkling or suspicion in any way of the matter. I did not know Mr. Washington was in Boston or intending to go there as I had just left him at Tuskegee. I had had no correspondence with Mr. Trotter for six months save in regard to a boarding place. When I arrived in Boston and heard of the meeting I told Mr. Trotter and Mr. [George] Forbes in plain terms my decided disapproval of the unfortunate occurrence and my conviction that it would do harm. Although I was unable at that time to defend Mr. Washington's position as I once had, I nevertheless took occasion to address a meeting of men at Mr. Trotter's home and remind them of the vast difference between criticizing Mr. Washington's policy and attacking him personally.

Nevertheless, brought into close contact with Mr. Trotter for the first time my admiration for his unselfishness, pureness of heart and indomitable energy even when misguided, grew. And, too, I saw how local jealousies were working to make mountains out of mole hills. So far as I could learn had it not been for Mr. Lewis,† the chairman of the Washington meeting, there would have been no riot—the disturbance could have easily and quickly [been] quelled and the dignity of the occasion saved. This same Mr. Lewis a few years ago was a rabid anti-Washington man and wanted to "burn down Tuskegee." I labored with him and Trotter and Forbes in past years and was instrumental in getting Mr. Washington and Mr. Lewis together

* Dr. Horace Bumstead was President of Atlanta University; his successor was Edmund A. Ware.
† William Henry Lewis, appointed Assistant Attorney-General by President Taft.

at a small luncheon so that they might understand each other. They evidently came to understand each other so well that Mr. Lewis got a political appointment and turning around proceeded to abuse his former comrades—a conversion in which I had as little faith as I had in his former radical stand.

There were a great many other things not generally known that made me pity and admire Mr. Trotter as well as condemn his lack of judgment and there were also things that made me have less and less faith in Mr. Washington. Nevertheless, I steadfastly condemned Mr. Trotter's action from that day to this—a fact which he will frankly testify to. When the matter was pushed to the extent of actual imprisonment I felt this was too much in view of all the facts and still feel so and I wrote an open letter to the [Boston] *Guardian* expressing my disagreement on many points with him but my admiration for his honesty of purpose.

While then I had absolutely no knowledge of the Washington meeting beforehand and no part, active or passive, in the disturbance and while I did then and do now condemn the disturbance, I nevertheless admire Mr. Trotter as a man and agree with him in his main contentions. When I think him in the right I shall help him, when his methods or opinions go beyond law and right, I shall condemn them.

As between him and Mr. Washington I unhesitatingly believe Mr. Trotter to be far nearer the right in his contentions and only pray such restraint and judgment on Mr. Trotter's part as will save our cause, his sincerity and unpurchasable soul in these days when every energy is being used to put black men back into slavery and when Mr. Washington is leading the way backward. . . .

Du Bois MSS.

[e]

Du Bois to Miss Force, 1910

The question as to whether the Negro should have simply an industrial education or should also be afforded the opportunity to the highest training depends entirely upon one simple question: Are you training the Negro for his own benefit or for the benefit of somebody else? If he has a right to be trained for his own benefit then he may demand the highest training to which his best minds are capable. If he is to be trained for usefulness to other people then his training depends, of course, on how they want to use it.

[f]

The National Negro Committee on Mr. Washington, 1910

To the People of Great Britain and Europe—
The undersigned Negro-Americans have heard, with great regret, the recent attempt to assure England and Europe that their condition in America is satisfactory. They sincerely wish that such were the case, but it becomes their plain duty to say that if Mr. Booker T. Washington, or any other person, is giving the impression abroad that the Negro problem in America is in process of satisfactory solution, he is giving an impression which is not true.

We say this without personal bitterness toward Mr. Washington. He is a distinguished American and has a perfect right to his opinions. But we are compelled to point out that Mr. Washington's large financial responsibilities have made him dependent on the rich charitable public and that, for this reason, he has for years been compelled to tell, not the whole truth, but that part of it which certain powerful interests in America wish to appear as the whole truth. . . .

Our people were emancipated in a whirl of passion, and then left naked to the mercies of their enraged and impoverished ex-masters. As our sole means of defence we were given the ballot, and we used it so as to secure the real fruits of the War. Without it we would have returned to slavery; with it we struggled toward freedom. No sooner, however, had we rid ourselves of nearly two-thirds of our illiteracy, and accumulated $600,000,000 worth of property in a generation, than this ballot, which had become increasingly necessary to the defence of our civil and property rights, was taken from us by force and fraud.

Today in eight States where the bulk of the Negroes live, Black men of property and university training can be, and usually are, by law denied the ballot, while the most ignorant White man votes. This attempt to put the personal and property rights of the best of the Blacks at the absolute political mercy of the worst of the Whites is spreading each day.

Along with this has gone a systematic attempt to curtail the education of the Black race. Under a widely advertised system of "universal" education, not one Black boy in three today has in the United States a chance to learn to read and write. The proportion of school funds due to Black children are often spent on Whites, and the burden on private charity to support education, which is a public duty, has become almost intolerable.

In every walk of life we meet discrimination based solely on race and color, but continually and persistently misrepresented to the world as the natural difference due to condition.

We are, for instance, usually forced to live in the worst quarters, and our consequent death rate is noted as a race trait, and reason for further discrimination. When we seek to buy property in better quarters we are sometimes in danger of mob violence, or, as now in Baltimore, of actual legislation to prevent.

We are forced to take lower wages for equal work, and our standard of living is then criticised. Fully half the labor unions refuse us admittance, and then claim that as "scabs" we lower the price of labor.

A persistent caste proscription seeks to force us and confine us to menial occupations where the conditions of work are worst.

Our women in the South are without protection in law and custom, and are then derided as lewd. A widespread system of deliberate public insult is customary, which makes it difficult, if not impossible, to secure decent accommodation in hotels, railway trains, restaurants and theatres, and even in the Christian Church we are in most cases given to understand that we are unwelcome unless segregated.

Worse than all this is the wilful miscarriage of justice in the courts. Not only have 3,500 Black men been lynched publicly by mobs in the last twenty-five years without semblance or pretence of trial, but regularly every day throughout the South the machinery of the courts is used, not to prevent crime and correct the wayward among Negroes, but to wreak public dislike and vengeance, and to raise public funds. This dealing in crime as a means of public revenue is a system well-nigh universal in the South, and while its glaring brutality through private lease has been checked, the underlying principle is still unchanged.

Everywhere in the United States the old democratic doctrine of recognising fitness wherever it occurs is losing ground before a reactionary policy of denying preferment in political or industrial life to competent men if they have a trace of Negro blood, and of using the weapons of public insult and humiliation to keep such men down. It is today a universal demand in the South that on all occasions social courtesies shall be denied any person of known Negro descent, even to the extent of refusing to apply the titles of "Mr.," "Mrs.," and "Miss."

Against this dominant tendency strong and brave Americans, White and Black, are fighting, but they need, and need sadly, the moral support of England and of Europe in this crusade for the recognition of manhood, despite adventitious differences of race, and it is like a blow in the face to have one, who himself suffers daily insult and humiliation in America, give the impression that all is well. It is one thing to be optimistic, self-forgetful and forgiving, but it is quite a different thing, consciously or unconsciously, to misrepresent the truth.

(*Signed*)

J. Max Barber, B.A., Editor of *The Voice of the Negro*.

C. E. Bentley, formerly Chairman of Dental Clinics, St. Louis Exposition.

W. Justin Carter, Barrister, Harrisburg, Pa.

S. L. Corrothers, D.D., Pastor African M.E. Zion Church, Washington, D.C.

George W. Crawford, B.A., LL.B., Barrister, formerly Clerk of Court, New Haven, Ct.

James R. L. Diggs, M.A., President of Virginia Seminary and College, Va.

W. E. Burghardt Du Bois, Ph.D., Author of *Souls of Black Folk*, &c., Fellow of the American Association for the Advancement of Science, Member of International Law Society and Secretary of the National Afro-American Committee.

Archibald H. Grimké, late U.S. Consul to San Domingo.

N. B. Marshall, B.A., LL.B., Barrister, Counsel in the Brownsville Soldiers Court Martial.

Frederick L. McGhee, Barrister, St. Paul, Minn.

G. W. Mitchell, B.A., LL.B., Barrister, Philadelphia.

Clement G. Morgan, B.A., LL.B., Barrister, formerly Alderman of Cambridge, Mass.

Edward H. Morris, Grand Master of the Grand United Order of Odd Fellows in America.

N. F. Mossell, M.D., Medical Director of Douglass Hospital, Philadelphia, Pa.

James L. Neill, Recording Secretary of the National Independent League.

William Pickens, B.A., Professor of Latin, Talladega College, Ala.

William A. Sinclair, Author of *The Aftermath of Slavery*, and Field Secretary of the Constitution League, which represents nine-tenths of the American Negroes, and has 15,000 coloured Ministers in affiliated relations with it.

Harry C. Smith, Editor of *The Cleveland Gazette*, for six years Member of the Legislature of Ohio.

B. S. Smith, Barrister, formerly Assistant States Attorney, State of Kansas.

William Monroe Trotter, B.A., Editor of *The Boston Guardian*.

J. Milton Waldron, D.D. Pastor of Shiloh Baptist Church, Washington, D.C.

Owen M. Waller, M.D., Physician, Brooklyn, New York.

Alexander Walters, D.D., Bishop of the African M.E. Zion Church.

A printed brochure entitled "Race Relations in the United States" in Du Bois MSS.

VI.

NEGRO ORGANIZATIONAL ACTIVITY, 1901–1910

The history of organizational activity among Negroes during the first decade of the twentieth century may be divided into three sections. The first marks a continuation of the type of work and groups of the past; the second concerns the appearance of the Niagara Movement in 1905 and its activities until 1909; the third consists of the immediate preliminary work for and the actual establishment of the National Association for the Advancement of Colored People, 1909–10.

A] Continuing Efforts

In this section are included five documents. The first [a] consists of the Address to the Country, in January, 1903, of the Executive Committee of the eight-year-old National Afro-American Council, whose chairman was Bishop Alexander Walters. Disfranchisement, discrimination, lynching and peonage were the particular targets of this Address.

In 1896, the National League of Colored Women and the National Federation of Colored Women combined to form the National Association of Colored Women. It affiliated with the National Council of Women of the United States in 1900 and thereafter was a very potent public influence. To indicate something of its work and viewpoint, the resolutions adopted by the Association at its fourth convention (1904) are published as the second document [b].

State-wide Negro Equal Rights Societies had existed, as we have seen, since the close of the Civil War. In 1906 there was revived the Georgia Equal Rights Convention and at its meeting, held in Macon, February 13–14, appeared five hundred locally elected delegates, men and women, from every corner of the state. The chairman was the Rev. William J. White, venerable editor of *The Georgia Baptist*, and present were figures like Bishop H. M. Turner, Dr. Du Bois and J. W. Lyons, Register of the United States Treasury. The convention's Address, militant and passionate, came from Du Bois' pen, and forms the third document [c].

In the fourth document [d] will be found summarized the work of the first twelve "Atlanta Conferences for the Study of the Negro Problem" spanning the years 1896–1907. These conferences were largely the inspiration of Dr. Du Bois and represented phases in his noble dream of resolving the Negro question through the sheer search for truth. The summary was written by Du Bois, June 7, 1907, and forwarded as a report to President Bumstead of Atlanta University, sponsor of the conferences.

In February, 1908, twenty-five Bishops of the African Methodist Episcopal, the A.M.E. Zion and the Colored Methodist Episcopal churches—with some two million communicants—conferred in the nation's capital. "An Address to the American People," of remarkable militance considering its source, came from these assembled dignitaries, and it forms the fifth document [e].

[a]

Address of The Afro-American Council, 1903

It is evident to the thoughtful among us that we are passing through one of the most critical periods of our existence in this country. Questions that immediately concern the liberty and well being of one-eighth of the population of the United States, and scarcely to less degree the whole population of the country are pressing for treatment as never before. A systematic effort has been inaugurated on the part of the South which has for its object the withdrawal of the franchise from the Afro-Americans of that section, and their reduction to a position of absolute subserviency in all the relations of life. It has been openly declared by some of the most prominent leaders of the South that it was the intention of the framers of the new constitutions to disfranchise as many Afro-Americans as possible and leave every Caucasian in full possession of the suffrage. The effect has been that not only has the Afro-American been disfranchised, but also a very large number of Caucasians, who, previous to the adoption of these constitutions, participated in elections, have ceased to register, to vote.

We contend for our constitutional rights on the ground that the right of suffrage has been conferred upon its citizens by the Federal government.

We heartily commend the Afro-Americans of Virginia, Alabama, Louisiana, and other states, who are seeking redress through the courts of the land, and we pledge them our moral and financial support.

We denounce the mob murders now so prevalent in this country.

We call the attention of the country to a condition of service on many farms in a number of Southern States resembling very much the old peonage system, and ask for legislation looking to the remedying of the evil.

We submit our protest against the unfair practices in the transportation of passengers in Southern States, discriminating unjustly against Afro-Americans; requiring of them the highest rates for travel and providing in return the poorest accommodations in carriage; and we invoke the exercise of the powers of the Interstate Commerce Commission, by that tribunal, to prevent discriminations in rates and accommodations against interstate passengers. . . .

A printed circular, "Special. The National Afro-American Council" in the papers of Dr. Du Bois.

[b]

The National Association of Colored Women, 1904

The National Association of Colored Women's Clubs in the fourth convention assembled, with gratitude acknowledge the Divine guidance of the Supreme Ruler of the Universe and thank Him for the preservation of our President, executive officers and other members.

We pledge renewed efforts and loyalty along all lines in this, our national organization, continuing to stand for adherence to our motto "Lifting as We Climb," for we believe that in it lies the future hope of the race.

In view of the fact of the numerous lynchings and the many victims burned at the stake, extending even to women, which have occurred in nearly every section of our country;

Be it Resolved, That we, the representatives of Negro womanhood, do heartily deplore and condemn this barbarous taking of human life, and that we appeal to the sentiment of the Christian world to check and eradicate this growing evil; and be it further

Resolved, That we do all in our power to bring criminals to justice, and that we appeal to all legislative bodies and courts of justice to see that all persons are protected in their rights as citizens.

Whereas, Our people throughout the South are discriminated against by railroads, being compelled to ride in offensive and inadequate cars, after paying first-class fares; and,

Whereas, Some of the Southern cities have introduced separate street cars,

Be it Resolved, That this body condemn such action, and that in all such states and towns the club women unite in trying to induce our people to refrain from patronizing street cars and running excursions from town to town, thus encouraging the railroads to continue their unjust discrimination.

Be it Resolved, That a vote of thanks be extended to Theodore Roosevelt, President of the United States, for his fearless and manly stand in defense of the Negro race, in declaring that he would not shut the door of hope and opportunity in the face of any one, on account of race, color or previous condition.

Be it Resolved, That we commend the action of the National Republican Convention in the adoption of that part of its platform which asserts that any state disfranchising its voters shall be limited in its Congressional representation.

Be it Resolved, That the women of our Association prepare themselves by the study of civil government and kindred subjects for the problems of city, state and national life, that they may be able to perform intelligently the duties that have come to some and will come to others in the natural progress of the woman's suffrage question.

Be it Resolved, That the Colored Women's Clubs endorse the W.C.T.U., and urge that we emphasize more fully the work among the young people, and do all in their power to create a sentiment against the practice of taking them to places of amusement where intoxicants are sold, and further that we do all in our power to prevent the diffusion of improper and pernicious literature that saps the vitality of the moral life of our young people.

Believing that the mother is the rock upon which the home is built, therefore, be it

Resolved, That we pledge ourselves to hold and encourage mothers' meetings whenever practicable, in order to instruct mothers in all that pertains to home building and child-life.

Minutes of the Fourth Convention of the National Association of Colored Women, held at St. Paul's Church, St. Louis, Missouri, July 11 to 16, 1904 (Jefferson City, Mo., n.d.), pp. 23–26. Copy in Du Bois Collection.

[c]

The Georgia Equal Rights Convention, 1906

We, colored men of Georgia, representing every district in the State and speaking for more than a million human souls send this statement and plea to the world:

Two races came to Georgia in the early eighteenth century and lived as master and slave. In that long hard apprenticeship we learned to work, to speak the tongue of the land, and better to know God. We learned this but we learned it at the cost of self-respect, self-reliance, knowledge, and the honor of our women.

This training left us above all ignorant. We are still ignorant, partly by our own fault in not striving more doggedly after knowledge, but chiefly because of the wretched educational opportunities given us in this state. The white and black school populations are nearly equal and yet out of every dollar of the state school money eighty cents go to the white child and twenty cents to the Negro child; each white child receives $5.92 a year, while the Negro child receives $2.27; white teachers receive over a million dollars a year, Negro teachers less than three hundred thousand. Less than half our children have school facilities furnished them and not a cent is given by the state to the higher training of Negro teachers and professional men. Of more than a million dollars given by the United States government for agricultural training, we who are preeminently the farmers of the state have received only $264,000, and the fund is at present being divided at the rate of $34,000 to the whites and $8,000 to the Negroes. We are a poor people. Poor in wealth and habit. We are not as efficient laborers as we might be. Yet the accumulated wealth of this great state has been built upon our bowed backs, and its present prosperity depends largely upon us. No portion of the community is giving more of its labor and money to support the public burdens than we; and yet we are not receiving just wages for our toil; we are too often cheated out of our scanty earnings; while the laws that govern our economic life and the rules of their administration are cunning with injustice toward us.

Especially true is this in the freedom of labor contracts; so much so that farm labor is almost reduced to slavery in many parts of the state. . . .

We do not deny that some of us are not yet fit for the ballot; but we do affirm that the majority of us are fit—fit by our growing intelligence, our ownership of property and our conservative, law-abiding tendencies—and in any case certainly disfranchisement and oppression will not increase our fitness, nor will they settle the race problem. The right to vote is in itself an education; and if Georgia had taken as much time and trouble to fit us for political responsibility as she has denying us our rights, she would have a safer and saner electorate than that which is today swaying her by appeals to her worst passions. Voteless workingmen are slaves; without the defense of the ballot we stand naked to our enemies, the helpless victims of jealousy and hate, subjected to, and humiliated by an unreasoning caste spirit, which grows by what it feeds upon. If we are good enough to be represented by five Georgia congressmen in the Councils of the nation, we are surely good enough to choose those representatives; and if we are not good enough to be represented, at least, as human beings, we are too good to be misrepresented by our enemies. We ask of this nation therefore the enforcement of the 14th and 15th amendments.

We do not desire association with any one who does not wish our company, but we do expect in a Christian, civilized land, to live under a system of law and order, to be secure in life, limb and property, to travel in comfort and decency and to receive a just equivalent for our money, and yet we are the victims of the most unreasoning sort of caste legislation. . . .

We ask for an abolition of Jim Crow cars on railroads and the substitution of first and second class cars, which would separate men according to condition, and not according to color.

The menace of the drunken unreasoning mob hangs ever above us. Since 1885, 260 Georgia Negroes have been lynched and burned without the semblance of a legal trial not to mention hundreds of unaccused persons who have been murdered.

We ask the right to enter the militia of Georgia. We have fought for this country in four wars and if we are good enough to fight we are good enough to be trained for fighting.

We ask, further, representation on the juries of the state. Trial by one's peers is one of the fundamental rights of common law and this is systematically denied in Georgia.

Far be it from us to claim any great and especial righteousness of our own. We are a sinful people who have not lived up to the fullness of our narrow opportunity. The sense of our shortcomings is heavy upon us, and there are those among us whose wicked ways shame us bitterly. We are not however as bad as the wilfully distorted and criminally unfair press reports picture us; on the contrary we can take honest comfort in the fact that we are growing daily in honesty, sobriety, industry and chastity; and God alone knows how much faster we might grow were it not for the open traffic in Negro crime which flourishes in this state, and were it not for the defenseless condition of our daughters. As long as public and private wealth in Georgia fattens on the sale of black criminals, so long will crime be encouraged and the outcry against it will ring with hypocrisy.

Colored men are punished in this state without intelligent discrimination; old and young, thug and mischief-maker and often men and women are herded together after unfair trials before juries who would rather convict ten innocent Negroes than let one guilty one escape. The sentences inflicted are cruel and excessive. Twenty-five per cent of the convicts are condemned for life and sixty per cent for ten years or more. White men escape conviction entirely or are promptly pardoned. These slaves of the state are then sold body and soul to private capitalists for the sake of gain, without the shadow of an attempt at reformation, and are thrown into relentless competition with free Negro laborers.

The fortunes of many a prominent white Georgia family is red with the blood and sweat of black men justly and unjustly held to labor in Georgia prison camps; the state today is receiving $225,000 a year of this blood money and boasting of her ability to make crime pay.

As long as any white man is openly taught disrespect for black womanhood so long will her degradation be the damnation of some black man's daughter. Let us black men then look to the care and protection of our wives and daughters. Let us, as far as possible, keep them at home and support them there, and defend their honor with our lives.

To stand up thus in our own defense, we must earn a decent living. We must work hard. We must buy land and homes. We must encourage Negro business men. And at the same time we must agitate, complain, protest and keep protesting against the invasion of our manhood rights; we must besiege the legislature, carry our cases to the courts and above all organize these million brothers of ours into one great fist which shall never cease to pound at the gates of opportunity until they fly open. Brethren of the white race, living together as we do, let us be friends and not enemies. Let us not stir up the darker, fiercer passions. Let us strive together, not as master and slave, but as man and man, equal in the sight of God and in the eyes of the law, eager to make this historic state a land of peace, a place of plenty and an abode of Jesus Christ.

The Voice of the Negro (Atlanta), March, 1906.

[d]

The Atlanta Conferences, 1896–1907

FIRST CONFERENCE

The series of Negro conferences at Atlanta University were instituted by President Horace Bumstead, Mr. George G. Bradford and others and began its meetings in 1896, taking for its subject, MORTALITY AMONG NEGROES IN CITIES. A report of 51 pages was printed which dealt with the statistics and causes of the excessive mortality among Negroes. This report led to a demand for better knowledge of actual living conditions.

SECOND CONFERENCE

The next conference in 1897 extended and systematized the work by house to house investigations in various cities. The results obtained were so voluminous and important that the United States Department of Labor under Commissioner Carroll D. Wright published a study of them in the *Bulletin of Labor* for May, 1897. The regular report of the conference was issued later and consisted of 86 pp. entitled SOCIAL AND PHYSICAL CONDITIONS OF NEGROES IN CITIES. This subject led to the query: How are Negroes themselves helping to better their social conditions?

THIRD CONFERENCE

The third conference in 1898, took up the subject SOME EFFORTS OF AMERICAN NEGROES FOR THEIR OWN SOCIAL BETTERMENT. A report of 66 pp. was published. Next to philanthropic efforts an enquiry into economic activities was felt to be necessary.

FOURTH CONFERENCE

The fourth annual conference in 1899, took up the subject, THE NEGRO IN BUSINESS, and published a report of 77 pp. From economics the conference now turned toward education.

FIFTH CONFERENCE

The COLLEGE-BRED NEGRO was the subject of this conference and a report of 115 pp. was issued in 1900. This report created widespread interest. An abridged second edition of this report was issued in 1903. The problem of the common school followed logically.

SIXTH CONFERENCE

The conference of 1901 took up the subject of THE NEGRO COMMON SCHOOL. The report was 118 pp. long and provoked wide discussion because of its striking conclusions. The conference now essayed to combine its two lines of economic and educational investigation.

SEVENTH CONFERENCE

The subject of study was the NEGRO ARTISAN and the report formed a book of 200 pp. Turning now from work and education the conference studied Negro moral life.

EIGHTH CONFERENCE

The eighth Atlanta conference was held May 26, 1903. The subject of study was the NEGRO CHURCH, and among the speakers were the Rev. Dr. Washington Gladden, Professor Kelly Miller, Mrs. Mary Church Terrell and the Rev. C. B. Wilmer. The report of this conference was the largest of all the volumes published, consisting of 212 pp. The next conference continued the study of morality among Negroes.

NINTH CONFERENCE

The ninth annual conference, held May 24, 1904 took up the difficult and important problem of crime. Difficulties in getting accurate statistics made it best to confine the research chiefly to Georgia. The conference itself was of unusual interest. Mr. Frank B. Sanborn, long prison commissioner of Massachusetts, was the chief speaker, together with the Rev. H. S. Bradley of Atlanta and Mr. M. N. Work, formerly of Chicago University. On account of the lack of funds the publication had to be curtailed to 68 pp. entitled NOTES ON NEGRO CRIME, PARTICULARLY IN GEORGIA.

TENTH CONFERENCE

The conference of 1905 was the tenth, and was devoted to a review of past work and a planning for the next decade. Among the speakers were Professor Walter F. Willcox of Cornell, Miss Francis Kellor and Miss Mary Ovington of New York, Professor T. J. Jones of Hampton Institute and Professor G. W. Henderson of Fisk University.

Here again the pressure of restricted funds was felt; it would have been desirable to publish a general resume of the decade's work at this time but this seemed impossible. It was decided therefore to let the year's publication take the form of a BIBLIOGRAPHY OF THE NEGRO AMERICAN. The conference had already published two bibliographies of 3 and 6 pp. and a number of special bibliographies. The report of 1905 was a list of books and pamphlets on the Negro arranged alphabetically by authors together with a list of articles in periodicals. It covered 71 pp. The work of the last and the following decade was outlined as follows:

The Atlanta University Studies

The First Cycle, 1896–1905	The Second Cycle, 1906–1915
A Vista of Results	A Vision of Work
1896 – Mortality	1906 – Physique
1897 – The Family	1907 – The Family
1898 – Social Betterment	1908 – Organization
1899 – Business	1909 – Economic Development
1900 – College-Bred Negroes	1910 – Economic Development
1901 – Common Schools	1911 – Education
1902 – The Artisan	1912 – Political Power
1903 – The Church	1913 – The Church
1904 – Crime	1914 – Crime
1905 – Methods and Results	1915 – Methods and Results
African Conditions	
Historical Research	
Statistics—Bibliography	

ELEVENTH CONFERENCE

The eleventh annual conference, May 29, 1906, was notable as beginning the second decade of these studies. The subject of the first conference was mortality, therefore the eleventh repeated this same subject but enlarged it to a study of the HEALTH AND PHYSIQUE OF THE NEGRO AMERICAN. At this conference the chief speaker was the eminent anthropologist, Professor Franz Boas of Columbia University. Others speakers were R. R. Wright of the University of Pennsylvania, Dr. C. V. Roman of Meharry and Dr. S. P. Lloyd of Savannah. The printed report of 112 pp. is now being distributed.

TWELFTH CONFERENCE

For the present year the conference has varied its program slightly at the request of the Carnegie Institution of Washington, D.C. The economic section of the Carnegie Institution has in hand an economic history of the United States and wishes for its information a study of ECONOMIC COOPERATION AMONG NEGRO AMERICANS, past and present. To aid such a study it has made a small grant to the conference. The work of collecting data for this is progressing and at the annual meeting May 28, Mr. N. O. Nelson, the founder of the Le Claire cooperative town, spoke. . . .

Du Bois MSS.

[e]

Address of the Negro Bishops, 1908

To enumerate the civil, social, moral, judicial and political injustices that today exasperate and annoy the members of our race, would be a hard task. We do not make for our people any claim that they are better than other classes or race groups of the citizens of the Republic. Nor yet do we assent to the imputation that they are worse than any other, and yet they compose in your midst an alien race in the land where they have lived and labored and loved for about three hundred years.

We speak the same language; we obey the same laws; we read the same books; we worship the same God; we have no blood in our veins which has not been American for centuries. This blood we have shed freely with you for our common country in four separate wars . . . we are American by right of birth; by the blood we shed; by the service we have freely given to achieve the independence and to preserve the life of the Republic against foreign and domestic enemies. . . .

We do not ask at your hands any special favors; we ask at the bar of this Christian Nation nothing to which we are not entitled under the Law and Constitution. We ask only for that which belongs to us as a right, for justice, for equality, for freedom of action and opportunity before the law and in the industrial life of the land, North and South alike. . . .

This also is a truth worth remembering, namely, that a labor class in an industrial Republic like ours, deprived of the right to vote or a voice in the Government is at the mercy of other laboring classes which possess that right and that voice: indeed, at the mercy of all thus privileged.

Now, badly as this race as a labor class needs the ballot, needs education at the public expense, needs industrial opportunities to see its labor freely like other classes in the Republic, in the South by one device or another it is almost universally deprived of the right to vote. In many cases our children are denied equal privileges and the whole race in the North and South is deprived of equal industrial freedom to obtain work with other labor classes.

We regret the fact that wherever this race turns that it is restricted within certain narrow limits by the "Color Line." It is "thus far" in the North, and "thus far" in the South. It hears this hostile, this terrible "no farther"

North and South alike. This Christian Republic cannot with safety look on with indifference at this state of affairs. . . .

We appeal to the friends of humanity to use their influence to rid this glorious country of mob violence which is sending so many to an untimely grave.

We appeal to all who believe in fair play to assist us in banishing from our land the peonage and convict labor system, which are degrading and destroying the very vestige of manhood and relegating many to the most galling serfdom.

We appeal to the liberty loving men in authority to lend us their assistance by influence, by legislation for the removal of the "Jim Crow" car laws which have placed a stigma upon the noblest and the best of our race, from the Bishops of the Church to the humblest, while at the same time, we are required to pay the same fare for inferior accommodation.

We appeal to the Judges of the Supreme Court to annul laws in violation of the Federal Constitution, to members of the several Southern States where disfranchisement laws have been enacted, and to the Congress of the United States to repeal the enactments which have robbed us of the rights guaranteed to us by the Federal Constitution which were gained upon the field of conquest by blood shed by black men as well as white men.

As leaders of the people, we finally appeal for all the rights guaranteed to the citizens of this great Republic.

The Christian Index, March 19, 1908. This publication, edited by the Rev. R. J. Brown at Jackson, Tenn., was the official organ of the C.M.E. Church.

B] *The Niagara Movement*

The jailing of William Monroe Trotter and the failure of the 1904 attempt at a Washington-Du Bois rapprochement were the immediate stimuli for the founding in 1905 of the Niagara Movement, which lasted until, and helped lay the groundwork for, the establishment of the National Association for the Advancement of Colored People.

Details as to its organization, personnel, platform, etc., will be found in the documents that follow. Here it is to be pointed out that the Niagara Movement was confined, in its limited membership, to Negro professionals—teachers, physicians, lawyers, ministers—and a few businessmen. Its general orientation of struggle, therefore, was in the direction of court litigation, occasional public meetings and annual conventions.

Some of the leaders, like Du Bois, himself, had been influenced, intellectually, by Marxism and this appears in some of the statements issuing from the Movement, but its class and social composition nevertheless confined it, in its activities, within the indicated orbits. Efforts were made to influence the growing Negro college population, and Negro women were by no means neglected, nor did they, in turn, neglect the Niagara Movement. The eleven documents that follow attempt to illuminate all these facets.

The first document [a] is the single most important statement presaging Niagara. It is Du Bois' "Credo" which first appeared in the influential New York periodical, *The Independent*, in October, 1904. It was reprinted very widely, especially in the Negro press, and later in scroll form was framed and hung in hundreds of Negro homes throughout the country. Indicative of the impact this statement had is the second document [b], a letter Jessie R. Fauset sent to Du Bois, dated Ithaca, N.Y., February 16, 1905. Miss Fauset, later a distinguished novelist (author of *There Is Confusion* (1924), *The Chinaberry Tree* (1931), and other works), had been assisted by Dr. Du Bois while she was still a student at Cornell in obtaining her first job—teaching American literature at Fisk University.

The third document [c] is the letter, dated Atlanta, June 13, 1905, which Du Bois sent to selected Negro leaders throughout the nation proposing the building of a new organization and outlining what he felt its purposes should be. As a result a call went out for a meeting to be held near Buffalo, New York in July, 1905. Du Bois hired a hotel on the Canadian side of the border and twenty-nine men from fourteen states met there July 11–14, 1905. To symbolize the power it was hoped the movement then founded would have, and because of proximity to the Falls, it was christened Niagara. Its "Declaration of Principles" forms the fourth document [d].

J. Max Barber was a charter member of Niagara and in his *Voice of the Negro* there appeared, in September, 1905, an excellent account of it by Dr. Du Bois. This is reprinted as the fifth document [e]. Niagara's second annual meeting was held in Harper's Ferry, West Virginia, in homage to John Brown, August 16–19, 1906, and reporting the event for Oswald Garrison Villard's New York *Post* was the young white radical social worker, Mary White Ovington, both of whom shortly played significant roles in founding the N.A.A.C.P. The "Address to the Country" from Harper's Ferry is the sixth document [f].

A Junior Niagara Movement directed specifically at Negro college students was established in 1906 and an "Open Letter to College Men" by Mason O. Hawkins, its secretary, constitutes the seventh document [g].

George W. Crawford, a Negro attorney of New Haven, Connecticut, was chairman of Niagara's Department of Civil Rights. His report, dated April 15, 1907, on the work of this department is offered as document eight [h]. Documents nine [i] and ten [j] concern the third annual meeting of Niagara held in Boston, August 26–29, 1907. The first of these is a letter, dated Brooklyn, New York, August 25, 1907, wishing the meeting well and signed by Sarah J. Garnet, Mary C. Cato and Lydia C. Smith on behalf of the Equal Suffrage League of the National Association of Colored Women. The second is the address to the American people of the meeting itself. The last document, [k] dated March 14, 1908, is a brief recapitulation of the work of the movement for the year from March, 1907 through February, 1908.

[a]

Du Bois' "Credo," 1904

I believe in God who made of one blood all races that dwell on earth. I believe that all men, black and brown, and white, are brothers, varying, through

Time and Opportunity, in form and gift and feature, but differing in no essential particular, and alike in soul and in the possibility of infinite development.

Especially do I believe in the Negro Race; in the beauty of its genius, the sweetness of its soul, and its strength in that meekness which shall inherit this turbulent earth.

I believe in pride of race and lineage itself; in pride of self so deep as to scorn injustice to other selves; in pride of lineage so great as to despise no man's father; in pride of race so chivalrous as neither to offer bastardy to the weak nor beg wedlock of the strong, knowing that men may be brothers in Christ, even though they be not brothers-in-law.

I believe in Service—humble reverent service. from the blackening of boots to the whitening of souls; for Work is Heaven, Idleness Hell, and Wages is the "Well done!" of the Master who summoned all them that labor and are heavy laden, making no distinction between the black sweating cotton-hands of Georgia and the First Families of Virginia, since all distinction not based on deed is devilish and not divine.

I believe in the Devil and his angels, who wantonly work to narrow the opportunity of struggling human beings, especially if they be black; who spit in the faces of the fallen, strike them that cannot strike again, believe the worst and work to prove it, hating the image which their Maker stamped on a brother's soul.

I believe in the Prince of Peace. I believe that War is Murder. I believe that armies and navies are at bottom the tinsel and braggadacio of oppression and wrong; and I believe that the wicked conquest of weaker and darker nations by nations white and stronger but foreshadows the death of that strength.

I believe in Liberty for all men; the space to stretch their arms and their souls; the right to breathe and the right to vote, the freedom to choose their friends, enjoy the sunshine and ride on the railroads, uncursed by color; thinking, dreaming, working as they will in a kingdom of God and love.

I believe in the training of children black even as white; the leading out of little souls into the green pastures and beside the still waters, not for pelf or peace, but for Life lit by some large vision of beauty and goodness and truth; lest we forget, and the sons of the fathers, like Esau, for mere meat barter their birthright in a mighty nation.

Finally, I believe in Patience—patience with the weakness of the Weak and the strength of the Strong, the prejudice of the Ignorant and the ignorance of the Blind; patience with the tardy triumph of Joy and the mad chastening of Sorrow—patience with God.

The Independent (N.Y.), October 6, 1904.

[b]

Miss Fauset to Dr. Du Bois, 1905

. . . . I saw your article "Credo" sometime ago . . . I meant to write you to tell you how glad I was to realize that that was your belief, and to ask you if you did not believe it to be worth while to teach our colored men and women *race* pride, *self*-pride, self-sufficiency (the right kind) and the necessity of living our lives as nearly as possible, *absolutely*, instead of comparing them always with white standards. Don't you believe that we should lead them to understand that the reason we adopt such and such criteria which are also adopted by the Anglo-Saxon, is because these criteria are the *best*, and not essentially because they are white? This kind of distinction would in the end breed self-dependence and self-respect, and subjective respect means always sooner or later an outcome of objective respect. You, I should say, are in an excellent position to inculcate this doctrine, and to illustrate it by your splendid example. I am so proud, you know, to claim you on our side.

Living as I have nearly all my life in a distinctly white neighborhood, and for the past four years as the only colored girl in a college community [Cornell] of over 3,000 students, I have *had* to let people know that we too possess some of the best—or else allow my own personality to be submerged. It has been with much pleasure that I have pointed to you as an example of the heights to which it is possible for some of us to climb. It is with the same pleasure and sincerity that I tell you this now—in the desire that in the hour when your work—always arduous—grows irksome through apparent lack of appreciation, you may take heart by remembering that somewhere afar off, some one or other is "rendering unto Caesar the things which are Caesar's."

Du Bois MSS.

[c]

Du Bois' Letter Launching Niagara Movement, 1905

The time seems more than ripe for organized, determined and aggressive action on the part of men who believe in Negro freedom and growth. Movements are on foot threatening individual freedom and our self respect. I write you to propose a conference during the coming summer for the following purposes:

1. To oppose firmly the present methods of strangling honest criticism,

manipulating public opinion and centralizing political power by means of the improper and corrupt use of money and influence.

2. To organize thoroughly the intelligent and honest Negroes throughout the United States for the purpose of insisting on manhood rights, industrial opportunity and spiritual freedom.

3. To establish and support proper organs of news and public opinion.

If you are in accord with the above objects will you kindly write me at your earliest opportunity as to whether or not you can join the movement indicated in the enclosed circular? Are there any other reliable men in your section, who do their own thinking, whom we could invite to join us?

Du Bois MSS.

[d]

Niagara's Declaration of Principles, 1905

Progress: The members of the conference, known as the Niagara Movement, assembled in annual meeting at Buffalo, July 11th, 12th and 13th, 1905, congratulate the Negro-Americans on certain undoubted evidences of progress in the last decade, particularly the increase of intelligence, the buying of property, the checking of crime, the uplift in home life, the advance in literature and art, and the demonstration of constructive and executive ability in the conduct of great religious, economic and educational institutions.

Suffrage: At the same time, we believe that this class of American citizens should protest emphatically and continually against the curtailment of their political rights. We believe in manhood suffrage; we believe that no man is so good, intelligent or wealthy as to be entrusted wholly with the welfare of his neighbor.

Civil Liberty: We believe also in protest against the curtailment of our civil rights. All American citizens have the right to equal treatment in places of public entertainment according to their behavior and deserts.

Economic Opportunity: We especially complain against the denial of equal opportunities to us in economic life; in the rural districts of the South this amounts to peonage and virtual slavery; all over the South it tends to crush labor and small business enterprises; and everywhere American prejudice, helped often by iniquitous laws, is making it more difficult for Negro-Americans to earn a decent living.

Education: Common school education should be free to all American children and compulsory. High school training should be adequately provided for all, and college training should be the monopoly of no class or race in any section of our common country. We believe that, in defense of our own institutions, the United States should aid common school education, particularly in the South, and we especially recommend concerted agitation to this end. We urge an increase in public high school facilities in the South, where the Negro-Americans are almost wholly without such provisions. We favor well-equipped trade and technical schools for the training of artisans, and the need of adequate and liberal endowment for a few institutions of higher education must be patent to sincere well-wishers of the race.

Courts: We demand upright judges in courts, juries selected without discrimination on account of color and the same measure of punishment and the same efforts at reformation for black as for white offenders. We need orphanages and farm schools for dependent children, juvenile reformatories for delinquents, and the abolition of the dehumanizing convict-lease system.

Public Opinion: We note with alarm the evident retrogression in this land of sound public opinion on the subject of manhood rights, republican government and human brotherhood, and we pray God that this nation will not degenerate into a mob of boasters and oppressors, but rather will return to the faith of the fathers, that all men were created free and equal, with certain unalienable rights.

Health: We plead for health—for an opportunity to live in decent houses and localities, for a chance to rear our children in physical and moral cleanliness.

Employers and Labor Unions: We hold up for public execration the conduct of two opposite classes of men:. The practice among employers of importing ignorant Negro-American laborers in emergencies, and then affording them neither protection nor permanent employment; and the practice of labor unions in proscribing and boycotting and oppressing thousands of their fellow-toilers, simply because they are black. These methods have accentuated and will accentuate the war of labor and capital, and they are disgraceful to both sides.

Protest: We refuse to allow the impression to remain that the Negro-American assents to inferiority, is submissive under oppression and apologetic before insults. Through helplessness we may submit, but the voice of protest of ten million Americans must never cease to assail the ears of their fellows, so long as America is unjust.

Color-Line: Any discrimination based simply on race or color is barbarous, we care not how hallowed it be by custom, expediency or prejudice. Differences made on account of ignorance, immorality, or disease are legitimate methods of fighting evil, and against them we have no word of protest; but discriminations based simply and solely on physical peculiarities, place of birth, color of skin, are relics of that unreasoning human savagery of which the world is and ought to be thoroughly ashamed.

"Jim Crow" Cars: We protest against the "Jim Crow" car, since its effect is and must be to make us pay first-class fare for third-class accommodations, render us open to insults and discomfort and to crucify wantonly our manhood, womanhood and self-respect.

Soldiers: We regret that this nation has never seen fit adequately to reward the black soldiers who, in its five wars, have defended their country with their blood, and yet have been systematically denied the promotions which their abilities deserve. And we regard as unjust, the exclusion of black boys from the military and naval training schools.

War Amendments: We urge upon Congress the enactment of appropriate legislation for securing the proper enforcement of those articles of freedom, the thirteenth, fourteenth and fifteenth amendments of the Constitution of the United States.

Oppression: We repudiate the monstrous doctrine that the oppressor should be the sole authority as to the rights of the oppressed. The Negro race in America stolen, ravished and degraded, struggling up through difficulties and oppression, needs sympathy and receives criticism; needs help and is given hindrance, needs protection and is given mob-violence, needs justice and is given charity, needs leadership and is given cowardice and apology, needs bread and is given a stone. This nation will never stand justified before God until these things are changed.

The Church: Especially are we surprised and astonished at the recent attitude of the church of Christ—of an increase of a desire to bow to racial prejudice, to narrow the bounds of human brotherhood, and to segregate black men to some outer sanctuary. This is wrong, unchristian and disgraceful to the twentieth century civilization.

Agitation: Of the above grievances we do not hesitate to complain, and to complain loudly and insistently. To ignore, overlook, or apologize for these wrongs is to prove ourselves unworthy of freedom. Persistent manly agitation is the way to liberty, and toward this goal the Niagara Movement has started and asks the cooperation of all men of all races.

Help: At the same time we want to acknowledge with deep thankfulness the help of our fellowmen from the Abolitionist down to those who today still stand for equal opportunity and who have given and still give of their wealth and of their poverty for our advancement.

Duties: And while we are demanding, and ought to demand, and will continue to demand the rights enumerated above, God forbid that we should ever forget to urge corresponding duties upon our people:

The duty to vote.

The duty to respect the rights of others.

The duty to work.

The duty to obey the laws.

The duty to be clean and orderly.

The duty to send our children to school.

The duty to respect ourselves, even as we respect others.

This statement, complaint and prayer we submit to the American people, and Almighty God.

Original brochure in editor's possession.

[e]

Du Bois on Niagara, 1905

What is the Niagara Movement? The Niagara Movement is an organization composed at present of 54 men resident in 18 states of the United States. These men having common aspirations have banded themselves together into an organization. This organization was perfected at a meeting held at Buffalo, New York, July 11, 12, and 13, 1905, and was called "The Niagara Movement." The present membership, which of course we hope to enlarge as we find others of like thought and ideal, consists of ministers, lawyers, editors, business men and teachers. The honor of founding the organization belongs to F. L. McGhee, who first suggested it; C. C. Bentley, who planned the method of organization and W. M. Trotter, who put the backbone into the platform.

The organization is extremely simple and is designed for effective work. Its officers are a general secretary and treasurer,* a series of state secretaries and a number of secretaries of special committees. Its membership in each State constitutes the State organization under the State secretary.

Why this organization is needed. The first exclamation of any one hearing of this new movement will naturally be: "Another!" Why, we may legitimately be asked, should men attempt another organization after the failures of the past? We answer soberly but earnestly, "For that very reason." Failure to organize Negro-Americans for specific objects in the past makes it all the more imperative that we should keep trying until we succeed. Today we have no organization devoted to the general interests of the African race in America. The Afro-American Council, while still in existence, has done practically nothing for three years, and is today, so far as effective membership and work is concerned, little more than a name. For specific objects we have two organizations, the New England Suffrage League and

* Dr. Du Bois and the Rev. J. M. Waldron of Washington, respectively.

the Negro Business League. There is, therefore, without the slightest doubt room for a larger national organization. What now is needed for the success of such an organization? If the lessons of the past are read aright there is demanded:

1. Simplicity of organization.
2. Definiteness of aim.

The country is too large, the race too scattered and the rank and file too unused to organized effort to attempt to impose a vast machine-like organization upon a wavering, uncertain constituency. This has been the mistake of several efforts at united work among us. Effective organization must be simple—a banding together of men on lines essentially as simple as those of a village debating club. What is the essential thing in such an organization? Manifestly it is like-mindedness—Agreement in the object to be worked for, or in other words, *definiteness of aim.*

Among ten million people enduring the stress under which we are striving there must of necessity be great and far-reaching differences of opinion. It is idle, even nonsensical, to suppose that a people just beginning self-mastery and self-guidance should be able from the start to be in perfect accord as to the wisdom or expediency of certain policies. And some universal agreement is impossible. The best step is for those who agree to unite for the realization of those things on which they have reached agreement. This is what the Niagara Movement has done. It has simply organized and its members agree as to certain great ideals and lines of policy. Such people as are in agreement with them it invites to co-operation and membership. Other persons it seeks to convert to its way of thinking; it respects their opinion, but believes thoroughly in its own. This the world teaches us is the way of progress.

What the Niagara Movement proposes to do. What now are the principles upon which the membership of the Niagara Movement are agreed? As set forth briefly in the constitution, they are as follows:

(a) Freedom of speech and criticism.

(b) An unfettered and unsubsidized press.

(c) Manhood suffrage.

(d) The abolition of all caste distinctions based simply on race and color.

(e) The recognition of the principle of human brotherhood as a practical present creed.

(f) The recognition of the highest and best training as the monopoly of no class or race.

(g) A belief in the dignity of labor.

(h) United effort to realize these ideals under wise and courageous leadership.

All these things we believe are of great and instant importance; there has been a determined effort in this country to stop the free expression of opinion among black men; money has been and is being distributed in considerable sums to influence the attitude of certain Negro papers; the principles of democratic government *are* losing ground, and caste distinctions are growing in all directions. Human brotherhood is spoken of today with a smile and a sneer; effort is being made to curtail the educational opportunities of the colored children; and while much is said about money-making, not enough is said about efficient, self-sacrificing toil of head and hand. Are not all these things worth striving for? *The Niagara Movement* proposes to gain these ends. All this is very well, answers the objector, but the ideals are impossible of realization. We can never gain our freedom in this land. To which we reply: We certainly cannot unless we try. If we expect to gain our rights by nerveless acquiescence in wrong, then we expect to do what no other nation ever did. What must we do then? We must complain. Yes, plain, blunt complaint, ceaseless agitation, unfailing exposure of dishonesty and wrong—this is the ancient, unerring way to liberty, and we must follow it. I know the ears of the American people have become very sensitive to Negro complaints of late and profess to dislike whining. Let that worry none. No nation on earth ever complained and whined so much as this nation has, and we propose to follow the example. Next we propose to work. These are the things that we as black men must try to do.

To press the matter of stopping the curtailment of our political rights.

To urge Negroes to vote intelligently and effectively.

To push the matter of civil rights.

To organize business co-operation.

To build school houses and increase the interest in education.

To open up new avenues of employment and strengthen our hold on the old.

To distribute tracts and information in regard to the laws of health.

To bring Negroes and labor unions into mutual understanding.

To study Negro history.

To increase the circulation of honest, unsubsidized newspapers and periodicals.

To attack crime among us by all civilized agencies. In fact to do all in our power by word or deed to increase the efficiency of our race, the enjoyment of its manhood, rights and the performance of its just duties.

This is a large program. It cannot be realized in a short time. But something can be done and we are going to do something. It is interesting to see how the platform and program has been received by the country. In not a single instance has the justice of our demands been denied.

The *Law Register* of Chicago acknowledges openly that "the student of legal and political history is aware that every right secured by men either individually or as a nation has been won only after asserting the right and sometimes fighting for it. And when a people begin to voice their demand for a right and keep it up, they ultimately obtain the right as a rule." The *Mail and Express* says that this idea is "that founded upon which the American white man has founded his success." All this but then have come the excuses: The *Outlook* thinks that "A child should use other language." It is all right for the white man says the *Mail and Express,* but black men— well they had better "work." Complaint has a horrible and almost a treasonable sound to the *Tribune* while the Chicago *Record-Herald* of course makes the inevitable discovery of "Social Equality." Is not this significant? Is justice in the world to be finally and definitely labelled white and that with your apathetic consent? Are we not men enough to protest, or shall the sneer of the *Outlook* and its kind be proven true that out of ten millions there are only a baker's dozen who will follow these fifty Negro Americans and dare to stand up and be counted as demanding every single right that belongs to free American citizens? This is the critical time, Black men of America; the staggering days of Emancipation, of childhood are gone.

The Voice of the Negro (Atlanta), Sept., 1905.

[f]

Niagara Address of 1906

The men of the Niagara Movement coming from the toil of the year's hard work and pausing a moment from the earning of their daily bread turn toward the nation and again ask in the name of ten million the privilege of a hearing. In the past year the work of the Negro hater has flourished in the land. Step by step the defenders of the rights of American citizens have retreated. The work of stealing the black man's ballot has progressed and the fifty and more representatives of stolen votes still sit in the nation's capital. Discrimination in travel and public accommodation has so spread that some of our weaker brethren are actually afraid to thunder against color discrimination as such and are simply whispering for ordinary decencies.

Against this the Niagara Movement eternally protests. We will not be satisfied to take one jot or tittle less than our full manhood rights. We claim for ourselves every single right that belongs to a freeborn American, political, civil and social; and until we get these rights we will never cease to protest and assail the ears of America. The battle we wage is not for ourselves alone but for all true Americans. It is a fight for ideals, lest this, our common fatherland, false to its founding, become in truth the land of the thief and the home of the Slave—a by-word and a hissing among the nations for its sounding pretentions and pitiful accomplishment.

Never before in the modern age has a great and civilized folk threatened to adopt so cowardly a creed in the treatment of its fellow-citizens born and bred on its soil. Stripped of verbiage and subterfuge and in its naked nastiness the new American creed says: Fear to let black men even try to rise lest they become the equals of the white. And this is the land that professes to follow Jesus Christ. The blasphemy of such a course is only matched by its cowardice.

In detail our demands are clear and unequivocal. First, we would vote; with the right to vote goes everything: Freedom, manhood, the honor of your wives, the chastity of your daughters, the right to work, and the chance to rise, and let no man listen to those who deny this.

We want full manhood suffrage, and we want it now, henceforth and forever.

Second. We want discrimination in public accommodation to cease. Separation in railway and street cars, based simply on race and color, is un-American, undemocratic, and silly. We protest against all such discrimination.

Third. We claim the right of freemen to walk, talk, and be with them that wish to be with us. No man has a right to choose another man's friends, and to attempt to do so is an impudent interference with the most fundamental human privilege.

Fourth. We want the laws enforced against rich as well as poor; against Capitalist as well as Laborer; against white as well as black. We are not more lawless than the white race, we are more often arrested, convicted and mobbed. We want justice even for criminals and outlaws. We want the Constitution of the country enforced. We want Congress to take charge of Congressional elections. We want the Fourteenth amendment carried out to the letter and every State disfranchised in Congress which attempts to disfranchise its rightful voters. We want the Fifteenth amendment enforced and no State allowed to base its franchise simply on color.

The failure of the Republican Party in Congress at the session just closed to redeem its pledge of 1904 with reference to suffrage conditions at the South seems a plain, deliberate, and premeditated breach of promise, and stamps that party as guilty of obtaining votes under false pretense.

Fifth. We want our children educated. The school system in the country districts of the South is a disgrace and in few towns and cities are the Negro schools what they ought to be. We want the national government to step in and wipe out illiteracy in the South. Either the United States will destroy ignorance or ignorance will destroy the United States.

And when we call for education we mean real education. We believe in work. We ourselves are workers, but work is not necessarily education. Education is the development of power and ideal. We want our children trained as intelligent human beings should be, and we will fight for all time against any proposal to educate black boys and girls simply as servants and underlings, or simply for the use of other people. They have a right to know, to think, to aspire.

These are some of the chief things which we want. How shall we get them? By voting where we may vote, by persistent, unceasing agitation, by hammering at the truth, by sacrifice and work.

We do not believe in violence, neither in the despised violence of the raid nor the lauded violence of the soldier, nor the barbarous violence of the mob, but we do believe in John Brown, in that incarnate spirit of justice, that hatred of a lie, that willingness to sacrifice money, reputation, and life itself on the altar of right. And here on the scene of John Brown's martyrdom we reconsecrate ourselves, our honor, our property to the final emancipation of the race which John Brown died to make free.

Our enemies, triumphant for the present, are fighting the stars in their courses. Justice and humanity must prevail. We live to tell these dark brothers of ours—scattered in counsel, wavering and weak—that no bribe of money or notoriety, no promise of wealth or fame, is worth the surrender of a peoples' manhood or the loss of a man's self-respect. We refuse to surrender the leadership of this race to cowards and trucklers. We are men; we will be treated as men. On this rock we have planted our banners. We will never give up, though the trump of doom find us still fighting.

And we shall win. The past promised it, the present foretells it. Thank God for John Brown! Thank God for Garrison and Douglass! Sumner and Phillips, Nat Turner and Robert Gould Shaw,* and all the hallowed dead who died for freedom! Thank God for all those today, few though their voices be, who have not forgotten the divine brotherhood of all men, white and black, rich and poor, fortunate and unfortunate.

We appeal to the young men and women of this nation, to those whose nostrils are not yet befouled by greed and snobbery and racial narrowness: Stand up for the right, prove yourselves worthy of your heritage and whether born north or south dare to treat men as men. Cannot the nation that has absorbed ten million foreigners into its political life without catastrophe absorb ten million Negro Americans into that same political life at less cost than their unjust and illegal exclusion will involve?

Courage, brothers! The battle for humanity is not lost or losing. All

* Colonel commanding the 54th Massachusetts Infantry who was killed in the storming of Fort Wagner, S.C., in 1863.

across the skies sit signs of promise. The Slav is raising in his might, the yellow millions are tasting liberty, the black Africans are writhing toward the light, and everywhere the laborer, with ballot in his hand, is voting open the gates of Opportunity and Peace. The morning breaks over blood-stained hills. We must not falter, we may not shrink. Above are the everlasting stars.

Du Bois MSS.

[g]

The Junior Niagara Movement

There came into existence in July, 1905, as doubtless you are aware, a national organization of colored men. From the place of meeting it took the name of Niagara Movement. Like the Falls, which suggested its name, away from the sordid dead-level of monotonous commercial life, out of sight of the popular gaze, regardless of the world's ideal of material success and its right of might, this national organization of colored men (the Niagara Movement), by its unostentatious force, by the manifested beauty of its unswerving manhood in its strivings for the highest human rights, by its appeal to those who know what truth and right are, and who dare be true and right, has called to itself the attention of the entire country, and sympathy and support from many quarters. . . .

Now it is the wish of the General Secretary of the Niagara Movement that this movement should become rooted in the fertile minds and fearless hearts of our college students. We want you as college men to become deeply interested in the affairs which vitally concern our race. We have been out of college long enough to learn that the saddest mistake that any college student can make is to shut himself off while in school from the questions and conditions which are with difficulty and hardship being worked out by the race. Of course you cannot take an active part in them. Such a course if practicable would not be desirable. You can and should, however, weigh in your minds every question together with the cause which gave rise to it, that concerns us as individuals and as a race. What is more, you should and doubtless do take a firm stand for what you after careful thought believe to be right. In other words, we want our college students to take a stand for the principles set down in the objects of the Niagara Movement. . . . We want you to do so because it will make you fearless men useful to the race.

Our brow-beaten race needs all the useful men it can get. Develop and make yourselves strong for the leadership which will come to you! Finally, we want you to adopt as your aim the objects of the Niagara Movement because the future of our race depends to a large extent upon its college men. This is not peculiar to the Negro race.

Students in our colleges and universities are discussing the same questions that United States congressmen are discussing, because they are soon to be the directors of their own community life and the future congressmen of the nation. Russian college students, and to a less degree German students, are among the foremost of those contending for the rights of their people. Above all, should young colored men, along with other men of similar training and thought throughout the country, take a stand for the ultimate attainment of all the rights and privileges that belong to us as men and as a race.

Such an attitude may cost you something. Everything worth having costs. But regardless of cost, whether you wish to or not, being as you are men of extraordinary training, having many talents, the race demands of you, its coming leaders, a wise, loyal, courageous, upright, manly attitude upon all questions of vital interest to the race.

Printed, undated, brochure in editor's possession.

[h]

Niagara's Department of Civil Rights, 1907

The Civil Rights Department desires to enlist your active co-operation in four lines of work to which it will mainly devote itself this year. These four lines of work are: 1. Securing the enactment of an effective Civil Rights Bill in each of the Northern States. 2. The organization in each of the Northern States of some sort of machine, like the Constitutional League, to be composed mainly of persons not members of the Movement. 3. To improve traveling accommodations on local carriers in the South. 4. To force the service of colored men on grand and petit juries in the Southern States.

The work of this Department will have to be done very largely by the Movement as a whole. The effectiveness of the work attempted will, therefore, depend upon the amount of co-operation which we secure. We offer the following ideas, briefly stated, to guide you in your efforts to help us:

1. Discrimination in places of public accommodation and amusement is increasing at an alarming rate in all parts of the North. This emphasizes the need of effective Civil Rights Acts. Have you a Civil Rights Act in your State? If so, is it effective? If not why not get it amended? If you haven't one, why not get one passed? Is your legislature in session this year?

2. It is but too evident that it will require a hard fight before we shall be able to get any sort of Reduction Measure * through Congress. We are going to fight. To fight effectively requires organization. In Connecticut we have

* That is, to reduce the South's congressional representation on the basis of its disfranchisement of the Negro.

organized a Constitution League the main purpose of which is the accomplishment of this very thing. The league was organized for the express purpose of enlisting in a common cause influential men who do not belong to the Movement. There must be a large number of good men in your State, outside the Movement, who could be used thru some such affiliated organization. Why not have one?

3. Our legal department is having much success in its "Jim Crow car" fight; but this fight relates mainly to interstate travel. For a long time to come, there will be "Jim Crow car" laws in the South which, if they are ingeniously drawn (and they will be), will be beyond attack so far as local travel is concerned—for over this the Federal jurisdiction does not extend. We cannot prevent separation, but we can improve conditions of local travel. The Federal Courts have held that the right to make a separation on a public conveyance, between white and colored passengers, can be upheld only when the carrier in good faith furnished accommodations equal in quality and convenience to both classes. A systematic bringing of suits on this point, should result in material improvement of local accommodations. Why isn't this a fine opportunity for our State movement in the South? How about your State? What kind of local passage do you get for first-class fares?

4. Exclusion of Negroes from Southern juries is one of the chief reasons for the too frequent miscarriage of justice in the trial of Negroes accused of crime. The United States Supreme Court has repeatedly allowed new trials for Negroes, where it has been shown that members of their race were excluded from the jury that convicted them. In those States where Negroes are excluded, why would it not be a splendid work for the local organizations to help Negroes in every worthy case to obtain new trials. An organized effort along this line would eventually result in the admission of Negroes to the jury. With the surety that new trials would be granted, the States would soon tire of the expense of fighting these cases. Are Negroes excluded from juries in your State? Are there any important cases pending in your locality? If so, why not give your jury system a whack on the head by taking them up and securing a new trial in case of conviction. Money? Take up a local subscription for the purpose. We are testing a law in our State, at this present time, by funds raised in this manner.

Now you can readily see that with the increasing expense of administration, and volume of its work, the National Organization will have neither means nor opportunity to attend to all these matters. It is evident that much of the work must be done by efficient State organization; and unless we are willing to confine our effort to a set of annual resolutions and an address to the Country, we must get busy. Don't sit down and wait on the initiative of the overworked General Secretary. Do something on your own initiative.

[i]

Negro Women Greet the Niagara Movement, 1907

We the members of the Equal Suffrage League, National Association Colored Women's Clubs, send greetings to you upon the glorious Cause for which you have assembled in Boston, the home of the noted pioneers and valiant philanthropists, who gave their *all* in the grand struggles for liberty and justice—our Attucks leading in the sacrifice of his life—his blood being the first spilled in the war of the Revolution.

These are auspicious times, and many violations of the laws of both state and Nation in the interest of the Negro for proper development as citizens are constantly occurring; yet these are grand incentives for us to accept in the name and service of the Lord, as His ammunition to assist us in the battle for justice.

Dear friends, these apparent obstacles which beset our pathway in our struggles are blessings in disguise; can we not look upon them as such? Therefore, be assured that we are with you in the spirit of the work to cooperate in any practical way.

Du Bois MSS.

[j]

Address of Third Annual Meeting of Niagara Movement, 1907

For the third time the Niagara Movement in annual meeting appeals to the world and to America. This has been a year of wrong and discrimination. There sits today in the governor's chair of a sovereign southern commonwealth a man stained with the blood of innocent black workingmen who fell in the Atlanta Massacre, and whose unavenged death cries to God for justice. What answer does Georgia return: The fraudulent disfranchisement of her citizens, and with the echo of her fell attack on democracy sound the eager voices of a great tribunal dedicated to industrial freedom, which has in unseemly haste scurried to uphold social slavery and the vicious and nasty Jim Crow car. And why not?

Has not the man in the White House set them brave example by bowing before the brown and armed dignity of Japan and swaggering roughshod over the helpless black regiment whose bravery made him famous? With such example why should not the lawless and vicious of the land take courage? Why should not the less civilized parts of our country follow this lead and spread the mockery of republican government in the South? But we will not follow. We are Americans. We believe in this land. We cannot silently see it false to its great ideals . . . We demand freedom from labor peonage. We demand a free and fair ballot. We demand the denial of national representation to States who deny the rights of citizens. We demand federal legislation forbidding exclusion of any persons from interstate cars on account of race or color. We ask common school training for every child, if necessary at national expense. We demand full exoneration and reinstatement of our shamefully libeled soldiers, and finally, in God's name, we ask justice, and not only do we ask and pray, but we back our prayer by deeds. We call on the 500,000 free black voters of the North: Use your ballots to defeat Theodore Roosevelt, William Taft, or any man named by the present dictatorship. Better vote for avowed enemies than for false friends. But, better still, vote with the white laboring classes, remembering that the cause of labor is the cause of black men, and the black man's cause is labor's own.

We are not discouraged. We thank God for life and health and property, for shade and shine, and above all for the opportunity in the twentieth century of Jesus Christ to fight the battle of humanity in the very van of His army. Help us, brothers, for the victory which lingers, must and shall prevail.

Printed circular, Du Bois Collection.

[k]

Niagara Activities, 1907–08

The chief items of interest in the work of the Niagara Movement this year have been as follows: . . .

Another Jim Crow car case, involving the Pullman service in the South, has been brought in Minnesota by the legal department under Secretary McGhee.

Public Meetings have been held in Washington, D.C., Baltimore, Md., New York, N.Y., Minneapolis, Minn., Cleveland, Ohio.

Letters are being sent to colored voters in the South urging a staunch anti-Taft campaign.

All legitimate influence was brought to bear on the late council of Negro Bishops, with excellent results.*

In the death of the late Mrs. Ida D. Bailey, the Niagara Movement sustains irreparable loss. Active to the last, Mrs. Bailey on January 1, 1908, after being offered the Secretaryship for Women in the South wrote, "I have decided to undertake the work." Despite the vision of death already in

* See document on p. 896.

her eyes she said, "I have many plans, and if I can get strong they may work out for good." Mrs. Carrie Clifford will take Mrs. Bailey's place as Secretary for Women in the South, and will carry on the women's work jointly with Mrs. Morgan.

The Massachusetts women have made a verbatim copy of John Brown's diary, and Secretary Mitchell of Pennsylvania is pushing the work of the John Brown Memorial Committee.

Secretary Hawkins has started a movement for scholarships in connection with his Students' Department.

We welcome to our ranks Bishop Alexander Walters, who joined as an associate member of the District of Columbia Branch. . . .

Lithoprinted sheet in editor's possession.

C] The National Association for the Advancement of Colored People

In its origins the N.A.A.C.P. represented a union of most of the Negro leadership involved in the Niagara Movement and white people of generally similar class and professional backgrounds and ideologies. The immediate stimulant for the white people involved was an anti-Negro outbreak in the summer of 1908 in Lincoln's home, Springfield, Illinois. This led to an article, "Race War in the South," by a leading publicist of the time, William English Walling, in *The Independent* of September 3. Here Walling called for a "powerful body of citizens" to assist the Negroes in their efforts to achieve "absolute political and social equality."

Mary White Ovington, a student of and a prolific writer on the Negro question, wrote to Walling and this resulted in her meeting with him and Dr. Henry Moskowitz in New York in January, 1909. It was then decided to issue, on February 12, 1909, a call for a meeting on the Negro question. William Lloyd Garrison's grandson, Oswald Garrison Villard, president of the New York Evening Post Company, wrote this call which was signed by fifty-three people, including six Negroes—William L. Bulkley, a school principal of New York, Mrs. Ida B. Wells-Barnett of Chicago, Dr. Du Bois of Atlanta, Rev. Francis J. Grimké of Washington, Bishop Alexander Walters and Dr. J. Milton Waldron of Washington. Among the white signers, in addition to the three already named, were Jane Addams, John Dewey, William Dean Howells, Lincoln Steffens, Florence Kelley, Charles Edward Russell, Rabbi Stephen S. Wise, Rev. John Haynes Holmes and Mary E. Woolley.

Thus was held a national conference on the Negro question in New York City, May 31 to June 1, 1909 at which in turn a committee was formed. This committee conducted several mass meetings in the ensuing months, and at a second conference in May, 1910, also in New York, there was organized a permanent body named the National Association for the Advancement of Colored People. Its first chairman was the distinguished Boston attorney, Moorfield Storey (formerly Charles Sumner's private secretary and a leader of the Anti-Imperialist League, later President of the American Bar Association), and Dr. Du Bois was its original Director of Publicity and Research. In November, 1910, under Du Bois' editorship, the first number of the N.A.A.C.P. organ, *The Crisis*, appeared.

Three documents dealing with these events follow. The first, taken from the proceedings of the May 31–June 1, 1909 conference, consists of four parts: a paper by Du Bois on "Politics and Industry"; remarks made by J. Max Barber and the Rev. George Frazier Miller; and a paper by Dr. J. Milton Waldron on "The Problem's Solution."

The second document is Dr. Du Bois' report on this conference which appeared less than two weeks after its close, while the third and final document is the statement of editorial policy by Dr. Du Bois appearing in the first number of *The Crisis.*

[a]

The National Negro Conference, 1909

1. "Politics and Industry" by W. E .B. Du Bois:

. . . . These qualifications [for voting] have been proposed with two reasons: (a) To keep the Negro from voting, (b) To eliminate the ignorant electorate.

Against both these excuses there were strong arguments, but at the time they were gathering force and momentum there came a counterargument that practically stopped all effective opposition to the disfranchisement laws. This argument was that the economic development of the Negro in right lines demanded his exclusion from the right of suffrage at least for the present. This proposition has been insisted on so strenuously and advocated by Negroes of such prominence that it simply took the wind out of the sails of those who had proposed defending his rights, and today so deeply has this idea been driven to most readers' minds [that it is believed] the Negroes of the land are divided into two great parties—one asking no political rights but giving all attention to economic growth and the other wanting votes, higher education and all rights. Moreover, the phrase "take the Negro out of politics" has come to be regarded as synonymous with industrial training and property getting by black men.

I want in this short paper to show that, in my opinion, both these propositions are wrong and mischievous. In the first place there is no such division of opinion among Negroes as is assumed. They are practically a unit in their demand for the ballot. The real difference of opinion comes as to how the ballot is to be gained. One set of opinions favors open, frank agitation. The other favors influence and diplomacy; and the result, curious to say, is that the latter party has today an organized political machine which dictates the distribution of offices among black men and sometimes among Southern whites. It is not too much to say that today the political power of the black race in America is in certain restricted lines very considerable. But those of us who oppose this party hold that this kind of political development by secrecy and machine methods is both dangerous and unwholesome and is not leading toward real democracy. It may and undoubtedly does put a large number of black men in office and it lessens momentary friction, but it is encouraging a coming economic conflict which will threaten the South and the Negro race.

And this brings me to the second proposition: that political power in the hands of the Negro would hinder economic development. It is untrue that any appreciable number of black men today forget or slur over the tremendous importance of economic uplift among Negroes. Every intelligent person knows that the most pressing problem of any people suddenly emancipated from slavery is the problem of regular work and accumulated property. But this problem of work and property is no simple thing—it is complicated of many elements. It is not simply a matter of manual dexterity but includes the spirit and the ideal back of that dexterity.

We who want to build and build firmly the strong foundations of a racial economy believe in vocational training, but we also believe that the vocation of a man in a modern civilized land includes not only the technique of his actual work but intelligent comprehension of his elementary duties as a father, citizen, and maker of public opinion, as a possible voter, a conservor of the public health, an intelligent follower of moral customs, and one who can at least appreciate if not partake something of the higher spiritual life of the world. We do not pretend that all of this can be taught each individual in school but it can be put into his social environment, and the more that environment is curtailed and restricted the more emphatic is the demand that some part at least of the group shall be trained and trained thoroughly in these higher matters of human development, if—and here is the crucial question—if they are going to be able to share the surrounding civilization.

This brings us to the matter of voting. It is possible—easily possible—to train a working class who shall have no right to participate in the government. Most of the manual workers in the history of the world have been so trained. It is also possible, and the modern world thinks desirable, to train a working class who shall also have the right to vote—both these things are possible although the overwhelming trend of modern thought is toward making workers voters. But the one thing that is impossible and proven so again and again is to train two sets of workers side by side in economic competition and make one set voters and deprive the other set of all participation in government. To attempt this is madness. It invites conflict and oppression. A nation cannot exist half slave and half free. Either the slave will rise through blood or the freeman will sink.

So far tremendous effort in the South has been put forth to keep down economic competition between the races by confining the Negroes by law and custom to certain vocations. But, for two reasons, this effort is bound to break down: First there is no caste of ability corresponding with the caste of color, and secondly because if every Negro in the South worked twenty-four hours a day at the kinds of work which are tacitly assigned him, he could not fill the demand for that kind of labor. Economic competition is therefore inevitable as facts like these show: In Alabama there are 94,000 Negro farm laborers and 82,000 whites. In Georgia there are 1,100 Negro barbers and 275 white barbers. In Florida there are 2,100 Negroes employed on railroads and 1,500 whites. In Tennessee there are 1,000 white masons and 1,200 black masons. And so on we might go through endless figures showing that economic competition among whites and blacks was not only existent but growing.

Moreover the schools that increase the competition are the industrial schools and this is both natural and proper. Negro professional men, teachers, physicians and artists come very seldom in competition with the whites. But farmers, masons, painters, carpenters, seamstresses and shoe-repairers work at the same work as whites and largely under like conditions. This competition accentuates race prejudice; when a whole community, a whole nation, pours contempt on a fellowman it seems a personal insult for that man to work beside me or at the same kind of work. Thus one of the first results of the denial of civil rights is industrial jealousy and hatred. Here is a man whom all my companions say is unworthy and dangerous as a companion on the street car or steam car, as a fellow listener at a concert, theatre or lecture, as a table companion in the same house or restaurant, often as a dweller in the same street or same neighborhood and always as a worshipper in the same church or occupant of the same graveyard. If all this is so—and this the Southern white working man is industriously taught from the cradle to the grave—if this is so then why should I be forced to work at the same job or be engaged in similar kinds of work, or receive the same wages? If we cannot play together why should we work together?

Not only is there this feeling but there is also power to act. After the Atlanta riot [of 1906] the police and militia searched the houses of colored people and took away guns and ammunition; while the sheriff almost gave away guns to some of the very men who had composed the mob. We think this monstrous but it is but a parallel of the action of the whole nation. They have put the ballot in the hands of the white workingmen of the South and taken it away from the black fellow-workmen. The result is that the white workman can enforce his feeling of prejudice and repulsion. Other things being equal the employer is forced to discharge the black man and hire the white man—public opinion demands it, the administrators of government, including police, magistrates, etc., render it easier, since by preferring the white many intricate questions of social contact are avoided and political influence is vastly increased.

Under such circumstances there is nothing for the Negro to do but to bribe the employer by underbidding his white fellow; to work not only for less money wages, but for longer hours and under worse conditions. No sooner does he do this than he is mocked as a "scab" from Mexico to Canada, and visited with all the consequent penalties. He is said to be taking bread from others' mouths and he may be, but his excuse is tremendous: he is dragging others down to keep himself from complete submergence and he is taking some of the bread from others' mouths lest his children starve. Does he *want* to do this? Does he like long hours? Ignorant as he is as a mass, has he not intelligence enough to perceive the value of the labor unions and the meaning of the labor movement? No, it is not because the black man is a fool but because he is a victim that he drags labor down.

Faced by this situation the next step of the white workmen is to enforce by law and administration that which they cannot gain by competition. In the past these laws have been laws to separate and humiliate the blacks, but more aggressive laws are demanded to-day and will be in the future. The Alabama child labor law excepts from its operation children in domestic service and in agriculture—i.e., Negro children. *They* may grow up in absolute ignorance so far as the law is concerned. The Alabama law makes the breaking of a contract to work by a farm laborer a felony punishable by a penitentiary sentence. Such a breaking of law in other industries is a misdemeanor punishable by a fine. Certain oppressive labor regulations in many southern states are only applicable to such counties as vote their enforcement. Counties with white workmen vote it down. Counties with disfranchised black workmen vote it in. In the state civil service no Negro can be employed at any job which any white man wants, for obvious reasons. More than that no white man whose business depends on public approbation, or political concession can dare to hire Negroes or if he hires them promote them as they deserve. He must often be content with a distinctly inferior grade of white help.

Judges and juries in the South are at the absolute mercy of the white voters. Few ordinary judges would dare oppose the momentary whim of the white mob and practically only now and then will a jury convict a white man for aggression on a Negro. This is true not only in criminal but also in civil suits, so much so that it is a widespread custom among Negroes of property never to take a civil suit to court but to let the white complainant settle it. In all public benefits like schools and parks and gatherings and institutions, Negroes are regularly taxed for what they cannot enjoy. I am taxed for the Carnegie Public Library of Atlanta where I cannot enter to draw my own books. The Negroes of Memphis are taxed for public parks where they cannot sit down. . . .

Even in serving his own people and organizing his own business the Negro is at the absolute mercy of the white voters. It is often said grandiloquently: let the Negroes organize their own theatres, transport their own passengers, organize their own industrial companies; but such kinds of businesses are almost absolutely dependent on public license and taxation requirements. A theatre built and equipped could by a single vote be refused a license, a transportation company could get no franchise, and an industrial enterprise could be taxed out of existence. This is not always done, but it is done just as soon as any white man or group of white men begin to feel the competition. Then the voters proceed to put the industrial screws on the disfranchised. Witness the strike of the white locomotive firemen in Georgia today. Negro firemen get from fifty cents to one dollar a day less than the white firemen and have to do menial work and cannot become engineers. They can, however, by good service and behavior be promoted to the best runs by the rule of seniority. Even this the white firemen now object to and say in a manifesto: the "white people of this state refuse to accept Negro equality. This is worse than that." The other day the white automobile drivers of Atlanta made a frantic appeal in the papers for persons to stop hiring black drivers. The black drivers replied, "We have had fewer accidents than you and get less wages," but the whites simply said, "This ought to be a white man's job."

This sort of thing is destined to grow and develop. The fear of Negro competition in all lines is increasing in the South. The demand of tomorrow is going to be increasingly not to protect white people from ignorance and degradation, but from knowledge and efficiency—that is, to so arrange the matter by law and custom as to make it possible for the inefficient and lazy white workman to be able to crush and keep down his black competitor at all hazards, and so that no black man shall be allowed to do his best if his success lifts him to any degree out of the place in which millions of Americans are being taught he ought to stay.

This is bad enough but this is not all. The voteless Negro is a provocation, an invitation to oppression, a plaything for mobs and a bonanza for demagogues. They serve always to distract attention from real issues and to ride fools and rascals into political power. The political campaign in Georgia before the last was avowedly and openly a campaign not against Negro crime and ignorance but against Negro intelligence and property-owning and industrial competition as shown by an 83% increase in their property in ten years.

It swept the state and if it had not culminated in riot and bloodshed and thus scared capital it would still be triumphant. As it is the end is not yet. The political power of a mass of active working people thus without votes is greater for harm, manipulation and riot than the power of the same people with votes could possibly be, with the additional fact that voters would learn to vote intelligently by voting. Fourteen years ago Mississippi began disfranchising Negroes. You were promised that the result would be to settle the Negro problem. Is it settled? No, and it never will be until you give black men the power to be men, until you give them the power to defend that manhood. When the Negro casts a free and intelligent vote in the South then and not until then will the Negro problem be settled.

2. Remarks by J. Max Barber:

It is because I wish to go on record, as regards the question which has been raised by one of my friends here, that I am so anxious to speak. I want to say that there is a great fundamental difficulty at the bottom of this problem; it lies not in economics but in politics . . . If you will give a man the right to vote, if you will put the ballot in his hands, if you will give him the right to protect himself, and if he will see that the proper man goes to Congress, a man who will see that American citizens are protected in their rights, then you will get these other things. If you want to solve the race problem, you have to get men who have the right to vote, to say who shall be the governor or the judge, with the right to sit on juries to protect themselves, the right to punish sheriffs for doing what they have done in office. And when you come to this place and tell me that economics and industry are going to solve this problem, I think you are radically wrong. Industry should be just merely a stepping stone to higher things in this republic, and I wish to say the thing that is needed more particularly in this problem is more backbone. If you are going to solve the race problem, you must have men of the William Lloyd Garrison stripe. You must have men that will be willing to stand up for humanity, and for their convictions on this question.

3. Remarks by George Frazier Miller:

We are fully convinced, from the address delivered by Mr. Du Bois this afternoon, that the millennium has not come as yet. But in seeking the solution of these questions we are confronted by the question as to whether Mr. Barber is correct in saying that it is not an economic, but a political point of view. Well, it depends largely on the point of view. I think economics is at the foundation of the whole thing. But we must come to economics through politics, so it depends upon the viewpoint largely as to the truth of the whole thing.

I have studied the colored man pretty well, and I find the greatest difficulty with the colored man as a rule is that he is true to one thing. I don't find him ordinarily true to his religion, I don't find him true to his friends, I don't find him true to his trusts. He is just as derelict in these things as the white man. But I find the one thing that the colored man is devoted to, and that ideal is Republicanism. That is his religion. Now it is not until a colored man can break away from this ideal, this religion of Republicanism, that he will get his liberty through economics. Of course, Mr. Taft, or Mr. anybody else, can treat the colored man as Mr. Taft treats him, and the colored man can be treated as the Supreme Court treats him, he can be treated as Congress treats him, as long as this colored man will stand firmly by the Republican ticket. We know that in various parts of the country they rebel, they say we will cut the party, we will organize an independent party, or we will stand by some other old party, but on the eve of election day, the great majority of them will come together and say, let us trust the dear old party one more time—and the Republicans know it.

Now, there is the great Socialistic party which stands for economic independence, which is the hope of the future today. I stand for rights. There are some people who say they want certain rights and do not want others. Some people say they are not looking for social equality. I want every kind of equality I can have. By that I do not mean that I want to force myself upon any man's presence. I never sought a man socially, and I don't expect to. I don't care whether he be rich as Carnegie, holy as St. John, wise as Socrates, or white as the Albanian fathers, but what I want is equality, and if I don't get equality, then I want superiority. Under Socialism we have economic independence. Everyone has the right to work and every man the full reward of his labors.

4. "The Problem's Solution," by J. Milton Waldron:
    . . . . The most recent solvent proposed for the race problem is the one brought forward by President Taft—which by the way is simply Dr. Washington's prescription revised and amended. Mr. Taft thinks that the Negro problem will be eventually solved if the colored man will make himself useful to the business interests of the community and keep out of sight and out of public office where he is by reason of his numbers or prominence offensive to white people. With regard to the President's solution for the race problem it ought to be said that the reaction in public sentiment in the last twenty years regarding justice to the Negro is as much the result of what is known as the prosperity of the country and the development of its resources as of anything else. In fact, the desire to put the Negro to one side, to segregate him, to assign him to a place at the bottom of the social scheme,

has its origin in and receives its support from the dominant commercial and industrial elements of the country. We have been told, and are still told that agitation concerning the Negro hurts business, frightens prosperity and arrests the development of material and commercial resources.

The usual plea now heard in behalf of the Negro and the one which President Taft makes is that his labor is necessary to a section of the country, and that his freedom, his happiness, his morals and his education are to be looked after to the extent that they add to the productiveness and efficiency of his labor and, as a consequence, the enrichment of his employers. It is regarded as good form to refer to the Negro as "an economic asset of the communities where he is found in large numbers," and the idea is spread abroad that whatever decency or consideration is extended to him is for the profit and advantage of others and not for him as a man. While chattel slavery is no longer upheld by the supreme law of the land, the habit and practice in thought and speech of looking at Negroes from the chattel plane still persists. President Taft's advice, if followed, may make slipshod servants of Negroes but it will not train them into good citizens or noble men.

Many solutions for the Negro problem have been proposed, but to our mind there is one and only one practical and effective answer to the question. In the first place we claim that the early friends of the Negro grasped the true solution, which is that his needs and possibilities are the same as those of the other members of the human family; that he must be educated not only for industrial efficiency and for private gain, but to share in the duties and responsibilities of a free democracy; that he must have equality of rights, for his own sake, for the sake of the human race and for the perpetuity of free institutions. America will not have learned the full lesson of her system of human slavery until she realizes that a rigid caste system is inimical to the progress of the human race and to the perpetuity of democratic government.

In the second place, the Negro must make common cause with the working class which today is organizing and struggling for better social and economic conditions. The old slave oligarchy maintained its ascendency largely by fixing a gulf between the Negro slave and the free white laborer, and the jealousies and animosities of the slave period have survived to keep apart the Negro and the laboring white man. Powerful influences are at work even today to impress upon the Negro the fact that he must look to the business men of the South alone for protection and recognition of his rights, while at the same time these influences inflame the laboring white man with fears of social equality and race fusion. The Negro, being a laborer, must see that the cause of his labor is his cause, that his elevation can be largely achieved by having the sympathy, support and cooperation of that growing organization of working men the world over which is working out the larger problems of human freedom and economic opportunity.

In the third place, wherever in this country the Negro has the franchise, and where by complying with requirements he can regain it, let him exercise it faithfully and constantly, but let him do so as an independent and not as a partisan, for his political salvation in the future depends upon his voting for men and measures, rather than with any particular party. . . .

Proceedings of the National Conference, 1909, New York (n.d., n.p.).

[b]

Du Bois on the National Conference, 1909

There must have been those who looked upon the recent Negro conference in New York with both apprehension and distrust. Many true and tried friends of the Negro were not there and at the same time the call was signed by men whose sanity and devotion to great human ideals was unquestioned. The conference was in fact a visible bursting into action of long gathering thought and brooding. Here is a nation faced with a group of tremendous social problems. What shall be done about them? The answer long forced on the American world has been: Let them alone; do not agitate, do not let loose dangerous forces and passions. So the *laissez-faire, laissez-passer* policy has been a growing insistent line of procedure until men who were willing to think and talk and know on nearly every racial question became suddenly dumb on the Negro problem, and foreigners viewed with increasing amazement a people willing to grapple with and study all their ailments save the most fatal.

When the call therefore went out on Lincoln's birthday to summon to council all those who felt that the great moral and social questions affecting the Negro American must be faced fairly and honestly, carefully discussed and a method of solution sought, there were many good men who refused to respond and the burden of the objection was: The situation is grave—even desperate, but don't agitate. They had before them the vision of wild-eyed irresponsible people, black and white, who without realizing the seriousness and delicacy of this racial muddle wanted to talk things right in a few long speeches and resolutions.

They refused to sanction such a movement. Others however said that free speech and sincere agitation have been the path whereby the modern world has ever sought salvation. And while they are no guarantee of successful search they are certainly worth trying, especially since they cannot in the long run be stopped. You may discredit certain earnest classes of

Negroes by calling them radicals consumed by petty jealousy, but this does not wholly answer their arguments nor prove the unrighteousness of their cause.

When therefore some two or three hundred persons of all shades assembled in the United Charities Building, New York, on May 31, there must have been many who looked into each other's faces with apprehension; who felt they were unleashing great and untrained forces, depths of bitterness and passionate feeling which might defeat the ends of human betterment.

Yet the conference did not look dangerous. The white folk there were well-known and earnest people like Florence Kelley, Anne Garlin Spencer, Oswald Garrison Villard, William Hayes Ward, Charles Edward Russell, Lillian D. Wald, John E. Milholland, and Rabbi Stephen S. Wise. But the curiosity of spectators was toward the darker and less known portion of the audience. What did they represent and want? How far were they earnest and unselfish men and women and how far did they possess the poise and balance necessary for a great forward movement of practical and efficient betterment? There were here conspicuous absences—Booker T. Washington, for instance; while among those present were J. M. Waldron, Bishop Alexander Walters, Monroe Trotter, J. M. Barber, W. L. Bulkley, Ida Wells-Barnett, W. A. Emilau, R. R. Wright, Jr., and L. M. Hershaw—all persons who mean much within the veil, but are less known without.

The conference began with emphasizing the very points around which the real race argument centers today, viz., from the standpoint of modern science, are Negroes men? The answers of Professor [B. G.] Wilder of Cornell and Professor [Livingston] Farrand of Columbia, stated with all care and caution, left no doubt in the minds of the listeners that the whole argument by which Negroes have been pronounced absolutely and inevitably inferior to whites is utterly without scientific basis. "Blood will tell" said Professor Farrand, "but we do not know just what it tells, nor which blood it is, which speaks." Turning from this, the conference took up political and industrial rights and organization. It was argued earnestly that industrial survival was impossible with political disfranchisement—that a body of workingmen could not progress "half-slave and half-free"; and the strike in Georgia was cited to prove this. Ida Wells-Barnett, who began a brave crusade against lynching ten years ago, spoke of the 3,284 men murdered by mobs in this country in twenty-five years and a former attorney general of Massachusetts [Albert E. Pillsbury] insisted on the wisdom and statesmanship of the war amendments.

Both in the conference and before the 1,500 listeners in Cooper Union, the white South was heard by two striking representatives—one, slight, angular and bitter, [Joseph C. Manning of Alabama] talking for his "poor white trash" and asserting that the enslavement and disfranchisement of the white workingman was already following the oppression of the black. The other representative, Prof. John Spencer Bassett, [of North Carolina] a man of culture with the quiet academic air, reminded the South that in its process of development it was submerging the exceptional Negro and retrograding from the ideals of its English ancestry and even of its American practice before the war.

There were many other speeches and talks—the strong straightforward confession of the old South by Judge [W. P.] Stafford of the District of Columbia, the fiery jeremiad of Jenkin Lloyd Jones, the earnestness of Bulkley and Walters and Milholland.

All this the waiting listeners heard with interest and sympathy. These men were earnest, they had heartbreaking grievances and they felt them. The policy of *laissez-faire* was not bringing moral, social, or even (as had been positively promised) industrial peace. But what was going to be done about it? How far could this conference find a practical path amid intense feeling, divergent views, bitter radicalism, impractical dreaming?

Thus the night session of Tuesday was of great interest and burning earnestness. The scientific calm, the repression and waiting were cast aside. The black mass moved forward and stretched out their own hands to take charge. It was their problem. They must name the condition. Three great thoughts were manifest: Intense hatred of further compromise and quibbling in stating this problem to the public; wavering uncertainty as to just what practical steps were best, and last but not least suspicion of the white hands stretched out in brotherhood to help. The first question was settled by straightforward resolutions:

We denounce the ever growing oppression of our 10,000,000 colored fellow citizens as the greatest menace that threatens the country. Often plundered of their just share of the public funds, robbed of nearly all part in the government, some murdered with impunity and all treated with open contempt by officials, they are held in some states in practical slavery to the white community. The systematic persecution of law-abiding citizens and their disfranchisement on account of their race alone is a crime that will ultimately drag down to an infamous end any nation that allows it to be practiced, and it bears most heavily on those poor white farmers and laborers whose economic position is most similar to that of the persecuted race.

To this was added an unequivocal demand:

As first and immediate steps toward remedying these national wrongs, so full of peril for the whites as well as the blacks of all sections, we demand of Congress and the executive:

(1) That the Constitution be strictly enforced and the civil rights

guaranteed under the Fourteenth Amendment be secured impartially to all.

(2) That there be equal educational opportunities for all and in all the states, and that public school expenditure be the same for the Negro and white child.

(3) That in accordance with the Fifteenth Amendment the right of the Negro to the ballot on the same terms as other citizens be recognized in every part of the country.

With these resolutions all seemed satisfied but the further question of practical work brought out the diversity of radical, disagreeing elements seeking unity but undecided and unsettled among themselves. The debate was warm and even passionate; the main points were often lost in clouds of words; impatience and anger appeared and out of all cropped suspicion. A woman leapt to her feet and cried in passionate, almost tearful earnestness—an earnestness born of bitter experience—"They are betraying us again—these white friends of ours." *

But through all this the mass of the conference kept calm and good-natured. They were not certain of everything but they had faith and they quietly voted through the plan of organization which the grandson of William Lloyd Garrison had ably outlined; a committee of forty on permanent organization and eventually a great central committee on the Negro problem, endowed, divided into carefully arranged and efficient departments of legal advice, social investigation, publicity, political propaganda and education.

So the conference adjourned. Its net result was the vision of future cooperation, not simply as in the past, between giver and beggar—the older ideal of charity—but a new alliance between experienced social workers and reformers in touch on the one hand with scientific philanthropy and on the other with the great struggling mass of laborers of all kinds, whose condition and needs know no color line.

The Survey (N.Y.), June 12, 1909.

[c]

The First Editorial of *The Crisis*, 1910

The object of this publication is to set forth those facts and arguments which show the danger of race prejudice, particularly as manifested today toward colored people. It takes its name from the fact that the editors †

---

* Probably Mrs. Ida B. Wells-Barnett. Such fears kept her and William Monroe Trotter from joining the N.A.A.C.P.
† Associated with Dr. Du Bois on the editorial board were: O. G. Villard, J. M. Barber, Charles E. Russell, Kelly Miller, William S. Braithwaite and Mary D. MacLean.

believe that this is a critical time in the history of the advancement of men. Catholicity and tolerance, reason and forebearance can today make the world-old dream of human brotherhood approach realization while bigotry and prejudice, emphasized race consciousness and force can repeat the awful history of the contact of nations and groups in the past. We strive for this higher and broader vision of Peace and Good Will.

The policy of *The Crisis* will be simple and well defined:

It will first and foremost be a newspaper: it will record important happenings and movements in the world which bear on the great problem of inter-racial relations, and especially those which affect the Negro-American.

Secondly, it will be a review of opinion and literature, recording briefly books, articles, and important expressions of opinion in the white and colored press on the race problem.

Thirdly, it will publish a few short articles.

Finally, its editorial page will stand for the rights of men, irrespective of color or race, for the highest ideals of American democracy, and for reasonable but earnest and persistent attempt to gain these rights and realize these ideals. The magazine will be the organ of no clique or party and will avoid personal rancor of all sorts. In the absence of proof to the contrary it will assume honesty of purpose on the part of all men, North and South, white and black.

The Crisis (N.Y.), November, 1910.

Index

(*The subjects,* Abolitionist, Civil War, Negro *and* Reconstruction, *are not indexed because they are clearly indicated in the table of contents.*)